# Human Communication and the Aging Process

Carl W. Carmichael
Carl H. Botan
Robert Hawkins

WAVELAND

PRESS, INC.
Prospect Heights, Illinois

For information about this book, write or call:

Waveland Press, Inc.
P.O. Box 400
Prospect Heights, Illinois 60070
(312) 634-0081

Printed in the United States of America

# List of Contributing Authors

Robert C. Atchley
*Scripps Foundation Gerontology Center*
*Miami University (Oxford, Ohio)*

Barbaranne H. Benjamin
*University of Toledo*

Carl H. Botan
*Rutgers University*

Robert N. Butler
*Mt. Sinai School of Medicine*

Carl W. Carmichael
*University of Oregon*

Frank E.X. Dance
*University of Denver*

Jerry Feezel
*Kent State University*

Paul Fritz
*University of Toledo*

Robert Hawkins
*Southern Illinois University*
  *Edwardsville*

Mark L. Knapp
*University of Texas*

Gary L. Kreps
*Northern Illinois University*

Jon F. Nussbaum
*University of Oklahoma*

Alan M. Rubin
*Kent State University*

Anthony B. Schroeder
*Eastern New Mexico University*

Janice E. Schuetz
*University of New Mexico*

Barbara B. Shadden
*University of Arkansas*

Teresa L. Thompson
*University of Dayton*

Anthony Traxler
*Southern Illinois University*
  *Edwardsville*

James R. Wilcox
*Bowling Green State University*

Leslie J. Young
*Bowling Green State University*

**Consulting Editors**

Joseph A. DeVito
Robert E. Denton, Jr.

# Contents

v

# Part III
# Aging and the Communication Process

# Part IV
# Meeting the Communication Needs of
# the Aging Individual

# Part V
# The Research Challenge

# Foreword

The study of aging in America has made important strides over the past two decades. One of the significant characteristics of this period has been the emergence of gerontology as an interdisciplinary field rather than a unified discipline with a particular focus. As knowledge in the field increased, it became apparent that the aging process touches the entire human condition and that all disciplines potentially have valuable contributions to make.

Several disciplines such as biology, psychology, sociology, and social work have been traditionally associated with gerontology, but other fields are beginning to offer their contributions as well. One of these, communication, has a relevant role to play in the study of aging.

The 1971 White House Conference on Aging had as one of its major themes "Communication Problems of the Elderly." In 1974, the Gerontological Society formed a Media Council to implement a grant-funded program to help bridge the gap between service providers to older people and the media. Now *Human Communication and the Aging Process* presents an overview of the recent research and thinking of this relatively new and emerging area within the interdisciplinary field of aging. Among the many topics it addresses are communication of attitudes and stereotypes, portrayal of older people through the media, administration of nursing homes, changing relationships in the elderly years, and effects of sensory losses on communication.

*Human Communication and the Aging Process* demonstrates that although the communication systems of our culture may be a part of the social problems of aging, they may also hold the solutions to those very problems—a positive message indeed.

*Robert N. Butler, M.D.*

Dr. Butler was awarded a Pulitzer prize for his book, *Why Survive?: Growing Old in America* and was the founding Director of the National Institute of Aging.

# Introduction

Since the mid-seventies there has been growing interest in the communication needs of the almost 30 million older persons and those who relate to them. We feel that attention to the communication aspects of aging is warranted because while the aging have communicative needs which are common to all people, these needs must be met somewhat differently as a result of the aging process and the images which people have of it. A number of scholars have been developing courses and conducting research on a variety of topics relating to communication and aging.

In response to this emerging interest, Carl Carmichael and Robert Hawkins organized an action caucus on communication and aging in November of 1979 at the Speech Communication Association convention in San Antonio. Fifty-four people from 20 states joined the caucus, the central purpose of which was to persuade SCA to promote research and teaching in communication and aging. As a result, SCA authorized a one-day pre-convention conference at the annual meeting in New York in November, 1980. The purposes of the conference were: (1) to identify research projects and courses of study relating to communication and aging that were already in place on college and university campuses, and (2) to identify new directions for research for the 1980s.

The high degree of interest generated among the participants and observers persuaded SCA to sponsor a national summer conference on communication and aging in July, 1981. The purpose of the conference was to provide a forum for representatives from the disciplines of speech communication and gerontology, as well as representatives from funding agencies, to deal with the following specific objectives: (1) to discover research topics of common interest to communication and gerontology scholars, (2) to stimulate interest in courses of study that might be developed jointly by departments of speech communication and gerontology, (3) to define political strategies for the obtaining of funds for joint programs in these two areas for research, training, and service, and (4) to discover how this emerging interest area could most effectively relate to the 1981 White House Conference on Aging.

Following this summer conference, the action caucus petitioned successfully for the authority to establish a commission on communication and aging (COCA). The commission convened for the first time at the SCA Convention in Anaheim, California, in November, 1981. The commission has also jointly sponsored panels with the American Speech-Language-Hearing Association on two occasions. Part II of this book grew out of these cooperative efforts with the help of Peggy Williams from the ASHA staff.

This book represents a concerted attempt by COCA members and other scholars to meet the central purpose of COCA—to promote education, research, service, and consulting in communication and aging.

## Goals

We have five goals in this book which the various contributions have been selected to fulfill. First, we seek to provide a foundation for scholars and students of communication and aging to branch out and address the multitude of issues being examined in communication and aging. Second, we hope to provide a reference resource for practitioners, professionals, and academics who need to develop specialized skills and insights in communicating with the aging. Third, we intend to provide a synthesis of the leading lines of research and conceptualization in communication and aging. The fourth goal is to provide a textbook to fill a long-term and growing need for the burgeoning number of courses in communication and aging at the undergraduate and graduate level.

The fifth goal of the book is to help the aging individual better understand communication relationships and breakdowns which they may be experiencing. In particular, our goal is to provide the aging individual with a comprehensive overview of what is happening to them as they age, from a communication perspective, and to provide some ideas for handling some of the communication situations with which they may be having trouble. We hope this fifth goal will help aging individuals to continue to enjoy fulfilling lives as they experience the natural aging process.

## Organization of Book

Based on the foregoing discussion of how communication and aging interact, this book is organized into four major sections. Part I, Foundations, attempts to provide an introduction to the fields of communication and gerontology for those readers unacquainted with either, or both, in Chapters 1 and 2. Chapter 3 introduces the interdisciplinary area of communication and aging and describes its perspectives, levels, and contexts.

Part II, The Aging Individual as Communicator, investigates the impacts which physiological changes associated with the aging process have on the aging individual's role as a communicator. Chapter 4 addresses the message processing (cognitive) aspects of how aging and communication interact and provides the bridge into analyzing major areas of aging and the communication process. The impact of the normal (non-pathological) aging process on both sending and receiving messages is addressed in Chapter 5. The impact of various expressive pathologies, the frequencies of which increase with aging, are addressed in Chapter 6.

Part III, Aging and the Communication Process, provides summaries and analyses of current research in several major areas of communication and the aging process. Chapter 7 examines how the various attitudes and stereotypes about aging impinge on the communication process. Chapter 8 looks at the ramifications which attitudes and stereotypes toward aging can have for interpersonal communication. Chapter 9 examines how the lifelong tool of non-verbal communication is employed both by and towards the aging, with particular emphasis on how it affects interpersonal communication and reflects attitudes and stereotypes. Chapter 10 addresses communication across generations, a particular need of the aging and one which usually occurs in an interpersonal context and is influenced by attitudes and the use of non-verbal communication. Chapter 11 looks at how organizations and aging individuals communicate and how better to facilitate that process. Chapter 12 examines how mass media contributes to the overall communication process for the aging and how that same media may inhibit the communication process.

Part IV, Meeting the Communication Needs of the Aging Individual, attempts to provide specific insights into communication and aging in critical situations. Chapter 13 looks at the broad question of the communication aspects of health care delivery to the aging. Chapter 14 addresses one particular aspect of health care delivery, the nursing home. Although less than 5% of the aging reside in nursing homes, the communication needs and research attention directed to this area is considerable. Chapter 15 addresses an often overlooked communication need of the aging — education. The erroneous stereotype that aging individuals cannot, or do not want to, learn new things is exposed. Chapter 16 concludes the section on communication needs of the aging by addressing the social issues which communication can help address, including elder abuse.

Part V, The Research Challenge, provides directions for scholars, practitioners, and students in pushing back the frontiers of our understanding about the unique aspects of communicating with and by the aging. Chapter 17 examines research relating to autonomy for the aging. Chapter 18 explicates the major methodological considerations which uniquely confront the communication and aging researcher.

Finally, the book concludes with a comprehensive bibliography that also serves as the references for the source citations in individual chapters. It is hoped this bibliography will assist future research in communication and aging.

*Carl W. Carmichael*
*Carl H. Botan*
*Robert Hawkins*

# Part I
# FOUNDATIONS

Part I presents a basic introduction to communication and aging. Rather than presenting large volumes of research, it presents an overview of the two major fields which make up communication and aging and explains how they come together. Chapters 1 and 2 provide the reader whose training is in one field with a basic introduction to the other field. Chapter 3 introduces the conceptual foundations upon which the rest of the book is based.

## ❧ 1 ❧

# Introduction to Social Gerontology

## Robert C. Atchley

### Gerontology: The Big Picture

(*Gerontology* is a multidimensional field of knowledge that brings together information about aging and older people that has been generated from both research and practice. Almost all academic fields and fields of professional practice have branches that deal with aging. In addition, gerontology is emerging as an academic field in its own right. Gerontology seeks to unite information about aging from a variety of sources into a cohesive whole.)

A full understanding of aging requires knowledge about physical aging, psychological aging, social psychological aging, and social aging. Knowledge about physical aging includes understanding the causes of the body's age-related declining capacity to renew itself, the physical effects of aging on the body, and what steps, if any, can be taken to prevent, stabilize, or reverse harmful physical effects of aging. Knowledge about psychological aging includes the effects of aging on sensory processes, perception, coordination, mental capacity, human development and coping capacity. Understanding social psychological aging requires knowledge about how aging influences interaction of the individual with his or her environment and includes information on attitudes, values and beliefs, social roles, self image, and psychosocial adjustment. Social aging deals with the nature of the society in which individual aging occurs, the influence that groups within society have on the experience of aging, social policies that affect aging or older people, and the impact that aging individuals have on their society.

*Social Gerontology* is the subfield of gerontology that deals mainly with nonphysical aspects of aging. Social gerontologists must take physical aging into account and must be able to define and measure it, but their primary focus of study is on the inner life of aging people and the interplay between individuals and groups as they deal with issues arising out of the fact that people age.

Many of the concepts, theoretical perspectives, factual information, practice concepts, and research issues in social gerontology are unique— largely unknown outside social gerontology. To be sure, social gerontology shares ideas with other social sciences, but it also has plenty of its own. In addition, many of the concepts borrowed from other social sciences must be modified substantially before they can be used effectively to inform research or theory in social gerontology. Outside gerontology, a great deal of what passes for "facts" about aging is actually the perpetuation of false stereotypes contained within the culture. And because social gerontologists attempt to fit their work into the "big picture" about aging in general, they are likely to be aware of research findings about aging from a wide variety of areas, which facilitates integration of information across topical boundaries.

*Human aging* is a broad concept that includes not only the physical changes that may accompany increased chronological age during adulthood but also psychological changes in our minds and in our mental capacities, and social changes with age in how we are seen by others, what we can expect from them, and what is expected of us.

Most people think about aging in terms of a simple biological metaphor. Organisms are seen as beginning life, going through a period of growth and maturation, achieving full maturity, maintaining full maturity, and then entering a period of decline or aging in which the organism gradually loses its vitality and eventually dies. Although this model applies well to physical aging in very simple organisms, its usefulness for understanding human aging is very limited indeed.

Biological aging is the result of many processes, most of which do not progress at the same rate, even within the same individual. For example, eyesight usually declines before hearing does. In addition, we do not merely accept physical aging. We attempt to prevent or compensate for negative changes. For instance, most people counteract the increased far-sightedness that usually occurs in one's 40s by using reading glasses. To complicate matters even further, most physical functions vary a good bit from person to person at all stages of life. For example, although diastolic blood pressure of 80 is considered "normal," among men age 18 to 24 it ranges from 45 to 105.

Psychological aging is just as complicated. Some functions decline with age while others increase or remain relatively constant. For example, problem solving ability generally declines with age (although declines can be compensated for to some extent), vocabulary usually increases with age, and habits and preferences remain relatively constant. The more closely a psychological function is tied to physical functions, the more likely it is to decline with age. Nevertheless, most of the normal decrements that occur with age are gradually accommodated to with little loss in social functioning.

On the other hand, social aging is largely an arbitrary process of defining what is appropriate for, or expected of, people of various ages. These definitions are usually not based on information about what people of various ages are actually capable of but rather on untested assumptions about the effects of aging. Because they are based largely on untested and often invalid assumptions, our rules which use age as a qualification or disqualification tend to discriminate unjustly against older people, a practice known as *ageism*.

Thus, aging is not one process, but many. It has many possible outcomes, some positive and some negative. On the one hand, aging can bring the opportunity for greater wisdom and skill, and later life can be a time of freedom and deep personal fulfillment. On the other hand, aging can bring physical or mental disability, loss of social position, or attrition within one's network of friends.

*Aging is neither predictably positive nor predictably negative.* For some it is mainly positive; for others, it is mainly negative; and for still others, aging is a little of both. Some scholars assert that aging is a difficult adjustment, yet others assert that it is not. Neither is wrong. Aging is difficult for some people and not for others. However, it is important to acknowledge that positive outcomes substantially outnumber negative outcomes. Most people encounter aging as a generally positive experience.

By now, you should have suspected that operationally defining *aging* or *the aged* is not a simple matter. We generally define age in terms of either chronological age or life stages. Chronological definitions dominate in research and laws and regulations, whereas life stage definitions are more frequently used in everyday social interaction.

Chronological age can be unambiguously measured by using birth certificates which conveniently identify who is or is not included in various chronological age categories. However, when chronological age is used as a proxy indicator of need, large proportions of the population can be misclassified. For example, age 65 is the age at which people become eligible for full retirement benefits under Social Security. Since age 65 has been the cultural norm for retirement for many years, it made some sense to use this age to begin eligibility. However, thousands of people become unable to work due to poor health prior to reaching age 65 and thousands more continue in full-time employment after age 65. Thus, the use of age 65 to define eligibility includes some people (such as the employed) who do not want or need benefits and excludes others who do need full benefits (such as those who are too ill to work but haven't reached age 65).

This problem is further compounded by the fact that a large variety of different chronological ages are used to define *aged, elder,* or *older.* Employees are defined as "older" by the U.S. Department of Labor at age 40. At age 60, widows are able to draw Social Security survivor's benefits; at age 62 people become eligible to live in housing for the "elderly" and eligible to draw actuarially-reduced Social Security retirement benefits. Other programs define "older" as beginning at age 67, age 70, and age 72. Nevertheless, age 65 dominates as the most commonly-used chronological age for defining the beginning of the older population.

Very often in everyday life, instead of chronological age, we use a combination of physical and social characteristics to categorize people into broad *life stages* such as young adulthood, middle adulthood, later adulthood, and old age. *Middle adulthood* is the life stage into which we classify people who are beginning to show physical slowing, who begin to seek less physically demanding activities, and who require longer to recover from exertion. We also classify people into middle age who have reached a job plateau of routine performance and whose children have left home (or at least reached legal adulthood). In middle age, physical changes are less important than the social changes occurring on the job and in the family. For most people, middle age is an exciting time, for many of its transitions make for a more satisfying, and sometimes less hectic, life.

*Later adulthood* is the life stage in to which we place people who have obviously been aging for a while but whose physical and social functioning have been affected by aging in only minor ways. Physically, the person in later adulthood has gray hair, less hair (especially in the case of some men), wrinkled skin, and sometimes slightly bent posture. Chronic illnesses are common but seldom disabling at this stage. Retirement usually occurs near the beginning of this stage. A large number of women become widowed in later adulthood, whereas most men who become widowed experience it in old age. Although later adulthood definitely has its losses, the subjective experience of this stage is much more positive than most young adults or middle-aged people suppose.

*Old age* is the last life stage and is associated with extreme physical frailty, slowed mental processes, greatly restricted activity, social networks decimated by the deaths of friends and relatives, the need for assistance in everyday activities such as bathing and dressing, and a subjective perception that death is near. Most people die before they exhibit these symptoms of old age. However, as our population continues to age, the proportion living to old age will probably increase.

The boundaries between the life stages are fuzzy, and life stage attributions depend to a large extent on the life stage of the person making the attribution. For example, young children often make amusing mistakes when they try to grapple with the issue of who is and who isn't "old." Life stage attributions also vary across ethnic groups and between genders. Although life stages are often used in everyday interactions, life stages are very difficult to measure and to use in research or in constructing laws and regulations.

Gerontological knowledge is growing at a very quick pace, and the rapid growth of the older population is keeping the pressure on to quicken the pace even further. In this book, you will be looking at how aging relates to communication. There are a number of direct benefits that you can expect from studying this relatively new area of gerontology.

Knowledge of aging can improve your interactions with aging or older people by helping you see the world from their viewpoints. Studying aging cannot tell you what a particular older person's viewpoint or experience is, but it can show you that older people vary so widely on so many dimensions that stereotypes of older people's viewpoints are not very useful as a basis for action. It can help you to be *open* to the older person's point of view. And the study of aging can motivate you to find out enough about an aging person to have a basis for genuine empathy.

Empathy is essential if you want to serve older people effectively. Serving the elderly is mainly a process of assisting competent people to pursue goals of their own choosing. Understanding their goals requires both knowledge of the other person and skill in setting aside your own point of view so that it does not interfere with your ability to see theirs.

Knowledge about aging can also improve your ability to make sound decisions, whether they be decisions about your own life, decisions about what social policies are needed, decisions about what programs should be developed, or decisions about whether current programs are operating effectively.

Finally, the study of gerontology can expose you to role models that can be used to fashion your own ideas about what successful aging means to you.

**Suggestions for Further Reading**

Atchley, Robert C. *Social Forces and Aging: An Introduction to Social Gerontology.* Fifth Edition. Belmont, CA: Wadsworth, 1988.

_____. *Aging: Continuity and Change.* Second Edition. Belmont, CA: Wadsworth, 1987.

Binstock, Robert, and Ethel Shanas (eds.) *Handbook of Aging and the Social Sciences.* Second Edition. New York: Van Nostrand Reinhold, 1985.

Birren, James E., and K. Warner Schaie (eds.) *Handbook of the Psychology of Aging.* Second Edition. New York: Van Nostrand Reinhold, 1985.

Maddox, George L. (ed.) *Encyclopedia of Aging.* New York: Springer, 1987.

Monk, Abraham (ed.) *Handbook of Gerontological Services.* New York: Van Nostrand Reinhold, 1985.

## ❧ 2 ❧

# Introduction to Communication

## Frank E.X. Dance

*Shoshin* is the Zen quality of taking a beginner's mind in approaching or considering a subject or behavior. When shoshin is present, the viewer sees that which is viewed as if for the very first time. One sometimes gets the feeling of shoshin when watching a movie. The photography, the quality of the camera work, the viewpoint of the director, or the excellence of the acting, can provide a new perspective on seemingly familiar objects. The image of the lake's surface in *On Golden Pond*, for example, seems novel and fresh. Another instance of shoshin might be watching a child experience something new; you find yourself reliving a similar encounter as if for the first time. Shoshin is important since "In the beginner's mind there are many possibilities, but in the expert's there are few" (Suzuki, 1970, p. 21). The expert says "it can't be done." The beginner, or the person with a shoshin approach, says "let's see how this can be done."

The shoshin approach becomes more difficult as familiarity increases. The closer, longer, and more intense our relation with something, the more difficult it is to step back to view with a beginner's mind. As organisms, we have been communicating since the moment of our coming into being. Each and every organism is interacting within itself and with the surrounding environment from the moment of conception. It is therefore most difficult to have a shoshin approach to communication. But let's try.

A key characteristic of communication is interaction. Whenever and wherever we find an instance of something called communication, we will also find an instance of interaction. The interaction or communication is within or between organisms. Through the human tendency to generalize a concept, communication is also used when discussing interaction between or among inanimate or inorganic objects so that the interactions between or among parts of a building are often referred to as instances of communication. Examples of such communication might be: "The doors in the corridor communicated between the different suites of the house," or "The elevators provided a swift means of communication between the floors of the apartment complex." While such usages are not uncommon we should always recognize them for what they are, extensions of the usage of communication as an organismic phenomenon.)

The very first interaction of an organism is between itself and its surrounding environment. This is true for *all* organisms. Slime molds, amoebas, embryos, all species interact with the surrounding environment. What goes on in this interaction between the organism and its environment is the quest to reduce uncertainty.

The organism scans its environment for nutrients, for other organisms, for signs of danger. Can the organism continue to exist? Can the organism reproduce itself? Can the organism protect itself against threats to its existence? These questions pose important uncertainties for the organism and cause the organism to interact with its environment in a quest to reduce the organism's uncertainty concerning the unresolved questions.

Information (a different commodity than communication) is a measure of the reduction of uncertainty. Because information automatically demands a change of level of uncertainty (from more uncertainty to less uncertainty), information is necessarily a process or processual. Information precedes communication. Communication acts upon information. Because all communication is fueled by or driven by information and because information is imminently processual in nature, all communication has a processual component.

Interaction is characteristic of communication and without it there is no communication. Interaction is designed to reduce uncertainty, to produce information. No organism can afford to take for granted that because nothing threatening is taking place *at* the moment, nothing threatening will take place *in* a moment. Interaction, the search for information, is an ongoing *process*. Information, processual in nature, is the basis for communication. Because communication is interactive and is fueled by information, all communication is also processual.

So far, trying to use the beginner's mind, we have isolated a number of characteristics that seem to be key to communication.

All organisms communicate.

Interaction is an intrinsic part of communication.

Interaction provides information which reduces uncertainty.

Communication acts upon information.

Information is processual and therefore communication is processual.

Therefore, communication is an organismic, interactive process acting upon information.

The initial communication is between the organism and its environment. The organism is the source of the communicative activity and the environment is the object of the communicative activity. As the organism interacts with other organisms in its environment, the communicative structure may extend to them.

To this point, all that has been said is true for all organisms, human or not human. To this point, there is no need to consider the presence or absence of intentionality, or of ethics, in the organismic communicative behavior.

In addition to the communicative structures available to all organisms in differing degrees, human beings are also capable of communicating through spoken language. Spoken language, which many argue is unique to human beings, is always intentional at its intrapersonal level and leads to the development of symbols, of choice, of values, and of ethics. Spoken language and its derivatives of written language, gestural language, and other symbolic codes enable human beings to handle possibilities in the abstract with reduced risk, with greater creativity and imagination. Spoken language and its symbolic derivatives provide the matrix for social relationships and for society in general.

When human beings began reflecting on the phenomenon of communication, they produced multitudinous approaches to the topic. One listing offers well over a hundred published definitions of communication (Dance, 1976), and that listing was restricted to language and printed sources and is already ten years old.

Human communication is a process (or an activity, or a behavior), interactive in nature, based on information (or the reduction of uncertainty), and utilizing both non-symbolic and symbolic vehicles (simple behavioral interaction as well as forms of spoken language).

Communication involves a sender, a message, and a receiver. The simple movement of a message between a sender and a receiver suggests what has been called a "linear" model of communication.

SENDER ─────────────► MESSAGE─────────────► RECEIVER

**Figure 1. Linear Model**

Some students of the communication process, dissatisfied with the one-way implications of the linear model, supported a "circular" model of communication.

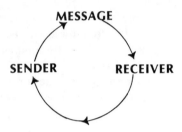

**Figure 2. Circular Model**

Although the circular model allows for feedback, it may be interpreted as suggesting that communicating ends at the very place it began. We know from simple experience that this isn't true. When we are finished with a communicative experience, things have changed. Whether imperceptibly or greatly, the situation has definitely been altered. Such common sense reasoning led to dissatisfaction with the circular model. This dissatisfaction occurred at about the time when the nature of DNA was being discovered and discussed. As a result, the circular model combined with the linear model plus the appreciation of the processual nature of communication produced a helical model of communication. The figure at the top right end of the helix is meant to suggest the never ending nature of communication. The helix evidences how a communicative event may start small, from a single organism, and then develop into ever widening ripples in the environment. If you imagine a helical "slinky" toy, you can also consider the possibilities for representing communicative breakdowns when the coils become tangled, or one section of the toy is compressed or stretched. In addition to a single helix, two or more helixes may be intertwined to suggest the complexity of communication when more than a single human organism is involved in the process.

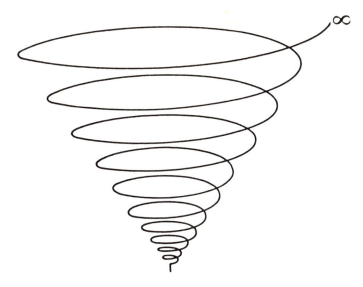

**Figure 3. Helical Model (Dance, 1967)**

All of these figures are geometrical models far more simple than the actual communication process they are intended to represent. The models do not accurately represent the whole process of communication. Rather, they are useful in isolating specific attributes.

In addition to the elements of the communication process already discussed, we have all experienced the reality that communication almost always is afflicted by noise. Noise is defined as something which tends to vary the message in an unpredictable and undesirable manner from what the sender originally intended. One of the better known graphic models of communication which factors in the component of "noise" is the Shannon-Weaver model. The Shannon-Weaver basic model describes an information *source* who creates a given *message* or selects one of a range of possible messages, and who *transmits* the message by generating *signals* which travel over a *channel* to be *received* and ultimately decoded by a *destination*.

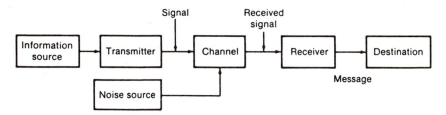

**Figure 4. The Shannon-Weaver Model (Shannon & Weaver, 1949)**

The source of this model suggests the point-of-view of the model's originators. The model is concerned with the fidelity or accuracy of message transference. The practical goal of the model was to parse out the message-sending process in order to measure the accuracy of information transferral with some degree of statistical predictability.

It might be interesting to try and produce your own model of the human communication process with shoshin as your guide.

As we orient our consideration to human communication rather than to organic communication in general, we need also to consider that as the human organism develops and matures it develops a withinness or an interiority. Communicative interaction takes place not only between and among human organisms but also within the individual organism. We often find ourselves talking to, or communicating with, ourselves.

Over the past 35 years, I have asked thousands of people to define communication. The question was posed not to scholars but to ordinary people—people with "beginner's minds." Ages ranged from adolescence to those in their sixties, seventies, and eighties. I have taken the responses and analyzed them for the most common components. Based upon this analysis I have put together what seems to be the most common definition of human communication.

> By human communication I mean the transference of something
> (a fact, a thought, an idea, an attitude, a theory, an emotion,
> et al.) from one person's interior to another person's interior
> with as little distortion of the meaning as possible.

Other components such as "feedback" and "noise" were mentioned from time to time. These components were not mentioned frequently enough to find their way into the overall definition. I would guess that if you asked some of your friends (not students of the formal fields of communication or speech communication or mass communication) to define human communication, you would hear a very similar definition.

So what? Well, a definition is a lot like a miniature theory. A theory is an effort to make sense out of something. A definition takes what we do, or think we do, analyzes it and then phrases the product of the analysis into a statement. So a definition is often a statement of what we do. Reversing the process, what we do is often a reflection of our definition. The result is that we most likely define human communication as we practice human communication.

Take the inductively arrived at definition given above. What are the elements of that definition? What then are the probable elements of the communicative behaviors of the definers? There are three elements in the definition:

1. Human communication works by transference.

2. Human communication takes at least two people ("from one person's interior to another person's interior").

3. Human communication takes place when both parties come away with pretty much identical understanding of the message ("with as little distortion of the meaning as possible").

Now we are where "the rubber hits the road." If you define human communication with the above three components, and if you actually communicate based upon that definition, you may be in trouble.

Human communication doesn't work on the basis of transference. As a matter of fact, you can't transfer anything to anybody except in terms of something with which they are already familiar. If I ask you to read "Man lernt nicht kennen als was Man liebt," and you don't know a word of German, then certainly I have not transferred the meaning of that statement to you. All I have transferred is visual stimuli. The transference of visual or auditory stimuli, purely as physical stimuli, does not usually meet anyone's definition of human communication. For you to understand that the statement means that a person only comes to really understand that which the person loves, you must know enough German to be able to associate the German words with their English equivalents.

If I want to communicate something to you, or to communicate with you, then we must both share some common referents, some common associations. Merely sending the stimuli in your direction simply does not do the trick of communicating. One of the most important things to do when we wish to improve the quality of our human communication is to check that we are putting together our message in terms of the receiver's experience, not just in terms of our own experience. We have to move away from egocentrism. Very young children are tremendously egocentric; they tend to see things and people only from their own viewpoint and they tend to put together and send messages only from their own viewpoint. Little children find it almost impossible to subordinate their own experience and wishes so as to communicate in terms of the experiences and wishes of the other person. Children are egocentric (which isn't the same thing as "selfish") by nature. Children have great difficulty in de-centering, in moving away from their own wishes as the center of their behavior and trying to ascertain the conceptual position of the other person.

Human communication does not work through transference. It succeeds through association, and association is a manifestation of decentering.

In order to communicate with other human beings we need to understand the concept of decentering and to work toward the development of our own capacity for benign decentering when formulating and sending messages. Even when we have developed our decentering capabilities we must always be on guard against what may be called the "egocentric seduction," the temptation to be so enamored of our own way of saying something that we simply "go with it" and thus avoid the constant effort of maintaining decentering.

The suggestion that it always takes two ("from one person's interior to another person's interior") to have human communication is in error. Everyone talks to themselves. The first level of human communication is not between two or more people but within oneself, when one serves simultaneously as the sender and the receiver. There are thought to be at least three levels of human communication:

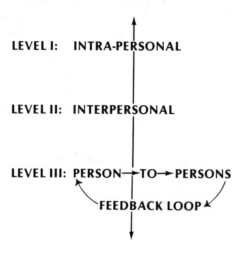

Some add levels such as group communication and organizational communication and cultural communication. Depending on your interests in studying human communication, you may find such additions helpful. For our present purposes, the three level model should prove sufficient. Later chapters of this book will deal with the intrapersonal and the interpersonal levels as they interface with the aging process. It may be noted that levels other than the three levels given are often not additional levels as much as they are settings in which the three levels are situated. The setting may affect the manner in which a level works without the setting constituting an additional level. Communication within nursing homes as well as communication and aging in organizations will be discussed later in this volume. Both qualify as settings within which levels of human communication are found. An organizational setting is composed of people in fairly formal relationships plus the informal network of those same people. The individuals use all three of the stated levels, but their utilization is most likely affected by the business setting. Theoretically speaking (my, how we have moved away from the "beginner's mind"), the fewer assumptions that must be made when dealing with a subject, the better. The fewer levels that satisfactorily serve the complexity of the behavior, the better.

**Level I,** as stated above, is when you are both the sender and receiver of your own messages. Some psychiatrists believe that the vast majority of mental illness is rooted on this first level. How you talk to yourself can materially affect how you feel as well as how you talk to others. One definition of "wellness" says that "wellness" is how a person talks to oneself about one's own physical condition. Some people may suffer serious physical or physiological handicaps yet consider themselves to be "well"; others consider themselves to be "unwell" although an objective point of view would say they were healthy. You tend to talk to others in terms of how you talk to yourself. If you, in your self-talk, stereotype all Irishmen as heavy drinkers, or all Blacks as musical prodigies, or all the elderly as senile or infirm, then it is quite likely that this self-talk is going to make itself apparent in the way in which you talk to others.

**Level II,** interpersonal communication, is when you are talking with one or a number of others in terms of their differences rather than in terms of their commonalities. If you are responding to a question from someone in a large audience, communication with that person is simultaneously being listened to by a large number of other individuals. Most considerations of breakdowns in human communication focus on Level II. It is important, however, to know that Level II is affected by Level I and in turn affects and is affected by the third level.

**Level III,** person to persons communication, is when one person is talking to a number of other persons in terms of their commonalities rather than in terms of their individual differences. When addressing a large audience, it is almost impossible to take into consideration and to evidence in one's speaking an appreciation of the different points of view of each of the audience members. Public speakers tend to talk in terms of things that the individual audience members have in common with one another rather than in terms of those things that set the individual audience members apart from each other. When speaking to a kindergarten class, the age commonality suggests a point of view for the speaker that may enable the speaker to meet some of the common expectations of the audience.

At this level, as well as at the other two levels, level interpenetration is evident. Each level affects the other levels and is, in turn, affected by the other levels. If I feel good about myself (Level I), I may find it much easier to be considerate of others on both Levels II and III. If someone speaks to me harshly (Level II), I may find myself re-evaluating my own self-esteem (Level I) or speaking nastily to someone else (Level II) or to many in a group setting (Level III). If, while attending a mass rally (Level III), I hear a motivational speaker who really makes me feel good about who I am, I may talk to myself (Level I) as well as to others (Level II) quite differently than I did before hearing the speaker. It is this level of interpenetration which is represented by the vertical line running down the middle of the three levels in the visual above. Human communication takes place in all three levels.

The last element that shows up in most peoples' definition of human communication is "with as little distortion of the meaning as possible." What this element suggests is that human communication, in order to be defined as human communication, should be successful. Not so. Again, shoshin testifies that we are not always successful in getting what we want when communicating with others. Our failure to get what we want doesn't mean that communication has not taken place. Not all human communication is successful human communication. *More* communication doesn't always mean *better* communication. Again we all can recall times when we would have been far better off if we had simply remained silent rather than tried to talk our way through a problem. Silence is a form of communication which is often quite salutary. Human communication is not always improved by being increased.

From the very beginnings of simple living organisms to the death of an individual human being, communication plays an important and essential role. Communication binds any organism, individual or social, together. In the human being, communication in general and spoken language in particular play a vitally important role in the sustenance and augmentation of self. There are those who suggest that when communication completely disappears or ceases operation, the decrements of life begin to outweigh the increments of life. The outcome of such a decremental process is the triumph of chaos. As one observer of communication and aging states:

> Energy bound into communication is peculiar to the life process. Perhaps it is this type of energy which controls the living organism as a whole and is dissipated in a flash at death. (Dunn, 1969, p. 114).

The study of human communication takes into consideration all of the things we have been discussing—components, elements, models, levels, decentering and much, much more. Although the field or discipline of human communication is fairly recent, the phenomenon or behavior of human communication is as old as the first human being. Today the discipline of human communication itself has a number of sub-disciplines affiliated with it. The study of organizational communication, the study of mass communication, the study of non-vocal (or non-verbal) communication (all three of these sub-areas will be treated in later chapters insofar as they interrelate with aging), and the study of spoken language are all speciality areas. The study of the interaction of human communication and human aging promises to be another, extremely important sub discipline.

When we all lived in an oral culture, a pre-literate world before writing, it was difficult if not impossible to hold human communication still enough to examine it closely. With the advent of writing and then of printing and then of electronic and mass means of communication, we find ourselves technologically enabled to hold things available for close examination and better theory construction. This is an example of technology driving theory so that we can bring ourselves to the point where informed theory can drive technology. As you will note, the last section of this book deals specifically with research questions. Research is a luxury of our age and a benefit of our technology. We profit from both the activity and the results of research. When it comes to the questions raised by the interface of aging and human communication, research is called for and its productive performance is needed immediately.

For many centuries, human communication was something everyone did but didn't think much about. Now human communication is something everybody does, some know about it and study it, and all should try to improve. There is a place for the "beginner's mind," for *shoshin*. There is also a place for well organized and highly focused academic disciplines. Those disciplines which study the processes of human communication and of human aging are in place and awaiting adequate funding of both talent and money. Lee Thayer once observed that if it is true that academic disciplines seem to emerge in inverse order of their importance to solving the essential questions of human interiority and human society, then a fully developed discipline of human communication may well be the last in order of emergence. We have waited too long, already. Let us get on with the quest!

# 3

# Communication and Aging
## Conceptual Foundations

## Carl H. Botan, Carl W. Carmichael, and Robert Hawkins

### Human Communication

The previous two chapters have introduced two important fields of study—gerontology and communication. These fields have much in common. Both are multidisciplinary fields. Both fields focus on social phenomena. Both fields deal with complex processes. Both fields are unquestionably socially relevant and are currently enjoying wide popularity, particularly in the mass media. This chapter looks at the relationship between communication and aging and explains the framework for the remainder of the book.

Understanding the relationship between communication and aging will take some effort on the part of the reader. Effort is required because aging is an immensely complex physiological, psychological, and social process. Communication is an equally complex physiological, psychological and social process. These two processes interact to produce the complex multidisciplinary specialization known as communication and aging—an area of study even more complex than either of the two composing processes. Because of the complexity of communication and aging, and its dependence on individual differences of interactants, the study of it is not a precise one.

There are no simple prescriptions which readers can memorize to become effective communication and aging practitioners. Rather, the reader will develop a general picture of how the two processes interact. This general understanding can then be applied to particular situations based on individual background and skills.

This chapter first addresses the two major perspectives which can be employed to explore human communication. Second, the five categories in which the relationship between communication and aging can be investigated are explicated. Third, the physiological, cognitive, interpersonal-social, and organizational-cultural contexts of communication and aging are discussed and other contexts are identified. Fourth, the communication needs of the aging are discussed. Finally, the organization of the book is presented. Succeeding chapters will address particular aspects of communication and aging and will offer suggestions as to how the reader might expand on the information in this basic volume.

## Perspectives

One major perspective on the study of human communication is the holistic, humanistic, approach of rhetoric. Rhetoric seeks to study human communication as a whole complex set of choices and actions and focuses on the human element in the interaction. From the rhetorical perspective, communication and aging is concerned with the array of factors affecting communication by and toward aging individuals.

A second major perspective is the communication theory approach which seeks to study human communication by investigating the various component parts of the overall communication process and how they relate to each other. From the communication theory approach, communication and aging is concerned with a wide range of specific questions which it addresses by treating aging as an independent or control variable and communication as an independent or dependent variable.

This book accepts both the rhetorical and communication theory perspective as useful for the study of communication and aging. Threads of both perspectives run throughout the study of communication and aging, although current research and writing tends to lean toward the communication theory perspective. As the study of communication and aging develops and draws the interest of more rhetorical scholars, there should evolve a more even balance between the two perspectives. Such a balance may be desirable because communication and aging may experience the same kind of benefits from employing two perspectives as the broader field of human communication has for many years.

# Categories for Analysis of Communication and Aging

Human communication occurs at several levels and in several contexts (see Chapter 2) which may be grouped together as categories. The two broad perspectives with which the communication discipline addresses communication and aging can be employed to analyze any one of five categories of communication. Approaching communication interactions as being from different categories is a long standing tool in communication research. Each category addresses different questions, may employ different methodologies, and can allow the investigator or reader to focus their attention on particular aspects of communication and aging. The most common set of categories is: (a) intrapersonal, (b) interpersonal, (c) group, (d) organizational, and (e) mass communication. This book makes some use of these categories, but it is not restricted to them.

## Intrapersonal

Intrapersonal communication (even though not accepted as communication by some) is of crucial importance to communication and aging. Those who would not accept an intrapersonal aspect in human communication tend to view the processes which go on inside an individual mind as psychology, not communication, because such processes do not involve the exchange of messages between people. However, our ability to perceive and process messages, an ability which is internal to the individual, is the foundation upon which all human communication is built.

As we age, a number of changes occur with respect to sensory functioning, memory, language facility, and other internal areas. These changes, discussed more fully in Chapter 4, set parameters on how older persons communicate and how they can be communicated with. The unique aspects of message processing which are associated with the aging process must be understood before the other categories of communication and aging can be successfully addressed.

## Interpersonal

The interpersonal category of analysis appears to have received the most attention by researchers investigating communication and aging. Interpersonal communication, often dyadic, focuses on the perceptions and responses of individuals, usually in oral face-to-face settings. Areas of research in interpersonal communication have included attraction, influence, non-verbal, commitment, and many others.

Aging involves alterations in virtually every aspect of interpersonal communication including content and frequency. Interpersonal communication in the family changes drastically as roles and economic status change. The huge set of interpersonal relationship communications associated with most workplaces may end with retirement. Those residing in nursing homes may find interpersonal communication is different from their earlier experience.

## Group Communication

Communication and aging on the small group level has not received very much attention from scholars although such areas as therapy, recreation, group joining, and family communication have been addressed. Group communication can be defined as three to about twenty people engaged in face-to-face communication, over time, in pursuit of some common goal. We spend much of our lives communicating in groups and such groups fill a large part of our communication needs.

Communication and aging scholars can find a fertile area of investigation if they address such topics as age and leadership in groups, age as a determinant of status in groups, and boundary setting (norming) behavior in older groups. Much more research is needed which investigates the specific role which groups can play in communication and aging.

### Organizational Communication

The organizational category of communication and aging has been largely ignored by both communication and gerontology scholars alike. Chapter 11 identifies current work and areas of need.

Organizational communication addresses communication within and by organizations. Organizational communication can be viewed as both a product (memos, etc.) and a process which produces the product known as an organization.

Organizational communication and aging occurs in two distinct sub-categories. The first sub-category is communication between an older person and an organization, with the older person occupying a position *within* the structure. This first sub-category can include communication between the aging and various service providers, employers, companies, and other organizational structures. The second sub-category is when the aging communicate *with* organizations that they are not members of. Dealings with government agencies, retailers, service providers, corporations, and other organizational structures are included in this sub-category. Organized advocacy efforts by the aging, such as consumer rights and patient rights groups as well as political and social organizations fit within this sub-category as well.

### Mass Communication

Mass communication and aging, as discussed in Chapter 12, has been researched extensively. Mass communication is one of the most pervasive communication influences in the lives of the aging, for better and for worse. Mass media (radio, television, newspapers, magazines, etc.) serve as a source of entertainment for the aging and help to maintain a reality orientation and sense of inclusion in society. But the same mass media also perpetuate many stereotypes, casting the aging as everything from villains to bumbling, dottering, senile creatures best communicated with as children.

It is ironic that the mass media serve these two antagonistic functions. On the one hand, they include the aging in the information flow of their society. On the other hand, they create in the minds of the aging, and those who would communicate with them, sets of images and expectations which tend to isolate the aging from the communication interactions which are the fount of life satisfaction and may even be necessary to life at a biological level.

## Contexts

Communication and aging can also be studied in the several contexts within which it occurs. This is a particularly convenient way to approach communication and aging because much of the research to date has been contextual in nature and seems to approach the questions in four major contexts: physiological, cognitive, interpersonal-social, and organizational-cultural.

### Physiological

The physiological aspects of communication and aging include both non-pathological and pathological impacts of the aging process on the communication process. Non-pathological impacts are effects of the normal aging process on the communication producing and receiving mechanisms. Included are changes in the musculature of the voice-producing mechanism and ears, as well as changes in the visual mechanism and all the other physical senses. Pathological impacts include the effects which pathologies, many of which become more common with older age, have on communication producing and receiving mechanisms. Finally, the effects of physiological changes on the capacity of the aging individual to process messages can be addressed as intrapersonal communication.

Both non-pathological and pathological physiological changes are discussed in Part II, Chapters 4, 5, and 6, and part of Chapter 9 on non-verbal communication. Chapter 4 addresses some of the ways in which aging affects the individual's capacity for processing messages and provides a basis for understanding how physiological changes affect the cognitive, social, and organizational-cultural contexts.

## Cognitive

The second context is cognitive—how communication relates to internal states of mind in the aging, and the behaviors which result. In this context researchers seek to find how communication can be used either to detect or to adjust internal states of mind and can be called the psychological approach.

In the cognitive approach researchers and practitioners might use communication as a diagnostic tool to detect changes in certain cognitive capabilities like memory loss or reduced speed of problem solving. Researchers and practitioners might also seek to detect and/or adjust internal mental states such as happiness, loneliness, satisfaction, and anomie.

The communication approach may be the most effective way to investigate internal mechanisms in the aging. When internal mechanisms are investigated with other than a communication approach, there may be a tendency to relegate communication to the role of an intervening variable with internal psychological mechanisms serving as determinant variables and overt behavior serving as the outcome variable. Such a methodology ignores the central role played by communication as the means by which individuals perceive their environment and respond to it, including responding to care providers, psychologists, and social workers. This in turn may lead to unreliable results. Cognitive questions are covered in Chapters 4, 7, and 9.

## Interpersonal-Social

The third context is interpersonal-social, how the aging participate as part of their social environment in one-to-one or one-to-a-few settings. In this context researchers seek to find how communication can be, and is, used to function successfully with the other individuals in the aging persons' immediate environment.

This large context actually operates within all the other contexts because individuals are exchanging messages in them. There are, however, questions which communication and aging researchers need to address which are particular to the interpersonal-social context although they may be transposed on other contexts as well. Issues of interpersonal and family relationships, friendships, and interpersonal aspects of service and health care delivery are all part of this context. Although physician-patient communication, for example, may occur in the organizational context of the hospital, it still retains aspects of a social relationship and can be addressed in that context as well. Social questions are addressed primarily in Chapters 7, 8, 9, and 10.

## Organizational-Cultural

The fourth context is organizational-cultural and addresses the communication needs and practices in the community as they relate to the aging. This more sociological orientation addresses message exchange as the means by which individuals are able to operate as functioning parts of their social environment. Included are the roles of communication, including mass media, in forming and maintaining communities, neighborhoods, and large living and working groups of aging persons. Questions of how practitioners can best go about communicating programs and services to aging members of the community are addressed here as are questions of communication in nursing homes and organizations. Organizational-cultural questions are addressed in Chapters 12, 13, 14, 15, 16, and 17.

## Other Contexts

Numerous other contexts have been discussed in the aging literature, but usually not from a communication perspective. Unfortunately, there does not appear to be a body of communication and aging literature sufficient to warrant the consideration of economic, political, racial and sexual contexts as separate contexts in spite of their crucial importance. Communication and aging researchers need to turn more of their attention to these contexts.

Economic and political needs are both assessed and addressed through communication. Issues of income, financial security, employment, and other economic aspects of life bring questions of communication strategy to the fore. Communication strategies should be formulated to access strategies for conversing with the aging and strategies for advocacy regarding issues of prime importance. The whole realm of political persuasive strategies in appealing to government bodies for programs and agencies which can address the particular needs of the aging requires more attention, as do strategies for appealing to private organizations through consumer advocacy approaches. Finally, the political rhetoric of those seeking, or eschewing, the older vote, needs investigation.

Racial discrimination against minorities in our society is endemic. Because our earlier lives serve as the foundation upon which our latter lives are built, patterns of discrimination to which minorities are subject throughout the life cycle may be expected to manifest themselves in later life (Golden, 1976). For example, there are more than 1½ million blacks over the age of 65 who, with other minorities, may have communication needs and opportunities for minorities which differ from those of aging whites.

Sexual discrimination is also endemic in our society. The economic situation of the 17 million women over 65 is often worse than the economic situation of men (U.S. Bureau of Census, 1985), possibly because women are discriminated against economically all their lives. Women may, therefore, be expected to have communication needs in latter life which differ significantly from those of males. Because women live longer than males, they also have such needs longer than do males.

The editors see expansion of research into the economic, political, racial, and sexual contexts of communication and aging as one of the most pressing needs in the field. In addition, communication scholars may be able to bring unique new approaches to society's attempts to address these aspects of aging.

## Communicating the Needs of the Aging

Meaning must be transferred in order to express, or meet, needs. The communication process is never 100% effective in transferring meaning. Therefore the process must be understood, and skills honed, in order to assure as efficient a transfer of meaning as possible. Physical, psychological, social, economic, political, and other needs, have to be expressed by the aging, and their advocates, in a manner which is both understandable and persuasive for their audiences. Therefore, communication training for the aging and their advocates is a desirable goal.

The ability to feel that we are expressing ourselves effectively is important for all people, including the aging. Communication training in interpersonal and organizational communication might, therefore, help the aging. Assertiveness training for the aging might be particularly beneficial given the tendency of some to adopt a "baby talk" mode when addressing dependent elderly.

Finally, the ability of care and service providers to communicate effectively with the aging can determine success in diagnosis, advocacy, social services, and other endeavors. Training in the aspects of communication unique to the aging process could, therefore, help both service providers and recipients.

# Part II
# THE AGING INDIVIDUAL AS COMMUNICATOR

Part II discusses the changes which occur in mental functioning, speech, and hearing as we age. All communication interactions require the exchange of messages through one of the five senses and the processing of those messages in the "central processing unit" of the brain. A clear understanding of changes in sending, receiving, and processing of messages is a necessary prerequisite to any study of how communication and aging takes place in particular settings or on particular questions.

## ⚜ 4 ⚜

# Intrapersonal Communication and Aging

## Carl W. Carmichael

While the study of the communication aspects of aging encompasses the whole spectrum of the communication field, a sensible starting point is with the most basic level in human communication: cognitive functioning within a single human being. All communication, on any of the various levels discussed in Chapter Two or in any social context, necessarily involves the processing of information by the participating individuals. The major components of human information processing—receiving, relating, storing, retrieving data, and symbolic encoding and decoding—are absolutely essential ingredients in every human communication situation.

The intrapersonal level of communication represents an important aspect of the aging process. Some of the most insidious, misleading stereotypes of aging have to do with various cognitive impairments, such as memory loss and intellectual decline, that are assumed to be directly attributable to the aging process. In this chapter, we will review the major issues and some of the research in the areas of memory, intelligence, language facility, and sensory losses. Two perspectives will persist in conducting this review. One is to analyze these areas in relation to aging in order to assess the validity of some relevant stereotypes. The other is to consider the research findings in relation to communication competence. Basic cognitive functioning is necessary for normal social existence. Communication effectiveness has not been the major criterion in much of the research in this area but certainly is of primary concern to the communication scholar.

## Memory

The myth of memory loss is one of the most deeply entrenched stereotypes in our cultural belief system, probably because folklore found support in early traditional gerontological research. "I just can't remember names any more" is one of the most common complaints of older people. The lapse of memory also applies to phone numbers, grocery prices, and numerous other bits of information processed daily. Does this experience represent a legitimate decline related to age or do we experience a kind of "self-fulfilling prophecy" having been programmed all of our lives with such cultural maxims as "You can't teach an old dog new tricks"? An examination of this question is warranted in a book on communication and aging. While memory is a major component in the human intrapersonal communication system, cultural belief systems that may contribute to the perpetuation of false beliefs are communicated through our primary (mediated and interpersonal) communication systems, Certainly, intervention in correcting widely held misbeliefs could not be possible without understanding and using the communication patterns and systems in the culture.

Is memory loss due to aging a misleading stereotype or reality? First, let's consider what memory is and how it functions; then, let's review what we know from the research literature.

Memory is not a troublesome word to define. Even when it is used in a stereotype that may be inaccurate, the concept of memory was probably used correctly. Memory has been equated with learning. Indeed, the two concepts would be difficult to distinguish, especially in classrooms where learning is operationalized by information retrieval rather than creativity. The best way to define memory may be to explore how it functions.

Researchers in this area usually represent memory in a three-stage model. The components comprising the model differ somewhat, however. One of the most common models of the memory process appears below (for example, Atkinson and Shiffrin, 1968; Hoyer and Plude, 1980; Murdock, 1960),

| Stage One | Stage Two | Stage Three |
|-----------|-----------|-------------|
| → **Sensory** | → **Short-term** | → **Long-term** |
| → **Stores** | → **Memory** | → **Memory** |

The first stage represents information that entered the human system but was never put into "memory" banks for later recall. In the information processing framework, such information may have been used briefly but was never really "processed." The second stage represents information that has been retained for relatively immediate use, while the third stage is believed to have a larger capacity and can hold information for a much

longer period of time. To confuse matters, different labels may be used—
for example, "Primary" and "secondary" instead of short-term and long-
term (Norman and Lindsey, 1972). Models of memory functioning may be
imbedded within the traditional three-stage model above. Botwinick's
Registration, Retention, Recall (Botwinick, 1967) model would be an
example; it includes the final stage of retrieving information but does not
distinguish among types of memory stores. The most comprehensive model
is Atkinson and Shiffrin's which combines both models. They posit three
stages:

**ENCODING ⟶ STORAGE ⟶ RETRIEVAL**

Within the storage stage, three types of stores appear—sensory, short-term,
long-term.

The relevant question remains. Does memory functioning decline with
age? Unfortunately, the question is more complicated than it seems. As
noted above, early research confirmed the cultural belief. This requires
some interpretation. On the one hand, it should be noted that most of this
research used cross-sectional designs and compared groups of younger (usually college age) and older subjects. This means that the aging process, per
se was not studied. Therefore, it could not be concluded that memory
declined as a result of aging. On the other hand, differences were found between young and old subjects, and those differences must be accounted for.
Also, in many of those studies, the differences increased as the age of the
older subjects increased (Poon, 1985). Research focusing on the encoding
stage (e.g., subjects are asked to learn lists of words) typically found differences, but those differences were reduced if subjects were trained to
organize the words into categories (Schmitt, Murphy, and Sanders, 1981), if
subjects were trained to use mnemonic devices (Hartley, Harker, and Walsh,
1980), or if subjects were instructed to use visual images (Rabinowitz,
Craik, and Ackerman, 1982).

Research focusing on the second stage of memory, storage, indicates little
difference between young and old in the sensory and short-term stores, but
significant differences in long-term memory. Of course, long-term store is
what we normally think of as memory, and therefore this conclusion should
not be taken lightly. However, psychologists have concluded that the
difficulty older people have with long-term memory is not one of capacity,
but rather either a problem of encoding (input) or of retrieval (output)
(Poon, 1985).

Research focusing on retrieval, the third stage, seems to argue for older
people having more difficulty. Two interesting conclusions emerge from
this literature. First, the distinction between recall and recognition is
apparently more pronounced for older people. That is, the differences
between older and younger subjects are reduced considerably when they are

asked to recognize the words either with a clue or with a direct question such as "Did you see the word *house* on the card?" When subjects are asked to recall words or factual information without the aid of any clues, age differences are significant (Poon, 1985). Second, the well-established belief that older people can remember distant events better than more recent events is not confirmed by the research literature. Rather, the concept of recency holds up consistently; older people are no different than younger people in remembering recent events better than events of the distant past. (Erber, 1981)

Most of this research is cross-sectional and therefore causes great concern. Many factors could account for such differences between younger and older people. An excellent example can be found in a recent experiment in which the amount of time subjects were given to study the stimuli was varied (Adamowicz, 1976). When subjects were given three seconds to study the card containing visual symbols, the usual age differences resulted. When they were given six seconds, the differences were not statistically significant but were in the same direction. However, when subjects were given the card for twelve seconds, although the differences were not statistically significant, older subjects retained slightly more information than younger subjects. If *learning time* is an important variable in accounting for memory differences between young and old, how many other variables may have similar effects? Motivation level? Test familiarity? Fatigue? Perceived relevance? Hopefully, future cross-sectional research will focus on such variables. Ideally, future research will include more longitudinal designs to enable a direct examination of the relationship between memory functioning and the aging process.

## Intelligence

Does age bring a decline in intellectual functioning? In answering that question we find much similarity with the memory loss question. The two questions are related in some relevant ways. A person cannot function very intelligently without the ability to retain information; intelligence and memory must function together to some degree. Intelligence is the ability to learn, to engage in logical thinking, to solve problems, to manipulate symbols on an abstract level. Intelligence goes beyond merely retaining information; it has to do with how one *uses* information. Regarding the question of relationship to age, the concepts of intelligence and memory are similar in that they are both cognitive functions that are victims of negative stereotypes deeply rooted in the cultural belief system.

Much that was examined earlier regarding memory applies to analyzing the question of intelligence and aging as well. Early gerontological research on intelligence mostly confirmed the negative stereotype of old dogs and new tricks. However, as is the case with memory, a close examination of the research raises many questions about methodology and confounding variables. The same issue of cross-sectional versus longitudinal research design is relevant, and a review of the few recent longitudinal studies on intelligence puts serious doubt on many of the old assumptions.

In a nutshell, the typical earlier study measured intelligence with an IQ test (e.g., the Wechsler or the Thurstone), used a cross-sectional design comparing a group of young people (usually college students) with a group of older people (usually over 65), and virtually always found significant differences in the stereotyped direction. Let's analyze each of these aspects.

First, the use of the IQ test raises some questions. Intelligence tests involve several subtests. The Wechsler Adult Intelligence Scale (WAIS), probably the most frequently used, has eleven subtests. Six are classified as "verbal" since they are heavily language oriented, while the remaining five are classified as "performance" since they emphasize problem-solving without relying on language. In spite of these arbitrary subdivisions, over half of the items on the test fall into a single category, usually referred to as "general intelligence" (51% of variance), as a result of factor analysis (Cohen, 1957). Thus, rather than incorporating a diversity of approaches to intellectual functioning, this particular IQ test primarily utilizes only one. If that dominant approach contains any age biases, the other minor categories of items will not be given sufficient weight to produce an unbiased total score.

Six other factors (or confounding variables) that we should consider in relation to IQ testing with older people are discussed below.

1. *Education level.* In one study, age was not a factor in analyzing the major component of General Intelligence, but education was (Birren and Morrison, 1961). Since education level is lower for older adults (70% over 65 have less than an eighth grade education), this would represent a serious age bias.

2. *Socio-economic status.* Similarly, socio-economic level could be a significant factor affecting IQ but was usually not reported in these earlier studies. The reasoning is that people with a higher socio-economic status tend to be on a higher intellectual level, tend to sustain that higher level since more intellectual activity is required in their lives, and tend to be more verbal. Therefore, people in this group are more likely to do better on a verbally oriented IQ test.

3. *Time limit as age bias.* Since IQ tests are timed, older people may be disadvantaged. Recalling the Adamowicz study cited above in which differences between young and old subjects disappeared when study time increased, time limitations in a stressful test situation could hinder adequate processing of the questions (Adamowicz, 1976).

4. *Test situation as age bias.* In addition to the time restraint, the pressurized test situation in general may be a biasing factor against older

people. The college students with whom the older people typically are being compared probably have sharper test-taking skills. They have been practicing taking tests for several years and are currently still in school where they frequently experience such situations. Most older people, on the other hand, have not taken a test in many years and may have forgotten some of the skills involved. Also, given less familiarity with the test situation, it may be much more anxiety producing for older people (Eisdorfer, Nowlin, and Wilkie, 1970).

5. *Fatigue.*   Common sense would argue that older people may be more likely to experience fatigue during a lengthy and complex test situation. Obviously, how well one does on a mentally demanding test is going to be affected by one's level of alertness.

6. *Motivation.*   Is it more likely that young people, perhaps students in college, would be more motivated to strive for the highest scores possible on an IQ test? They may have been conditioned to believe the test outcome could affect their careers in some way. Is it logical that an older person would feel the same sense of urgency to perform? Common sense would argue again that the older subject may not be as highly motivated to do as well as the younger subject.

The most significant issue, of course, is the use of cross-sectional research designs comparing younger with older subjects. It is not surprising that age differences in IQ are found consistently. The above factors, especially in combination since any number might be operating simultaneously, should make age differences in IQ as measured in these tests quite predictable. Fortunately, several studies have been conducted using a longitudinal design that may reveal more about intellectual development in the later years.

One of the earliest longitudinal studies of intelligence took advantage of the fact that by the 1950s there were middle-aged people who had taken IQ tests as college students, a practice that began in the early 1920s (Owens, 1966). Owens found that, rather than the decrease in IQ after age twenty-five that had been indicated from the cross-sectional studies, the longitudinal study actually showed an increase in IQ—at least up to age fifty. However, a major criticism of this study was that the college-educated subjects probably were of higher intelligence and were in careers that required maintaining intellectual skills. Later longitudinal studies confirmed the validity of that criticism. That is, when subjects at all levels of intelligence and education were used, the increase in IQ was more prevalent with the higher educated population. However, even with the lower educated subjects, these studies did not find a decrease in IQ through the adult years and well into the later years (e.g., Eisdorfer and Wilkie, 1973).

Probably the best study to date is one that used a combination of both cross-sectional and longitudinal designs to enable a comparison (Schaie, 1979, 1983a; Schaie and Hertzog, 1985). This study began in 1956 using 500 subjects ranging in age from 21 to 70, with three replications in 1963, 1970, and 1977. In the case of "Verbal Meanings," for example, one of the "Primary Mental Abilities" tested, the cross-sectional comparisons between the younger and older subjects showed a sharp decrease. The longitudinal data showed increases until age 60, with only a small decrease thereafter.

There has been a consistent pattern over the last thirty years. Cross-sectional studies indicate a decline in intelligence with age; longitudinal studies show no decline and, in some cases, an increase in intelligence as the subject ages. This apparent discrepancy is probably a result of cohort or generational differences in average IQ scores. One explanation may be that the development of our information processing abilities is directly related to the level and complexity required to process information in the culture. That is, when the production of information in the culture was slow, relying primarily on print media, the processing of that information matched the demand. As information dissemination increased and media became more sophisticated, the requirements for processing by the individual receiver may have become more sophisticated as well. When one considers that each generation currently alive in our culture has experienced very different systems of mediated communication during the early developmental years, generational differences in cognitive abilities are not surprising. The oldest generation in America was weaned on print media primarily; the next oldest generation grew up with radio; the middle-aged folks bridged the gap between radio and television; young adults represent the "television generation"; and, today's children are perfectly at ease in front of a computer terminal at home as well as in school. With each succeeding generation, the primarily used media in the culture have become more sophisticated, and the amount and speed of information production has increased (Carmichael, 1976).

In any case, there is ample reason to doubt the cultural myths on intellectual decline. The most recent longitudinal evidence indicates that healthy people who stay mentally active need not experience any decline in their intellectual abilities well into their eighties.

## Language Facility

Probably the most important cognitive ability for ordinary people to possess is the ability to function linguistically—to speak their native language and to communicate effectively with others in their social systems. There appears to be very little research directly on language use in the professional journals on aging. However, the discussions about memory and intelligence also apply to the language area.

Most of the memory research used verbal stimuli in the testing procedures, usually lists of words but not in any meaningful verbal context. Literally all of the intelligence research directly applies here. Many of the test items on the IQ tests are language use items (e.g., vocabulary, or verbal analogies). Moreover, it could be argued that the entire IQ testing procedure is really language testing because the tests are conducted in a linguistic framework and use language to give test instructions and to communicate the test questions. Test items in problem-solving or logic may not be focusing on specific aspects of language use such as vocabulary, grammar, or syntax, but a minimum level of competency in linguistic functioning is certainly required in order to understand and to respond intelligently to any of the test items. Thus, the conclusions reached regarding intelligence and aging are applicable to language facility and aging as well. The language related items, a major part of what Schaie referred to as "Crystallized Intelligence," showed the most dramatic increase with age in longitudinal designs (Schaie, 1983b).

The concept of "language facility" may best be understood in this context. Rather than focusing on grammatical correctness or linguistic devices, language facility refers more directly to the ability to function verbally on a minimum level of competency.

This is not a new concept in developmental psychology. A variety of measurement techniques have been devised (e.g., the Utah Test of Language Facility) for which there are national test data. Unfortunately, all of these have been devised for, and tested with, children. One study adapted this procedure for older subjects (Pearson, 1977).

Pearson's adaptation involved showing a photograph to subjects and asking them to describe what they saw. The photograph displayed a kitchen scene containing a variety of usual items—appliances, sink, cupboards, children, cookie jar, etc. Analysis of the subjects' verbal responses involved determining the level of verbal complexity on a multi-level scale ranging from single-word responses on one end to complex, coherent sentences intricately organized at the other end.

For data analysis, subjects were grouped chronologically in increments of five years from age sixty to eighty-one plus. Pearson reports a negative correlation (-.26) between age and language facility, with no education differences and no sex except in the eighty-one plus category. Women scored higher than men in the oldest category (Pearson, 1977).

The central concept in this chapter should be what has been referred to as communication competency—the ability to communicate at a level that enables a normal social existence. While this has not been a criterion of concern in the numerous research studies reviewed, normal social survival represents the perspective of this book. The issue of competence is obviously a moot point in interpreting the longitudinal research that found increases, or no decline, in cognitive functioning in older people.

Communication competence becomes a significant phenomenon, however, in interpreting the apparent negative findings of the cross-sectional studies that report "significant differences." We must remember that statistically significant differences between younger and older subjects in such a study does not in any way tell us how competently the subjects are functioning. What if an eighty year old has more difficulty retaining a list of words presented by a researcher than does a twenty-five year old? Does that mean the older person cannot communicate competently? How does that finding relate to the reality of the older person's everyday existence?

So far in this chapter, we have briefly reviewed research in the areas of memory, intelligence, and language facility. As major components of human cognitive functioning, they represent significant aspects of information processing that determine communication competence. The conclusion from this review can only be that the general evidence indicates that aging, per se, does not necessarily produce cognitive impairment until the very elderly years. There is apparently some decline of memory function through the middle years, increasing with age, but not enough to impair normal communication processes. In the case of general intellectual functioning, the evidence from recent longitudinal research debunks the cultural myth that aging brings an increasing loss of IQ level. Rather, the major aspects of intelligence (verbal skills, problem-solving, etc.) increase in acuity over the years, while there may be some decline in some of the minor areas such as visuo-motor flexibility. Language facility may be the least researched area of those reviewed, but it shows promise as a central concept in assessing the communication competence of normally aging older adults. The language oriented categories in the intelligence tests may relate to this concept enough to conclude from the IQ research that language facility also does not appear to be a problem in the normal aging process.

## Sensory Losses and Aging

The fourth area, and the focus of this section, has been subject to a great deal of research. The relationship between sensory losses and aging has been well documented in the literature (e.g., Colavita, *Sensory Changes in the Elderly,* 1978; and, Carmichael, 1983). Therefore, this topic will be reviewed only briefly here, primarily for the purpose of noting the effects of sensory losses on the communication process for older normally aging people.

### Visual Perception

The first area considered, visual changes and aging, has received the greatest attention in the literature, rivaled only by hearing losses. A number of literature reviews in this area have already been done, with the two most comprehensive being by Fozard, et al., in which they cite 183 studies, and the chapter on visual changes in *Sensory Changes in the Elderly* (Colavita, 1978).

Age relates to two types of changes in the structure of the eye. The first concerns changes in the transmissiveness and accommodative power of the eye that begin to assume importance between the ages of 35-45 years; such changes affect distance vision, sensitivity to glare, binocular depth perception, and color sensitivity. The second change affects the retina and nervous system and begins to be important between 55-65 years of age, producing changes in size of the visual field, sensitivity to low quantities of light, and sensitivity to flicker (Fozard, et al., 1977). In fact, numerous eye-related physical changes have been documented. It seems, just as a good veterinarian can tell the age of a horse by looking at its teeth, so your ophthalmologist may be able to detect your age by examining your eyes. "A strong subjective impression of an individual's age is provided by the physical appearance of the eye and its surrounding tissue" (Fozard, et al., 1977).

Surrounding tissue includes the eyelids, eyebrows and eyelashes. They, too, change with age. For example, the eyelids lose their skin and subcutaneous fat which make them appear to be wrinkled and more transparent. Loss of muscle tone reduces the eyelid's ability to move tightly over the eyeball; irritation and reddening are common. These changes, along with the typical nose growth, may make the older person's eyes appear to be more sunken.

The eye itself may experience many age-related changes (details of which can be found in the sources cited above). Major changes include:

      Cornea:  development of a gray ring (arcus senilis)
               increase in thickness
               reduced refractive power
         Iris: decrease in permeability
         Lens: hardening, yellowing, development of cataracts
        Pupil: decrease in size
       Retina: reduction of visual field
               increase in blind spot
               development of macular disease (accounting for nearly
                  half of vision problems in old age)

Blindness and visual acuity are unquestionably related to aging. In the case of blindness, one study found that the number of cases of legal blindness increases from about 250 per 100,000 in the 40-64 age group to 500 per 100,000 in the 65-69 age group and to 1,450 per 100,000 in the 69+ group. In other words, the incidence of blindness doubles from the middle-aged group to the upper 60s group and triples in the oldest group (National

Society for the Prevention of Blindness, 1966; reported by Fozard, et al., 1977).

There is also a pronounced relationship between age and visual acuity. The number of older people experiencing a decrease in normal visual functioning rises dramatically with each age bracket. Using both the United States National Health Survey (1968) and the Duke University longitudinal study (Anderson and Palmore, 1974), we see a dramatic change from age 60 to 80. The percentage of older individuals having the optimal 20/20 vision goes from about 40% at age 60 to 10% at age 80; those suffering from 20/50 acuity (considered serious enough that some states impose restrictions on drivers' licenses) goes from about 8% at age 60 to 32% at age 80.

A number of conditions (intraocular pressure and glaucoma, pupil size decrease, lens hardening, cataracts, etc.) are only indirectly related to aging. However, a number of conditions are directly related to aging: diabetic retinopathy (characterized by accelerated aging of the arteries), senile miosis, and yellowing of the lenses. The most common age-related conditions would be changes in adapting to degree of luminance and sensitivity to glare and flicker. The practical significance of these findings is in tasks that require partial adaptation. For instance, the operation of motor vehicles at night under conditions of unpredictable changes of luminance or movie attendance would be activities requiring adjustment.

## Auditory Perception

The topic of hearing loss and aging has similarly received considerable attention and has enjoyed several literature reviews. This topic is covered more fully in Chapter 5 of this book, so this will be a brief overview. By now, the term "presbycusis" should be familiar. The term denotes a condition characterized by a progressive bilateral loss of hearing for tones of high frequency due to degenerative physiological changes in the auditory system as a result of age. As John Corso points out in his review article, "the problems related to presbycusis and other hearing disorders emerge in new perspective since the implications of these disorders cannot be isolated from the aging person's total repertoire of behavior" (Corso, 1977).

One point that should be made at the outset is that auditory problems are increasing in our culture irrespective of age. Trend studies from the 1960s and 1970s predict that there will be 80% more "hard of hearing" persons in the U.S. in the year 2000 than exist today. Approximately 13% of the 65 and over population show advanced signs of prebycusis, and this should increase as well. A number of age-related conditions have been documented. A common finding in the elderly (but also in young children) is the accumulation of fluid in the middle ear due to an obstruction in the Eustachian tube, usually in conjunction with a cold. In addition, a number of classes of disorders may be observed as a function of age in the morphological structures of the inner ear—from atrophy and degeneration of hair cells to loss of auditory neurons. Hearing loss has been related to noise exposure (no surprise here); the best studies have chosen non-noise exposed subjects for age comparisons since this would be a very "noisy" (confounding) variable relating to occupation, neighborhood, population density, family norms, etc.

In presbycusis there is not only a decrease in auditory sensitivity but a decrease in the ability to understand speech. Reduced speech perception in the aged seems to be due, in part, to the increase in the time required to process information in the higher auditory centers. The magnitude of the effect has been studied by presenting individuals with accelerated speech (compressed speech), i.e., an increase in the word rate per minute. For young subjects, it is possible to offset the decrease in discrimination by slightly increasing speech intensity. This equalizing effect is not possible in older subjects. For those over 70 years, 100% intelligibility can be obtained for normal rates (140 words per minute) if the intensity is high enough, but for accelerated speech (350 words per minute), intelligibility does not exceed 45% regardless of intensity. Thus, when speaking to older people, getting louder might not help, but speaking more slowly may!

Listening is required for effective communication. Hearing impairment, even to a small degree, can seriously affect the communication process. The functional changes in speech and hearing that may be experienced in the later years are likely to reduce older people's communicative involvement.

**Taste, Smell and Tactility**

The sensory modalities of taste and smell are much more controversial in relation to aging. Not only are there fewer research studies in these areas, but some of them report no age-related changes. Although the research has increased during the 70s, there is not as yet enough information to make generalizations which may be useful, for example, in diagnosing sensory problems or improving diets. In fact, there has been more emphasis on measuring taste and smell preference than on measuring sensitivity. The most widely cited conclusion is that taste sensitivity decreases with age; not all experiments have been able to verify it, however. Odor sensitivity seems to be very stable over age (Engen, 1977).

The last area to be reviewed is somesthetic or tactile sensitivity. The most recent findings of the effect of age on somesthetic acuity are no different than those from the early studies in the 30s—uniform decreasing sensitivity. Loss in touch sensitivity (e.g., appreciation of cotton or wool applied to the hairy skin) has been reported to occur in approximately 25% of the aged population. More controversial, but still somewhat related to age, are sensitivities to vibrations, temperature changes, puffs of air, pain, and the two-point limen test. A major factor emerging is that different body parts vary in sensitivity levels. In relation to aging, the lower extremities decrease in sensitivity before the upper extremities (Kenshalo, 1977).

## Communication and Sensory Losses

The relationship between sensory losses and various aspects of the communication process has not received research attention. Many obvious and not so obvious questions can be raised concerning the implications of age-related sensory losses on the social-interactive functioning of the normally aging individual.

Obviously, the information processing aspects of communication must be affected somewhat when the amount of information input has been reduced. Could sensory losses account for the "having trouble keeping up" gap cited in early communication and aging research? How many misunderstandings and other failures to communicate have been attributed to generational differences when sensory losses might have caused a correctable problem?

Logical thinking requires good information input. Could erratic behavior or apparent problems in rational thinking be a result of sensory losses? Since decision making in general, logical or otherwise, requires information, experiencing sensory losses could result in an older person's indecisiveness and, therefore, loss of control over the environment.

Perhaps the most significant effect of sensory losses on an older person could be a reduction in communication efforts. Observation of communication deprivation, now made by numerous communication researchers in nursing homes, should not lead to remedial actions such as manipulations of increased interaction, environmental changes, staff training on conversation initiation, etc. until sensory loss data are obtained on the subjects in question.

A few observations are worth noting from the literature. First, when communication problems are experienced, multiple factors may be operating. We are cautioned by the researchers in this area that usually a number of other age-related variables may be affecting the condition at the same time that sensory losses are being experienced. Remember, too, more than one type of sensory loss may be experienced simultaneously.

The literature also indicates that one of the most difficult communication problems relating to sensory losses is to convince the affected older person to seek rehabilitation. Sensory losses have become a "sign" of aging and may therefore be denied. "I can hear fine—you're not talking loud enough!"

Of all the sensory functions, vision and hearing have the most significant impact on behavior. Hearing loss is probably the most serious. An interview study of 270 centenarions confirmed that loss of hearing is more gradual than loss of sight, but adjustment to loss of hearing is more difficult (Beard,

1969). As one reviewer in this area wrote, "With advancing years, the functional changes in speech and hearing significantly interfere with the communication process and the aging individual is, therefore, inclined to restrict the degree and scope of his social interaction" (Corso, 1977). Indeed, this may be one of the most significant areas of study in communication and aging.

In conclusion, here are a few suggestions for improving communication with older people:

1. Don't assume an older person is experiencing a decline in mental functioning simply because they are older.
2. Monitor your talk with older people. Are you speaking in a manner that is more appropriate for communicating with children? Include in your observations such items as vocaulary choice, sentence complexity, vocal intonation, voice intensity, and topic choice.
3. If an older person appears to be hard of hearing (i.e., has asked to have something repeated more than once), speak more slowly and distinctly rather than louder.
4. Encourage older friends or family members to get regular examinations for visual and hearing changes, especially if they drive. If correction is needed, express positive attitudes toward getting the correction. For example, mention how this would improve communication and how important this is to you.

# ❧ 5 ❧

# Aging and Normal Changes in Speech-Language-Hearing

## Barbaranne H. Benjamin

The ability to communicate is vital to the well-being of humans. The concept of self, for example, is largely constructed through social interaction in which others communicate expectations of role, personal value, ability, etc. In addition, the very fabric of society depends on communication to facilitate contact among individuals for social, educational, and productive endeavors. Clearly, changes which affect the ability to communicate significantly impact every aspect of daily life.

Throughout our life span, ordinary changes occur which potentially affect communication. Major growth and development occur in the early formative years of the child with finer development of communication skills typically occurring throughout later childhood and adolescence. Even for the adult, changes in cognitive functioning, memory, and linguistic skill have a subtle though pervasive influence on communication abilities after adolescence. These changes occur normally, separate from illness, disease, or pathological condition which also may affect communication by and with elderly individuals.

Incidence of chronic conditions is highest in the older adult population because chronic conditions are cumulative through the life span (Ward, 1984). For instance, while severe visual disabilities occur in .1% of individuals below the age of 45 years, the percentage increases to nearly 6.5% in adults between the ages of 75 and 84 years and to 18% in adults over the age of 85 years (Hess, 1984). Arthritis, hypertension, and hearing loss—all conditions that potentially impact communication—are the three most common conditions affecting the elderly population in the United States (U.S. Congress Senate, 1980).

Certain physiological changes which occur normally with aging subtly impact the ability of older adults engaged in communication interactions. This chapter examines the impact of these changes on the efficiency and effectiveness of the receiver-sender roles of older communicators. Before dividing the role of receiver and sender to facilitate ease of examination, we will explore the changes in the neurological system which are central to both receiving and sending messages.

Certain changes in the neurological system associated with normal advanced aging may have an impact on both reception of information and expression of messages in communication interactions. Although the onset and rate of aging differs between as well as within individuals, significant anatomic and physiological changes typically occur in the central nervous system (Ordy, Brizzee, & Beavers, 1980). For instance, by the ninth decade of life, brain weight has decreased by 10% (Appel & Appel, 1942). Although the reason for this decrease is unclear, changes in neural structure affect those areas of the brain associated with various language functions.

A decrease in the number of cells in the precentral gyrus, postcentral gyrus, and superior temporal gyrus is significant with progressive age. Reductions are greatest for the frontal and temporal lobes although changes also occur in the visual cortex and hippocampal areas (see: Kemper, 1984). These areas are associated with specific components of motor movements and sensory feedback involved in speech production: the superior temporal gyri, frontal lobes, and temporal lobes are involved in various aspects of coordination, production, and processing of language; the hippocampus is associated with memory, a prerequisite ability for effective communication during normal daily interaction.

In addition to brain functioning, the nerve paths of the central nervous system are affected by the normal aging process. Reduction in the length of dendrites, the number of dendrite branches, and efficiency of synaptic contacts occurs with advanced age (H. Brody, 1985). An increase in neurite plaque, neurofibrillary tangles, and granulovacular degeneration occur in the brains of normal elderly persons although excessive increases are associated with dementia and other pathologies in which language and speech disturbances are apparent (Kemper, 1984).

Such changes in neural tissue may systematically affect an individual's ability to use and to understand speech and language. In the normal older person, these changes in speech and language functioning are subtle; they are insufficient to cause deterioration of communication in most daily activities. Nonetheless, consistent patterns of change are found in older communicators' abilities both to receive and to send messages. These patterns are examined in the following sections of this chapter.

## The Older Adult as Message Receiver

Sensory disability can affect individuals at any age. Deafness or blindness may occur at birth, may be the result of trauma, or may be due to an accumulation of disease-related defects, drug side-effects, or accidents throughout the life span. Sensory disabilities are more prevalent in the older population than in other age groups. In addition to an accumulation of chronic defects, normal changes in anatomy and physiology as a result of aging alter sensitivity of the various sensory systems.

The ability to receive information from other communicators and from the environment requires an intact sensory system. Aging older adults normally experience a reduction in sensory abilities. Senses are less acute so some stimuli must be of greater magnitude or of longer duration to be perceived by older individuals. Reduction in sensory ability has a debilitating impact on communication which may be out of proportion with the extent of the sensory deficit. The more difficult the communication process becomes, the more likely communicators will opt to withdraw from such demanding situations. Changes in sensory systems can impede the efficiency of communicators, reduce adaptation to environmental conditions, and contribute to a decrease in communication contacts (Tamir, 1979). Ultimately, the quality of life can be adversely affected by decreased communicative contact (Jacobs-Condit & Ortenzo, 1984).

## Changes in Auditory Ability with Advanced Age

Reduction of hearing ability begins at about age 30 with reduction for males beginning between 26-32 years and about age 37 for females. By age 51-57 years, females have a more significant reduction of hearing ability for low frequency tones while males exhibit less sensitivity for high frequency tones (Corso, 1963).

Not only does the ability to sense auditory stimuli decrease with age but a deterioration in the ability to discriminate speech is a recognized characteristic of age-related hearing impairment. Speech discrimination difficulty is related to the normal aging process, to changes in peripheral or conductive hearing, and to degenerative changes in the sensory and central auditory nervous system (see: Orchik, 1981). These factors, contributing to hearing impairment in older individuals, include cumulative etiologies which cause hearing loss throughout the life span (Nadol, 1981) as well as particular changes attributable to advanced age. Consider the example of otitis media, a middle ear infection which primarily affects young children but may occur in anyone whose eustachian tube does not provide sufficient ventilation of the middle ear cavity.

Ototoxic medicines result in hearing loss; infections may also cause reduced hearing sensitivity. Chronic sensory neural loss from exposure to noise pollution is a primary contributing factor to reduction in auditory sensitivity in the older population. These etiologies of hearing impairment may occur at any time in life, but the cumulative effects of a lifetime of exposure to infections and noise pollution are most pronounced in the older population.

Older adults also tend to produce excessive cerumen, or ear wax, which can block the auditory canal and occlude the transmission of sound waves to the internal hearing mechanism. Improper cleaning of the ears with a cotton swab can perforate the eardrum or impact the cerumen in the ear canal. The resulting conductive hearing loss further contributes to reduced hearing sensitivity for many older adults.

Presbycusis, typical hearing loss in older adults, refers to the gradual reduction in hearing ability as a result of the aging process. Corso (1981) did not consider presbycusis a pathological condition but the normal reduction of sensitivity due to normal aging. Presbycusis is not necessarily the result of a single causal factor but may be due to several etiologies. For instance, physical changes in the mechanism of the ear itself may contribute to the typical hearing impairment experienced by older adults. While reduction of tympanic membrane elasticity and alterations in the ossicular chain have minimal influence on hearing ability, changes in functioning and degeneration of cells in the inner ear can result in significant hearing impairment with advancing age. According to Orchik (1981), presbycusis is primarily due to changes in the internal functioning of the ear rather than changes in the transmission of sound waves to the sensing mechanism. Of course, any changes in the transmission of sound waves through the outer and middle ear mechanism are superimposed upon the hearing loss due to alterations in the inner ear's sensory capability. Epithelia atrophy, deterioration of supporting cells, and degeneration of nerve cells affect the structure and functioning of the cochlea; reduction in the number of neurons in the auditory pathways including the eighth cranial nerve and higher auditory pathways occur with advanced age; biochemical and bioelectrical properties of the endolymphatic fluid of the inner ear also occur (Corso, 1981). These changes, as well as stiffening of the inner ear structures, result in the typical types of hearing loss found in many older persons.

Changes in the sensory cells which occur with aging generally result in a high frequency hearing loss — an impairment of hearing in which speech is sensed but is difficult to understand. The high frequency component of speech provides information necessary for the differentiation and discrimination of speech sounds. Persons with this type of presbycusis can sense speech but cannot easily discriminate among the different sounds. In addition, recruitment may coincide with hearing loss. The person with recruitment superimposed upon a hearing loss has a reduced range of loudness for comfortable listening to speech. Soft to moderate speech may be barely heard but moderate loudness is perceived as too loud for comfort.

In metabolic presbycusis, all sound frequencies are equally reduced. This results in softer sounds but not distorted sounds. As a consequence of metabolic presbycusis, discrimination among sounds is preserved only if the sounds are loud enough to be sensed. There are many other types of presbycusis (see: Nadol, 1981; Schow, Christensen, Hutchinson, & Nerbonne, 1978) which result in different types of hearing impairment affecting communication.

Reduction in the sensitivity of the auditory mechanism, limitations on the "comfort" range of hearing by recruitment, and difficulty in speech discrimination combine to restrict older communicators in their roles as receivers of messages. Although supplementary strategies are available to aid older communicators in the reception of auditory messages, the individual must expend additional effort to attend to and to incorporate visual cues from the speaker's face and body for speech reading,[1] or cognitively to filter the extraneous sounds amplified by a hearing aid to attend to the spoken message.

Even with the use of supplementary aids, the older individual may answer questions inappropriately or respond to communication situations in unexpected ways. For example, one older individual with a mild hearing loss was asked, "Are you a member of the union?" and responded, "No, I carry my lunch." Since the older individual may not hear the full, undistorted message, a possible though incorrect message may be inferred, and an inappropriate response may be offered. The resulting *non sequitur* may be erroneously interpreted as lack of attention, inability to follow a conversation, confusion, or even senility in the older communicator.


**Changes in Other Senses with Advanced Age**

Although hearing is often considered the most important sense in daily communication, the visual system provides the communicator with a magnitude of information. Decreased sensitivity of the retina and the thickening, yellowing, and reduced flexibility of the lens affects visual functioning in older adults (Schaie & Geiwitz, 1982). Similar reductions in the perception of touch, pain, and temperature changes have been found in older adults. Chapter 4 details the impact on intrapersonal communication which occur with changes in these sensory systems.

Although these senses are not extensively involved in daily

---

[1]Similar to "lipreading" but including the entire communication situation, linguistic knowledge, and all cues from the speaker to infer the message.

communication of information, they do contribute to the totality of information available to older communicators. The quality of life is affected reduced sensitivity to environmental stimuli. The typical older adult does not experience the same "world" as do younger adults. The full flavor, texture, and intensity is muted or distorted to some extent. The resulting differences in experiential environments affect emotional outlook, selection of communication topics, and ultimately the quality of the life experience.

## The Older Adult as Message Sender

The speech production mechanism consists of a complex system of (1) muscles which regulate a controlled airstream, (2) the larynx, and (3) the suprelaryngeal structures of articulation which intricately alter the size, shape, and coupling of the oral and nasal cavities. Airflow through the larynx is modified by the movement of these supralaryngeal structures to produce the sounds of speech. The myo-elastic aerodynamic theory of speech production is based upon physical laws describing modifications and movements of the anatomical mechanism which result in alterations of the acoustic output of the speech production system, the speech signal.

Since the speech mechanism of older adults has generally undergone gradual anatomic and physiological modification, typical alterations of the acoustic speech signal also occur. Normal changes in the aging speech mechanism result in typical vocal productions that listeners identify as characteristic of older speakers. Listeners are quite proficient in judging speaker age based upon vocal characteristics alone (Ptacek & Sander, 1966; Ryan & Capadano, 1978).

Although there is not a one-to-one correspondence between anatomic changes and acoustic production, complex yet subtle changes in all the subsystems of the entire speech mechanism result in an identifiable older voice. The remainder of this chapter describes the typical changes in the subsystems of respiration, laryngeal phonation, and articulation which affect the older individual's production of speech.

### Respiratory Changes with Advanced Age

Muscular activity is less forceful with advancing age. This reduction of force affects the muscles of respiration. In addition, the thorax becomes more rigid with calcification and ossification of cartilage and therefore is less pliable for active expansion by the weakened muscles of inhalation. Decreased elasticity of the lungs themselves profoundly affects respiratory effort by reducing the recoil of the lungs, an important passive force of exhalation used in speech production (Kahane, 1981). The overall result of these changes is a decrease in maximum respiratory ability with advancing age.

These changes in the respiratory system of older adults are linked with demonstrable changes in respiratory functioning. Vital capacity, the ability to inhale and exhale a maximum volume of air, is significantly affected in older adults. Reduction of vital capacity is reflected in increased residual volumes of air remaining in the lungs after maximum exhalation (Kahane, 1981). Older speakers may not exert the fine control of air expenditures at maximum air volumes that young adult speakers do. This reduction would be evident in a reduced ability to shout or to sustain a monologue on one breath of air.

Although reduction of maximum respiratory support for speech is common in older adults, normal older speakers do not use fewer words per breath unit, nor do they need additional breaths to complete an utterance in normal speaking situations. Normal speakers rarely use maximum respiratory capacities in daily speaking situations; mid-lung volumes are used for typical speech production. Older speakers' difficulties in regulating maximum air volumes does not extend into the mid-lung range. Changes in mid-lung respiratory efforts are not a function of advanced age but are associated with disease or pathological conditions.

## Phonatory Differences with Advanced Age

The phonatory component of the speech signal is altered by anatomic and physiological changes in the larynx. Changes in laryngeal structures with advanced age include loss of elasticity, atrophy of the vocal fold muscles, decrease of muscle tone, and ossification and calcification of the laryngeal cartilages (Jacobs-Condit & Ortenzo, 1984; Kahane, 1981). Such extensive changes in the anatomy and physiology of the larynx have significant effects on the phonatory component of older adult voices.

The phonatory functioning of older speakers has been more extensively studied than other subsystems supporting speech production. In general, the fundamental frequency at which the older adult male vocal folds vibrate is higher than that for middle-aged or young adult males. Changes in the older female fundamental frequency are less clear with reports of lower frequencies with advanced age to nonsignificant changes in fundamental frequency with advanced age (Benjamin, 1986; Kent & Burkard, 1981).

The perturbation or jitter of the older voice, a measure of period variation between adjacent cycles of vocal fold vibration, is greater than that of young adult speakers (Wilcox & Horii, 1980). Jitter is an objective measure of the smooth-rough quality of a voice; increased jitter is associated with a perceived "rough" voice quality. The increased perturbation in regular vocal fold vibration may explain the perception of roughness, hoarseness, breathiness, and even the tremor which listeners indicate as typical of the older-sounding voice (Kent & Burkard, 1981; Ptacek & Sander, 1966; Ryan & Burk, 1974).

The larynx also controls pitch variations in discourse. The number of pitch inflections and maximum intonational change in speaking increase with advancing age. Fine control of the larynx within phonemic segments may be susceptible to changes in neuromuscular control due to physical condition and/or aging while the prosodic features of controlled intonation may be attributed to factors other than physical change. Age-related differences in reading style may explain the increased use of objectively measured inflections by older adults without a listener judgment of abnormal intonation pattern. The older adults tend to read more dramatically than do young adults (Benjamin, 1986).

While there are wide variations in vocal quality, listeners are surprisingly effective in identifying speakers' ages based solely on vocal production. The acoustic signal of phonation is sensitive to variations in vocal fold density, tension, mass, etc. As a result, the phonatory component of voice is most sensitive to changes in general health as well as changes typical of the aging process. Ramig and Ringel (1983) have suggested that phonatory changes are not necessarily associated with actual chronological age but are attributable to illness and/or physical condition of the speaker.

Subtle changes in vocal quality may be indicative of poor physical condition or a combination of advanced age with changes in physical condition. These changes, although noticeable in older adults, are not sufficient to indicate a disorder of speech production. Pervasive hoarseness, reduced use of inflection, and loss of pitch control are not perceived in the voices of normal older communicators who are unaffected by diseases or pathological conditions.

### Articulation Alterations with Advanced Age

Changes occurring in the supralaryngeal oral structures have been documented in the aged population. Changes in oral mucosa, muscle tonus of the tongue, and orofacial support occur with advancing age. Loss of dental structures, reduction of oral sensitivity, and decreased salivary function may contribute to modification in older speakers' articulatory functioning. Finally, reduced neuromuscular support of the superlaryngeal structures may also affect older speakers' abilities to articulate speech sounds (Jacobs-Condit & Ortenzo, 1984; Kahane, 1981).

Older adults are perceived as speaking more slowly and/or less precisely by listeners. Increased latency times, slower motor speech, and/or reduced neuromuscular support, contribute to the fact that older adults perform more slowly on diadochokinetic tasks such as rapid repetition of syllables (Ptacek et al., 1966; Ryan, 1972). In addition, older speakers are perceived as speaking more imprecisely than younger speakers (Hartman & Danhauer, 1976; Ryan & Burk, 1974), and actually exhibit a greater number of disfluencies and hesitations (Yairi & Clifton, 1972). It is possible that the articulatory abilities of older speakers lie along a continuum from dysarthria, a motor disorder of speech, to effortless speech exhibited by normal, young adult speakers (Ryan & Burk, 1974).

Differences in articulatory movements with age are most noticeable in the speech of older males (Benjamin, 1986; Kukol, 1979). Older females do not exhibit the amount of articulatory imprecision found in the speech of older male speakers; they appear to compensate for physiological differences by using more prestigious, more carefully articulated phonological variants (Benjamin, 1986). Consequently, perceived imprecise articulation in older females is not normally associated with advanced age. By contrast, older males, in general, appear to be less careful and fastidious in their articulation of speech sounds.

## Suggestions for More Effective Communication

Normal anatomic and physiological changes of advancing age which affect the sensory and motor speech systems with advanced age subtly influence an older individual's ability to act effectively as a participant in communication exchanges. In the role of receiver, older communicators may be unable to discriminate sounds necessary for understanding a message or may be totally unaware that someone else is talking. Reduction in auditory sensitivity can be most frustrating to the individual who must listen intently to follow what is being said or who may be entirely left out of a conversation. It is no wonder that presbycusis, reduced hearing acuity due to aging, can isolate older adults from others.

With sensitivity to the older communcator's reduced sensory abilities, speakers may facilitate message reception through several dimensions. The environment may be changed or arranged to provide an optimum setting for communication. Noise and distractions are counterproductive to message reception and such adverse communication environments are particularly disadvantageous for older adults who have difficulty in discriminating speech from background noise (Olsho, Harkins & Lenhardt, 1985). Sensitivity to background noise, locating a quiet environment, and minimizing environmental distractions are ways in which speakers can alter the environment to accommodate the deterioration of older adults' reception of speech (Dreher, 1987).

Speaking in a slightly louder voice without shouting can help older listeners perceive sufficient clues to interpret the intended message. Speakers should be sensitive to their facial expression when speaking loudly (Kopac, 1983). Even though one's facial expressions may be unintentionally exaggerated when deliberately speaking in a louder voice, a speaker should take care to maintain a pleasant facial expression while increasing speaking volume. A slightly slower speed of speech production may also help older listeners, but over articulation of speech sounds is not helpful. In speaking with older adults, communicators do not want to offend older listeners by unintentionally "talking down" to them, but speakers should make minor adjustments to the volume and rate of their speech to provide a clearer, more perceptible speech signal.

When speaking to older adults with impaired hearing, speakers should face older listeners to permit maximum use of lip movements, facial expression, and posture to supplement a partially heard message. Speakers should maintain a three to six foot distance from the older listener; adequate light must fall on the speaker's face to enhance the older listener's perception of facial and body expression. Gestures can also be used to reference and reorient older listeners to the topic.

Other useful reorienting devices are linguistic in nature. Repetition of a message may be requested by older listeners; paraphrase of that message provides an alternative form which may contribute necessary clues for interpreting the intended meaning (Dreher, 1987). Redundancy of the message is also helpful. Speakers can orient listeners to a topic by verbally and nonverbally directing attention to a new topic before beginning the detailed message. Verbal and nonverbal clues to reorient the older listeners to a topic, to maintain a topic, or to change a topic not only structure the communicative exchange but also provide the older listeners with several opportunities to discern what the speaker intended to communicate.

In the role of sender, the normal older speaker is quite capable. Although changes in the speech mechanism may reduce the maximum range of speaking, these changes do not appreciably affect the older adult's ability to communicate in daily life. Although these changes in normal older speech are subtle and do not indicate a pathological or abnormal condition, they are noticeable and provide cues to the speaker's age. These changes affect the form but not the character of the message.

Listeners attribute personality characteristics to speakers based on vocal production; perceived age in voice is most productive in generating these perceptions (Bassili & Reil, 1981). The stereotypical characteristics evoked in listeners' minds by older voices are not accurate but may often serve to reinforce negative stereotypes held by listeners.

Since communication is a two-way process, listener attitudes, expectations, and reactions have an important impact on the communication interaction. Listeners must become aware of their attitudes toward aging. The tendency to attribute stereotypical characteristics to speakers based n the sound of the aged voice must be counteracted. The accuracy of such personality attribution is questionable and creates a needless barrier to effective communication. Just as "there may be snow on the roof but there is fire in the furnace'' counteracts unfounded stereotypes of older adults' sexual desires and activities, ''there may be variation in the voice but there is meaning in the message'' should become the watchword for counteracting unfounded assumptions regarding older adults' communication abilities.

## ❧ 6 ❧

# Barriers to Sending Messages

## Barbara B. Shadden

One of the major life crises faced by older persons is the onset, gradual or abrupt, of a speech-language disorder. Speech disorders involve impairment in the selection, organization, and execution of neuromotor commands to intact body structures which produce the acoustic output we call speech. Language disorders result from a breakdown in the processing, central organization, and formulation of language symbols (written or spoken) for communication purposes. Thus, speech-language disorders can be understood from the perspective of either the system component that is affected (cognitive, linguistic, neuromuscular, and/or anatomical) or the specific form of speech-language disruption (e.g., aphasia, language impairment in dementia and right hemisphere damage, dysarthria, apraxia, and alaryngeal speech). Both perspectives will be integrated in this chapter.

Although it is believed that there are currently over eight million speech-language-hearing impaired older persons (Sayles & Adams, 1979), precise estimates of prevalence are difficult to establish. For example, Fein (1983a) notes that, according to the 1977 National Center for Health Statistics Survey, approximately 212,000 noninstitutionalized persons over the age of 65 years evidence a speech impairment. Since the term "speech" (not "speech-language") was used in this study and since the prevalence of all handicapping conditions is much higher in institutionalized subgroups, it is assumed that these figures radically underestimate the occurrence of speech-language disorders. It has been suggested that there may be as many as one million speech-language impaired persons in this country (Sayles & Adams, 1979).

The magnitude of this problem can be understood by considering the degree to which the elderly are represented in the general population of speech-language impaired individuals of all ages. Currently, it is estimated that the rate of occurrence of speech-language disorders in the elderly is exceeded only by the rate of occurrence in children 5-14 years of age (Fein, 1983a). The elderly are believed to constitute 20% of the speech-language impaired population. It is projected that 39% of the population will be over the age of 65 by the year 2050 (Fein, 1983b). These figures suggest a major demand for professional services in coming years, along with a need for increasing levels of awareness on the part of older persons and those in their communication networks. At present, levels of awareness among the elderly concerning all forms of communication impairment are extremely low (Shadden, 1982).

It is essential that the reader remember that communication disorders do not occur in a vacuum. They exist against a background of *normal* changes in speech-language-hearing functions (as outlined in Chapter 5). In addition, the individual's response to the disability will be influenced by the varied social, economic, psychological, and physiological changes associated with aging. Such changes affect the frequency and quality of communicative interactions, skills, and opportunities (Maurer, 1984).

In the following pages, the reader will be introduced to the most common speech-language disorders associated with aging. Emphasis will be placed on developing an understanding of both the distinguishing characteristics of each disorder and the consequences of speech-language impairment. The impact on the handicapped individual, the family, and community will be addressed. Basic management considerations and strategies will also be described within the context of the entire communication network of the speech-language impaired older person.

## Distinguishing Speech-Language Disorders

The diagnosis of a particular speech-language disorder is the responsibility of the speech-language pathologist. A variety of communication assessment tools will be supplemented by available medical and case history data to reach this determination. Some of the more important diagnostic considerations include:

1. The site of lesion (damage) or of physical impairment;
2. The onset characteristics of the disorder—gradual or abrupt;
3. The underlying functions disturbed—cognition, language input, language output, neuromotor systems, structural integrity;

4. The nature and severity of impairment of language comprehension and of speech-language output; and,

5. The nature of interpersonal (social) communicative behaviors.

Of particular importance is an understanding of the site of system damage and the associated functions disturbed. For a message to be received and understood fully, the original signal must pass through a series of stages. To review briefly, a spoken (or written) message must first be received peripherally by the appropriate sense organs. It then travels through the central nervous system where a variety of perceptual analyses are used to interpret the electrical signals and convert them into familiar patterns. Once the analysis is complete, it is possible for the brain's central language processor to assign meaning to this message. This assignment of meaning, however, is also dependent upon other neurological processes involved in analysis of situational context (who is saying what where), motivation to communicate and relate, and basic cognition.

Having interpreted the message, a response can be formulated. The intent (desire) to communicate must be present first. Access to various associative areas of the brain which generate the content of the message then follows. Once this content is established, the language processor can select the appropriate words and rules for ordering words and submit these to the motor programmer, a computer-like center which works out the necessary sequence and timing of motor gestures needed to coincide with the desired linguistic utterance. The resulting program is passed on to the motor pathways, beginning at the motor cortex, and conveyed down to the muscles and associated speech structures for speech production.

A breakdown in any stage in this rather complex process can and typically will result in a communication impairment. Chapter 4 has already discussed the results of disruption in functioning related to auditory peripheral sensation and perceptual processing. In this chapter, we will focus on aphasia (dysfunction in the language processor), secondary language disorders (dysfunctions in cognitive and perceptual components of the system in right hemisphere damage or dementia), the motor speech disorders of dysarthria and verbal apraxia (dysfunction in the transmission or programming of neuromotor commands for speech), and structural impairments (primarily laryngectomy).

## Language Disorders — Primary (Aphasia)

### Characteristics

Aphasia is an impairment in the ability to process and/or to use language in any or all modalities due to focal damage to the language centers of the brain, typically in the left hemisphere (Brookshire, 1986; Darley, 1982). The term *primary language disorder* is used to distinguish aphasia from other disruptions in language functions. Language disorders which result from damage to right hemisphere brain centers controlling nonverbal skills (essential in utilizing language in context) or from the more diffuse neurological deterioration in dementia (affects basic cognitive processes contributing to language) are considered secondary and do not warrant the label "aphasia" (Davis & Baggs, 1984).

Sources of neurological damage leading to aphasia generally take three forms: cerebrovascular accidents (CVA), head trauma, and brain tumors (Davis & Holland, 1981). However, age differences in common etiologies are evident. The young adult is most likely to become aphasic as a result of traumatic head injury, whereas the older adult's aphasia typically results from a CVA. A CVA or stroke occurs when blood supply, and consequently oxygen, is cut off from any portion of the brain sufficiently long to produce the death of brain cells. Although CVAs can be caused by both hemorrhage and blockage of an artery, the latter is more common. In older individuals, an increased likelihood of stroke is frequently associated with cerebrovascular disease (atherosclerosis), high blood pressure, and cardiac disease.

Strokes occur in about 800,000 Americans each year, with 2.7 million adults reporting some history of stroke. Almost 75% of all strokes occur in persons over the age of 65 years, and close to 60% of the noncomatose survivors of such strokes evidence some form of communication impairment (Weinfeld, 1981). Although the exact percentage of older persons with aphasia is unknown, incidence is probably highest among the elderly in institutions. In one study, it was estimated that 11% of nursing home residents have some form of aphasic deficit (Mueller & Peters, 1981).

Central to an understanding of aphasia is an appreciation of its variability; there are many forms and consequently numerous classification systems. It is common, for example, to subdivide the aphasias into those that are fluent (grammatically complete with effortless speech flow) and nonfluent (grammatically deviant and effortful). Other designations refer to aphasias as anterior or posterior, signalling the broad area of the brain-damaged and certain common language characteristics. Perhaps the most common classification system today is a neurological one based on site of lesion (Goodglass & Kaplan, 1983).

Diagnostic classification systems are useful in determining prognosis and defining intervention programs. However, communicating with an aphasic individual requires an understanding of certain basic characteristics relating to level of comprehension, grammatical output and fluency, the extent of word retrieval problems, and daily social communication. Most aphasic persons have trouble understanding what is said to them, although the severity of this disturbance may vary considerably. Comprehension difficulties increase with longer, more complex, and less common linguistic material and are aggravated in group conversations, under conditions of distracting stimuli, or when the patient is fatigued. It takes an aphasic individual longer to process information heard or read. Memory span is typically reduced which further aggravates comprehension. All of these problems fall under the heading of receptive language disorder or aphasia. Ironically, if an individual has severely impaired reception, he may be unable to monitor his own expressive language and may appear unaware of his errors.

Most aphasic individuals experience some difficulty finding the names for things. These problems in word finding or word retrieval (anomia) can be observed with any content word. It is common to hear, "I know what I want to say but I can't find the right words." Some individuals may talk around the subject to describe a missing word, a process called circumlocution.

Two commonly described forms of aphasia, Broca's and Wernicke's, are best distinguished by the fluency and grammatical completeness of speech versus the degree of impairment in comprehension. For example, when listening to a Wernicke's aphasic, one feels that the language should be making sense because the flow, grammar and intonation are normal sounding. Only the content is deficient, filled with indefinite words such as "this" or "it" and jargon words. These individuals have severe deficits in comprehension. In contrast, expressive language in Broca's aphasia can be so effortful and lacking in grammatical continuity that one struggles to put together the meanings. Speech output is frequently described as telegraphic, meaning that the small, connecting parts of speech are omitted. Comprehension is typically only mildly to moderately impaired. The Wernicke's form of aphasia increases in prevalence with advancing age (Holland & Bartlett, 1985), as does another aphasic type, global aphasia. In global aphasia, language comprehension and expression are so severely limited as to make any one modality difficult or impossible to assess. Typically, global aphasia is associated with extensive brain damage.

Finally, all but the most severely impaired aphasic individuals are able to produce some social or "automatic" speech. Familiar greetings and responses are produced casually, leading the listener to believe that the language deficit must not be that profound. Unfortunately, automatic speech reflects relatively overlearned, meaningless behavior patterns that do not indicate the extent of language facility or deficit.

**Consequences**

The emotional and behavioral consequences of aphasia can be traced to both the communication disorder and to the concomitant brain damage. Among the common manifestations of brain damage are emotional lability, attention disturbances, and shifts in personality (Brookshire, 1986).

Emotional lability refers to the excessive and seemingly inappropriate emotional responses demonstrated by many neurologically impaired individuals, presumably the product of the loss of higher (cortical) brain control of emotional reactions. Lability can be both embarrassing and frightening to the patient and family, particularly if the aphasic individual is one with a history of limited emotionality. Other behavioral patterns include inconsistency in responding, distractibility, and shortened attention span. Many families also express concern about shifts in personality which are probably exaggerations of premorbid personality traits that can no longer be inhibited. In addition to these general changes, stroke patients frequently must contend with motor deficits (such as paralysis or weakness of one side of the body) and visual deficits (losing part of the field of vision or experiencing perceptual problems).

These changes coupled with impairment in communication, the primary tool for personal expression and social interaction, may produce profound emotional reactions. Some common responses include: depression, anxiety, guilt, excessive reliance on defense mechanisms, feelings of isolation, loss of identity, and dependency. These reactions can be exaggerated by restrictions in former activities, reduction in social contacts, and loss of role identities (e.g., Buck, 1978; Eisenson, 1973).

Both the aphasic individual and the immediate family members may experience a sense of loss and grief, with any or all of the stages of grieving emerging during the weeks and months post onset. Family members must also cope with increased responsibility, role reversals, and fears that the person is "losing his mind." Financial concerns may become overwhelming. Feelings of fear, frustration, helplessness, and anger are commonly reported (e.g., Chwat & Gurland, 1981; Czvik, 1977; Linebaugh & Young-Charles, 1978; Malone, 1969).

## Language Disorders — Secondary

As noted earlier, primary language disorders (aphasia) are associated with focal damage to the language centers in the dominant hemisphere. In recent years, however, recognition is growing that neurological impairment to other centers of the brain controlling perceptual and cognitive functions can produce a communication impairment. The resulting deficits are sometimes considered secondary language disorders, since communication breakdown evolves *indirectly* from dysfunction in components of the neurological system that support effective language processing or production. Secondary language disorders include those associated with damage to the right (or nondominant) hemisphere and those associated with the dementias. Each will be discussed briefly below.

## Right Hemisphere Communication Impairment

*Characteristics.* Adequate estimates of the prevalence of communication impairment following right hemisphere damage are lacking, primarily due to the recency of interest in identifying and treating such deficits. Davis and Baggs (1984) describe right hemisphere disorders as "focal nonverbal impairments," and Myers (1986) defines them as:

> ...an acquired disorder in the expression and reception of complex, contextually based communicative events resulting from disturbance of the attentional and perceptual mechanisms underlying nonsymbolic, experiential processing. (p. 446)

Regardless of one's definition, there is considerable agreement concerning the characteristics of right hemisphere impaired patients. These include linguistic, nonlinguistic, and extralinguistic deficits (Myers, 1986).

Linguistic impairments, as measured on formal language tasks, are not pronounced. The right hemisphere patient typically performs well on simple language comprehension and production tasks at the word, phrase, or short sentence level, but performance may break down as linguistic length and complexity increase. It is probable that visuospatial and attentional factors are responsible for this breakdown. These observed high level linguistic deficits do not normally create major barriers to daily communication (Myers, 1984). However, additional difficulties may be found in reading and writing activities because of the right hemisphere's role in visual analysis and pattern recognition.

Nonlinguistic deficits are more evident. Common characteristics include impaired facial recognition (prosopagnosia), impaired geographical and spatial orientation, and unilateral neglect (patient fails to respond to stimuli on the left side of the body). All of these characteristics can have an indirect impact on communication. The most immediate consequence may be confusion and disorientation resulting from the lack of consistency in environmental perceptions and the difficulties of creating and maintaining a clear image of the spatial surroundings. In addition, neglect of one side of the body and of space may impair responses to auditory or visual language information presented to that side.

Extralinguistic deficits include impairments in comprehending and expressing emotional tone as well as disturbances in situational and social processing and in the use of language skills (pragmatics). Both of these sources of disturbance have a pronounced effect on daily communication. The impairment of affective processing and production can involve the modalities of facial expression, body language, and speech prosody (intonation, verbal stress, and rhythm). Patients are described as having a flat affect facially and vocally. They may not smile or may not respond with concern about their condition or emotional events. Intonation is reduced and monotonous. Inappropriate responses to affective input are common.

Jokes, metaphors, and irony may be misinterpreted.

The latter observations also pertain to the pragmatic aspects of extralinguistic behavior. Pragmatics refers to the appropriate and purposeful use of language in social contexts. The right hemisphere patient's inability to make effective use of contextual cues leads to frequent misinterpretations of messages or overly literal responses to language content. An inability to organize incoming or outgoing data is compounded by difficulty in distinguishing critical points or logical steps from irrelevant detail. In effect, the nondominant hemisphere's ability to interpret the gestalt of a situation (linguistic or otherwise) is impaired, and responses become inappropriate and illogical.

*Consequences.* Although there is considerable variability in the pattern and severity of linguistic and nonlinguistic dysfunctions presented by right hemisphere patients, the consequences for daily functioning are pronounced. It is particularly important to remember that these individuals may look and sound relatively normal. In some respects, this is one of their greatest handicaps, since initial hopes for recovery of normal functioning are usually high (Myers, 1986).

One of the major consequences of right hemisphere impairment is an erosion of interpersonal relationships, particularly if members of the social network do not understand the individual's behavior. The lack of emotional affect, inappropriate communicative interactions, and occasionally bizarre behaviors may disturb and distance friends and relatives. In addition, many activities previously taken for granted (e.g., moving around familiar and unfamiliar environments) may now require considerable effort and major compensatory adjustments. Motivation to effect these changes is sometimes reduced, consistent with the low levels of concern and emotion displayed by the individual in other arenas.

Occupational and recreational activities requiring multiple steps, visual and attentional skills, and/or complex ideation may no longer be accessible to the right hemisphere patient. Frequently, the family may be more distressed by these changes in life style than the neurologically impaired individual. Both patient and family may become fatigued by the need to cope with periods of confusion and with the demands for repetition, relearning, and simplification of some tasks.

## Communication Impairment Related to Dementia

*Characteristics.* The various dementias are associated with another cluster of secondary language disorders. Unfortunately, defining the different dementia types and their communication sequelae is a difficult task. Some conditions which resemble dementia are reversible through medical and rehabilitative treatments (e.g., those conditions due to depression, overmedication, vitamin deficiencies, etc.). Our discussion in this chapter will be restricted to the irreversible forms of dementia characterized by progressive deterioration of intellect, memory, personality, and communicative function (Bayles, 1986). Although prevalence figures vary, it is estimated that 10% of persons over the age of 65 years evidence mild dementia, with 1% being severely demented (Bayles, 1984).

Within the group of irreversible dementias, it is possible to subdivide the many precipitating conditions into cortical and subcortical nonvascular dementias and the vascular dementias (Cummings & Benson, 1983). The most common form of cortical dementia is Alzheimer's disease, a progressive disorder that can begin any time after middle adulthood. Alzheimer's disease accounts for approximately 50% of all dementia cases and is notable for its primary impairments in orientation, intellect, memory, and judgment in the absence of major motor or sensory deficits. Even in the earliest stages, patients may be confused, forgetful, and may show emotional disturbances such as apathy and irritability.

In contrast, Parkinson's disease, the most common form of subcortical dementia, is most notable for its distinctive motor components of tremor, rigidity, and movement impairment related to inadequate production of the neurotransmitter dopamine. Parkinson's patients have trouble initiating movement and have a characteristic shuffling, bent-over gait and masklike facial appearance. Speech disturbances in the early stages of this disorder assume the characteristics of a dysarthria (see next section in this chapter). However, in the later stages, the majority of Parkinson's patients evidence some intellectual degeneration.

The third most common form of dementia is typified in the multi-infarct patient, the individual who has suffered multiple strokes which cumulatively erode cortical and subcortical functions. Because these strokes can occur anywhere in the brain, the characteristics of this group of dementia patients are less predictable.

Bayles (1986) makes a convincing case for stating that dementia patients are not truly aphasic. Certainly, observed linguistic and communicative deficits result from underlying and diffuse cognitive impairments. Nevertheless, there are several commonly described linguistic dysfunctions. The most frequent include: anomia (naming or word retrieval deficits), verbal dysfluency, jargon, verbal perseveration (involuntary repetition), and circumlocution (talking around a topic). The extent and manner of disruption of linguistic functioning is markedly dependent upon the stage of progression of the disease (Obler & Albert, 1981). In addition, it is apparent that the various elements of language—sounds, words, grammar, content, and use—are impaired differentially. For example, the sound system (and to a lesser extent the grammatical rules) are well-preserved, in contrast with the semantic system (words and word meanings) and pragmatics (social uses of language), which are affected. In the early stages, a typical dementia patient will produce grammatically and phonologically correct utterances with key words omitted, word retrieval problems, noticeable topic shifting, and loss of focus. Conversational give and take may be inappropriate, and abstract or figurative language comprehension may be impaired. In the later stages, however, only the sound system is somewhat preserved, grammatical comprehension is poor, and sentence fragments are common. Word comprehension and usage are severely impaired, and jargon is often substituted for key words. Ideational content for speech is totally lacking and frequently bizarre, with no meaningful social, context-appropriate communication.

*Consequences.* The consequences of dementia are devastating for both patient and family. There is a gradual but steady erosion of most daily functions, resulting from the progressive deterioration of prerequisite intellectual, memory, and communication skills. Normal vocational and recreational activities become inaccessible and, with time, even daily self help skills (e.g., hygiene, dressing, eating) may become impaired. Concurrently, the major personality changes in the dementia patient frequently mean families are providing total care for a loved one who is virtually unrecognizable in temperament and behavior.

Previous individual and familial routines are disrupted, and major shifts in family roles and responsibilities occur. The resulting emotional reactions of caregivers range from guilt and denial to hostility and blame. High levels of stress and associated mental and physical health problems are reported by primary caregivers (Jenkins, Parham, & Jenkins, 1985). Demands are constantly placed on the family to learn new ways of communicating with the dementia patient, new ways of managing behavior, and alternate strategies for structuring the environment to ensure safety and maximize functioning (Glosser & Wexler, 1985). Financial pressures may accumulate. Although the grieving process for the loss of both a person and of specific functional skills must be encouraged (Tanner, 1980), the losses continue and accelerate, so that it is difficult to reach a point of acceptance and homeostasis.

## Motor Speech Disorders

The terms motor speech or neuromotor speech disorders are used to describe a cluster of speech problems resulting from impairment of the neurological systems responsible for programming, initiating, and transmitting commands to the muscles for the physical execution of a language message. These disorders are distinguished from other communication problems by their primary effects on speech output. The two primary forms of motor speech disorders are dysarthria and apraxia of speech.

Data concerning the prevalence of neuromotor speech disorders in the elderly are difficult to find. Both dysarthria and apraxia of speech may result from stroke, head trauma, and brain tumors and may co-occur with aphasia. As Kurtzke and Kurland (1973) indicate, there is a geometric increase in cerebrovascular disease with age. Thus, it is appropriate to assume that a similar increase in the incidence of motor speech disorders will be seen. In addition, the dysarthrias are frequently associated with degenerative disorders or conditions beginning in adulthood. In some instances, peak incidence for these disorders occurs above 55 years of age (e.g., Parkinson's disease, 70 to 80 years; amytrophic lateral sclerosis, 57 to 61 years). In nursing homes, it has been estimated that 19% of the observed communication disorders consist of dysarthria or other articulation difficulties, with another 21% reflecting voice disorders that may indicate a dysarthric component (Mueller & Peters, 1981).

## The Dysarthrias

*Characteristics.* The dysarthrias can be defined as a group of motor speech disorders resulting from central or peripheral nervous system impairment of muscular *control* for speech (Rosenbek & LaPointe, 1981). These disturbances may affect aspects of respiration, phonation, resonance, articulation, and prosody and can influence muscular control whether or not the system is being used for speech purposes. For example, the dysarthric individual with impairment in motor function involving the throat (oro-pharynx) may have difficulties swallowing (dysphagia) as well as controlling the nasality of his speech. Common patterns of dysarthric involvement include weakness, slowness, and incoordination of muscles. The individual with a pure dysarthria possesses an adequate language system, knows what he wants to say, but lacks the speed, strength, or coordination necessary to produce the message.

Because dysarthria can develop at any time and can result from damage to any component of the central or peripheral nervous system that involves impulse transmission to the muscles, there are a wide range of characteristics and systems for classifying these disorders. Most systems combine the underlying component of the impaired neuromotor system and the resulting perceptual and acoustic characteristics (Darley, Aronson, & Brown, 1975). Individuals who experience dysarthria following a cortical stroke may present slow, labored speech with slurred articulation and disturbances of speech prosody. Those who experience ataxic dysarthria secondary to damage to the cerebellum show impairments in controlling the range, speed, and direction of speech movements, resulting in inconsistent misarticulations and unusual intonation and stress patterns. Parkinson's disease damages structures deep within the brain and produces a hypokinetic form of dysarthria in which speech is characterized by problems in initiating and terminating movement, tremor, reduced range and inconsistent speed of speech movements. In addition, there are a variety of mixed dysarthrias produced by degenerative neurological diseases. For example, amyotrophic lateral sclerosis (ALS) often begins between 40 and 60 years of age and progresses rapidly. In ALS patients, speech is markedly impaired, characterized by extremely slow rate, short phrases, excessive nasality, and a harsh or strained vocal quality.

*Consequences.* If an individual's primary problem is dysarthria, he or she frequently can be intelligible to others with effort and training or with the assistance of compensatory tools such as communication boards and electronic devices. In such instances, the primary difficulties encountered by the patient and his family involve adjustment to the pronounced alterations in quality of voice and speech. Since a person's identity often is associated with his speaking patterns, this adjustment may be difficult initially. However, dysarthria rarely occurs without other problems. In addition to its frequent appearance with aphasia after a stroke, it may also be associated with a more general system impairment of neuromotor functioning. Thus, in addition to the communication deficits, the dysarthric individual and his family may be faced with radical shifts in daily functioning, roles, independence, and even life expectancy.

## Apraxia of Speech

*Characteristics.* The nature and causes of apraxia of speech (or verbal apraxia) are less widely agreed upon clinically than those of dysarthria. Nevertheless, most definitions include the following elements:

> ...a neurogenic phonologic disorder resulting from sensorimotor impairment of the capacity to program the positioning of the speech musculature and the sequencing of muscle movements for the volitional production of phonemes. (Rosenbek & LaPointe, 1981, p. 160)

Apraxia of speech results from neurological damage to the speech motor programming centers of the brain, usually believed to be in the frontal lobe near the area associated with Broca's aphasia (Halpern, 1986). Thus, aphasia and verbal apraxia can occur simultaneously; causes of damage typically parallel those identified for aphasia. Since the programming element of speech production involves the selection, sequencing and coordination of intended motor gestures, only speech articulation and prosody are affected. Vegetative functions (use of the oral structures for non-speech purposes, such as eating) are not affected, since there is no weakness, paralysis or incoordination of the form found in dysarthria.

Some typical speech characteristics of the verbal apraxic individual include the following (Halpern, 1986; Rosenbek & LaPointe, 1981):

1. Better functioning on automatic, overly used forms of speech (e.g., social greetings) than on highly propositional speech (e.g., retelling a complex story).
2. Problems initiating any speech effort, associated with hesitations, audible or inaudible groping for articulator targets, restarts, and repetitions. (Some patients' degree of effort and struggle here tends to resemble that of the stutterer.)
3. Substitutions and additions of one phoneme (speech sound) for another, with occasional production of a non-English phoneme due to inappropriate pairing of articulatory gestures.
4. Inconsistencies in articulation from one occurrence of a sound or word to the next.
5. More errors at the beginning of words than at any other position.
6. Increasing errors as the complexity of articulatory adjustments increases (e.g., more errors on a consonant blend than singleton).

As with dysarthria, the individual with a verbal apraxia knows what he wants to say, correctly selects the appropriate words and grammatical ordering of words, but is unable to program the necessary motor movements to match his intended language target. For example, he may plan to say "supper" but the commands for lip closure for the "p" become mixed up with the tongue elevation for "s". The resulting motor confusions may produce an unintended phoneme or may result in repetitive efforts to correct the anticipated or perceived error. The individual whose primary deficit is apraxia of speech is unable to monitor his speech for inaccuracies.

*Consequences.* It is commonly agreed that verbal apraxia can be one of the most frustrating of speech-language disorders. Frustration results from the individual's clear understanding of what he wishes to communicate and his potentially intact language system, in the face of a devastating lack of control of speech movements. In addition, the oral motor system works normally when non-speech activities are attempted. These inconsistencies in performance, coupled with a severe disruption in the ability to communicate, lead to a number of different personal consequences.

Some apraxic individuals virtually stop trying to speak because the lack of success is so overwhelming emotionally. Others persist in struggling blindly, refusing to use therapeutic suggestions or alternate means of communication. Since verbal apraxia frequently appears concurrently with aphasia, speech programming deficits can be complicated by language impairments. Communication options such as writing messages become less than effective. All activities involving verbal communication must be drastically curtailed or modified. Interpersonal relationships suffer as the person is unable to express his feelings and even his needs.

# Anatomical Disorders

## Characteristics

Although normal aging affects the anatomical structures involved in respiration, phonation, and articulation (see Chapter 5), the resulting changes in speech output are not typically considered disordered. Older individuals do experience laryngeal problems (e.g., vocal nodules, polyps, and contact ulcers), but there is no evidence that these occur with greater frequency in the elderly than in other age groups (Batza, 1977).

The most common form of anatomically-based speech disorder found in older individuals is alaryngeal speech. The term alaryngeal speech refers to the consequences of removal of the larynx. The surgical procedure is termed a total laryngectomy, and the individual is usually referred to as a laryngectomee. In most instances, the total laryngectomy is performed as treatment for laryngeal cancer. Other treatments—partial laryngectomy, radiation, and laser surgery—may also be employed in the treatment of laryngeal carcinoma and may, in fact, be preferred for the elderly due to increased risks in surgery (Davis & Baggs, 1984).

Regardless of the treatment methodology utilized, the result is an impaired or absent vocal mechanism that cannot be used normally for the production of speech. Although specific estimates of the incidence of laryngeal cancer in all older persons are lacking, there is a close relationship between advancing age and the occurrence of laryngeal cancer. The average age of laryngectomized individuals is 55 years (IAL, 1975), with incidence rising dramatically from 9.2 per 100,000 in the mid 30's to 41.9 per 100,000 in the mid 60's (American Cancer Society, 1984). There are currently around 30,000 laryngectomees alive in the United States (IAL, 1975). Other forms of head and neck cancer may also exist in the older population and may require surgical interventions radically altering the speech mechanism. However, the variability in such problems makes it impossible to provide accurate assessments of prevalence.

Individuals who have undergone a total laryngectomy are effectively without a voice. Prior to any speech-language intervention, they can only communicate with oral movements and writing. Communication options take one of three basic forms (Prater & Swift, 1984).

The individual may be taught to use esophageal speech, in which a substitute sound source is created using existing structures. The laryngectomee learns to produce a consistent, sustained burping-like noise that can be used as an alternate sound base for speech. Although people vary in the degree to which they become facile with this mode of communication, common characteristics of esophageal speech include: markedly lowered vocal pitch, reduced loudness, aberrant vocal quality, and a generally fixed and monotonous intonation pattern. Esophageal speakers are sometimes described as having robot-like speech. Reductions in pitch are particularly distressing to female laryngectomees because of social expectations for the female pitch range.

A second option involves the use of an artificial larynx or electro-larynx. The artificial larynx provides an external sound source. Battery operated devices produce a buzzing sound. The device can be held against the neck, directed into the oral cavity through a tube, or built into dental appliances. An alternative pneumatic device involves inhaling air through a tube placed in the stoma (the breathing hold in the neck) and then redirecting the air into the oral cavity.

The third set of options includes attempts to create a new sound source within the patient. Surgical construction of a tissue vibrating source (e.g., Asai, 1972), or surgical reconstruction to allow attachment of a removable prosthetic device (e.g., Blom & Singer, 1979), have been successful with certain patients.

*Consequences.* The laryngectomee faces a relatively unique situation. Literally overnight he or she is transformed from a speaking to a nonspeaking individual with all other faculties for language and communication presumably intact. The initial shock and subsequent depression can be major sources of interference in communication training and in acceptance or an alternate voice source. Many laryngectomees, particularly women, resist the sound of the various voice substitutes. In addition, use of esophageal speech in particular is extremely fatiguing and may tax the energy levels of an elderly individual. Some alternatives produce voice with low intensity levels that would be hard for hearing impaired older family members and friends to hear.

In addition, the surgical removal of the larynx leaves some disfigurement in the neck region and a permanent stoma (breathing hole) that can alarm the unfamiliar viewer. The respirations of the laryngectomized person through the stoma are also noisy, particularly when phlegm accumulates. These physical changes may lead to low self image and avoidance of social contacts (Prater & Swift, 1984). The alaryngeal speaker must also contend with other life alterations. Changes in smell, taste, eating and hygiene patterns as well as physical activities may be required. If a previous job or leisure activity required frequent verbal communication, temporary restrictions may be imposed. Finally, there is always the fear of a recurrence of the cancer that precipitated the surgery. The communication channel is disrupted and social contacts endangered at a time when the laryngectomee may be most in need of support.

## Suggestions for Improving Communication

Although speech-language pathologists are the primary professionals responsible for assessment, diagnosis, and treatment of speech-language impairments, management of communication disorders requires participation and cooperation on the part of all members of the impaired individual's communication network. Any individual therapy program is potentially doomed to failure without the participation and cooperation of family members, friends, neighbors, and other professionals. These members of the communication network complete the programming cycle by ensuring that basic communication needs of speech-language impaired older persons are met. These needs are depicted in the *speak* model in Figure 1 and include:

1. *Skills:* speech, language, hearing, social communication;
2. *Partners:* who are available, compatible, and knowledgeable about communicating with speech-language impaired individuals;
3. *Environments:* that ensure privacy, are adequately arranged physically to promote social interaction, are acoustically treated and well-lit, and are free of unnecessary sensory distractions;
4. *Activities:* that are appropriate, functional, and allow meaningful communication to occur;
5. *Knowledge:* on the part of all participants of the basic elements of good communication, prerequisite skills, and the nature and consequences of specific speech-language disorders.

### Speak

### A Model for Communication Success

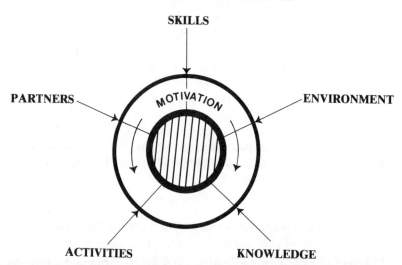

**Figure 1.** Communication needs of speech-language impaired older persons.

Meeting these communication needs requires sensitivity to the interaction between age-related social, phychological, and physiological changes and the specific impact of a speech-language disorder. For example, an older individual with reduced visual acuity will experience difficulty perceiving some stimulus materials used in aphasia assessment or intervention and may be unable to use a communication board with small print or finely drawn pictures. Dysarthric individuals with a hearing impairment may be unable to monitor their speech output with complete accuracy. The hearing impaired companions of laryngectomees will not be able to discern clearly their partner's new esophageal speech. Aphasic nursing home residents depressed by the erosion of their social support systems may not be motivated to participate in therapy. The list of possible interactions between aging and speech-language disorders is endless. The message, however, is simple; we cannot treat the disorder alone but must consider the whole individual and his/her social and physical environment in designing management strategies.

## Treating the Speech-Language Impaired Individual

Speech-language interventions take many forms, depending on the nature of the underlying disorder and the theoretical perspectives of the clinician. All speech-language impaired individuals should be referred for assessment and therapy to a speech-language pathologist certified by the American Speech-Language-Hearing Association. Excellent summaries of current treatment approaches can be found in a variety of sources (c.f., Beasley & Davis, 1981; Chapey, 1986; Jacobs-Condit, 1984).

Regardless of the treatment approach, three primary management goals can be identified: a) to facilitate the individual's use of speech structures and residual speech and language skills to maximize effective communication; b) to develop techniques and equipment that allow the individual to compensate for irremediable deficits; and c) to enhance strategies for coping with the consequences (social, emotional, vocational) of impaired or altered communication.

Current trends in speech-language pathology suggest increased emphasis upon interventions designed to maximize the individual's social communication in real-life situations and settings outside the therapy environment. Examples of such interventions include: a) reducing environmental physical and psychological barriers to communication; b) designing, managing, and/or supervising communication enhancement programs; c) utilizing new technology to improve social communication (e.g., alternate or augmentative communication devices, prosthetic speech aids, portable amplification systems); d) developing maintenance programs to delay the deterioration of communicative functioning; and e) increasing involvement in the management of right hemisphere and dementia patients.

One important aspect of management for speech-language impaired elderly individuals is the provision of counseling and support. Although individual counseling is presumably carried out routinely in daily therapy sessions, group sessions have been found to be particularly effective in meeting one or more of the following goals:

1. to enhance willingness to engage in therapy;
2. to encourage willingness to use all available modalities for daily communication and to provide opportunities for practice;
3. to facilitate emotional adjustment and promote socialization;
4. to provide a mechanism for problem solving daily difficulties in functioning;
5. to ensure realistic expectations concerning recovery.

Kearns (1986) has described the wide range of psychosocial and treatment groups that have been proposed as model programs in the literature. One of his major pleas is for multidisciplinary participation in the provision of counseling experiences to individual clients and their families.

## Significant Others

In the broadest sense of the concept of support, it is clear that interventions must extend to the significant others of speech-language impaired older individuals. Although it has been argued that the term "significant other" should include the spouse, other family members, friends, and even the social support network provided by the community (Florance, 1979), it is used here to refer to those primary caregivers who provide significant social and emotional support. These significant others play a critical role in the treatment process because they:

1. provide the primary source of emotional support for the speech-language impaired individual (a major consideration when the reduced social networks of the elderly are considered);
2. serve as the primary communication partners to speech-language impaired individuals and typically must assume a disproportionate portion of the communicative burden; and,
3. can become a major partner in the therapeutic process— implementing treatment procedures, facilitating carryover to the home environment, enhancing communication interactions, etc.

In designing management strategies utilizing significant others, it is important to remember that family members and primary caregivers also need assistance in coping with the effects of speech-language disorders on their own lives and emotional adjustments. As Buck (1978) has indicated, stroke (and presumably other communication disorders) is a family illness. The onset of any communication disorder constitutes a crisis of major proportions (Lubinski, 1981). Family homeostasis is disrupted and roles and life styles are disorganized (Webster & Newhoff, 1981). Emotional responses may include: anxiety, frustration, helplessness, depression, pity, hostility, and guilt (Linebaugh & Young-Charles, 1978). Adjustment and participation in treatment is complicated by the fact that family members frequently underestimate the extent of an individual's communication deficits and report little or no information about communication disorders prior to a personal experience with an impaired relative (e.g., Helmick, Watamori, & Palmer, 1976; Vogel & Costello, 1985).

Management options for significant others can take various forms. Counseling should be provided in both individual and group contexts, as needed and must consider the nature of pre-existing family patterns of communication and relationships (e.g., Bardach, 1969; Derman & Manaster, 1967; Newhoff & Davis, 1978). According to Webster and Newhoff (1981), the four primary functions for such counseling should include: a) receiving information the family wishes to share; b) giving information; c) helping individuals clarify ideas, emotions, and attitudes, and d) providing family members with options for changing communication patterns. Research clearly supports the need for counseling of family members at the outset of coping with a speech-language disorder and dealing with ongoing needs expressed by many (Linebaugh & Young-Charles, 1978).

In addition, significant others may be involved directly in the client's treatment program through direct participation in therapy sessions and carryover activities and/or through specific programs designed to utilize the significant other as a therapy aide (e.g., Florance, 1979). Finally, various support groups have proved to be particularly effective in meeting the needs of family members for information, emotional venting, and exploration of coping strategies (e.g., Sanders, Hamby, & Nelson, 1984; McCormick & Williams, 1976; Carey & Hansen, 1985/86; Tardelli & Bocage, 1985).

## The Role of Other Professionals

Professionals other than speech-language pathologists must assume responsibility for contributing positively to the identification and management of older persons with speech-language disorders. Frequently, a speech-language pathologist is not a member of the immediate health care team serving the older individual or may not be on staff in facilities serving the elderly. As a result, other professionals may be the first to recognize the presence of a speech-language disorder and may be among the few communication partners of the impaired older individual. In these capacities, the professional must become informed about the nature of speech-language disorders and their communicative consequences as well as techniques for communicating effectively with this client group. In addition, professionals must be willing to participate in interdisciplinary planning to meet the needs of such persons and must be prepared to cooperate in direct interventions for individuals and/or families that involve a multidisciplinary team. The last responsibility is particularly important. There is a critical role for communications professionals in programming involving group counseling and communication training, environmental modifications, inservicing, and mass media outreach.

## Community

The gerontological literature is replete with references to the importance of informal social support systems to the elderly (Biegel, Shore, & Gordon, 1984). The need for support networks is particularly critical for communicatively-impaired older persons. When one looks beyond the immediate family and/or primary caregivers for informal support systems, one must turn to the community. The term community is used here to encompass those persons, services, activities, and physical surroundings that constitute the total communication environment of the older person. Defined in this manner, the community becomes an important resource in meeting the holistic communication needs of all elderly persons by acting as a major facilitator of communicative interactions.

The major barrier to effective community response to the needs of its speech-language impaired older members is lack of information. The neighbor of an aphasic stroke victim may avoid visiting because he is uncomfortable with communication problems and is unsure of family needs or desires. A laryngectomee's critical first visit to a restaurant with a group of friends may never be repeated because of the attitudes of the staff or the failure of the facility to place the group in a quiet section where the person's fledgling esophageal speech can be heard. The church group's weekly bridge club may be puzzled by a former member's refusal to return, not recognizing that bidding out loud or scorekeeping have become too difficult whereas an alternate, simpler card game might be manageable.

The answer to many of these problems lies in community education— through any medium and in any setting possible. One program that has already been developed to meet this need is a series of pre-crisis intervention workshops concerning communication disorders (Shadden, Raiford, & Shadden, 1983). The purpose of pre-crisis intervention is to provide participants with information and experiences that allow them to understand the nature and consequences of communication disorders, as well as effective ways of coping with these consequences, *before* major barriers to communication and adjustment have been allowed to develop. The program targets the community of older persons but is suitable to any group.

Any educational program should encourage the development of a community action plan for reviewing the needs of communicatively impaired residents and for implementing appropriate environmental modifications. In addition to basic education, communities would benefit from the development and maintenance of a central clearinghouse of information. Helpful ingredients might include a library of appropriate literature, a complete listing of agencies, professionals, and services, and possibly a hotline for assistance.

## Summary

Dowd (1980) has stated that the lives of the elderly are largely dependent upon the relative power resources of the actors in any social interaction. The primary medium for exchange of resources and status in such interactions is conversation. According to exchange theory, the elderly are disadvantaged with respect to the personal resources they bring to communication events which are critical to enhance a sense of positive self worth and to achieve basic needs and services from others. When a speech-language disorder is superimposed upon existing resource limitations, a true communication crisis occurs. The implications for social and personal adjustment are far-reaching.

This chapter has reviewed some of the more common speech-language disorders found in older individuals. It has been suggested that these disorders affect whole communication networks and must consequently be the concern of family members, friends and neighbors in the community, and service providers in all professions and settings. Every one of us has a responsibility to understand the nature of speech-language impairment, its consequences, and effective strategies for coping with communication breakdown and for obtaining appropriate and comprehensive services.

# Part III
# AGING AND THE
# COMMUNICATION PROCESS

Part III looks at the issues which have received the most attention in communication and aging research. This section constitutes a state of the art review of current research in communication and aging, divided by subject area.

## ❧ 7 ❧

# Myths and Stereotypes
## Communication Breakdowns

## Jerry Feezel and Robert Hawkins

*You're 65? Wow! I didn't know you were that old!*
*Oh well, you can't teach an old dog new tricks.*
*Why is grandpa marrying again? I mean, what's the point?*
*I just hate getting behind an old codger in rush hour traffic.*
*If you live long enough, your entire family will finally abandon*
*you.*

These statements reflect some common myths about aging and aging persons. Many young people have grown up with such perceptions and, unfortunately, cling to them well into adulthood. What is even more unfortunate is that many older adults have come to perceive these myths as realities in their own lives (see Dreher, 1987; Hendricks & Hendricks, 1977). The purpose of this chapter is to (1) examine some common myths and stereotypes about aging, (2) discuss their impact on the communicative lives of elders, and (3) suggest some realistic attitudes that may foster more positive communication with elders. We shall begin with a general overview of the role of attitudes in communication and aging, then look at negative and positive attitudes, and conclude with some realistic communicative approaches with older people.

Attitudes toward aging is the conceptual category of the research dealing with myths and stereotypes. An attitude may be defined as an evaluation of a given object, event, person, or group. In the case of aging, we are focusing on evaluations of older adults, individually or as a group. Attitudes are mental states of views, expectations, feelings, beliefs and judgments which may be kept hidden or expressed (intentionally or unintentially). Perhaps you have heard someone explain remarks similar to those at the beginning of this chapter by saying: "I didn't really mean that" or "a lot of people say things like that." Of course, our intentions are not always accurately reflected in what we say; the words may come out wrong. However, words, looks, or actions may also betray our true feelings about "old folk" which we do not want to admit and try to disguise. Remarks such as the examples given should not be taken lightly.

Attitudes may determine our behavior toward older persons. The connection between attitudes and behaviors has been well established in research (see Fishbein & Ajzen, 1975; Steinfatt & Infante, 1976). In fact, an earlier definition which has been accepted by most theorists treats an attitude as a somewhat enduring set of beliefs "predisposing one to respond in some preferential manner" (Rokeach, 1970, p. 112). The importance of attitudes is that they predispose us to behave in certain ways consistent with our feelings. If you believe that all elders are hard of hearing, you are likely to speak much louder to anyone over 60 (or, with more disastrous effects, to whisper about them in their presence as if they can't hear you).

An insidious consequence of attitudes may be the attendant response of older people. If they see themselves in terms of the expectations of others, a self-fulfilling prophecy may be set in motion. The amazing life of Grace Murray Hopper provides an illustration which, fortunately, combats the frequently debilitating stereotype. Ms. Hopper, a math professor, joined the Naval reserves in 1943; she was informed she was too old for active duty after the war. In civilian life she developed the breakthrough computer language COBOL and was recalled to active duty at age 60. Now 79 and just retired from the Navy, she speaks with wry humor of the earlier attitude: "It's just as well to be told you're too old at 40. Then you're over it" (Medina, 1986).

Attitudes underlie and give direction to communication. Since the act of communicating (both verbally and nonverbally) is behavior, an attitude leads us to communicate in certain ways to an older person. If our attitude toward them is an accurate and valid evaluation, then we may behave appropriately in our communication. If we hold false or distorted beliefs, we are more likely to communicate inappropriately or even in a harmful manner. Although people can and do behave in ways not consistent with their mental states, they are much more likely to communicate in accord with their attitudes.

When looking at positive and negative attitudes toward elders, it is important that we keep in mind some of the components of attitude theory which may apply. One set of constructs, which has been drawn from the work of Milton Rokeach (1970), identifies a kind of hierarchy of interrelatedness for *values, beliefs, and attitudes.* Values may be seen as a set of superordinate, fundamental beliefs from which more specific beliefs about life derive; attitudes are particular predispositions toward the attitude object which derive from those beliefs. It is important to note, then, that an attitude toward older people may be a reflection of much deeper underlying beliefs and values for life. As such, it may be very entrenched and difficult to change.

In addition to the related components of attitude, we can examine attitudes toward elders in terms of who holds them or their loci. The attitude may be located in *Self, Significant Others, and/or Society* (Clarke & Feezel, 1982). Self-attitudes are those that older persons believe about themselves individually or about people their age (cohorts). The significant others for an elder may include spouse, offspring, grandchildren, other relatives, friends, clergy, doctors, etc. — anyone who relates closely to the older adult on a regular, noncasual basis and has some role in his/her well-being. The attitudes felt or expressed by such other people are obviously quite important in day-to-day communication. Societal attitudes, in contrast, are those evaluations of older people by large groups and institutions (health care professionals, insurance companies, government agencies, etc.), service providers (clerks, cashiers, receptionists), and the public as a whole (drivers, audiences, shoppers, etc.) who have somewhat casual contact with an elder as mere acquaintances or even strangers. In such situations, people will probably communicate with a given elder in terms of societally pre-programmed attitudes toward aging.

Whatever the dynamic of the attitude components and location, such evaluations of persons may be relatively positive or negative, valid or invalid, accurate or distorted, helpful or harmful. In other words, as evaluations, attitudes may vary on several dimensions which we summarize as either detrimental to or facilitative of healthy communication with and among elders. *Detrimental attitudes* would be those myths, stereotypes, lies, delusions, or any type of misinformation that restricts growth through communication for the elders as well as those around them. *Facilitative attitudes* are positive, accurate perceptions which foster growth for elders and others in their communicative relationships, whether momentary or long-enduring. The following sections discuss these two categories of attitudes toward elders.

## Detrimental Attitudes Toward Elders

The topic area of attitudes on aging has been the focus of much research over some 45 years. It is beyond the scope of this chapter to enumerate all of the pernicious attitudes about older adults and aging. Rather, we shall limit our coverage to those myths, stereotypes, lies and distortions which, as attitudes, are significantly detrimental to communication with and among elders. The term "age-ism" was used by Butler (1969) to refer to a stereotypic attitude toward older persons based on a "distaste for growing older" (p. 243). Butler and others have found that negative attitudes toward aging are perpetuated by media images (Francher, 1973; Greenberg, Korzenny & Atkins, 1979) and by language used (Nuessel, 1984; Barbato & Nuessel, 1984). Surveys repeated over several years by Palmore (1977, 1980) and Harris & Associates (1975) have detailed negative perceptions or myths and stereotypes of aging and elders. Many of the findings of attitudes on aging research were summarized by gerontologist Anthony Traxler (1980b) into the following 15 representative myths, which serve to organize the discussion of detrimental attitudes.

1. *Myth of the dominance of chronological age.* Once an individual reaches the age of 65, she/he is too often assumed to be "old" simply because society equates "old" with "65 and above." This chronological perspective "ignores the tremendous heterogeneity and diversity displayed by the elderly in such areas as interests, aptitudes, personality, and attitudes" (Traxler, 1980b). Consider the 20-year-old who seems completely bored with himself and others and who asks of life: "Is that all there is?" Consider also the 80-year-old who accepts each new day and each new acquaintance as Christmas gifts to be opened and relished and who exclaims: "What a wonder life has been and continues to be." Indeed, the myth of the dominance of chronological age stifles the urge to grow communicatively, to open up to everything within the self as well as with others. A note about the song "Memories" in the highly successful musical show *Cats* is relevant at this point. With an eloquent metaphor involving the lives of humans and cats, the artists write movingly about the need that older and younger beings have for remaining in touch to celebrate the memories of earlier years ("if you touch me, you'll know what happiness is").

2. *The senility myth.* This myth posits that if you live enough, eventually you'll become senile. Gerontological researchers tell us that senility is a disease process which afflicts only about .5% of those over 65. Yet the myth prevails, and we avoid contact with the elderly because we think they are too crazy to engage in dialogue. As a result, many of us limit our conversations with older adults to simple, often inane words and phrases that serve only to test the communication channels and nothing else: "Hi, gramps! How are you? Isn't that nice! Well, it's nice talking to you. See you around!" What is worse, "gramps" accepts this prophecy about himself and makes no attempt to recognize himself as a perfectly sane, non-senile individual whose opinions are valuable.

3. *The decline in intelligence myth,*

4. *the learning myth* (or you can't teach an old dog new tricks), and

5. *the incompetence myth.* These are three related myths (addressed more fully in Chapter 4) which directly assault the older person's self-concept and feelings of worth; they are indeed debilitating. Put simply, they tell us that the older you get, the dumber you get. The truth is quite the opposite; ability to learn remains intact well into advanced old age and the wisdom of elders has been evident in generations of leaders in many nations (Baltes and Schaie, 1974; Green, 1969). Research tells us that what has been labelled as a "learning deficit in the elderly" may be more correctly a difficulty in performance or response.

> What this means then, is that the elderly's learning capacity and mental ability hold up well into old age and when there is a decline in learning performance, it is more likely caused by such factors as lack of time to respond, health impairment, motivational differences, lack of confidence, or cultural role expectations (e.g., the elderly are not supposed to be competent human beings!) rather than a decline in mental or learning ability. (Traxler, 1980b, p. 14).

The problem is that so many people continue to communicate with the elderly totally unaware of the foregoing realities. How often we hear younger people say, "Why bother trying to say anything to old Mrs. Green? She's so mentally slow and dense about learning new things, even if she wanted to." Again, as is the case of the senility myth, the decline in learning and intelligence myths tend to become internalized by older adults with the result that they close themselves off to communicative contact with younger friends as well as with each other.

Finally, the incompetency myth establishes the notion that, even in the face of research findings which dispel the myth, "old" translates into "incompetent." This myth gives rise to the attitudes expressed in the following: "What's the point in trying to communicate with old persons? They're incompetent! You'd have to look after them constantly and worry about them when they're out of sight. What kind of a communication relationship is that? Why bother!"

Moreover, when this myth and its resulting attitudes are believed, older persons are robbed of the opportunity, in intergenerational communications, to demonstrate their competency. In "My Children are Coming Today," Elise Maclay very poignantly suggests how well-meaning adult children make it difficult for their aged parents to function fully as communicative human beings simply because the children are fearful of the risks the parents must assume in living by themselves.

### My Children Are Coming Today

My children are coming today, They mean well. But they worry.
They think I should have a railing in the hall. A telephone in the kitchen.
They want someone to come in when I take a bath. They really don't like my living alone.

Help me to be grateful for their concern. And help them to understand that I have to do what I can as long as I can. They're right when they say there are risks. I might fall. I might leave the stove on. But there is no challenge, no possibility of triumph, no real aliveness without risk. When they were young and climbed trees and rode bicycles and went away to camp, I was terrified. But I let them go. Because to hold them would have hurt them.

Now our roles are reversed. Help them see.

Keep me from being grim or stubborn about it. But don't let me let them smother me. (p. 3)

In addition to the myths discussed, there are others that Traxler has summarized. These will be simply listed with brief comments to suggest how other myths can restrict growth through communication in the lives of older adults.

6. *Rigidity and resistance to change myth.* These two factors are not age related; thus we can expect to find many seniors who will not fight our ideas as we converse with them. In fact, some communities have noted increases in the older adults taking courses and supporting progressive programs.

7. *Institutionalization or nursing home myth.* Only about 4% of persons over 65 are living in nursing homes rather than the higher percentages that many younger people assume. Thus, most people over 65 are relatively healthy and fully capable of interacting and communicating meaningfully in independent living situations.

8. *Pain myth or pain is normal and to be expected as one grows older.* Again, pain is not necessarily age-related. Thus, we don't need to worry about conversations with older adults who seem preoccupied with their aches and pains. This communication pattern is characteristic of some but not most elders, and is more likely to be a function of life satisfaction.

9. *Old people are rejected by their children myth.* This probably derived from earlier studies in which older parents reported that their offspring rarely wrote, called or visited. Subsequent studies to verify the information found it was not necessarily accurate. People in "midlife crises" frequently find their elders can be a source of information.

10. *Second childhood myth.* Not all folks lapse into second childhood as they grow older. This means that senior citizens need not be perceived by younger persons as silly and childish communicators. The prevalence of baby talk to elders found by recent research shows the persistence of this myth (Caporael & Culbertson, 1986).

11. *The loneliness and social isolation myth.* Many older folks are just as gregarious and involved as younger people are. They, therefore, are good conversational partners.

12. *Preoccupation with death myth.* The aged members in our society are probably less concerned about their oncoming death than younger persons are. The communication topics need not be overly morbid.

13. *The retirement myth.* Older persons, in general, do not withdraw into themselves during their retirement and some actually expand their involvements and interests. Thus we can count on them to be interesting communication partners.

14. *The physical handicap myth.* Being old does not necessarily mean that one is physically handicapped. Thus, we can expect to interact with them easily, go for walks, ride bicycles, and communicate on the way.

15. *The asexual elderly or "the myth of the sexless senior citizen".* Again, being old does not necessarily mean that one's sex life has come to an end. Harmful assumptions about intimate relationships can unfairly constrain our conversations with the elderly.

The foregoing myths, when extended to encompass all older age groups, become stereotypes which inhibit social interaction with and among the elderly. The problem is becoming increasingly serious as the segment of our population comprised of older persons grows dramatically.

Unfortunately, these detrimental attitudes may be perpetuated through problems which occur on levels ranging from interpersonal to mass communication. Infrequency of daily interpersonal contact between young and old people results in the perpetuation of negative attitudes not only about the elderly but the young as well.

In perhaps more dramatic fashion, this perpetuation in societal attitudes is carried out through images and language in the mass media. Johnny Carson's pathetic and not-very-funny "Aunt Blabby" is a prime example of the way television communicates the notion that older adults (in this case, women) are silly-acting, bizarre, and weird simply because they are old. Newspaper and magazine ads in very subtle ways suggest that all old people are run down, lifeless and uninteresting without Geritol (or some other similar tonic) to restore their energy level to make them act younger and, therefore, be more acceptable. Put briefly, the basic media message is simply this: to be old is to be stoutly resisted since it carries so many negative connotations.

## Facilitative Attitudes Toward Elders

Once we have set aside the myths and stereotypes, we can begin to get at the realities of aging. Our purpose is to paint a truer picture of older adults, one which will help foster accurate and effective communication with and among them. This does not mean arriving at a "pretty" picture with only positive attitudes. Not all aspects of the reality of aging can be good or positive, but our point here is that a more realistic perception, free of myths and distortions, will facilitate growth or healthy communicative experiences. Proper attitudes toward aging facilitate:

1. a just and humane treatment by society,
2. empathic, helping relationships with significant others, and
3. a self-realization of productive growth in later years.

This latter may be the most important; elders must view themselves positively as capable of growth. All older adults need to keep the healthy belief that "yes, there *is* life after retirement" or even that life *can* begin at 80.

Valid and accurate evaluations of elders will help break down communication barriers and thus facilitate more effective communication. Much of the research on attitudes toward aging has identified valid beliefs, feelings, and actions along with the myths and stereotypes. The surveys conducted periodically by Palmore reveal, through his "correct answers" to the true/false questions, some information about the facts of aging as synthesized from research (see Palmore 1977, 1980).

It is interesting to note that some recent research suggests that the attitudes of younger adults and society generally have become more positive toward elders (Austin, 1985). Palmore's comparison of his results with those of several other similar studies in the seventies implies a trend to more positive views of aging. To adapt a line from a cigarette ad, "you've come a long way, old folks," from the largely negative attitudes held by graduate students in a Tuckman and Lorge study in 1953.

In a similarly positive perspective, the 1975 Louis Harris and Associates poll found that one-third of those over 65 felt their lives had turned out better than they expected. Only one-tenth described their situation as worse than they expected (pp.111-117). Although the positive outcome was related to income and race, Blacks and those earning under $7,000 still rated their lives "better" rather than "worse" by nearly three to one. Those who see their lives as better identify the reasons as financial security, good family life, good health, and comfortable life with fewer problems or worries. These all suggest some needs of elders for continued growth in advanced age. Generally, when people of any age feel secure and comfortable in stable relationships with others, they will be more likely to communicate honestly and openly.

The notion of facilitative attitudes was treated by Traxler as "developmental characteristics" (1980b, pp. 19-22). He identified seven valid characteristics of older adults which facilitate understanding them. These are summarized here as statements of attitudes that are generally accurate evaluations. Elders:

1. desire to leave a legacy of themselves after death,
2. want to fulfill the elder function by sharing their years of experience.
3. have a strong emotional attachment to familiar objects,

4. change their sense of time and perspective on the entire life cycle,
5. tend toward slowness of behavior in contrast to the speed of society,
6. develop a sense of presentness or living one day at a time, and
7. tend toward self-reflection and reminiscence, a kind of life review.

Together, these attitudes facilitate the older person taking time to make sense of his or her life experiences and to make a contribution to society and the significant others around them.

Another approach to facilitative attitudes toward elders was developed by Clarke and Feezel (1982). Such needs may be viewed as attitudes held by elders themselves, by others, and by society which enable continued growth through communication. The following three principles of facilitative attitudes have been developed from the Clarke/Feezel discussion of needs (1982, pp. 14-21).

*Productive Principle of Self: the self is capable of independent productive growth even in later life.* With advancing age, we come face-to-face with ourselves and the need arises to look within in order to make sense of our lives. Self-engagement theory (Chellam, 1977-78) views this as a healthy turning point in later life from outer orientation to inner direction to synthesize a meaning, purpose and personal satisfaction in one's life. A second kind of self-need is that of detachment or independence. As we grow older, the world seems to move faster and the losses of other people close to us increase. In order to cope with these changes, some detachment and inner reliance is necessary (see Feezel & Shepherd, 1987). Disengagement theory shows the validity of this need by positing that as we grow older there is a need to maintain some detachment from social relationships, not a total withdrawal or denial of feelings, but a strength of independence (Cumming & Henry, 1961). The elder needs to disengage from others somewhat in order to self-engage for the synthesis of life experiences into a positive self-satisfaction.

In other words, the older adult may legitimately take this attitude: I don't have to rely on others; from my life of experience, I am capable of making the most of my remaining time on "this mortal coil." Such a position was espoused by Kalish (1979) in his Personal Growth model of old age. He felt the later years could be a period of optimum personal growth if elders took the attitude to do so, because they:

1. do not have so many responsibilities as earlier,
2. no longer need to be constrained by what others think of them,
3. have learned through their problems the priorities for satisfaction,

4. have lots of discretionary time to do so things, and
5. may be motivated by the knowledge of a finite future.
    (p. 401)

*Productive Principle of Other: the significant others who relate to elders should cultivate empathic helping relationships with them.* In seeming contrast to the disengagement theory, activity theory maintains that "psychological well-being is attained in one's later years through activity, especially social intercourse" (Harris & Bodden, 1978, p. 325). The needs of older people include (1) to maintain interdependence with family and friends, (2) to share one's life experiences with others, and (3) to engage in some forms of activity. Significant others can empathize with elders and provide the support for fulfilling these needs.

*Productive Principle of Society: the collected people and groups who make up society must achieve a just, humane, respectful treatment of elders.* The institutions and the anonymous people on the street that exert the pressures of society on each of us have practically exiled elders from the community through retirement, diminished power and control, and ageism generally. Therefore, societal attitudes must be changed to enable the following needs of elders to be met:

1. a positive sense of place of function in society after retirement,
2. opportunities provided for societal input,
3. treatment as competent, both cognitively and affectively, and
4. education as to resources available, such as government and legal agencies.

The reforming of societal attitudes to fulfill these needs would allow increased power and control, with elders having significant input into the environment in which they live and move.

The facilitative attitudes attendant to the self, other and societal needs discussed above, is well summarized in the responses of older people studied by Offenbacher and Poster (1985). The elders in this study seemed to follow a four principle "code of conduct":

Don't be sorry for yourself.
Try to be independent.
Don't just sit there; do something.
Above all, be sociable.

Although these principles were focused on attitudes the elders themselves should maintain, the people around must also assist them to follow these principles.

## Implications for Communication

Perhaps the most important overall attitude (belief or value) to maintain is that each older person is first and foremost a *person*, and wants to be treated as such, communicatively and otherwise. Remember, it is a myth that all old people are alike, (dominance of chronological age myth) and this myth leads to stereotyping which denies individuality. If we communicate with each older adult as a person, the primary attitudes which should guide our communications would be as follows:

*P*ositiveness
*E*mpathy
*R*espect
*S*ecurity
*O*penness
*N*onjudgmental stance

Each of these six attitudes will be examined specifically in relation to recommended communication behaviors involving elders.

Communication is a mutual transaction involving the constant, simultaneous interplay of factors in the behavior of all parties to the communication. As applied in this chapter, the parties would be an older person and one or more other persons (other elders, sons, daughters, doctors, clerks, agency staff, etc.). Again, using the tripartite division of self, significant others, and society would indicate that the attitudes located in all three will mutually impact the communication behaviors of the situation. Facilitative attitudes on the part of self, other(s), and society become a kind of S.O.S. to "save our sanity" in elder communication.

*Self* is the beginning point; how the older person chooses to behave is central to the communication interchange. First, as an older person, you must have some *positive regard* for yourself; you must take the attitude that "Yes, I am someone who counts and I can do it." Believe that your ideas should be heard and be willing to "open" up and share them. *Openness* refers to being assertive enough to let your feelings or thoughts be known to others. Be careful of being too wide open when the situation is risky or the occasion is not appropriate, but speak up for your rights. Don't let them be trampled into silence. If you don't feel you know how to do this effectively, assert yourself to find the help. There are assertiveness training workshops available in many areas. If speaking in front of groups is a concern, then look into a public speaking course at the local college.

*Other* people close to an elder are important to the communication. Their attitudes will affect how they speak and listen. Significant others often choose to "feel with" or "resonate" with older persons, encouraging them to share their pains as well as their joys of long and eventful lives. Thus, *empathy* becomes an important attitude and value. Typically, empathic communication is manifested in such warm, personal expressions as, "Gee, it sounds like you've had a really rough time. Want to tell me about it?" or "what a marvelous time that must have been during the St. Louis Exposition of 1904!"

Such language as this promotes a sense of *security* for the elder, of safety in the midst of life's storms much as a harbor provides refuge for the beleagured sailor. *Respect* is another positive attitude that may be seen in deferential postures taken toward older folks. This is not shown in fawning behavior nor that of "let's humor the old codger"; rather, it reveals a feeling of genuinely prizing the elder as a worthwhile and competent being.

Closely related to respect, we may say that the attitudes that significant others have for older people should be *non-judgmental* in nature. This means an attitude that affirms the rights of the older person without judging the merit of his/her ideas, opinions and feelings. This does not mean to avoid or never to disagree with an elder (that could be seen as humoring or condescension), but hear them out or listen openly to them before confronting differences. Even so, disagreements should be founded in mutual respect and regard.

*Society* is not the least of the parties to the communication process. The attitudes instilled in you by society affect interaction between you and the other person(s); many dispositions may be subtle or hidden. We will focus here on those casual, short-term relationships between strangers as one of the realms of an elder's interaction with society.

A recent case of following societal myths or stereotypic attitudes was detailed in a *Time* magazine story on the high incidence of AIDS in Belle Glade, Florida. Although the Atlanta-based Center for Disease Control had attributed the incidence to sexual activity or drug use (not to mosquitos), the local director of the Tropical Disease Clinic disputed that with the following quotation. Many of the victims "are older individuals who are way past their sexually active years." (Medina, 1986) Here the societal myth that older persons are not sexually active may so blind people in power positions that tragic decisions are the result.

Essentially, these relationships may be viewed as microcosms of the more expansive interactions with society as a whole. Suppose you are a driver or a pedestrian or a clerk dealing with an older adult; what is the first step? Try to listen with *empathy* and be *nonjudgmental* (at least for a while). Try to set aside your biases or initial reactions to hear the older person out. It may take them a while to make themselves clear because (a) some may feel inadequate and unsure of themselves, (b) they may have a physical problem affecting speech or breathing, (c) they may enjoy and want to prolong the contact with someone who will listen, or (d) they simply aren't in any hurry. The reasons may be as diverse as older people are. Try to put yourself in their "shoes" to feel what they may be feeling, to understand what their life is like, before you respond. In terms of judgments, you may eventually have to tell them they did something wrong or reject the request, but try to avoid instant conclusions before you have tried to empathize with them fully.

We are talking here of short lived encounters in life where you don't need or want to get to know the older person well, so you don't want to prolong the agony of an uncomfortable situation. However, a 2-3 minute episode can linger and have impact for days or even longer, for you and the other person. Life is too short for all of us to make the short interactions more difficult than they need be.

Finally, we may consider two more implications for practitioners and scholars in the discipline of speech communication. The first is that the aging-related phenomena we've discussed above under the categories of detrimental and facilitative attitudes suggest a somewhat specialized interpretation of Jack Gibb's study of defensive and supportive climates of communication. For example, Gibb (1961) tells us that, to minimize defensiveness, certainty ("the issue is black or white; there is one way, and one way only, to approach this problem") must give way to provisionalism ("let us consider tentatively a variety of ways of approaching the problem"). The implication here is that often it's too easy a temptation for the service provider to assume that the nursing home resident cannot be trusted to develop provisional solutions to such a problem as the presence of a pet in his/her room. Therefore, the resident must be controlled by the certainty of a no-pets-in-resident's-rooms rule.

Another implication concerns the phenomenon of relational deterioration. Special attention must be given to caregivers to help them overcome the trauma that accompanies all of the painful "goodbyes" they experience in interactions with the frail elderly (Feezel & Shepherd, 1987). Moreover, we need to work with seniors themselves of all ages to help them work through their expiring relationships with siblings, confidants, and other significant others.

Shakespeare once wrote: "There's nothing either good or bad, but thinking makes it so." Since attitudes represent, in part anyway, what we think, we might modify Shakespeare's statement to read: There's nothing good or bad, but attitudes make it so. Finally, we may add that the goodness and badness of communication are not inherent in the nature of communication, rather they stem from the attitudes that underlie that communication.

We have seen in this chapter that detrimental and facilitative attitudes affect the communication with and among older adults. Thus, the person who has the attitude that older adults are incapable of learning anything new will probably communicate in a negative and condescending manner. On the other hand, the person who believes that older adults, if given the opportunity, are perfectly capable of learning "new tricks" will probably communicate in a positive tone and in an open and accepting manner.

Moreover, older adults themselves often will communicate among themselves in patterns—both positive and negative—which reflect how younger people communicate with them.

# Interpersonal Communication
## Intimate Relationships and Aging

## Teresa L. Thompson and Jon F. Nussbaum

We are who we are through the relationships we build with other people. Of particular importance are the intimate relationships we develop. Our meaning for "intimacy" here is not intended to refer to sexual relationships exclusively, although many of those are indeed intimate. Rather, we are referring to any emotionally close relationship. Typically, this includes marital, familial, and friend relationships.

The notion that satisfaction with intimate relationships is important for the elderly is substantiated by work such as that conducted by Traupmann, Eckels and Hatfield (1982) and Nussbaum (1983a). These researchers concluded that satisfaction with an intimate relationship is related to life satisfaction and psychological well-being, especially for elderly women. In another study, Lowenthall and Haven (1968) determined that one intimate, stable relationship is more closely associated with high morale than are overall high levels of social interaction. Similarly, Genevay (1986) found that intimacy is essential for self-esteem and emotional health for aging individuals.

Relationships between people, intimate or otherwise, do not develop out of nothingness. They are created through what the two people involved in the relationship *do* with each other—how they communicate. Messages are sent and reacted to as the individuals go through the process of defining a relationship. It is a negotiation process. Each message relationally

(Watzlawick, Beavin, and Jackson, 1967) offers a definition of the relationship. Depending upon the other person's response, that definition is accepted, rejected, or modified. All of these behaviors are communicative, in that messages are offered. Together, the two people build their relationship. Indeed, many have argued that communication not only defines, creates and reflects relationships, but that communication *is* the relationship. After all, what else can be seen about a relationship between two people but how they communicate with each other? One's feelings and other internal processes *influence* how we communicate with each other, but you cannot see those. All that you can see about a relationship is the communication shared by the two people.

The relational perspective briefly articulated above will guide our discussion in this chapter. To keep the length of the chapter within acceptable ranges, our review must be representative, rather than comprehensive. We will confine our review to published work to which the reader will likely have access, rather than including much research that has been presented at conventions but has not found its way into print.

We had originally planned to organize this review in a rather traditional method by discussing each of the types of intimate relationships which are potentially a part of the life of an elderly individual. This would include a section on marital relationships, one on familial relationships, one on friendships, etc. Such a breakdown would imply more separation between the relationships than actually exists. A spouse or family member, for instance, can also be a friend. So we instead decided to discuss some *themes* that appear to emerge as one investigates intimate relationships and the elderly. Ten themes stood out in our analysis of the existing literature: 1) conversations; 2) relationship development; 3) relationships and the quality of life; 4) functions of relationships; 5) relationship styles; 6) confirmatory communication (including such issues as helping, affect, expressiveness, and disconfirmation); 7) control and power; 8) relationship termination; 9) aloneness; and 10) relationships and successful aging.

Prior to beginning our discussion of this research, we should mention a couple of limitations found in much of it. As in the case with many of the areas reviewed within this book, much of the research on which this review was based is cross-sectional rather than longitudinal. Thus, the conclusions are somewhat limited. Further, much of the research on relationships is rather demographic in nature, rather than focusing on the *process* of relationships. While some would defend this perspective by arguing that the demographic questions are the first ones that should be asked by researchers, we question whether those are the *most important* questions—whether they tell us much that is important about relationships. People study relationships and aging because they are interested in how those relationships work—what keeps a marriage going for 50 years, for instance? The demographic studies tell us little about this. Similarly, some of the research to be found appears to begin from the perspective that younger people are at fault for any problems occurring in communication with the elderly. Such a view not only ignores the transactional nature of communication but is not consistent with much of the literature. We will attempt to minimize our discussion of the demographic research in this review and will emphasize the research that tells us a little more about the process of relationships. Thus, we begin our discussion by focusing on a truly communicative issue—conversations. What do people say to each other in their relationships?

## Conversations

A few studies found in the literature have examined the content of conversations within various relational contexts. For instance, Treas (1975) reported that older married couples focus their conversations differently than do younger couples. Later-life couples talk about their kids much less than they did when they were younger. They are also more likely to focus on rather conventional topics, such as church, home upkeep, and health. Similarly, Troll (1982) concluded that there is a great deal of concern for and discussion of health in middle-age and older marriages. In particular, women exhibit much concern about their husband's health—they are more concerned about their husband's health than they are about their own.

The issue of *reminiscence* as a conversational topic has probably been the focus of more research than any other topic. Although Butler (1968) argued that a "life review" is helpful whether done privately or in conversation, other research indicates that such a review done in solitude *can* be depressing (Evans, Millicovsky & Tennison, 1984; Tamir, 1979). Reminiscence is seen by some people as a tiresome self-indulgence (Moody, 1984), but it does serve several important functions. Reminiscence can be used as a coping mechanism, which usually focuses on unresolved conflicts and fears (Butler, 1974). It also apparently helps one cope with the fear of death, with grief and depression, and with a loss of self-identity and self-esteem (McMahon & Rudrick, 1964). Other work has indicated that reminiscence helps one defend one's self-esteem and beliefs (Priefer & Gambert, 1984), feel loved (Becker, Blumenfield & Gordon, 1984), gain self-awareness and self-understanding (Kiernat, 1983), disengage from society (Kaminsky, 1984), adapt to stress (Priefer & Gambert, 1984), and see one's part in the larger historical/cultural context (Kaminsky, 1984). The therapeutic value of reminiscing has been well documented (Baum, 1980; Belsky, 1984; Perrotta & Meachan, 1981; Sable, 1984).

The focus of reminiscence is usually the family, although one's work also comes up frequently (Unruh, 1983). Recollections usually show identity in some way—the recaller tries to recreate his or her identity, since it is no longer immediately apparent. Younger old people focus on the recent past, while older old people focus on the distant past (Unruh, 1983).

Some other studies of conversation in the elderly have examined unique characteristics found in their communication. In most ways, of course, there are few differences between the communication of older people and that of younger people. Nevertheless, there are some differences. For instance, the elderly are a bit more cautious in their communication than are younger people (Botwinick, 1973). Older people desire greater certainty, and are more reluctant to suggest courses of action. They are more likely than younger people to say "I don't know" or to express no opinion about issues.

The elderly may also take longer to react during conversation (Tamir, 1979), and sentence comprehension abilities decrease somewhat throughout the life-span (Feier & Gerstman, 1980). Summarizing much of this research, Tamir (1979) pointed out that the elderly may have difficulty asking appropriate, strategic questions or synthesizing information. When the elderly do express opinions, their verbalizations tend to be more dogmatic and idiosyncratic, and somewhat less sensitive than the norm.

Tamir argues that some of these changes may occur because there is less *need* for verbal skills in the elderly since their world has become so restricted. Welford (1983) concurs with this suggestion but argues that there are some factors that make social skills even more important for the elderly than for younger people. These factors include dependency upon others and reduced mobility. Physiological factors such as loss of hearing or memory can make communication more difficult and create a need for compensatory social skills. In addition, living in close proximity to others, which occurs in many residential facilities or when living with adult offspring, leads to a need for effective interaction. Zaks and Labouvie-Vief (1980) and Isquick (1981) developed and tested methods of improving perspective-taking, empathy, and communication skills in the elderly for just such reasons.

## Relationship Development

The kinds of communication skills mentioned above are particularly important in new, developing relationships. Little research has examined the development of friendships or familial relationships, although study of the growth of such relationships would certainly be interesting. However, research has investigated the development of "romantic" relationships among the elderly. This research has focused on dating/courtship and remarriage.

Although we usually associate dating with younger people, its importance for the elderly is growing. As Bulcroft and Bulcroft (1985) point out, "In a world of shrinking social roles, dating relationships in late life may have heightened importance" (p. 116). While for younger people dating is frequently a prelude to mate selection, this is not necessarily the case for older people. The elderly do not have the pressure to get married experienced by those who are younger — indeed, the pressures may be in the opposite direction. Some older people, however, do use dating to find a mate (Bulcroft & Bulcroft, 1985).

Mate selection is, thus, one of the motives for dating in older people. Some people report enjoying their new-found freedom and are reluctant to give it up for a new mate. Bulcroft and Bulcroft (1985) found that dating also provided opportunities to meet *other* potential dating partners! Other motives included an exchange of intimacies, remaining socially active, relearning to interact with persons of the opposite sex, prestige, and maintaining a stable identity. These last two motives are particularly important for women (Bulcroft & Bulcroft, 1985).

Older people on dates engage in a greater variety of activities than do younger people. They also "move the relationship" along more quickly than youngsters do (Bulcroft & Bulcroft, 1985). Although Huyck and Hoyer (1982) argue that sex becomes less important in older dating relationships, Bulcroft and Bulcroft's interviews indicated that sexuality was a vital part of the dating relationship, and was expected by the fourth or fifth date.

An earlier study (Vinick, 1978) concluded that older people are less likely to go out "looking for" someone to date than are younger people. Older people are usually introduced by mutual friends, happen to meet in public places, or have known or been related to each other during previous marriages.

At the present time, older males are more likely to initiate dating relationships than are older women (Bulcroft & Bulcroft, 1985; Vinick, 1978). This, of course, may change as younger cohort groups grow older.

Some dating relationships do develop into marriages. Among the elderly, marriages are most likely to be remarriages (Treas & Van Hilst, 1976). As implied above, however, there are some barriers to remarriage among the elderly. These include: 1) concerns from offspring that a deceased parent will no longer be sanctified or that an inheritance will be jeopardized (Huyck & Hoyer, 1982; Troll, 1982); 2) stereotypes about other elderly being senile that cause elderly individuals themselves not to consider remarriage (Vinick, 1978); 3) feelings of loyalty to a deceased spouse (Huyck & Hoyer, 1982); and 4) negative feedback from friends (Vinick, 1978).

Reasons for remarriages are several: companionship, lasting affection and regard, anxiety about health, and not wanting to depend on children

(Troll, 1982). Men usually look for companionship and care in remarriages (Huyck & Hoyer, 1982; Vinick, 1978). Women, while they may in some ways be readier to remarry than are men (Troll, 1982), may also be somewhat reluctant to remarry because they know that they will have a good chance of having to care for an ailing spouse (Huyck & Hoyer, 1982).

Remarriages are frequently successful, especially among those who have known each other a long time (McKain, 1969). Despite this, there are some individuals who never remarry. Bell (1979) has categorized these into a typology:

1. The bitter: "He'll be as bad as the old one was!"
2. The frightened: "I don't want to risk another personal failure."
3. The overdemanding: "I can't find anyone good enough."
4. The rejected: "I can't find anyone who will have me."
5. The adjusted: "I have accepted being single and enjoy it."

Overall, the percentage of men remarrying is much higher than the percentage of women who remarry (Treas, 1975).

## Relationships and the Quality of Life

Once again, we find that most of the research regarding this theme— relationships and the quality of life—has focused on the marital relationship. In one way, this focus makes sense, in that this relationship is a primary one for those who are married. But a large number of elderly individuals are not married. Nonetheless, we will review this research.

Much of the research has examined satisfaction with the marital relationship itself. The early research on this topic was not very encouraging. Much of it indicated growing disenchantment in the later years of marriage (Blood & Wolfe, 1960; Pineo, 1961). More recent research has uncovered different trends, however. Work by both Deutscher (1968) and Stinnett, Carter and Montgomery (1972) described increased satisfaction in the later years of marriage. Overall, it appears that the earliest years of marriage—the honeymoon—are the happiest (Troll, 1982). This is followed by decreasing satisfaction during the child-rearing years (Burr, 1970), then an upswing in satisfaction (Rollins & Feldman, 1970; Steere, 1981). More specifically, Schumm and Bugaighis (1986) reported a serious decline in satisfaction during the child-rearing years for a small number of women who were working full time and had little opportunity to talk about daily matters with their husbands.

There are also, of course, gender differences in the evaluation of marital happiness. Middle-aged women are not as happy with their husbands nor are they as happy as are younger or older women, and middle-aged men realize that they do not meet their wives' needs (Troll, 1982). Women are also the dyad members who are most likely to make adjustments and changes in order for a marriage to continue (Ahammer, 1973). Overall, however, most research indicates a fairly high amount of satisfaction in older marriages.

Being married is also related to several other variables. Married older people are typically: 1) better of financially (Gilford, 1986); 2) less sensitive to density changes (Rosow, 1967); 3) better adjusted (Philblad & McNamara, 1965); 4) in better health (Palmore, 1981); 5) happier (Altergott, 1985); and 6) less depressed (Livson, 1983). They also experienced fewer psychoneurotic symptoms (Busse & Eisdorfer, 1970) and have more primary relationships (Longino & Lipman, 1981). One recent study, however, found that marital status is *not* the most important variable determining life satisfaction. Mouser, Powers, Keith and Goudy (1985) concluded that, when such variables as having a confidant, affiliation with a voluntary organization, and personal resources such as health are taken into account, marital status does not seem to make any difference in life satisfaction. The marital relationship does seem to provide self-concept confirmation at a time when, because of retirement and other role changes, it is sorely needed (Blau, 1973). Blau also argued, however, that those with a spouse *and* other relationships are in the best position.

That other relationships are important is also indicated by two studies by Nussbaum (1983a, b). He reported: 1) a relationship between the network of closeness of communication in elderly people and life satisfaction; and 2) that conversational content covaries with life satisfaction. Those discussing topics indicating less preoccupation with self showed higher levels of mood tone and more zest for life.

## The Functions of Relationships

Different relationships serve different functions for all of us. Some research has examined the functions served by marital, familial, and friend relationships for the elderly. Some of the functions that appear repeatedly in the literature are *expressiveness* and *helping*. We turn now to a review of this research.

Decker (1980) points out that the American family has always formed around the conjugal (husband-wife) bond, rather than the consanguineal (blood) bond. Within the marital dyad, research has tended to focus on the helping function. Johnson (1983) determined that, "the most comprehensive and unstressful support was provided by a spouse" (p. 377), although Burke and Weir (1982) found that older wives seek the help of someone other than their spouse for handling stress. This may be consistent with Keither and Schafer's (1985) finding that older husbands frequently feel overbenefitted in their marriages, since the husbands both receive more help and are more satisfied with the relationship.

In second marriages among older people, the notion of companionship is a function that surfaces in the literature (Treas, 1975). Some of the other functions served by remarriages and dating relationships were mentioned above.

For widows and widowers, grieving and helping (Litwak, 1985) are needed functions served by their relationships with others. Heinemann (1985) found that kin and friend relationships serve somewhat different functions here, with relatives giving socioemotional insurance, financial aid, and identity and friends providing *mutual* gratification, socialization, socializing, and confirmation. Further, new friends help the widow cope, while older friends help keep memories alive (Litwak, 1985).

Two basic functions seem to be served by the elderly parent-adult child relationship: affect and mutual aid. Both Singh and Williams (1982) and Beckman and Houser (1982) discovered that the positive affect provided to the elderly by their children significantly increased their feelings of well-being. Involvement with family activities also increases with age (Sussman & Burchinal, 1962a, b).

Positive affect can sometimes be hurt by demands for aid (E. Brody, 1985; Cicirelli, 1981). Aid, however, frequently is *mutual* — aid is given by both parents and children. Frequently, parents give more aid to their children than children do to their parents (Troll, 1986). In later years, a shift occurs such that children, particularly daughters, give more aid to their parents (Cicirelli, 1983b).

Grandparenthood, an important relationship for many elderly individuals, also serves some functions. Grandparents serve as "watchdogs" for the family, to comfort during times of crisis (Troll, 1983). Grandmothers typically have warm, close relationships with their grandchildren (Hagestad, 1978). Advice may be offered by grandparents (Thomas, 1986), and some grandparents serve as mediators in the family.

The sibling relationship seems to be guided by affect, or feelings of closeness (Cicirelli, 1977, 1979), especially amongst sisters (McGhee, 1985). Cicirelli (1977) wrote that the sibling relationship can involve encouragement, morale-building, counseling in time of crisis, serving as a confidant, and supply information. Further, sisters provide emotional support for their elderly brothers and challenge and stimulation for their elderly sisters. Help is also provided by siblings (Troll, 1980). Sibling rivalry does not seem to continue into older age (Allan, 1979).

Finally, friendships serve two basic functions for the elderly: psychosocial well-being (Roberto & Scott, 1986) and informal support (Litwak, 1985; Adams, 1985/1986). This informal support differs from that provided by families, in that there is no feeling of obligation present. Several explanations have been offered for the strong relationship between elderly friendship and psychosocial well-being: 1) homophily (Matthews, 1986); 2) mutual choice (Blau, 1981; Roberto & Scott, 1986); 3) maintaining social activity (Nussbaum, 1983a); and 4) self-disclosure (Nussbaum, 1983a). This research has been nicely summarized by Adams (1986).

## Relationship Styles

Several of the possible intimate relationships in which elderly individuals participate have been categorized by researchers according to various relationship styles or types. Focusing on marital dyads, Cuber and Haroff (1965) found four types: 1) Devitalized, characterized by unexcited dependency; 2) Conflict-habituated, those very used to fighting and very good at it; 3) Passive-congenial, a relationship of convenience, but one in which the couple gets along well enough; and 4) Vital, characterized by a great deal of sharing, intimacy, and interdependence.

Later, Atchley and Miller (1983) categorized couples based on the similarity of their family orientations, particularly the value of close family ties and intimacy. The most common couple type they found was "Divergent," in which the two couples did not totally agree on the values. This was followed by "Integrated," where both values were important, "Family-centered," and then "Self-centered," where neither was valued and "Couple-centered," where intimacy was paramount. Atchley and Miller's findings present a more positive view of older couples than did Cuber and Haroff.

Grandparenting styles have been described by four sets of researchers. Neugarten and Weinstein (1964) listed formal, fun-seeker, surrogate parent, reservoir of family wisdom, and distant figure as possible approaches to grandparenting. Wood and Robertson (1976) conceptualized grandparenting by focusing on two sets of needs—personal and social. "Apportioned" grandparents are high on both needs. "Individualized" were high in personal needs and low in social needs. "Symbolic" grandparents were low in both needs, while "Remote" grandparents rarely interact with their grandchildren. Kivinck (1981) listed five styles—centrality, valued elder, immortality, reinvolvement, and indulgence—but assumed that each grandparent manifests some of the behaviors within each style. Most recently, Cherlin and Furstenberg (1986) discussed three grandparenting styles: remote, compassionate, and involved.

In an attempt to describe friendship styles among the elderly, Matthews (1986) interviewed over sixty older individuals. The first friendship style that emerged was labeled "The Independents," who alluded to *circumstances* when friendship was important. These people had only a few close, and very loyal, friends. The second group was labeled as the "Discerning" style. These individuals were not affected by circumstances in regard to friendship, but were very vulnerable to their friends being unavailable. They also found it hard to make new friends in old age. The third group of people has been "Discerning," but had, over the years, become more "Independent." The last group, "Acquisitive," had kept friendships from the past and remained open to new ones.

Similarly, Lopata (1977) found three types of friendship styles among widows: 1) those who keep their old friends and develop new friendships; 2) those who keep their old friends and don't develop new ones; and 3) those who never had any friends and don't develop any after widowhood. Widowhood is hardest on the third group, who rely primarily on the family for support.


## Confirmatory Communication


Several concepts have been investigated in the communication and aging literature which relate roughly to the notion of confirmation. We are using confirmation in a rather loose sense to refer to any behavior that communicates acceptance or validation of one's sense of self. The research to be discussed in this section includes issues such as expressiveness, helping, and affect. We will also provide a brief discussion of *dis*confirmation involving the elderly.

Expressiveness—a willingness to share feelings—is a major function of the family (Lasch, 1977). In "traditional" relationships, expressiveness has been seen as being consistent with the woman's role, while men have been expected to be more instrumental, or task oriented. Research on the elderly provides some indication of increasing convergence on expressiveness/instrumentality with age. Several studies have concluded that wives become more assertive and instrumental and husbands more affiliative and expressive in the later years of marriage (Chiriboga & Thurner, 1975; Grunebam, 1979; Levinson, 1978). Other researchers, however, indicate that both husbands and wives become more expressive as they grow older (Lipman, 1961, 1962; Lowenthal & Robinson, 1976). In either case, we are seeing more similarity emerge within couples over the years. This increasing similarity can help mitigate other sources of strain in older marriages.

The notion of help, or mutual aid, has been referred to in some of the research reviewed in earlier sections. This, too, can be a confirming behavior. While we have discussed help from family and friends, neighbors also provide help in some circumstances (Goodman, 1984).

The sharing of positive affect provides confirmation for most of us (Cohler, 1983; Henderson, 1980; Mueller, 1980). This comes from many relationships, but researchers have found it to be particularly important in the elderly parent/adult child relationship (Singh & Williams, 1982; Beckman & Houser, 1982) and among aged siblings (Cicirelli, 1977).

The notion of disconfirmation stems primarily from the work of philosophers such as Martin Buber (1957) and R.D. Laing (1961). Disconfirming statements communicate a lack of acceptance or validation of another person. The ultimate disconfirmation would be completely ignoring someone, which happens to elderly people who are avoided by others (Levin & Levin, 1981). More subtle forms of disconfirmation include imperviousness ("I know you better than you do") and tangential communication in which my reply to you does not really address your message. Disconfirmation weakens one's self concept. Indeed, Tamir (1979) concludes that, "The older adult finds his identity difficult to maintain, for the image that he holds of himself is not the image that others perceive" (p. 143) — disconfirmation through imperviousness. Talking to an older adult as if he or she were a child (Ferguson, 1977) is also disconfirming.

Disconfirmation, of course, is not just a problem from younger people to older people. In some cases, the behavior of the elderly can be disconfirming to others. Forgetting is an example of this. We do know that elderly memory is not as consistent as is memory in younger people (Belsky, 1984; Walsh, 1975).

## Control and Power

One of the key factors influencing how communication creates relationships is interactional control. This notion refers to control of conversation and interaction, not control of the person, per se. Control is exercised in all interactions, including control over the definition of the relationship and over the direction the conversation will take.

The notion of interactional control is relevant to the elderly, in that they are frequently allowed little such control (Tamir, 1979). Decreasing power or control is a major issue for the elderly (Rosow, 1974; Sussman, 1976). The prerogative for initiating interaction typically is controlled by the younger person in the interaction. Hampe and Bievins (1975) found that frequent visits from children are not comforting if the parent feels that he or she has no control over the initiation of the visit. Several other studies concluded that older people find it difficult to change interaction patterns when they want to initiate new relationships or renegotiate older ones (Britton & Britton, 1972; Chown, 1977; Fitzgerald, 1978).

Several other indications of one-down or noncontrolling behavior are also seen in the elderly. The cautiousness in communication cited earlier would be one such example; another is seen in the fact that the elderly may be more easily persuaded than are others (Bennett & Eckman, 1973). Agreement is a one-down behavior. Bengston & Cutler (1976) found that elderly people often become deferring for fear that the other person will stop initiating contact.

Power differences have also been uncovered *within* elderly relationships. While Smith (1965) argued that men have more power in older marriages (because of the scarcity of older men!), Treas (1975) concluded that women acquire more power with increasing age. Several other studies have indicated that higher marital adjustment and happiness is found in marriages with equality in the power structure (Atchley, 1980; Brubaker, 1985; Smith, 1965).

## Relationship Termination

Although relationships can end in many ways, research on the elderly has examined only two kinds of relationship termination—divorce and death. That emphasis is perhaps understandable, because those kinds of relationship termination may be the most traumatic. We will first discuss the research to be found on divorce among the elderly.

Although only 1% of divorces in 1975 went to those over 65 (Gilford, 1986), every year nearly 10,000 Americans over 65 divorce (Troll, 1982). An unfortunately small amount of research has been conducted on divorce in older marriages. From the research that has been done we can draw a few conclusions:

1. Older divorced people are less happy than younger divorced people (Troll, 1982);
2. Divorce is a particular problem for displaced homemakers (Troll, 1982) who suffer economically and in terms of self-esteem (Huyck & Hoyer, 1982);
3. The younger people are when they first marry, the more likely they are to divorce (Troll, 1982);
4. Divorced women are much worse off than divorced men (Troll, 1982);
5. Divorced individuals are frequently worse off than are widowed individuals (Hennon, 1983).

This last finding may be due to the fact that, for the elderly, widowhood is a well-defined role with established norms. Divorcees, however, feel more alienated and restricted socially, and receive less social support (Hennon, 1983). Among some elderly, divorce is still somewhat stigmatizing.

Divorce, of course, does not *necessarily* produce an end to a relationship. The divorced people may still continue to see each other. Relationship termination by death is more definitive, although the relationship may still continue in the mind of the living participant.

Much of the research on relationship termination through death has examined either the communication of dying people or communication to dying people. Our fear of death (Kalish, 1976) may cause us to avoid those who are known to be dying. Even if that does not happen, the dying person is placed in a bind of sorts (Erickson & Hyerstay, 1974) because family and friends emit incongruent verbal and nonverbal messages to the dying person. One set of cues says, "You're dying," while the other set, typically the verbal, communicates, "Everything's just dandy." The dying person is then placed in the position of appearing paranoid or defensive if he or she doesn't believe the verbal cues.

Most dying people prefer to discuss their approaching demise (Simmons & Given, 1980). Indeed Kalish (1976) concluded that it is difficult for patients to maintain relationships with significant others unless the topic of death can be discussed. One study, however, found that only 35% of married couples had openly shared their awareness that the spouse could be dying. Freer communication about dying occurred if the spouse considered the relationship "Average" or "Poor" rather than "Very good." (Hinton, 1981). Dying individuals also talk about their families quite frequently (Kastenbaum & Aisenberg, 1972). The interested reader is referred to a particularly fascinating article on relational conclusion with intimates vs. nonintimates for further information (Fieweger & Smilowitz, 1984).

A great deal of research, much too voluminous to review here, has examined the effects of widowhood on both men and women and on their relationships with others. Of particular note is the work of Helen Lopata (1973; 1977; 1981).

## Aloneness

Following our discussion of relationship termination it seems appropriate to mention briefly some of the research that has been conducted on the *absence* of relationships among the elderly. Some elderly individuals, for instance, have never been married. Gubrium (1976) points out that isolation (the absence of social contacts) is not the same as desolation, with its negativity and loneliness. While older single people are isolated, most are not lonely. Indeed, never-married older people *resent* the commonly held assumption that they are lonely. They also tend to be more independent than do other people (Gubrium, 1976).

While never-married people may miss some of the benefits of marital and familial relationships, they also miss some of the disadvantages. They are much less likely to go through the pain and suffering of grief and bereavement (Atchley, 1980; Gubrium, 1976; Troll, 1982). Troll also points out that never-married women are usually better off than are never-married men.

Some single people are, of course, lonely. Suggestions for alleviating loneliness in older people who have few intimate relationships have been provided and tested by Andersson (1984).

## Relationships and Successful Aging

As we grow older, each of us will attempt to cope and adapt to the inevitable changes which occur as we age. Social gerontologists for the past several decades have put forth several theories of successful aging to guide our thinking as to just what behaviors or lifestyles lead to satisfaction with the aging process. Although the various theories of successful aging can at times be quite disparate, for instance activity theory versus disengagement theory, each theory of successful aging has at its core the importance of relationships throughout the entire life span.

The great majority of research which has attempted to predict successful aging stresses the importance of maintaining close, intimate relationships in old age. From the early research of Lowenthal and Haven (1968) to the more recent research of Nussbaum (1983a; b), close relationships have been a significant factor in predicting elderly satisfaction with life. Since human beings are inherently social, relationships will continue to develop and change as long as individuals live. The successful maintenance of close relationships may be a key to successful adaptation to the aging process.

## Conclusions

This chapter has presented a brief overview of existing knowledge on the topic of intimate relationships and the elderly. Ten themes were discussed to bind the massive amount of information concerning intimate relationships which has recently found its way into the gerontological literature. As a way to conclude this chapter, we would like to suggest several areas where communication scholars can conduct much needed research.

An initial area of future research can incorporate how relationships which have lasted for 70 or 80 years are able to be maintained. What can we learn from relationships which have sustained themselves throughout the life span? What relational strategies were utlilized to keep the relationship functioning? How did the relationship change throughout the life span?

A second area of future research involves the initiating of new relationships in the elderly population. How do friendships develop in old age? Are the processes of relational development similar for teenagers and those in their seventies? Can close friendships be replaced when a friend dies? How do intergenerational relationships work?

A third area of future research can uncover the various communicative functions of differing relationships. How do differing relationships such as marriage, parental relationships, sibling relationships, grandparent-grandchild relationships, etc., function to aid successful adaptation to aging. How does divorce affect the grandparent-grandchild relationship? Does relational definition in older marriages continue in the same way it did in the earlier years?

Obviously, the potential research questions in the general area of intimate relationships and the elderly are far too numerous to be listed one by one. We hope that your reading this chapter has ignited a flame of interest so that you can ask exciting questions and seek to discover the answers to produce more knowledge about the nature and functions of intimate relationships within the elderly population.

## ❧ 9 ❧

# Nonverbal Aspects of Communication and Aging

## Carl W. Carmichael and Mark L. Knapp

As noted in other chapters in this volume, the aging process often brings with it dramatic changes in physical features, patterns of body movement and adaptations to new environments. These processes—commonly called nonverbal behavior—accompany corresponding age-related changes in verbal behavior and will be the focus of this chapter.

Generally, nonverbal communication embraces a wide variety of "non-word" signals which may repeat, substitute for, contradict, or reinforce verbalizations. This close relationship with verbal behavior makes it difficult to formulate a general definition of nonverbal communication which would apply to the diversity of signals included and also clearly distinguish it from verbal behavior. There are too many points of overlap (Knapp, 1978a). We can, however, specify the various "non-word" signals which will be discussed in this chapter:

- The physical features of the communicators

- The patterns of behavior (vocal and body movement) which are associated with pathologies common to this age group

- The environment within which older citizens communicate

- The patterns of behavior (vocal and body movement) which combine in order for interactants to accomplish important goals (intimacy, understanding, control, and identity)  // /

Although the literature on nonverbal communication has been steadily accumulating during the last twenty years (Burgoon, 1980; 1985; Harper, Wiens, & Matarazzo, 1978; Heslin & Patterson, 1982; Knapp, 1978a), there have been very few studies specifically focused on the older population. The "developmental" studies in this area are, for the most part, studies of infants and children (Aiello, Nicosia, & Thompson, 1979; Allen, 1981; Feldman, 1982; Mayo & LaFrance, 1978; Oster & Ekman, 1978; Ragsdale & Dauterive, 1986; Scheman & Lockard, 1979). Therefore, what follows will be an attempt to summarize the work on the aged per se and to extrapolate hypotheses for future research from studies using younger subjects for research. It should also be noted that we can only assume that some behaviors occur more or less frequently with increasing age; we cannot state with certainty that any given behavior is solely the province of a particular age group. With the preceding in mind, let us explore the manifestation and role of nonverbal signals among the elderly.

## Physical Features

Hundreds of studies have been conducted on the perceptions of physical attractiveness and its role in human interaction. The results of these studies have been summarized in other sources (Hatfield & Sprecher, 1986; Berscheid & Walster, 1974), but one finding repeatedly occurs: *initially, people tend to characterize physically attractive people as more popular, successful, qualified for employment, persuasive, and possessing more positive personality characteristics than people judged to be physically unattractive.* This conclusion has been confirmed with children and adolescents as well as young and middle-aged adults. What about the elderly? There is very little research available, but preliminary indications suggest similar findings.

Facial photographs of men and women between the ages of 60 and 93 which had been rated for attractiveness were used as the stimuli for judgments by two groups of raters—one aged 18–36 and one 60–84 (Johnson, 1985; Johnson & Pittenger, 1984). The photographs of the elderly subjects who were rated attractive were judged to possess more desirable personality characteristics, assumed to have had more positive life experiences, and to have attained more occupational status than their less attractive counterparts. A study conducted by Adams and Huston (1975) obtained very similar results using photographs of men and women between the ages of 48 and 52 as the stimulus photos. Thus "being old" like "being young" means people may perceive you as either attractive, unattractive or somewhere in-between. If you are perceived as attractive, you will be presumed to have a host of positive characteristics too.

All of the studies cited in the preceding paragraph used both older and younger judges to rate the photographs, and each found substantial agreement between the generations on who was and who wasn't an attractive older person. Thus, the age of the persons doing the judging and the age of the persons being judged does not seem to alter significantly the physical attractiveness stereotype for this culture. The often cited negativity associated with older persons portrayed on television programs and in commercial advertisements (Greenberg, Korzenny & Atkin, 1979), does not seem to prevent people of all ages from distinguishing attractiveness and unattractiveness among the elderly. Nevertheless, the United States is still a culture which reveres youth and attractiveness. Thus, perceptions of unattractiveness among the young would not be nearly as socially and personally damaging as perceptions of unattractiveness among the elderly (Adams, 1985).

What specific features of the elderly are considered attractive and unattractive and why? Johnson (1985) used the photographs of 28 white males and 28 white females who were judged by 45 white elderly males and 45 white elderly females. Judges were asked to identify physical features such as eyes, nose, hair, and mouth which they perceived as attractive or unattractive and to state why they perceived them as such. The adjectives used to describe attractive and unattractive features of the elderly were then clustered and the results are shown in Table 1. These descriptors give some insight into the criteria being used by the elderly in judging their peers on attractiveness.

**Table 1**

**Perceptions of Attractiveness in the Elderly
By the Elderly**

| Adjectives Describing Most Attractive Features | Adjectives Describing Least Attractive Features |
|---|---|
| Firm - for males, big, strong, rugged for females, firm, full, steady | Gross - flabby, large, thick, wide |
| Fresh & Youthful - bright, clear, sparkling | Deformed - humped, crooked, protruding, elongated |
| Gestalt - well shaped, natural, full-formed | Old - unsteady, wrinkled, cloudy, gray, loss of |
| Pleasant - nice, good, kind, sweet | Worn - weak, saggy, jagged, floppy |

Even though both young and old are able to identify different levels of attractiveness among the elderly, some evidence suggests a general decline in attractiveness over the lifespan. Deutsch, Clark & Zalenski (1983) used photographs of elderly men and women in swimming suits which were taken at three different age periods (19-24; 40-50; and over 60) and had them evaluated by both young and elderly men and women. Ratings of attractiveness declined over the three age periods. A similar study suggests facial attractiveness has more stability over the years than body attractiveness (Adams, 1977).

While physical attractiveness is perceived to decline as one moves into the upper age groups, this does not mean that physical attractiveness is any less important to the elderly. Interviews with people aged 18 to 90 about the importance of physical attractiveness found older respondents rating physical attractiveness as more important than younger ones in marriage selection, friendship formation, marital happiness, and general success (Jones & Adams, 1982). Older citizens, like younger ones, are also concerned about their body image. Perceptions of one's body image is closely linked to one's happiness at every age that has been tested (Berscheid, Walster, and Bohrnstedt, 1973).

Is there a double standard in judgments of physical attractiveness as people age? More specifically, are aging women measured against the standards of youth while aging men are measured against the standards of their age group? Sontag (1972) argues that women are taught from childhood to care in a "pathologically exaggerated way" for their appearance. Masculinity, on the other hand, often carries with it a rule that caring about one's appearance is less important than other things. Men, then, the argument goes, are valued for the things that come with age— money, status, experience; women are devalued because their resource—appearance—declines with age. One of the goals of the cosmetics industry is to help a woman maintain a youthful appearance:

> The purpose of makeup is not to make a woman look *younger*, but to look better, more attractive, healthier, and to show that she cares. Usually she will also look younger. If she looks like "today" instead of like "yesterday," she will look younger. (Roberts, G., 1985, p. 251)

Two studies have examined the issue of differential ratings for men and women as they age. Adams and Huston (1975) examined middle-aged people and used both elderly and youthful respondents to rate them. Unattractive females seemed to suffer the most. Physically unattractive middle-aged females were rated lower than both the unattractive male group and as the attractive male and female groups on achieved vocational status and in self-esteem perceptions. They were perceived as more honest, however. Deutsch, Clark & Zalenski (1983) compared the attractiveness ratings of people's pictures from three different times in their life—youth, middle-age, and elderly. The ratings for both men and women declined with age, but the ratings for women were sharply lower than those for men in the elderly group. More evidence is needed, but there are indications that physical attractiveness does have different implications for women than for men during the aging process.

Thus far, we have been talking about the "normal" population of older persons and the role of physical attractiveness. We also know, however, that as one grows older, the chances of acquiring a handicap or being confined to a hospital bed increase. There is a sizeable body of literature which has examined the role of disfigurements, amputations, and other handicaps as they affect social relations (Bull, 1985; Kleck & Strenta, 1985). These features of one's appearance do affect the expectations of both interactants. Sometimes the handicapped person is so expectant of a certain reaction that he or she behaves in a way that elicits such behavior. The British Red Cross has had, for over 25 years, a Beauty and Camouflage Service which helps hospitalized patients improve their appearance through makeup and clothing. It is based on the premise that looking good will make a person feel better (R. Roberts, 1985).

In sum, the work done on physical attractiveness and the aged has been minimal but there are indications that: 1) young and old alike can and do evaluate the elderly on the basis of physical attractiveness; 2) like all other age groups, judgments of physical attractiveness among the elderly are accompanied by a host of other positive evaluations; 3) adjectives describing attractive elderly people include firm, strong, fresh, youthful, natural, pleasant; 4) adjectives describing unattractive elderly people include gross, deformed, old, worn; 5) while facial attractiveness has some stability over the lifespan, one's general attractiveness declines; 6) the elderly believe physical attractiveness is an important factor in successful living; and 7) there seems to be a double standard for aging men and aging women with women being judged more harshly and by the same criteria usually applied to younger people.

Despite these findings, there is much work to be done. Most of this work was done within the person perception paradigm; not an interaction paradigm. The person perception paradigm is primarily limited to facial attractiveness, to photographs as the object of judgment, and to a single observation of each person. Hence, the effects of verbal behavior, movement, repeated observations, and behavior by one's interaction partner remain unexplored (Knapp, 1985).

## Nonverbal Aspects of Age-Related Pathologies

Until now, we have explored the nonverbal aspects of a *normally* aging older person's existence. Unfortunately, many older people experience special problems during their later years; pathological problems can have a profound effects on their abilities to communicate with those around them. One of the most common pathologies is a stroke where the body is partially paralyzed and the speech production centers are damaged. Typically, the greatest problem is the inability to speak. Stroke victims are unable to let their loved ones know their feelings and needs. Obviously, in such cases, the person will have to rely primarily on nonverbal means of communicating and perhaps will have to develop new techniques of nonverbal communication since the whole body may not be available for bodily expression as a result of the paralysis.

Virtually no research has been done on the special nonverbal communication needs, patterns, etc. of the stroke victim. Yet, several conclusions about nonverbal communication with persons experiencing a stroke are obvious and should lead to specific research in this area.

1. Reliance on nonverbal means of communicating should increase significantly.

2. Nonverbal patterns of communication may have to change drastically from the lifelong normal patterns. Body expression may be reduced dramatically as a result of paralysis. There should be more reliance on facial expression, use of the eyes, and use of the unaffected portions of the body.

3. New systems of nonverbal communication may have to be developed for more efficient communication with the stroke victim. Some of the simplest, ordinary, everyday messages may require new ways to be communicated. The expression of basic needs could be excruciatingly difficult following a stroke but could be facilitated with simple one-handed gestures and facial expressions.

Caregivers to older people, whether family members or professionals, need to be aware of these changes and find compensatory ways to enable easier communication.

Another serious pathological problem experienced by the elderly population, especially those in the very elderly years, is senile dementia. Obviously, the typical cognitive impairments that lead to the diagnosis of senile dementia could be defined as communication impairments as well. Most relevant to this chapter is that research on the social interaction problems of senile dementia patients reveals that the most extreme cases are more restricted in verbal than in nonverbal interchange (Luke, 1973). Significantly, this research indicates that such cases are extremely isolated socially; there is a high correlation between social isolation of senile dementia patients and disproportionate restriction of verbal over nonverbal communication abilities.

The implications should be obvious. Communicating with older people who are suffering from senile dementia may require significantly more use of nonverbal means. Certainly, in extreme cases, social isolation is not likely to be reduced if meaningful nonverbal social contact is not made. Since research does not yet reveal specific patterns of nonverbal communication with senile dementia patients, and since individual variation can be expected anyway, caregivers and family members need to explore various nonverbal signals with the patient to discover what patterns are meaningful. Observations of nonverbal behavior should be made of the use of facial expressions (upper and lower), bodily movements (trunk, extremities—looking for stereotypic movements such as rocking) or self-directed actions (e.g., touching own face, clothing, hair), as well as for attempts to make contact with others. Such information would be valuable in maintaining meaningful contact with the senile dementia patient even after the verbal facilities are severely restricted.

One particular form of senile dementia, known as Alzheimer's Type Dementia, has received a great deal of attention recently with television specials, talk shows on radio and television, and increased coverage in general in all the media. Alzheimer's Disease is diagnosed with clinical signs of memory loss, spatial and environmental confusion, time and place disorientation, and inattention to personal hygiene. Advanced stages may include types of aphasia, agnosia, apraxia, and perceptual distortions (Burnside, 1979). One of the few studies focusing on nonverbal communication with Alzheimer's patients was conducted by a nurse with the purpose of improving communication with these almost incommunicative patients (Bartol, 1979). Bartol did an intensive qualitative study of 10 males in an Alzheimer's ward. This study is significant for two reasons.

First, she documents the importance of nonverbal behaviors in understanding older people suffering from Alzheimer's (ATD). She concludes from these systematic observations that communication is facilitated by the use of anatomical positioning of the body parts. In the face of language dysfunction, ATD patients use their head, face, eyes, torso, upper and lower extremities, hands, and feet to give valuable cues to what intellectual and emotional messages they are trying to communicate (Bartol, 1979). More specifically, she writes:

> ATD patients tend to avert their eyes, look down, back away, and increase hand gesturing when they do not understand. Frustration, hostility, aggression, and fear are often communicated through increased general motor activity (pacing), rattling door knobs, kicking doors, waving arms about, shaking fists, frowning, increasing voice volume, raising voice pitch and tone, eyes widening, pupils dilating, lips pursing, tightening of jaws, lips and facial muscles (Bartol, 1979).

A second contribution of this study is that Bartol provides specific suggestions for improving communication with ATD patients. While these suggestions are quite general, including verbal considerations and general behavioral guidelines, several prescriptions focus on nonverbal behaviors:

> Convince yourself that your nonverbal style can be felt all the way across the room and by several people, not just the patient or staff person you are addressing.
>
> Every verbal communication is delivered by proper nonverbal gestures.
>
> Stand in front (or directly in line of vision) of person.
>
> Maintain eye contact.
>
> Move slowly.
>
> If person starts or continues to walk while you are talking to him, do not try to stop him as your first move. Instead, keep moving along in front of him and persevere.
>
> Use overemphasis and exaggerated facial expression to emphasize your point, particularly if vision and/or hearing is impaired (Bartol, 1979).

Nonverbal communication research has also been conducted with older people suffering from Chronic Brain Syndrome (CBS). Preston found that nurses were assisted considerably by relying on the most basic nonverbal signals that are learned in early childhood—touching, gesturing, smiling (Preston, 1973). Such research is not surprising but is comforting in that it supports the general pattern of nonverbal findings among the various age-related pathologies. Very little research has been done with CBS patients with a focus on specific nonverbal dimensions. A notable exception, however, focused on the specific impairment of the ability to recognize facially expressed emotions (Kurocz, et al., 1979). The research team named this condition Prosopo-Affective Agnosia. Using CBS patients that were relatively intact in neurological functioning in underlying perceptual-verbal-motor processing and comparing them with a group of normal persons and with a second group of patients with a history of schizophrenia or other major affective disorders resulted in significant differences. The normal group made no errors (100%), the schizophrenic/affective disorder group did almost as well (95%), but the CBS group did very poorly in recognizing emotions from facial expressions (66%). The researchers conclude that "CBS patients may be impaired with respect to receiving and appreciating elementary aspects of social communications such as recognizing a smile, anger, sadness, or disapproval on the faces of people who surround them. This disability requires understanding and a special attitude on the part of the therapeutic team toward such patients" (Kurocz, et al., 1979).

These are some of the most significant age-related pathologies for which nonverbal communication may play an important role in improving communication with older people who suffer from such conditions. There are, of course, a variety of inflictions that could render an older person severely disabled and confined to a wheelchair or a bed. Such severe restrictions cannot help but pose serious communication problems for older victims. The paucity of research in this area represents a major neglect in the communication field. The few studies focusing on the special communication problems of the severely handicapped older person have been conducted primarily by gerontology professionals (as is the case with all of the sources cited above in this section). One such study developed and tested a communication system with geriatric patients who have severe physical disabilities. The system included three communication boards ranging from a simple basic communication system to an advanced board capable of sentence transmission (Hardiman, et al., 1979).

The implications relative to nonverbal communication for older people with any of these pathological problems are important. In some cases, language dysfunction necessitates increased importance of nonverbal behaviors; in others, pathological conditions have changed the nonverbal behaviors and therefore have changed the older person's lifelong communication patterns. Without knowledge of such changes, communication with older people suffering from any of these problems may be very difficult indeed.

## Environments and Aging

All human beings exist within a contextual framework of some sort; we cannot live in a vacuum. Without full awareness, we interact with our environment, are affected by it, and even become a part of it. Environmental factors have long been considered a major category of nonverbal elements in our lives.

Special attention to environmental aspects of aging is warranted for all the obvious reasons, but two stand out: 1) There are special environments created uniquely for older people, and 2) all environments, no matter how ordinary, potentially can present special problems for older people. Whatever the environment, from a nursing home to a private home, consideration should be given to the needs of older people and how those environments address those needs. Attention to the cultural, social, physiological, and psychological aspects of architectural design by gerontologists increased considerably in the decade of the 1970s. Some of the most significant works are Carson and Pastalan, *Spatial Behavior of Older People* (1970); Robert Sommer, *Personal Space* (1969) and *Design Awareness* (1972); M. Powell Lawton, *Planning and Managing Housing for the Elderly* (1975); Joseph A. Koncelik, *Designing the Open Nursing Home* (1976); and Betty Ann Raschko, *Interior Design for the Elderly* (1982).

Consideration of older people's needs in relation to their living environments produces numerous important issues.

Privacy. Environmental factors may affect the person's ability to choose to be totally private in their activities. A separate entrance, a private bathroom, and bedroom door locks are commonplace examples.

Personal Comfort.   Environmental factors can enhance or detract from a comfortable existence in daily living. Operating windows, for example, could give better control over temperature and light.

Accessibility.   Environmental factors can determine whether or not an older person is able to use all necessary and desirable spaces in the environment. Narrow doorways or showers that do not permit wheelchairs or steep stairs without handrails would affect access.

Safety.   The environment may present many hazards that can be seriously detrimental to older people's personal well-being. Attention to details such as properly placed electrical switches, non-slip floors, and shower handrails can dramatically improve the safety environment for the elderly.

Architectural barriers.   How an environment is designed may have profound effects on human activity. The effect may be psychological ("It just doesn't feel comfortable sitting in that room."), or physical ("I don't get to play games with the family because the rec room is down those steep stairs."). Human interaction may be affected both psychologically and physically by architectural design.

Utilization of space. Architectural design should reflect the spatial needs and patterns of the inhabitants. Older people's needs may change in the later years, and the environment should reflect that, but the more serious problem may be when the assumption is made that older people need less space so they are given a claustrophobic environment much smaller than they had enjoyed for many years. Moving from the four bedroom family home to an apartment is one thing while moving to a small room off the garage is quite another.

These and many other nonverbal factors in the environment can impact the general happiness and well-being of older people. Not all of these factors can be analyzed here, but they provide a framework for discussion of environmental aspects of aging. In this section we will consider special environments, the home environment, and special problems in ordinary public environments in relation to older people.

## Special Environments

A variety of types of environments have been created especially for older people. Examples of such environments are: 1) nursing homes offering full-time health care, 2) live-in facilities with part-time health care available, 3) retirement condominiums which may be newly built or remodeled apartment buildings, 4) retirement "villages" which are residential neighborhoods with ownership limited to people over a specified age (usually fifty-five), as well as numerous variations on these.

One of the most significant decisions to be made affecting an older person's life is whether or not to move into a nursing home. This is not the appropriate context in which to discuss this decision-making process, but we should stress that the decision is essentially based on the need for health care beyond the capabilities of the family. (see *Your Home, Your Choice,* 1985, for a practical guide for the family on this problem.) This means the nursing home is basically a health care environment and, as such, is somewhat limited as a "normal" living environment.

The nursing home, traditionally defined as a 24-hour, skilled, health care facility, usually has the look, smell, and feel of a hospital rather than a home. No wonder most nursing home residents (usually referred to as patients) assume that this is the end of the road. The focus is on death instead of life. The patient-resident feels like this is a place to die rather than a place to live (Koncelik, 1976). It probably goes without saying, but the difference between an environment focusing on living and one oriented toward dying is a communication phenomenon determined primarily by nonverbal, environmental factors. If the rooms look like wards, the beds look like hospital beds, and the workers wear white uniforms, the place is not going to look like anybody's home.

The concept of the "open" nursing home, developed by Koncelik, stresses rehabilitation and the positive aspects of living. There should be a sense of residency in a comfortable surrounding that gives the individual as much control as possible. Koncelik's book is literally filled with specific recommendations in every category imaginable that would improve the lives of nursing home residents. He includes suggestions on basic design (e.g., having restrooms accessible to the lounge areas), on furnishings (e.g., chairs with appropriate back support and height), on improving communication (e.g., round tables in the dining room instead of long rectangular ones that restrict interaction), on use of accessible outside areas (e.g., walkways, decks, atriums with seating), and on increasing personal control over residents own lives (e.g., with the bed as control center, having reachable controls for light, sound and music, television, communications, temperature and air control, natural light screening, nurse call, and other signaling devices) (Koncelik, 1976).

A sensible housing compromise for many older people who find they cannot keep up with the maintenance requirements of the family home (which may also have become too large and inconvenient) and who do not require daily health care is to rent or to purchase a studio or one-bedroom apartment in an apartment building specifically designed for the needs of older residents (Haynie, 1983). These living environments, of course, would not contain symbols of institutionalization, although limited health care could be available within the building or a medical facility may be in the neighborhood. Most of the positive aspects of the open nursing home design would apply as well to the retirement apartment complex. Recreational areas, lounge areas, access to all spaces, safety in the design of details such as electrical devices, convenience in the use of door levers instead of knobs, are just as relevant in the apartment environment. Every floor should be a center of activity and should contain a small lounge where residents can meet visitors or neighbors.

The concept of "retirement living" would also include residential neighborhoods, sometimes referred to as retirement villages. A single family dwelling, smaller than the family home and perhaps more conveniently located, may be the most desirable living situation for some older people. Like the retirement apartment, it allows for much more independence than an institutional situation, probably as much as the previous family home living situation allowed. Of course, most of the design characteristics already discussed relating to safety, accessibility, and convenience, apply here as well, but site location becomes more important. Since most necessary services are not contained within the building structure, location of the residence to provide proximity to services and opportunities for community/social involvement would be essential (Green, et al., 1975).

## The Home Environment

At any one time, most people over the age of sixty or sixty-five are living in a private home. In most cases, a dwelling that was not designed for any special occupants by age or impairment. Many people feel very strongly that to do otherwise would be to buy into stereotypes or to further segregate older people from the mainstream of society. Within this category, there are several alternatives: 1) Staying in the family home, which may contain memories of many happy years of children growing up and a long-term marriage; 2) Living with older friends in a house sharing situation, perhaps a growing trend in the eighties (McConnell, 1979); 3) Moving in with family, usually middle-aged children with a family of their own. This may also be a recent trend, but certainly not a new one since the "extended family" may be the oldest known method of elder care; 4) Moving into a pre-fab "granny flat" constructed on the children's property. It may or may not be attached to the main house (Lipman, 1984).

In all of these home living situations, similar issues arise. As the older person becomes more frail, how should the environment be changed to adapt to the changing needs of that person? How is the environment affecting the older person's life, what changes would be important for their well-being? Actually, the same issues apply as discussed in the previous section, but present serious problems because adaptations are required— perhaps even complete remodeling. These structures were not designed and built for special problems of any kind.

Older people have a number of alternatives available for personal living situations. They vary in the degree of independence allowed and the amount of health care offered. Whether the most appropriate housing choice is to continue living in the family home, to move into another home with family or friends, to buy a better located house, to rent a retirement apartment, or to go to a nursing home, the individual's personal living will be affected in many ways by the subtle, nonverbal aspects of their environment. A major concern should be to meet the personal and social needs of older people within their living environments. As a concluding comment, from our perspective, one important need that is often neglected is the need to maintain normal healthy relationships and communication with others. In designing any living space for older people, the mobility requirements, etc., of potential visitors need to be considered also. The older person in question may not be severely impaired at the time of remodeling or housing selection; however, not only could that change in the near future, but older friends who may be impaired should be able to visit in order to facilitate the maintenance of friendships.

### Public Environments

Any environment can present problems for older people, even if they are not seriously impaired in any way. A good exercise for a class or seminar is to have the students select a public environment that may be frequented by older people and analyze the salient features, the special problems, and the communication barriers of that environment. Consider, for example, the following;

Restaurants
Theaters
Public Transportation Terminals
Transportation Carriers (Bus, plane, car, train, subway)
Beach Facilities
Doctor's Offices
Grocery Stores
Department Stores
Shopping Centers/Malls
Social Service Agencies
Churches

Similar questions can be asked with most of these. Is the print on the menu or the pricing label large enough to be read by older people with some visual impairment? Are the restrooms accessible? Can the sign marking the restrooms be seen clearly? Is there visual interference from inadequate lighting? Is there auditory interference from background "noise" that prohibits normal conversation? (Remember that loud music may be pleasurable to some people and "noise" to others.) Is the ventilation adequate? Is the seating comfortable? Are all products in the stores accessible? Do these environments help an older person to feel as though they are more impaired than they may actually be? Or, do they help them to feel somewhat normal and an integral part of their culture?

## Aging and Nonverbal Communication Goals

In everyday life, the individual nonverbal signals discussed earlier combine as we seek various communicative outcomes. Four common goals or outcomes include: self-presentation, relationship to others, influencing others, and achieving accuracy and understanding.

*Self-Presentation.* We use a variety of nonverbal signals to communicate to others who we are—our identity. Our sex, age, personality, socioeconomic status, occupation, geographical background, group membership, and social attitudes can all be communicated through nonverbal signals. Sometimes these signals accurately reflect a person's identity, but sometimes we manipulate these signals in order to communicate a special part of our identity or to communicate who we are at a particular moment in time.

We can communicate "being old" at any time of life by the way we move, talk, and dress. We are able to speculate on what these signals might be, but in the absence of systematic research we have much to learn.

There are studies, however, which show that age, along with sex and socioeconomic status, are often accurately judged from photographic or vocal samples (Nerbonne, 1967; Davis, 1949). The characteristics associated with attractive and unattractive photographs of elderly persons were reported earlier in the section on physical features. Two studies have examined the characteristics of the voice of older citizens. There seems to be a general lowering of pitch level among males from infancy through middle-age. Then a reversal occurs and pitch level rises slightly with advancing age. Mysak (1959) found his 80–92-year-old study group had higher fundamental pitch levels than males 65–79. McClone and Hollien (1963), in a similar study, found no differences among females in these two age groups. The speaking pitch level for women probably varies little—certainly less than men—across the life span. In any case, voices do change in pitch flexibility, rate, loudness, vocal quality, articulatory control as well as other characteristics and this is what we are hearing in the voices we label "old." The second author plays tape recordings made by speakers of all ages for his students and asks them to judge the ages within five years. The greatest variance is always with speakers in the 60–90 age range. If students do not perceive a vocal stereotype for "old," judging accuracy declines sharply. Judging accuracy for any of these studies is, of course, partly dependent on how precise the judgment task is.

Up to this point we have been discussing what Helfrich (1979) calls "sender age markers." These are characteristics with which a speaker's voice is endowed. There are also "receiver age markers." These are vocal variations made by the speaker when he or she is talking to particular listeners—e.g., an adult speaking in a higher pitch when talking to young children. In all of our assessments of the behavior of the elderly we should remember this distinction. There may be some behaviors which occur as a result of the person's physical abilities, but there are other behaviors which can occur with particular listeners. From this perspective we view the elderly as capable of a great deal more change potential than some people commonly attribute to them.

Personality characteristics are the most difficult to judge, although on some occasions judgments are quite accurate. Some characteristics are easier to judge than others. A person's neatness, conformity, practicality, and need for attention may be judged from the way a person dresses and behaves while other characteristics may be much more difficult to assess. Accurate or not, people do tend to judge personality characteristics according to body shape (Wells & Siegel, 1961; Cortes & Gatti, 1965). Very thin people are perceived to be withdrawn, tense, suspicious, and sensitive; fat people are perceived to be sympathetic, dependent, sociable, and sluggish; muscular types are often believed to be assertive, active, adventurous, and determined. No one has used a sample of elderly body types for these studies, but it is likely that stereotyped responses exist for these as well. Vocal cues, in studies with younger subjects, have been found to provide an accurate reading of personality characteristics like energetic/ lazy, but far less accurate readings for characteristics like independence/ dependence (Scherer, 1979).

*Relationship to Others.* Nonverbal scholars have looked closely at how people communicate their relationship to others through nonverbal signals (Mehrabian, 1969). None of these studies have focused on the elderly, however. It is likely that the findings from this body of research will need to be modified as the behavior of the elderly is closely examined. For example, there may be instances in which some forms of touching among young and middle-aged adults carries romantic and/or sexual meanings—meanings which do not accrue when performed by the very young or the very old. This does not mean that romantic and/or sexual meanings are not a part of the social life of the elderly. It does suggest that the type of signals and the performance of these signals may differ from other age groups. It is an empirical question. Do we continue to perform messages of liking, dominance, and involvement differently at different ages?

Certainly dominance, status and power are messages central to the relational life of the older citizen—as they are received and as they are given. In the United States a person has traditionally been accorded less power as he or she acquires the label, "elderly." Often there is less space and territory—a common status/power marker of earlier age periods. The methods for nonverbally asserting dominance may also change with age. The stereotypical behavior for seeking dominance such as speaking with a louder voice, assuming a position of height, using expansive gestures and engaging in a forceful gaze may not be actions used by the elderly to achieve dominance. But we don't know. Nor do we know how power or dominance is maintained once it is achieved. We do know that in studies with younger people, the methods used to maintain a relationship differ greatly from the methods used to build it or restore it when it is threatened.

*Influencing Others.* Getting others to do things for us is partly the result of the message content and partly the result of the context in which the message is delivered. Nonverbal signals also play an important role. Most of the speculation about persuasion and old age has to do with the older person as a receiver rather than a sender. Some argue that the elderly person is more rigid in his or her beliefs and is therefore harder to persuade. Others point out that older persons often feel very insecure in this society and are willing to go to great lengths to accede to the wishes of others because they have less inclination and strength to fight against them.

Several factors combine to make a person an effective persuader—likeability, perceptions of expertise, similarity to the persuadee, and the ability to believe in one's own argument. Nonverbal signals may play a role in each of these factors. We already posed the question of whether the liking/disliking nonverbal signals are the same for people of all ages—e.g., more forward leaning toward the other, more touching of the other, more openness of arms and legs, closer proximity to the other, more eye gaze toward the other, a more direct body orientation toward the other, more postural relaxation, and more positive facial and vocal expressions. Perceptions of expertise are often based on fluency of speech, rate of speech, authoritativeness of tone, a slightly relaxed posture, gazing at the other frequently, and variations in intonation, gestures and facial expressions. For both the liking and the expertise messages, one might speculate the largest differences between the elderly and other age groups might occur on "activity" dimensions. Since similarity of persuader and persuadee is also a key to influence, we might speculate difficulties in inter-generational communication. Experience tells us that grandparents and grandchildren often have a strong affinity and influence on one another.

Systematic research can tell us whether our observations are true and perhaps help to explain this form of influence. The belief in one's own argument often occurs with "self-priming" behavior. Talking to oneself is part of it, but gesturing and speaking aloud with varying vocalizations is important as well. Feeling good about yourself often means feeling good about yourself as a persuader. To what extent the nonverbal behavior of elderly persons in priming themselves for an attempt at influence occurs in a similar fashion as with other age groups remains open for study.

Persuasion research in general has not focused strongly on long-term efforts to influence others. It has been primarily a science of one time encounters. One might speculate that older citizens may have more patience and may be more likely to seek a gradual campaign of influence. On the other hand, the elderly may believe they have less time for long-term campaigns and will become disappointed if the initial effort does not succeed.

*Accuracy and Understanding.* A key feature of being able to communicate accurately and to achieve understanding is the ability to coordinate properly both verbal and nonverbal channels toward one's intended goals. When verbal and nonverbal channels are out of sync or when they do not complement one another, greater risks of error occur. Similarly, as a receiver, accuracy and understanding are increased as one is able to process more signals. Certainly for those older citizens who have hearing and vision losses or who have other infirmities, we can expect a decrease in both sending and receiving accuracy. It would be of interest to know the methods used to cope with these deficits. For example, one 90-year-old woman we know looks intently at her interaction partners and nods at junctures in the speech flow. She smiles frequently in a knowing way. But if the interaction partner ends with a question, it is clear the woman did not comprehend what was being said. For those elderly people without severe sensory losses, we don't know how accurate they are as senders or receivers. We can speculate that coordination of verbal and nonverbal systems may be more difficult; that postural shifts used to indicate topic changes may not be used as frequently; that pauses may be used more frequently to segregate smaller information units; and that gestures may be used less frequently to demarcate clauses. On the other hand, conversations which are high on intrinsic motivation for the elderly may reflect very similar patterns to younger adults.

# Conclusion

The topic of nonverbal communication and aging is far broader than can be covered in one chapter. Studies of nonverbal behavior have produced compelling evidence about the strong but underrecognized impact of subtle nonverbal and paralinguistic behaviors on everyday interactions. Most of the previous research is directly applicable to the aging population even though it may not have been conducted with older subjects. Many questions arise that have not been discussed in this chapter and need to be dealt with in future research:

1. patterns of nonverbal behavior exhibited by health care providers
2. awareness of nonverbal cues while communicating with older people
3. effect of nonverbal behaviors on creating a "self-fulfilling prophecy" of aging
4. effects of the physical setting on sensory decline in old age
5. communication of power and control over older people through nonverbal behaviors.

These are but a few of the many issues that can be added to this discussion. Unquestionably, anyone who relates to older people could profit from increased knowledge of the numerous personal, social, and environmental dimensions of nonverbal behavior that relate to the aging process.

# ✤ 10 ✤

# Communication Across Generations

## Anthony B. Schroeder

## Introduction

As a result of increased longevity, the multigenerational family is no longer a rarity. It is not uncommon to find four and five generation families, which extends the possibility of the family as a resource for the elderly. As people age, they depend more on family relationships, often due to forced separation from the work force. The family is a suitable channel for integration and participation since it can provide emotional support and a link with the community. An extended network bridging elderly parents with their adult children provides economic and social functions, "...such as the mutual exchange of services, gifts, advice, and financial assistance between the generations in as many as 93% of families" (Johnson & Bursk, 1977).

Multigenerational or intergenerational exchanges function as primary relationships. These interactions provide intimate communication, a caring relationship with mutual concerns about welfare, accompanied by bonds (Sussman, 1983). Intimacy is the need to be close, to be part of, to be familiar with another person. The need for intimacy does not change with age. Most adult children and their elderly parents maintain a relationship based on an "affectional bond" (Cicirelli, 1983a). Among the elderly, maintaining and developing relationships often becomes increasingly difficult because of negative attitudes which devalue them and assign them to "roleless" roles. As a result, familial bonds become even more essential. This chapter will focus on various aspects of communication across generations.

## Generation

Each generation or contemporaneous grouping of individuals is considered to participate in common values and attitudes which are different from the next generation. Generation differences in themselves do not create problems; however, society often attributes communication problems between children and their parents to this factor. It is considered a "generation gap" if we, as adults, do not understand our aging and elderly parents. "Intergenerational" deals with communication between generations, while "multigenerational" refers to layers of intergenerational communication. Within families, representatives of four or five generations may be present. According to Weeks (1984), "A five generation family is rare, but a four generation family is now quite common."

As children mature, they request understanding from their peers, parents, and grandparents; as people age, the desire for understanding remains equally important. The understanding so often denied youth by their parents may be reversed between elderly parents and adult children.

## Age Segregation

Today's fast-paced lifestyle combined with the quest for success and material comforts can result in focusing attention inwardly on one's immediate environment. Daily activities and objectives often take precedence over communication with elderly parents. Relocation for business purposes may prohibit frequent face-to-face interactions with parents and grandparents. As years progress, the adult child may find the family has not talked about concerns significant to those involved. Conversations tend to focus on the mundane while philosophical issues are put out of mind; contact with family ideals and struggles are often forgotten.

Knapp (1978b) refers to this stage as "differentiating," referring to "...the paradox of being simultaneously separate and connected in family relationships." Separation from the parent is unavoidable in our modern society as young adults pursue an education and career. Often, the idea of an education and career in a field different than the parents' image for their child may result in conflict. The discord prompts the realization that differentiating ourselves is important for our own well-being. Cicirelli (1983a) argues that to deal with this necessary separation and attachment the adult child establishes symbolic closeness and contact with the parents through identification.

Differentiating may also have a destructive side, if the individual chooses to break contact or destroy links with family members. Knapp (1978b, p. 246) states, "As one grows older, maintenance of intergenerational communication bridges may increase in difficulty.... Older citizens have been treated as a separate and distinct group in this society for so long, it must be difficult for each of us to avoid mentally differentiating ourselves as we feel age accumulating."

The effect of differentiation (Bowen, 1978) may be a simple matter of not communicating, or it may signal the intentional avoidance of a discussion thus signaling the rejection of family values. All that may be necessary to avoid segregation of the elderly is to take an active interest in the concerns of the elderly parent. Bowen provides an illustration by relating a personal family encounter. He discovered homestead records for a branch of his father's family in a neighboring county. While traveling to see the property, he and his father discussed many topics not normally included in their daily conversation. The opportunity for extended dialogue during the long ride and the focused purpose of the trip created fertile ground for inter-generational communication.

## Myths Affecting Interaction

Attributions about elderly parents are generally the result of stereotyping. The loss of contact, especially on a daily basis, often results in making inaccurate assumptions about the elderly. Myths are perpetuated as a result of lack of information about the elderly. (see Chapter Seven.) Common myths regarding aging are that the majority of elderly are senile, the majority of old people are socially isolated and lonely, and the majority of old people are bored (Zarit, 1982). Myths affect our attributions and our communicative behavior. Tuckman and Lorge (1953) found widespread acceptance of stereotypes about old people. Beliefs that the elderly exhibit physical ugliness, sadness, sorrow, loneliness, poverty, boredom, and uselessness (Barrow and Smith, 1979) create damaging myths. Most of the research indicates an acceptance of stereotypes across all age groups. Kastenbaum and Durkee (1964), Hickey and Kalish (1968), and Weinberger and Millham (1975) corroborate negative attributes towards the elderly. However, Ivester and King (1977) found a positive attitude towards the elderly in the rural community (most previous research on elderly stereotypes has been done in large cities). Ivester and King attribute this to the rural community's tendency for extended families to remain intact, which increased contact among generations. Rozencranz and McNevin (1969) found that frequent contact with the elderly resulted in more favorable attitudes. However, Ivester and King note that the poor held less favorable attitudes than the more wealthy. Possibly the elderly represent financial burdens for this group.

Simos (1973) reported that "Some children were uncomfortable about visiting their parents, and complained 'there is nothing to do; we just sit there.' It was incomprehensible to them that they might be supporting their parents emotionally, merely by their presence and interest." Three-fourths of his subjects (adult child) reported familial problems resulting from parental aging. The adult child usually attributed long-standing intergenerational and interpersonal problems to the elderly parent's personality.

## Role Changes

Roles within the family change dramatically as a person ages. For women the process typically progresses from daughter, lover, wife, mother, to widow. These role shifts are "functional" in nature, defining self and the interaction others expect. A well-defined relationship reduces the amount or degree of uncertainty in the relationship (Berger and Bradac, 1982). Since each role involves defining the new relationship and the attendant interaction, identity shifts necessarily occur. Clausen (1972) asserts, "The departure of the last child is likely to be the most traumatic." The trauma results from increased uncertainty as to self worth, role, and the future. A departure is assimilated differently by each individual; for many, the alteration will be positive, for others, it will be difficult at best. For everyone, it involves the realization of aging. Males may not have such overt shifts in their roles; aging may merely mean different duties or responsibilities. Retirement or physical failures mark the dramatic and traumatic role change for the male and for some working women. The ability to maintain social contacts is extremely important in the process of redefining ourselves after retirement. Retirement increases the degree of uncertainty in the relationships with the family and the community. Many elderly differentiate themselves from the younger or middle-aged person to help in the process of uncertainty reduction.

According to Itzin (1983), there is, "...abundant evidence that physical and geographical segregation of the elderly has progressed rapidly...due to increased financial resources, and partly to the out-migration of younger people leaving concentrations of the elderly." Itzin (1983) refers to this exit of the young adult from an area as being responsible for the creation of "senior" communities, a characteristic which is becoming typical of much of rural America.

Separation is a natural and normal phase through which the family progresses. This is especially true in the United States where career decisions may result in the young adult moving hundreds of miles for purposes of an education, special training, and/or employment. Families in smaller rural communities may feel the effects of this separation more so than families in metropolitan communities, because many small communities do not plan for social services or future growth and expansion. As Simos (1973) points out, "The lack of recreational facilities and the inadequate public transportation system contributed to the isolation of many parents."

Age stratification implies that conflict is inevitable, as Foner (1974, 1979) suggests with the phrase "structured social inequality." Age is a determinate of social position; cohort and common experiences, acquisition of specific material goods, and shared ideals which reflect similar struggles unify a particular chronological group. Separation of ages is enhanced due to these segregated environments and the reduced amount of contact across age groups. Thus, the potential for age conflict increases (Ward, 1984). Williamson (1981) considers these age conflicts to be power oriented and attributable primarily to the hierarchical nature of the family. He asserts that power has driven members of the family away and that, before the adult child and the elderly parent can improve on their relationship, personal authority needs to be renegotiated or the adult child will use the same generational power dynamics once used by the elderly parent.

Society places heavy emphasis on differentiation of youth from the older population. Mass media focuses on the young with its messages of the "Pepsi generation," and "Yuppies," speaking in terms of the individual need to be part of what is happening socially. These messages are designed to disrupt the contentedness of self and community and to solve the problem with a quick solution: a soft drink, the latest fall fashion, a trip to Hawaii, or the new wonder drug "used for years in Europe." This message of differentiation is designed to sell products and to promote careers and lifestyles. The message classifies much of what the elderly know and did as out of date or "old-fashioned." If the elderly parent hears a derogatory or demeaning message about his or her occupation and former lifestyle, the perception of being roleless assumes greater significance.

## Communicative Behaviors

With communication focusing on the "here and now," stereotyping, and separation from the elderly parent, it is consistent to conclude that the adult child/aged parent relationship is lacking in consistent and relationally productive communication. According to Johnson (1978) "... when elderly parents have few resources to bring to play, when their income is inadequate, their health is poor, their living situation is undesirable, or their attitude toward aging somewhat negative,... [they] may be forced to act compliantly with their children in order to preserve a relationship for which there are often no alternatives. On the other hand, elderly parents who possess adequate resources, either intrinsic or provided to them by the community, may feel less need to suppress themselves in their relationship with their children." In an earlier study Johnson and Bursk (1977) reported " . . . a significant association between a positive elderly parent-adult child relationship and health and attitude toward aging factors associated with the elderly parent."

## Interaction with the Elderly

The solution to the intergenerational communication problem is the development of a positive, flexible, and healthy role which is able to function in a variety of family communicative settings. Research by Conner, Powers and Bultena (1979) found that the morale of the elderly individual was influenced "... not by 'how often' or with 'how many' one interacts, but rather under what circumstances, for what purposes, with what degree of intimacy and caring the interaction takes place." Herr and Weakland (1979) indicate that the parent-child relationship "assumes great intensity" when parents are of advanced age. The adult child is now caught in a dichotomous situation of being both child and parent. The relationship takes on more intensity as members of the family are made aware of the need to change the environment. The parent with years of experience as a decision maker is now the concern of the family's decision making.

Johnson and Bursk (1977) observed "... in today's society there are no cultural guidelines, no specific norms for behavior in the area of inter-generational relationships.... There is no socialization mechanism available for aiding elderly parents or adult children with their new roles at this life stage."

The intergenerational communication problem is a recent one, for many of the early settlers and even some more recent immigrants could never hope to return home to see their parents. Bengston (1979) asserts, "Much more contact takes place between generations today than at any other time in American history." With our increased longevity we now have families dealing with a unique situation which previous generations had not faced in this magnitude. According to Treas (1979), "While aging parents are not new to the twentieth century, they are newly commonplace in American families. Surer survival has ushered in an era of intergenerational relations unprecedented in scope and predictability, because today's middle-aged adult is more likely to have an aging parent than was his counterpart in yesteryear.'' Thus for both the adult child and the elderly parent, the repertoire of communicative behaviors often seems inadequate.

The development of an appropriate set of behaviors would involve training in intergenerational communication. An appropriate interaction style requires an understanding of the role and its reversal. Styles of communicative behavior for dealing with the elderly parent involve observation of positive behaviors exhibited by others and the sharing of experiences which have proven to be successful in the past (Schroeder, 1977). The observation of different roles is instructive for both the child and the adult child when interacting with the elderly parent. If the opportunity to interact with the parents and grandparents is restricted, role models may be eliminated from the child's immediate field of experience. The removal of adequate role models due to death, divorce, etc. may result in a disfunctional family unit where individuals do not develop a sense of family. Galvin and Brommel (1986) state, ''Every family creates its own identity.... Communication, the symbolic, transactional process of sharing meanings, undergirds and illuminates the structure of kinship relationships. The form and content of family messages combine to create a family's view of itself and the world. Family members, through their interdependence and mutual influence, create meanings based on their interaction patterns.... [C]ommunication regulates cohesion among family members, and this distance regulation interacts with the family's adaptive processes. Over a period of time, family members come to have certain meanings for one another.''

Other signs of changing family relations include circumscribing, stagnating, avoiding, and terminating. Generally, each stage marks a change in the content and nature of interaction. ''Circumscribing'' communication is characterized by messages that redefine the family and family roles, as well as individual roles. Often this may mean more intentional management of communication by limiting topics, less disclosure, and/or even withdrawal from new and different social encounters. ''Stagnating'' communication involves an altered self-concept and society plays a critical role in the process. Our future may be limited or destroyed by actions taken by employers, family members, or physicians. Who we are and what we are involves interaction; this interaction involves interdependence when we are able to contribute. If the ability to contribute has been taken away or redefined, the elderly individual may begin to show a great deal of resentment and anger. Likewise, with the redefinition of role may come fewer meaningful contacts and activities with old friends.

The ''avoiding'' stage of communication is characterized by a further reduction in the frequency and length of time spent in communicating. Initial stages of avoiding communication may be very subtle. Family members might find that they are extremely busy, resulting in less time to sit and discuss issues. Avoiding communication with others may also be a function of how emotionally difficult it is to deal with the situation, i.e., terminal illness, cancer, death. Actions initially taken to make a family member more comfortable (for example, setting up another television for more "viewing enjoyment," eating separately, or separate bedrooms) may lead to the extremes of avoiding. Because of this lack of social contact, the elderly individual often becomes passive as a communicator and expects the other person to initiate conversation. "Boring" conversation may result from this passivity on the part of the elderly and may reflect the attitude of "you communicate with me." Such an attitude indicates that reciprocity (Gouldner, 1960) is not viewed as important. Reciprocity refers to the commitment to maintain the relationship which defines one another (Cushman and Cahn, 1985). In conversation patterns, reciprocity involves "turn taking," according to Cappella and Street (in Street and Cappella, ed., 1985). Altman and Taylor (1973) note, ". . . wherever people are forced to deal with one another and are unable to leave a relationship their inter-action is likely to be quite restrained." If the elderly parent chooses not to answer, many unfavorable conclusions may be drawn by the adult child.

## Social Disability

Many elderly exhibit what Sussman (1983) refers to as "social disability," which is an incongruity between familial and social norms for the elderly. Social disability is the failure to adjust to and to achieve normative values and goals and to accept alternative structures. Often, family conflicts are due to social disability. Social disability is not necessarily a function of age; it involves the ability to adjust to changing values and social structure. The elderly may simply not be prepared to accept a new environment and the new relationships this environment will include.

Herr and Weakland (1979) illustrate the communication problems of the adult child and the elderly parent. As previously noted, the intensity of the relationship increases when the behavior of the elderly parent indicates the need for greater dependency. Next, the intensity of the interaction may further increase due to communication problems characterized by "denial or concealment of communicational contradictions" (Herr and Weakland, 1979). An example of this is when an elderly woman, against her son's advice, tries to carry a pot of geraniums into the house. She falls and injures herself. When confronted about the accident, she denies trying to carry in the geraniums. The adult child will assume a management position, supervising activities for the elderly parent. If the parent acts in-dependently, the adult child may communicate the concern, suggesting that prior approval or at least informing the adult child of the activity is necessary. If the elderly parent should seek prior approval, the adult child will interpret it to mean more dependency, thus contributing to the notion of helplessness on the part of the parent. As the relationship is redefined, the elderly parent is further confined by the rules. Herr and Weakland indicate that the contradictory rules make it nearly impossible for the elderly person to feel comfortable in their independent environment. The contradictory message given is "We will help you to remain independent. If you refuse our help (by not following all our advice and directives) this will be a sign to us that you are unable to continue living independently. Thus the mother is cast into the paradoxical position of having to take orders to remain living independently. If she questions these orders she is admitting that she is no longer able to take care of herself." Friends and neighbors will notice a change in behavior, resulting in comments about the elderly person being senile, unsure, confused, lacking in direction and motivation. This description characterizes a "double bind" relationship with its circular causality (Herr and Weakland, 1979).

The adult child is placed in a developmental relationship with his/her parent as problems of health and psychological well-being develop. Establishing and maintaining channels of communication is difficult because both individuals must be involved in the process of uncertainty reduction (Berger and Bradac, 1982). In 1961, Cumming and Henry introduced the disengagement theory of aging. This idea is based on the notion of decreased interaction. Decreased interaction is not immediate; the retired individual will maintain association with cohorts and will participate in the same activities. Often the retired individual will develop new hobbies and interests, make new friends, and participate socially more than any other time period in their life. However, for a portion of the elderly, the poor, ill, isolated, and abused, the experience of disengagement is real. If the elderly individual is facing a terminal illness or if members of the family die preceding the parent, many elderly will withdraw from society. "Terminating" communication according to Knapp (1978b), signals an even further decrease of involvement in the relationship with less spontaneity in conversation and negative messages about the future of the relationship. Messages about how personal effects and property are to be distributed and comments about the final visit illustrate "terminating" communicative behavior.

## Conclusion

Modern America has an increasing number of elderly resulting in a number of four and five generation families. Elderly parents frequently become more involved with their families as an appropriate channel for integration, to serve as a link with the community, and for emotional security. Adult children are commonly confronted with those pressures which will grow as the aging of America continues.

Generation differences in themselves do not create problems for families. The problem is with communication or more precisely with the *lack* of communication, with the style of interaction dominant within the family, and with the lack of understanding about roles. As our roles change, so does the amount and nature of communication. Individuals central to an organization, business, or family are highly involved in interaction on a daily basis. Social interaction structures society and our daily communicative habits. Retirement and other aspects of aging change the social interaction resulting in age segregation which, for many, means less communication.

The elderly in many cases are treated as separate and distinct. Our language refers to age differences, our media sells products based on the needs of age groups, and parents tell their children to be on their best behavior when visiting grandparents. Myths are created and perpetuated due to a lack of interaction and understanding about the elderly. The elderly differentiate themselves by communicating more with cohorts than with younger or middle-aged individuals.

The adult child is now caught in the conflicting roles of being both child and parent. The situation is equally disquieting for the parent. After years of experience as a decision maker, the parent is now the object of the family's decision making. Often our communication becomes contradictory and establishes a circular style of communication which is destructive to both the adult child and the elderly parent.

Much more contact takes place between generations today than at any other time in American history. Establishing and maintaining channels of communication is difficult because both individuals must be involved in the process of uncertainty reduction. Developing styles of communicative behavior for dealing with the elderly parent involves observation of positive behaviors exhibited by others and the sharing of experiences which have proven to be successful in the past. If the adult child or the elderly parent are socially disengaged, communication is both the problem and the solution.

## Suggestions for Improving Intergenerational Communication

Improving communication between generations is dependent upon the development of good interpersonal skills and a genuine desire to share experiences and feelings without criticism of the person or the content of the conversation. The experiences of past generations should be valued and serve as useful to future generations.

Knowledge of our personal family heritage will generally not be found in history books nor will it be lectured about in the classroom. If the information is to be gained for ourselves and our children, it is necessary for us to take the initiative in developing an oral history, a family tree with comments about as many of the individuals as possible. What historical events did your ancestors participate in or observe? If a homesteader is in the family history, what motivated the family to move, to settle? What problems did the homesteader overcome? If he was a sailor, where did he sail? What cargo did he transport? What battles did he fight? If she was a teacher, what did she teach? What were her responsibilities? What was her schedule? What did she dream?

Memories of childhood or activities as a young adult may remain detailed and rich even though short-term recall may be faulty. Reminisce with the elderly about their experiences or moments you have shared with them. What were their proudest moments or their most embarrassing? Attempt to discover new topics of conversation to discuss. For example, you could walk through a museum and discuss the various displays. Just as the most important step in a long journey is the first, establishing a long, mutually satisfying conversation begins with the first question. The first question we should ask ourselves about our communication with the elderly is: Are our communication skills sufficient to respond to changing needs while maintaining and strengthening bonds which cross generations?

# Communication and Aging in Organizational Contexts

## Carl H. Botan

The relationship between communication and organizations is so intimate one researcher has suggested that "human beings developed the ability to speak because they had to in order to form and sustain organizations" (Fry, 1977). Communication has been explored and studied for centuries; organizations have been probed since their early beginnings. Some have studied the interaction of the two and called the endeavor the study of organizational communication.

The aging process impacts on how we communicate within organizations just as it impacts on how we communicate in intrapersonal, interpersonal, group, and mass situations. This chapter addresses communication and aging in organizations. Of course, organizations also communicate with the aging outside of the organization through advertising, public relations, sales, client relationships, and a myriad of other forms. Such external communication is also organizational communication, strictly speaking, but space does not permit a full examination of external communication by organizations in this chapter. This chapter is therefore divided into three parts. The first part introduces organizational communication as it relates to aging. The purpose is to provide the reader with an understanding of basic terms and concepts in organizational communication. Part two examines the kinds of organizations aging people communicate in and how communication functions in them. Part three offers some recommendations which may contribute to more effective organizational communication with, and by, the aging.

## Foundations of Organizational Communication

Understanding the organizations within which the aging communicate requires understanding four characteristics of organizations: how big they are, what role communication plays, what role shared goals play, and what role division of labor plays. These four characteristics will then be used to define the organizations in which the aging communicate.

### Size

It is often assumed that the term organization refers to large hierarchical structures composed of many people; this is not the case. Organizations can be made up of a very few people. Half a century ago, Chester Barnard (1938) defined an organization as a system of consciously coordinated activities or forces of two or more persons. More recently, Phillips (1982) took the position that whenever two or more people are required to share time or space, goods or services, an organization is formed.

Organizations within which the aging communicate are therefore composed of at least two people. They do not have to be large hierarchical structures; rather, they can be a neighborhood association or a church with only one part-time minister.

### Communication

Organizations are often mistakenly thought of as being made up of a building, bank account, or incorporation papers, but organizations are actually constituted by two or more people communicating. Haney (1967) referred to communication as "the sine qua non of the organization" (p. 10). Haney's stance was based on the fact that there can be no coordination of efforts between two or more people without communication. Wilson, Goodall and Waagen (1986) supported Haney's analysis when they referred to organizations as manageable communication environments.

Organizations within which the aging communicate must therefore have provisions for ongoing communication. Such provisions define what the organization is and who is in it much more descriptively than a building, bank account or corporate papers. This communication often follows consistent patterns within the organization. Thus the real structure of the organization is provided by its communication patterns rather than the official organizational charts.

## Goals

Organizations are two or more people communicating about shared goals. Robbins (1983) defined an organization as "The planned coordination of the collective activities of two or more people who, functioning on a relatively continuous hierarchy of authority, seek to achieve a common goal or set of goals" (p. 5). To agree on common goals and to coordinate efforts in pursuit of those goals requires communication.

Organizations within which the aging communicate must therefore have common goals. These common goals determine the importance of the organization to the aging person and the importance of the aging person to the organization. For example, an organization whose goal is to build a bridge will value a person, young or old, who has training as a structural engineer over a person who has training as a chef.

## Division of Labor

In addition to communication about shared goals, organizations have a formalized system for division of labor. Many groups of people who communicate together and have a common goal are not organizations because there is no formal division of labor. Farace, Monge, and Russell (1977) suggested that in organizations "Coordination refers to the strategy that seeks to make each member of the organization, each component part of it, work in harmony with the others" (p. 18). Similarly, Katz and Kahn (1978) said that "Social organizations move toward the multiplication and elaboration of roles with greater specialization of function" (p. 29).

Organizations within which the aging communicate must therefore have a division of labor which is expressed in both formal job descriptions and informal cues as to what is expected" of each person. The individual's role and status in the organization is determined largely by his/her position within the framework for the division of labor. For example, one whose role is to coordinate and to evaluate the way others fulfill their roles may be called an executive and hold higher rank than those whose roles are to tighten nuts on an assembly line.

## Definition

Based on the preceding four characteristics, we have defined the organizations within which the aging communicate as: two or more people within a formalized division of labor framework communicating about shared goals. Such a broad definition includes many kinds of organizations within the life experience of the aging. This means that communication and aging scholars and practitioners must expand their focus beyond the nursing home to include other organizational experiences of the aging such as work (for both large and small employers), and memberships in civic, religious, fraternal-sororal, recreational, and other organizations.

## Perspectives on Organizational Communication

The communication which the aging engage in within organizations can be examined from several perspectives, each of which provide the communication and aging scholar or practitioner with unique advantages and disadvantages. The scholar or practitioner selects a particular perspective because it highlights one of the aspects of organizational communication which they feel is important. Four popular perspectives are the systems, product, process and cultural approaches.

### Systems

The systems perspective highlights the interdependent nature of the relationship between organizations and aging members. Addressing the aging experience from a systems perspective, while rare, is not new. In 1978, Harel presented an analysis of institutions for the aging essentially from a systems perspective.

A systems analysis is a holistic view which sees an organization as a gestalt — the whole is greater than the sum of the parts. The view holds that an organization is made up of composing sub-units which are interdependent in that each must rely on the others to do their part (cf. Katz & Kahn, 1978). This interconnectedness is the key characteristic of organizations with respect to communication and aging. The concept of interdependence holds that a change to any one composing unit of a system will bring about some change in the system as a whole and therefore will result in changes to other sub-units and to the relationships between those sub-units.

As employees age, both physically and socially, they change (see Chapters 1, 3-7, and others). These changes are manifest in, and cause change in, the communication behavior of the aging individual (see Chapters 4-9). These changes have an effect on other parts of the organization and on the organization as a whole. With a clear understanding of the role of the aging individual and how to communicate effectively with them, the organization can adjust to age-related changes. This will allow aging organizational members to continue as useful parts of the system. Some adjustments are discussed in the final section of this chapter.

### Product

A second perspective on organizational communication, which can be used alone or in conjunction with a systems analysis, is viewing organizational communication as a product. Memos, letters, advertisements, newsletters, manuals, speeches, and the like, are all examples of organizational communication as a product. In this sense, organizational communication is what is produced by organizations in order to get their messages across (cf. most older organizational communication books). The product is what carries the message. From this perspective, the aging are receivers, and occasionally senders, of organizational communication. Every time aging persons receive a letter or memo, listen to a presentation, or read a bulletin from the organization, they are receiving organizational communication.

When viewed from this perspective, the messages which organizations produce and direct to their aging members must take into account the specific communication needs of the aging receiver. Organizational messages which are concrete, moderately paced, related to the life experience of the aging, and which reflect the opinion that the aging member is valuable are more likely to be successful than those which do not contain those ingredients or which communicate age-related biases on the part of the organization. In some cases, organizations may even have to make mechanical adjustments to their messages such as larger print, broader lines, better illumination, use of illustrations, and delivery of the message in an environment with a minimum of extraneous stimuli (noise).

## Process

A third perspective, often used in conjunction with a systems perspective, sees organizational communication as a process. This perspective holds that people, including the aging, engage in an ongoing process of exchanging, organizing, and coordinating communication. Out of this process comes the product called an organization. This is, the thing called an organization is the product of the communication process and exists only so long as coordinating communication continues (cf. Farace, Monge, & Russell, 1977). From the process perspective, the aging are part of the creation and perpetuation of each organization in which they communicate. The aging person may play a central role by coordinating other's efforts or a peripheral role. But in each case, the aging person is playing some role in determining the shape, function, and even existence of the organization in question. Ironically, from this perspective, the aging person helps create and perpetuate the organization which may discriminate against him or her. However, this perspective, unlike the product perspective, prescribes a role for the aging person and allows the possibility of some power.

## Cultural Approach

A fourth perspective is called the cultural perspective. This view sees an organization as a "mini-culture" and has been gaining in acceptance in recent years (cf. Wilson, Goodall, & Waagen, 1986). One reason for the gain may be the current high level of interest which the business world is showing. This perspective may be particularly useful for the communication and aging scholar or practitioner because it helps develop insight into the environment or "feel" of an organization and may therefore help in understanding the total communication experience of the aging organization member.

*Culture.* An organization's culture is the sum total of its beliefs, values, codes of conduct, role definitions, and purpose as communicated both verbally and nonverbally. Unfortunately, the culture of many American organizations today includes a distinct anti-age bias which is communicated both verbally and nonverbally.

*Socialization.* The process of learning and adjusting to an organization's formal and informal beliefs, values, codes of conduct, and role definitions is called socialization. Socialization interacts with communication and aging in at least two ways.

First, as employees age they may receive messages from the organization which suggest that they are losing their value and should accept new, often less important, roles. This can happen because many organizations stereotypically assume that when individuals reach the age of 65 or 70 they somehow lose the capacity to do what they have been doing successfully for 40 or 50 years. This assumption is part of the culture and is communicated to the aging person both verbally and nonverbally. For example, refusal to allow older employees to participate in valuable training programs because they are too close to retirement would communicate organizational worthlessness.

Second, one of the communicative roles of older employees is to socialize new employees. Since older workers have normally been members of an organization longer than younger workers, it is logical that they would serve this function. As Stagner (1985) noted:

> In every plant, older workers indoctrinate newcomers with regard to company rules (it is safe to break this one, but don't take a chance on that one), supervision (habits and soft spots of different supervisors, probability of discipline), and a variety of other issues. As the Hawthorne studies and many replications show, older workers may impose production norms on new employees and enforce these by a variety of sanctions (p. 794).

Given their experience, it would be reasonable to expect that the organization would use older workers for more than just an informal socialization role. This is not the case according to Stagner, who says that "constructive personnel policies calculated to involve older employees in helping new workers fit into the work environment seem to be lacking" p. 794).

# Organizational Communication in the Lives of the Aging

## Channels

### Formal Channels

Formal communication is that which is an official part of the functioning of the organization and follows the paths prescribed by the organization. Formal communication is divided by most scholars into upward, downward, and horizontal (cf. Goldhaber, 1986). The aging are part of the formal flow of communication by virtue of their role in the organization.

Formal communication can be both written and spoken and can include memos, bulletins, training films, videos, computer data banks, electronic mail, and other forms. Because of changes in the rate at which the aging can process information (discussed in Chapter 4), and because the aging were born into a generation which did not use some of these newer forms, they may not be as comfortable with them as younger members of the organization. Every adult who has been through the trauma of learning to use a computer for word processing envies today's youth who are as much at home at computer keyboards as today's 70 year olds were with manual transmissions. Learning to use today's communication channels is one thing; feeling ''at home'' with them may be another. Formal communication with the older organizational member may, therefore, be more successful in an oral face-to-face mode and at a slower pace.

Access to formal communication is also important. In organizations, information is power. If an organization has a discriminatory attitude toward aging members, it may use denial of formal communication as a means of isolation. Such policies may not even be conscious. If an organization's leaders subscribe, even subconsciously, to disengagement theory, they may restrict the access which aging members have to the flow of formal communication. Of course, anyone who claims to be doing the older organizational member a favor by lightening their formal information load would never acquiesce to ''help.'' Access to communication channels is mandatory in organizational life.

### Informal Channels

Informal channels of communication are those which are not part of the official functioning of the organization. Often called the ''grapevine,'' informal communication in organizations is principally, but not solely, oral and face-to-face (cf. Goldhaber, 1986). Organizational members differ throughout life in their level of participation in the grapevine, so it is sometimes difficult to isolate age-specific behaviors.

Since the aging organizational member may have been in the organization longer than others, he/she may have a broader network of friends and contacts and therefore be more able to engage in informal communication. This advantage may be counterbalanced by the loss of members of their personal network due to retirement, sickness, or other cause. Because of prejudices against the aging there may be a tendency to exclude older organization members from some informal channels of communication, possibly contributing to a sense of isolation.

## Location

### Non-work and Voluntary

Participation by the aging in voluntary and non-work organizations has not received adequate attention in either the organizational communication or aging literature, although many aging individuals belong to several such organizations. Oyer (1976) detailed a few of the non-work organizations which the aging either belong to or communicate with:

> Economic organizations, such as large corporations and chambers of commerce.... Vocational groups such as nurses' associations, labor unions, farmers' cooperatives, banks and professional organizations such as the American Medical Association.... Government sponsored organizations [such as the] Administration on Aging and the Social Security Administration with their various regional and area branches.

> Educational organizations... religious, cultural, fraternal, recreational, civic, health and welfare, community service and planning, as well as advocacy, lobbying, and research organizations... neighborhood groups, the concerned block police officer, the landlord... (p. 291-92).

In one study of voluntary organizations, Babchuk, Peters, Hoyt and Kaiser (1979) addressed the subject of communication when they reported that such organizations "not only provide fellowship and diversion for members but also critical services and information, act as important agencies and pressure groups on behalf of their constituents, provide an arena in which expressive behavior takes place, educate and perform a wide variety of functions" (p. 579).

Babchuk, et al. (1979) reported that 79.8% of their aged subjects were affiliated with a voluntary organization. 58% belonged to more than one association with 40% being in three or more groups. Surprisingly, 65.5% of those 75-79 years of age belonged to at least one voluntary organization and 75.9% of those 80 or older had at least one membership. The higher percentage of those 80+ in organizations may be an artifact of the relatively small sample size, or it may suggest that those active in organizations tend to reach the age of 80 more frequently than those not similarly active.

Babchuk, et al. also provided a classification system for the voluntary organizations to which the aging belong and in which they communicate.

*Instrumental* organizations, such as the Chamber of Commerce or American Association of Retired Persons, are groups which seek to maintain the status quo or to change the social order. *Expressive* organizations, such as a garden or music club, provide gratification for their members. *Instrumental-expressive* organizations, such as the American Legion or Shriners, seek to combine both functions in one organization. Babchuk, et al. concluded that the aging who belong to an organization have more favorable self-images, avoid feeling powerless and alienated, and sometimes become politically active.

Clearly, the non-work and voluntary organizations to which the aging belong play a major role in their lives, both as locations where the aging communicate and as products of the communication activities of the aging. However, the most important organizations in which the aging communicate are employment related. The critical importance derives from the fact that many aging persons are employed. There has been considerable research done on aging individuals in the workplace. Lessons drawn from this research might also be applied to voluntary organizations.

## Work

The aging are usually thought of as retired. This image is at least partially false. The most recent year for which complementary sets of statistics are available is 1981. The Bureau of the Census (1984) reported that in 1981 there were 26,826,000 people 65 and over comprising more than 11% of the population. The same source predicted that the aging population would rise to a possible 31,989,000 in 1990 and 36,246,000 by the year 2000.

Malcolm Morrison, Director of National Studies of Mandatory Retirement, U.S. Dept. of Labor, analyzed employment of the aged and found that 16% of the 65 and over population had reported some work experience during 1981. Contrary to long standing myth, a higher percentage of the aged were employed in some capacity than were below the poverty line for income. There were slightly more part-time than full-time workers among those 65 and over, but more than ⅔ of the 1.9 million full-timers worked 50-52 hours per week. Half of the males worked full-time while most of the females worked part-time (Morrison, 1983).

Possibly the most revealing information in the Morrison (1983) analysis was the type of work the aging do. In 1981, almost ⅔ of the working men 65 and over were employed in the wholesale and retail trades or in services such as repair, personal, and professional service. Only about 40% of the younger age groups were concentrated in similar kinds of work. Morrison summarized the work of both males and females by saying that "In terms of occupations, older workers are heavily employed as managers and administrators, professional and technical workers, service workers, and farmers" (p. 17). Most of these areas of employment have communication as their central function suggesting that communication skills are even more important for older workers than for younger ones.

## Importance

Organizational communication plays a central role in the lives of the aging. Most aging individuals belong to one or more voluntary organizations and many are still employed. According to the U.S. Dept. of Health and Human Services (1982), even more would like to work. The ability to communicate effectively in organizational settings is as important for the aging individual as it is for the younger individual. Unfortunately, organizations often overlook the importance of communicating effectively with the aging individual or assume that the aging individual can no longer communicate effectively. Worse yet, some organizations assume the elderly no longer have anything valuable to communicate.

# Problems

## Discrimination in the Workplace

One overwhelming fact of life for the aging individual, particularly in the workplace, is discrimination by reason of age. In fact, an American worker files an age discrimination complaint every 25 minutes each day of the week. The number of federal age discrimination complaints has risen from 5,000 in 1979 to 10,000 in 1981, and to 21,000 in 1983 (Reiter, 1985). The aging person's communication interactions in the organization are damaged on both the task and social dimensions by such discrimination (see also Chapter 7).

Why does such discrimination take place? Part of the blame lies in assumptions made about the aging worker's competence. Negative opinions are commonplace concerning slowed performance, decreased ability to learn new skills, being prone to accidents, rigidity, resistance to supervision, irritability, lack of creativity, inability to cope with stress, and poor health (Doering, Rhodes, & Schuster, 1983; Stagner, 1985).

Older employees often do not have opportunities for new training (Doering, Rhodes, & Schuster, 1983). This denial is rationalized either by stereotypical assumptions that the aging employee cannot learn as well as the younger employee or by the assumption that the aging employee has less time left than the younger person. Thus, an "investment" in their training would not pay as many "dividends." Both of these rationalizations are specious.

The aging can, and do, learn as effectively as the younger worker (Doering, Rhodes, & Schuster, 1983). Sometimes, they may have to be communicated with differently in order to achieve the same results. (See

Chapter 8 for a discussion of how the aging learn and how best to teach them.) The notion that the aging employee may not represent the same return on training investment as the younger employee ignores rapid technological advances which frequently render the most sophisticated training programs obsolete before any employee returns to work! In modern society, projections too far into the future can be disastrous. Aging employees have a greater reservoir of experience which may allow them to adapt skills more readily than younger employees.

Stereotypes of the aging are a major source of workplace communication problems for both the aging and for the organizations attempting to communicate with them. The problems are exacerbated by ignorance of specific communication needs of aging members. Attention to simple details such as better light, slower pace, and less extraneous noise would alleviate much of the difficulty.

## Performance

Many stereotypes which lead to discrimination and unsatisfactory communication are based on the presumed inability of the aging to perform at the level required in the workplace. The research on the topic an be summed up simply: "Older workers can perform as well as their younger counterparts but external and psychological conditions associated with aging, such as negative cultural expectations, lower self esteem, high anxiety, and cautiousness, sometimes affect job performance and motivation" (Bourne, 1982, p. 37). Likewise, Panek, Barrett, Alexander, and Sterns (1979) reported that "Though sparse, research on the relationship between age and work productivity suggests that older employees tend to be as productive as younger workers" (p. 183).

Research into the work performance of aging workers has been conducted since at least the mid-60s. Griew (1964) reported that in tasks requiring good vision, older workers were less efficient than younger ones, but he went on to point that "it is usually possible to compensate for [vision decreases] by adapting the environment slightly" (p. 53). Griew also reported that it is unlikely that changes in the sense of touch in older workers will cause a very important impairment to the older worker. While hearing also declines with aging, it too can be counterbalanced. Older workers do, however, prefer a slower pace of work (Panek et al., 1979) and their performance will decline if the pace is too fast or too continuous (Bourne, 1982; Griew, 1964; Panek, et al., 1979).

On the other side of the coin, older workers have some advantages on the job. Panek, et al. (1979) reported "a positive relationship between age and experience on the job; that is, older workers are able to compensate for productivity declines by taking advantage of improved skills and knowledge gained through experience" (p. 183). The same authors also reported that older workers' quality of performance was equal to younger employees when both were performing unfamiliar tasks, although they were somewhat slower. One other advantage of the older employee should be noted in view of the increase in the aging population. Older employees tend to relate better to older customers (Root, 1985). For this reason, one bank in Arizona has actively sought older persons for jobs as tellers and in customer relations.

## Alternatives

The organization cannot meet its needs without relying on and communicating with its members. As the aging process changes the ways in which aging members communicate, the organization must adapt its communication strategies and practices because it is partially dependent on those aging members.

Most of the adaptations organizations and their representatives must make are the same as those covered extensively in other chapters. There are, however, some adaptations which are unique to the organizational setting. These relate to environmental adjustments, message construction and channels, and tapping into the experience of the aging employee.

### Environment

Organizations often have some control over their environment. Simple precautions like good lighting, comfortable temperature, regulated noise levels, or placement of aging members at the front of larger groups can be very beneficial. More sophisticated adjustments may include arranging seats so aging communicators can see the face and hands of all speakers (to allow audio and visual input to complement each other) or the use of electronic message pickup and transmission devices for the hard of hearing.

### Messages and Channels

With respect to message content, careful watch should be kept to make sure no age biases slip into organizational communications. This is particularly difficult because biases against the aging are deeply ingrained in most organizations. While the prejudice might not be readily apparent to a younger person, the aging member will surely detect the prejudgment. The elder employee may suffer a drop in motivational level or self-esteem. The negative impact will eventually be detrimental to both the aging individual and the organization.

Careful message construction can be a major contributor to effective communication with aging organization members. Messages should be related to the life experience of the aging wherever possible and should avoid using unfamiliar terms. Spoken messages should be delivered in a low tone of voice (most hearing loss is in the higher ranges, see Chapter 5).

The most important adaptation with respect to channels is to try to use more than one channel or medium whenever possible. As we age, our physical senses experience a decline and all organizational communication must pass through one or more of these senses. Aging individuals may experience increasing numbers of communication breakdowns when forced to rely on a single sense. If the message is received through more than one channel (such as a formal written memo and informal conversation) communication breakdowns are less likely to occur. Of course, this is true for communicators of all ages; the need for duplicate channels and duplicate mediums is greater with aging individuals.

In addition to questions of duplicate channels, organizations should remember that aging individuals are part of a generation which is comfortable with certain channels such as memos and meetings. Other channels, such as computerized electronic mailboxes, may be foreign. These less familiar channels can sometimes be sources of frustration and intimidation for the aging organizational member.

### Experience

The experience of aging members can be harnessed to the benefit of both the organization and the aging individual. As indicated earlier, older employees can, and probably should, be used to help socialize newer organizational members. Their knowledge of the norms and values of the organization can be used to shorten the length of the socialization process and to reduce the number of errors made by younger employees. This use of experience also would communicate to the older employee that they are of value in the eyes of the organization.

Root (1985) has reported several innovative mechanisms which have been developed to make constructive use of the vast organizational experience of retired employees, Some firms, such as The Travelers Companies, hire their retirees on a part-time basis, sometimes on 4-hour "mini-shifts," to meet temporary personnel needs. Aerospace Corporation hires its retirees on a project basis to take advantage of their "institutional memory" (Root). If pension eligibility is endangered by employment with a past employer, it may be possible to use an intermediary as the employer of record or to develop a contractual consulting relationship.

## Conclusion

On the whole, how organizations communicate with the aging should be a major area of concern for scholars and practitioners. Unfortunately, the area has been largely ignored. As a result, many of the simple adaptations which organizations and their non-aging members should make in order to communicate more effectively with the aging are left undone, often because of age-related biases. Aging organizational members are able to communicate and to function effectively when these adaptations are made; they may even contribute special talents and insights which are a function of their age.

# ❖ 12 ❖

# Mass Media and Aging

## Alan M. Rubin

The mass media provide important communication links for all segments of the population. During the past 25 years, the elder population has been the focus of much research assessing the role of the mass media in people's lives. This is especially the case with television. This chapter summarizes pertinent media and aging research, identifies methodological problems with past research, and suggests future research directions. The focus is on television because television reaches the broadest audience and is considered to be the most relied upon medium of information (Roper, 1987). Readers also are referred to other summaries published since the mid-1970s (e.g., Atkin, 1976; Davis, 1980; Kubey, 1980; Rubin, 1982).

The foundation for much media and aging research evolves from social gerontology research of the 1960s and 1970s. That research looked at the social and cultural stereotypes of aging and the leisure time behavior of elder persons. In particular, these studies considered advertising and other media content such as television programming.

The *social stereotype* research suggests that media depictions produce stereotypes of aging that deprive elders of social roles and social status enjoyed in earlier years (Rosow, 1974; Tibbitts, 1962). Investigators have found that children and adolescents view old age unpleasantly and develop negative attitudes about elders (Aaronson, 1966; Britton & Britton, 1970).

These findings have been extended to consider the formation of older persons' self-conceptions in line with these social definitions of aging (Peters, 1971) and the relationship of television viewing to the self-concepts

155

of older persons (Korzenny & Neuendorf, 1980). This research suggests that elder persons live in relative structural isolation with the loss of communication and social contacts because of retirement and deaths of friends and spouses. Mediated messages, therefore, play a prominent role, not only in societal views of aging, but in the formation of the self-perceptions of older persons (Comstock, Chaffee, Katzman, McCombs, & Roberts, 1978; Hess, 1974).

The *leisure behavior* research suggests that media use is a primary leisure time activity of older persons (DeGrazia, 1961; Schramm, 1969). Early writings noted that reading newspapers, magazines, and books was a popular leisure activity for older persons (Cowgill & Baulch, 1962; DeGrazia, 1961). However, by a decisive margin, elders spend more time with television than any other mass medium (Cowgill & Baulch, 1962; Harris & Associates, 1975) and watch more television than do younger persons (Bower, 1973).

In addition to watching more, older persons are largely satisfied with what they see on television. Davis and Westbrook (1985), for example, found that over 70% of the elderly in their sample were satisfied with the entertainment on television. The elderly, in fact, have been labelled television "embracers" (Glick & Levy, 1962).

Adhering to the stereotype and leisure activity research, then, there have been two primary areas of focus for media and aging research: (a) media content, especially the portrayal of elder persons on television; and (b) the media experience, especially the viewing behavior of and the television functions for elder persons. Curiously, these two areas present an unusual contrast for television in society. Although many older persons spend substantial time with television and have been found to exhibit an affinity with the medium, the elder population has been a relatively insignificant factor in commercial television programming decisions. In general, programmers and advertisers typically have ignored the needs and wishes of over 20% of the population (i.e., those past the age of 54), a potential and growing audience in excess of 40 million persons.

## Media Content

Analyses of advertising and other media content point to two general conclusions about elder role portrayals in the media: (a) quantitative discrimination and (b) qualitative discrimination.

### Quantitative Discrimination

First, the *quantity* of older persons is underrepresented in the media. The elderly are presented in the media less frequently than is justified by actual population figures. In essence, media consumers are given the impression that there are few older people in society. Gantz, Gartenberg, and Rainbow (1980), for example, found that with only 5.9% containing an elder person, magazine advertisements underrepresented the elderly. Aronoff (1974) and Northcott (1975) noted that elder roles accounted for only 4.9% and 1.5%, respectively, of all examined roles portrayed on prime time commercial television drama. More recently, Gerbner, Gross, Signorielli, and Morgan (1980) reported that only 2.3% of all roles on fictional, prime time television portrayed older persons. Calling the process "symbolic annihilation," these researchers observed that viewers are led to believe that "old people are a vanishing breed" (p. 37).

Older women are even less visible. Petersen (1973), for example, found that prime time television presented eleven elder male appearances to every elder female appearance. The actual societal pattern was three older women to every two older men. Several years later, Gerbner and his colleagues (1980) observed that men outnumber women three to one on prime time television drama.

## Qualitative Discrimination

Second, the *quality* of roles presented in the media often offer unflattering depictions of elder persons being incompetent, helpless, unattractive, and suffering from health, crime, and relational problems. Northcott (1975) observed that the elderly are portrayed as being unable to cope with these problems, needing to rely on younger characters to overcome the dilemmas. From their sample of network television programs, Harris and Feinberg (1977) described the portrayals of elder persons as being one-dimensional and lacking well-developed characterizations (i.e., without a range of emotions). They noted that older characters were ten times more likely to have health problems as compared to other adult characters. Francher (1973) found that television commercials emphasize youth, and that television advertising invalidates an elder person's self-esteem.

Carmichael (1976) observed that the mass media portray older persons as being "slow, less intelligent, decrepit, sick, sexless, ugly, and senile" (p. 126). This view is supported by other researchers who found the elderly to be presented in the media as being eccentric, unhappy, lazy, useless, rigid, closed-minded, comical, unintelligent, and powerless (e.g., Aronoff, 1974; Gerbner et al., 1980; Harris & Feinberg, 1977). The myth of old age that is often perpetuated by the media, then, is an image of frailty, infirmity, and incapacitation. According to Harris and Associates (1975), "The media, with coverage of the elderly poor, the elderly sick, the elderly institutionalized and elderly unemployed or retired, may be protecting and reinforcing the distorted stereotypes of the elderly and myths of old age" (p. 193).

Some have argued that consumers of these media presentations adopt these negative images of older persons. In other words, they feel that the media perpetuate the negative cultural images of aging. Gerbner and his associates (1980), for example, argued that the elder roles that are presented cultivate negative images that older persons are not bright, alert, industrious, open-minded, or adaptable to change. And, living in somewhat greater social-structural isolation than many other members of society, the elderly may be unable to test the validity of these negative media images against actual societal trends. Therefore, Comstock and his colleagues (1978) suggested that, as a primary medium of information, television is likely to affect the values and behaviors of elder persons.

Still, somewhat surprisingly, many feel that elder roles are presented fairly in the media. The 1975 Harris and Associates national survey, for example, reported that about two-thirds of the sample (which included an overrepresentation of those aged 65 and above) felt that elder roles are portrayed fairly in the print media: 68% felt that way about newspapers, 66% about magazines, and 66% about books. In addition, a majority (56%) agreed that elder roles are presented fairly on television programs, and about half (48%) felt that way about television commercials. Davis and Westbrook (1985) present similar findings in a more recent survey about television: 59% felt the aged are "honestly and factually presented in television drama," and 40% felt that way about television commercials (p. 212). These authors argued that this is understandable if we consider that roles are presented more sympathetically in drama, but more stereo-typically in commercials.

## The Media Experience

Studies of the media experience have concentrated on the use of media content and the functions that the media serve for elder individuals. Researchers have focused upon older persons' media exposure levels, preferences, and perceived importance. Once again, this is especially the case regarding television.

### Media Behavior

Those age 65 and over spend almost as much time with television as with the other traditional mass media (i.e., radio, newspapers, magazines, books, film) combined. Back in 1961 Meyersohn reported that the proportions of those persons who attended movies and listened to popular music were lowest for the 50 and over age group. In their national sample, Harris and Associates (1975) found that those age 65 and over spent a median 2.2 hours "yesterday" watching television, 1.0 hours listening to radio, 0.9 hours reading newspapers, 0.4 hours reading magazines, and 0.3 hours reading books. As compared to those below age 65 in the sample, these media exposure amounts were higher for television viewing, the same for newspaper reading, and lower for radio listening, book reading, and magazine reading. Barton and Schreiber (1978) concluded that the leisure time of the aged is dominated by media use, especially television, with radio being used more selectively. According to Young (1979), "radio listening declines with advancing age and typically consumes less than one hour a day" (p. 127).

Of all the mass media, television plays the most prominent role in the lives of many older persons. For the past three decades, television has been identified as the preferred mass medium of many elderly and television viewing as the principal leisure activity (DeGrazia, 1961; Schramm, 1969). Investigators have noted that older persons watch more television than do other adults, viewing about 3 to 6 hours of television each day, with a daily average approximating 5 hours (Bower, 1973; Cowgill & Baulch, 1962; Davis, 1971; Davis, Edwards, Bartel, & Martin, 1976; Korzenny & Neuendorf, 1980; A. Rubin & R. Rubin, 1981, 1982b; Schreiber & Boyd, 1980). Other researchers have reported a consistent increase in viewing levels from around mid-50 to about mid-70 ages (Chaffee & Wilson, 1975; Harris & Associates, 1975).

In addition to the amount of media use, there are clear media content preferences of older persons. Older persons listen to radio for news summaries, weather reports, and local affairs information (Comstock et al., 1978; Young, 1979). They also listen to talk radio (Turow, 1974). A definite affinity is evident with informational media content, such as news, talk, magazine, and documentary television programs (Bower, 1973; Davis, 1971; Meyersohn, 1961; A. Rubin & R. Rubin, 1981, 1982b; Wenner, 1976).

As Meyersohn (1961) observed, elder persons are partial to "concrete, nonfictional entertainment, in which they or people like them play an important role" (p. 268). Television, then, plays an important role in disseminating not only information but also entertainment to the older audience. On television, these entertainment preferences also include family dramas, mellow music programs, and game shows; there are gender differences with women preferring daytime serials and men preferring sports programs (Bower, 1973; Davis, 1971, 1980; Davis et al., 1976; A. Rubin & R. Rubin, 1981, 1982b; Young, 1979).

There are, though, some inconsistencies in research findings about the relative positions of newspapers and television in the aged's seeking of information. For example, some have observed that, although newspapers are still important to older persons, newspaper reading declines with increasing age and that older persons prefer television news and public affairs programs (e.g., Williams, Evans, & Powell, 1982). Carmichael (1976), on the other hand, concluded that television is the preferred and more credible mass medium for the over 65 population with the exception of newspapers as the preferred and most believable medium for local public affairs. Clearly, newspapers do serve an important function by providing information about the local community for older people.

There also are certain demographic relationships that are as apparent for the older age group as they are for other age groups. In particular, education is a strong predictor of media use. In fact, education has been noted to be a better predictor than age of news media use (Doolittle, 1979). Schramm (1969) observed that the more educated a person is, the more likely he or she is "to prefer information programs on television, read public affairs news, and use print relatively more than television" (p. 366). Better educated older people have been found to regard the print media to be better sources of world and national affairs information (Hwang, 1972). This is consistent with Barton and Schreiber's (1978) conclusion that the "more educated aged rely less on electronic media than print for world and national affairs information" (p. 176).

## Media Functions

In addition to media behavior, it is important to understand why the media are so important for many elderly. Research has determined a variety of uses and roles of the media in the lives of elder individuals. There have been consistent explanations of the importance of the media, especially television, as vehicles of information and entertainment.

About two decades ago, Schramm (1969) suggested how disengagement and the need to maintain contact with the surrounding environment lead to reliance on the mass media. He reasoned that, to compensate for lost interpersonal communication channels, the mass media are used by the elderly to combat loneliness and alienation. According to Schramm, older people use the mass media to keep "in touch with environment, combat the progressive disengagement, [and] maintain a sense of 'belonging' to the society around them" (p. 373).

Combining media and content, such as reading newspapers and magazines and listening to radio news and talk shows, can be used for these purposes. Turow (1974) noted, for example, that callers to a talk radio station were older, less mobile, and more isolated. Talk radio programming encourages the development of parasocial relationships, or a sense that the listener is interacting with the talk show host and callers. Parasocial interaction — a sense of interpersonal involvement with media personalities — also is evident with television news and entertainment programming such as soap operas and game shows (e.g., Rubin, Perse, & Powell, 1985).

Others have offered related explanations for the important use of the media. Graney and Graney (1974), for example, proposed that the media are "valuable and socially acceptable" resources for older people "because they can be used anonymously, inexpensively, and more or less at will" (p. 89). Graney (1975) observed that certain behaviors were exchanged for other activities so, for example, increased television viewing substituted for decreased reading and attendance at meetings. He concluded that "television use seems to be a substitute of last resort" for those who disengage from a more active life (p. 363). In addition to allowing a sense of keeping active, Barton and Schreiber (1978) identified several other reasons for using the media including acquiring information about the surrounding world, seeking companionship, and passing the time.

These explanations of media use are closely related to the reasons provided as to why the television medium is so important for older persons. Davis (1980) suggested that television serves four functions for the older audience: (a) involvement—providing a "window to the world" and a means to share common experiences, (b) companionship—enabling a substitute for reduced interpersonal contact, (c) time demarcation—providing a means to structure the time of day, and (d) time structure—filling time.

These functions have been observed by others who have offered similar explanations for elder persons' television use. These include: releasing tension; surveying the environment; providing a daily record of events; combating loneliness, alienation, and disengagement; fostering parasocial interaction and companionship; consuming time or relieving boredom; and substituting for interpersonal communication (Atkin, 1976; Davis, 1980; Graney & Graney, 1974; Hess, 1974; Schramm, 1969). Obviously, such uses are not limited to television, but relate to other media as well. For example, older persons listen to radio to seek news and information about the surrounding environment (A.M. Rubin, 1980). And, Young (1979) suggested that newspapers help older persons structure activities by providing a listing of local events such as local meetings and shopping sales.

In addition, findings from recent research suggest that television is watched for several major reasons. These include: information, entertainment, economics, convenience, companionship, relaxation, and time consumption (Rubin, 1986; A Rubin & R. Rubin, 1981, 1982a, 1982b; R. Rubin & A. Rubin, 1982). In other words, television is used by older persons because it is an accessible, economical, and relaxing vehicle for learning, amusement, companionship, and boredom relief. This portrait of television reliance by the elder viewer is not very different from the profile of adult television use.

Television reliance, however, is often more pronounced for the older consumer. In addition to easy accessibility of the television medium, several factors contribute to television dependency, especially for the "old old": social isolation, infirmity, immobility, and economic insecurity. Hwang (1972), for example, found that the disengaged elderly relied more on the broadcast media than the print media for public affairs information. In a recent study, the less mobile, more infirm, less socially active, and less life satisfied watched more television, watched it ritualistically (e.g., to pass the time conveniently), and felt television was more important in their lives (Rubin, 1986). Davis and Kubey (1982) also noted that sensory declines that accompany aging may restrict choices among media and lead to television dependency: "Reading may be restricted by failing eyesight, and hearing impairment may limit the use of radio. Television, because it provides both auditory and visual information simultaneously, allows an older person to fill in perceptual gaps that might otherwise have been missed" (p. 202).

## Methodological Difficulties

Early media and aging research provided a valuable, descriptive portrait of media content and the media experience. The description includes negative presentations and omissions of significant elder roles in the media. Despite this, however, the portrait also includes satisfaction with content and a considerable reliance on the media, especially television, by older persons for information, amusement, boredom relief, and companionship.

Many early media and aging studies, though, had some methodological difficulties that may limit their utility. A few of these limitations are summarized below. They include definition, categorization, sampling, and analysis. It must be noted, however, that these problems are by no means limited to media and aging research. They surface in many communication and social science research studies. Investigators need to remedy these limitations when designing future studies.

First, there have been inadequate definitions of important terms such as "old" and "aging." *Age* presents an individual difference and not a social categories variable. A chronological definition such as "65 years of age" ignores important communication, social, psychological, physical, and economic variations among people. Alternative conceptions of aging, such as activity (Knapp, 1977), disengagement (Cummings, 1963; Cummings & Henry, 1961), and personality theories (Havighurst, 1968; Neugarten, 1972), have partially recognized this limitation. Only within the past several years, though, has the problem been addressed in some communication and aging research (Dimmick, McCain, & Bolton, 1979; Rubin, 1986; A. Rubin & R. Rubin, 1982a, 1986; R. Rubin & A. Rubin, 1982).

Second, a related problem is the assumption that the elderly are a universally homogeneous group. Investigators err when they assume that all older persons are in failing health, immobile, dissatisfied with life, economically poor, or television embracers. Research has, indeed, been able to differentiate, for example, between discriminate and indiscriminate television use based on life-position factors such as communication activity, isolation, dependence, and mobility (Rubin, 1986; A. Rubin & R. Rubin, 1982a; R. Rubin & A. Rubin, 1982; Schalinske, 1968; Swank, 1979; Wenner, 1976).

Third, atypical, but easily accessible, confined elderly have comprised some samples for media and aging research. With fewer than 5% of those age 65 and over confined to institutions or communal living facilities at any one time, it is difficult to generalize findings from confined groups to the older population. Few studies are able to assess the influence of communication contexts and patterns. One investigation, for example, found evidence that differentiates television use in contexts of confinement and nonconfinement (Rubin & Rubin, 1981). In a hospital environment of confinement, for example, television use reflects fewer differences between older and younger consumers in why television is viewed.

Fourth, there are measurement and analytic problems in much media and aging research. Few content analyses of role portrayals in the media even mention coding validity and reliability. Also, most early media and aging studies relied on univariate statistical techniques that ignore the interrelationships among life-position and media use variables. And, given the population being studied, most media and aging investigations are one-shot field studies or surveys rather than longitudinal designs.

## Research Directions

From this brief review of research and methodological difficulties, several promising directions for future research can be identified. Several recommendations respond directly to the stated limitations in past research. In general, these directions build on past findings and consider some of the gaps in our analysis and understanding of communication and aging. Once again, some suggestions are not restricted to the realm of media and aging research.

One direction is to use individual difference, life-position variables to define the aging process. *Contextual age* research indicates that the number of years a person has lived is only part of an explanation of aging. Other important factors include a person's health, mobility, life satisfaction, social activity, interpersonal interaction, and economic security (Rubin, 1986; A. Rubin & R. Rubin, 1982a, 1986; R. Rubin & A. Rubin, 1982). There are other factors, as well, that should affect one's life position. These include a person's locus of control, self-concept, psychological health, and alienation.

A second research direction considers the interaction of personal and mediated communication channels. Research needs to consider, not only media channels, but also the role of interpersonal communication in satisfying the needs and wants of aging and aged persons. We require a more comprehensive understanding of how personal and mediated communication interface to fulfill people's needs and wants (Rubin & Rubin, 1985). One aspect of this is to examine mediated substitutions for personal communication, such as using television news or talk radio for parasocial interaction. In addition, life-position components, such as physical health and mobility, need to be assessed as they affect one's ability to communicate interpersonally and to use mediated communication channels. For example, some life-position variables foster dependence on or less discriminating use of certain media.

A related research direction is to expand consideration of the use of mediated channels other than television. As the earlier summary of research indicates, there is limited data about older persons' uses of other communication media such as radio and print. Communication motives and consequences are not restricted to television. Talk radio, for example, provides prime subject matter. Researchers would be remiss to ignore evolving technologies such as cable television, videocassette recorders, and personal computers. We know that, similar to the more traditional media of radio and magazines, older persons have made less use of these technologies than have younger persons (e.g., Cabletelevision Advertising Bureau, 1987). Regarding these technologies, research could address why adoption has been slower for older persons, as well as issues of availability, technological literacy or competence, use, impact on an individual's information- and entertainment-seeking strategies, learning, attitude and value formation and alteration, and communication behavior.

It also would be of interest to consider how traditional and newer technologies are affected by the shifting composition of consumers. To a large extent, the mass-appeal media have been able to turn aside the needs and wants of the older segment of the population. Given the availability of additional communication media, smaller potential audiences for the presented content, and greater economic visibility at retirement age, it is important to reconsider how older consumers now fit into the plans and practices of programmers, advertisers, and media developers.

Communication policy provides another area for research. How will the traditional and evolving media respond to the needs and wants of different segments of society, especially in a climate of broadcast deregulation? In the past, the usual answer has been largely to ignore those segments not regarded as economically valuable. It would be useful to explore how decisions are made about the "creative" portrayal of roles, the sensitivity to age-related content, the addressing of aging-related issues, and the provision of media access.

Future research must seek to address limitations found in past research and to answer questions produced by the earlier media and aging research. Methodologically, for example, what are the multivariate relationships among life-position and media use variables? Given restricted samples in past research, how comparable would the data be across different time periods and geographic regions? More sophisticated data treatments, replication of research studies in different settings, and longitudinal research designs are needed.

Also, based on earlier research we need to know more about certain issues. For example, research has located ritualized and instrumental uses of television among aging and aged viewers (Rubin, 1986; A. Rubin & R. Rubin, 1982b, 1985). Such media use patterns should be examined in more depth. The meaning and implications of using a medium ritualistically or instrumentally should be determined. For example, how do such patterns grow out of different life-position variables, and do the effects of using a medium ritualistically or instrumentally differ?

This latter question leads to further consideration of media influence. Past research often has presumed attitudinal and behavioral effects of the media on consumers, including older persons. We need to use more sophisticated analytic techniques to assess whether media content, such as older role portrayals, influences an audience, as well as whether dependence on a single medium, such as television, affects an older individual's perceptions, attitudes, and behaviors.

Media and aging research has produced some valuable descriptions and explanations of media content and media use. The research has shown signs of maturation but needs to progress further to provide us with a better understanding of the role of communication in the lives of older persons.

# Part IV
# MEETING THE
# COMMUNICATION NEEDS
# OF THE AGING INDIVIDUAL

Part IV is a review of research in major applications areas of communication and aging. This part examines how the communication needs of the aging are being met, or not being met, in health care, nursing homes, education, and with respect to elder abuse.

# ✤ 13 ✤

# Communication Aspects of Health Care

## Gary L. Kreps

## Introduction

In recent years, there has been growing interest in the role communication plays in health and health care (Thompson, 1984). One of the populations that is most dramatically affected by the quality of human communication in health care is the aged (Kreps and Thornton, 1984). Since the aged are disproportionately high utilizers of health care services, they represent a significant segment of the total number of people seeking health care (Pegels, 1980; Gifford, 1983; Weg, 1975). In 1977, the United States Department of Health, Education, and Welfare (p. 53) reported that age was one of the most important population characteristics in identifying the groups of people seeking health care treatment in the United States:

> Age is one of the characteristics which can be used to predict health status and judge the need for health services. In general, older people are less healthy and tend to utilize health services more frequently than younger ones. Approximately 10 percent of the U.S. population is 65 years of age or older and approximately 4 percent is 75 or older. In areas where there is high in-migration of retired persons or high out-migration of young people these proportions may be much higher. In these areas there are likely to be higher death rates, greater prevalence of chronic conditions and greater utilization of health services, especially long-term care services.

Hepner and Hepner (1973, p. 15) further explain how the aged find themselves increasingly more dependent upon the health care system:

> Scientific medical knowledge has extended the average life-span creating
> new problems. There are 22 million Americans, or about 11% of the
> total population that are age 65 years or over. This is a critical factor
> when one considers the need for medical care in the senior citizen group.
> After the age of 45 years the health needs of the individual begin to
> increase; after age 65 years the incidence of illness is usually twice as
> great and the length of hospital stay twice as long. These senior citi-
> zens presently consume 27% of all health care resources. The health
> problems of the elderly are usually residual and of long term duration
> after the acute illness has been *cured*.

There is abundant evidence of inadequate and often inhumane treatment of
the elderly within the health care system (United States Senate Special
Committee on Aging, Subcommittee on Long Term Care, 1974, 1975;
Mendelson, 1974; Stannard, 1973; Fontana, 1980). Kreps (1982) identifies
five primary, interrelated health communication problems confronting the
aged in seeking health care services: 1) their loss of social status within the
health care system; 2) their loss of personal independence and control over
their health care treatment; 3) limitations in the availability of health care
services to the aged; 4) the growing alienation, loneliness, and boredom of
the elderly within the health care system; and 5) the increase of fraud and
misrepresentation in health care for the aged. This paper will further
explicate each of these five issues concerning health communication with
the aged, identifying contributions of relevant literature in understanding
each problem area, and suggesting future directions for health care policy
and practice to help relieve these health communication problems facing the
aged.

## Stigma: The Loss of Social Identity

A primary problem facing many people seeking health care, but
especially elderly health care recipients, is what Goffman (1963) refers to as
"stigma" or the loss of social identity and status. Stigma is a social
situation that occurs when a person's public image is "... reduced in our
minds from a whole and usual person to a tainted, discounted one"
(Goffman, 1963, p. 3). Parsons (1958, 1951) has identified the person
seeking health care treatment as an individual perceived as a deviant by
society who loses his or her normal social role and image, adopting a role
defined by his or her illness, a "sick role." "The sick person is considered
deviant in the sense that he is incapable of performing his social roles and
must be encouraged to seek help in order that he may return to a state of

normalcy or health'' (Crane, 1975, p. 131). Due to the perceived deviance associated with the sick role, those seeking health care services often suffer from stigma (Cassata, 1979; Friedson, 1966).

Before the aged even enter the health care system, they are already branded by the stigma of being old in our youth-oriented society (Hess, 1974). Entry into the health care system as a patient brings an additional stigma, that of the ''sick role,'' for the already stigmatized elder. The stigma of being old reduces the social value of the elderly health care consumer. The sick role compounds the level of stigma surrounding the aged, transforming the limited social image of the elder from that of an ''old codger,'' to an even more stigmatized social role of a ''sick old codger.'' This double stigma of being both aged and sick can have deleterious influences on health care treatment.

Stigma significantly impacts the way elders are perceived and perceive themselves and is undoubtedly a major problem confronting the aged seeking health care today. Sudnow (1967) reports that health care practitioners' perceptions of the social status possessed by a health care client will strongly influence the kinds of health care treatment that person will receive. Age of client is one of the most important criteria used by health care providers in judging social value (Sudnow, 1967; Coe, 1980). The greater the social value of the client, the greater the health care efforts expended by practitioners in health care treatment. It is not uncommon to hear health care practitioners react to an aged patient's failing health and poor response to treatment with a comment like, ''He was pretty old anyway.'' Stigma deprives many aged of the social status they need to receive the highest quality health care treatment.

Stigma not only limits the social status of the aged in the eyes of health care providers but also leads to the deterioration of elders' self-images. Lowered self-image contributes to many elders' passive acceptance of organizational repression in health care; as a result, the aged may fail to direct their own health care treatment. The stigma surrounding aging presents a societally reinforced stereotype of the elder as a low prestige individual with limited abilities and control over their actions and their environment. Bradford (1981), in a study of the portrayal of the elderly in advertising in public media identified five negative societal stereotypes presented: 1) ''persons over the age of 65 are unproductive'' (stereotype of uselessness); 2) ''... prefer to disengage from society'' (stereotype of seclusion); 3) ''... are inflexible'' (stereotype of obstinacy); 4) ''... have no sex drive'' (stereotype of impotency); and 5) ''... are serene'' (stereotype of indifference). These stigma-induced stereotypes can become self-fulfilling prophecies when the elder is encouraged to live up to the stereotype (Francher, 1973). The elder begins to believe he or she is not an important individual and cannot make active decisions about his or her life due to the limited social expectations for these activities. The stigma encourages the elder to perform in accord with limited social expectations.

## Loss of Independence and Control

Loss of independence and control in making health care decisions and seeking health care services is a direct extension of the stigma and loss of social status experienced by elderly health care recipients. Oyer and Oyer (1976, p. 9) describe the loss of independence experienced by many elders, "When older persons are no longer in a position to make those decisions that affect him/her, or that affect the behaviors of others, they suffer a loss of power and status and frequently withdraw from social situations." Aged health care recipients quickly became dependent upon the health care system due to the many decisions made for them by paternalistic health care providers and others who "know what is best" for the elder. "Paternalism refers to an action that is seen as advocating a person's interests but which in reality limits that person's behavior, desires, or freedom of choice" (Kreps and Thornton, 1984, p. 206). Paternalistic behaviors can dehumanize elders, because paternalism infers elders are not capable of making choices for themselves and are no longer independent human beings. An incredibly broad spectrum of decisions surrounding health care treatment for aged consumers are regularly made and enforced by paternalistic health care personnel (including social workers, therapists, administrators, pharmacists, dieticians, physicians, and nurses), family members (often offspring), insurance companies, or government agencies.

Entry into health care systems, such as hospitals or nursing homes, severely constrains elders' freedom of choice. As a patient, the elder is generally "assigned" a patient number, a patient chart, a bed, a room, a medical regimen, and sometimes even given institutionally approved garments to wear. The patient must adapt to the health care system's schedule of events rather than choose their own activities, including many hygienic schedule choices they are used to making for themselves, (such as when to eat, when to sleep, and when to use the toilet). Daily events are often scheduled for the elder, with little or no heed for the individual's wishes. Elderly patients are often given little choice about what foods they want to eat; (dieticians make those choices for them). Hospital personnel take the elder for lab tests, therapy sessions, and even surgical operations according to a schedule prepared for the patient, often with little or no collaboration with the elder. The elder is regularly told when to sit up, when to lie down, or when to stand up, regardless of their own wishes.

A study by Keller and Rozema (1981, p. 7) indicated that older persons (those over age 65) "... were more persuaded to change their behaviors on the basis of interpersonal appeals by physicians than were younger patients." Age-related susceptibility to health provider influence can complicate elders' loss of independence and control in health care situations where they are given many persuasive messages by health professionals and few opportunities to make active choices for themselves. After a lengthy stay in a health care organization where decisions are often made for the elder, the elderly patient may forget how to make decisions on their own, leading to ever increasing levels of elderly patient passivity (Pegels, 1980).

## Availability of Health Care Services

The health care system is not always easily accessible for elderly health care recipients (Elmore and Elmore, 1982). One part of this problem is the difficulty many elders may have in physically getting to health care facilities. Often it is difficult for the aged person, who may not be able to drive a car or to walk very well, to get to health care organizations. Public means of transportation may be too difficult for the elder to negotiate, and the health care organization may not be within walking distance. Commercial means of transportation, such as taxis or ambulances, can be difficult to arrange as well as very expensive for the elder to use.

Even if the elder is able to get to the health care facility, the accessibility of health care services may continue to be a problem. In large hospitals and medical centers, the elder often is confused about where they should go to seek help. Many of these health care facilities are huge, sprawling complexes of buildings with long hallways, many elevators, and a myriad of waiting rooms that all seem to look alike. It is easy for anyone unfamiliar with the specific health care facility to get lost. Even if an individual does know where to go in the health care facility and how to get there, it is often a long walk, which may be troublesome for the elder.

Perhaps the elder has to go to the emergency room or to the outpatient clinic to seek treatment. Once at these units there is often a long, unpleasant wait until health care treatment is rendered. A typical health system entry situation would begin with a barrage of forms that must be filled out, often in triplicate. The busy receptionist/admitting clerk is often unconcerned with the problems and feelings of the elder, wishing only to get the bare data from the patient and to send the individual on to the waiting room. The elder is directed to sit in the waiting room (if they are lucky enough to find a seat) and await treatment along with other patients with health problems who are restlessly waiting for their names to be called so they can be helped. This is not an inviting situation and can discourage the elder from seeking health care services.

Another part of the problem of accessibility of health care for the aged is the expense of modern health care treatment. The costs of modern health care services have risen dramatically over the past decade (Fuchs, 1974; Illich, 1976). Many elders live on fixed incomes that only cover their normal living expenses and cannot afford expensive health care treatment. Illich

(1976, p. 76) reports,

> Old age has become medicalized at precisely the historical moment when
> it has become a more common occurrence for demographic reasons;
> 28 percent of the American medical budget is spent on the 10 percent of
> the American population who are over 65. This minority is outgrowing
> the remainder of the population at an annual rate of 3 percent while the
> per capita cost of their care is rising 5 to 7 percent faster than the over-
> all per capita cost.

Hepner and Hepner (1973, p. 15) describe the extent of this situation,
"Living on fixed retirement incomes, in an inflationary economy, the aged
often lack financial resources to pay for health care. Despite the Medicare
program, nearly 11 million persons, or half the total population aged 65
years and over, still pay for private health insurance policies to supplement
Medicare." Public and private medical payment and insurance plans are
extremely prescriptive about the kinds of health care treatment they will pay
for and the specific amounts of money they will pay, making it difficult for
elders to seek health care services for all of the different health problems
they may experience (Somers and Somers, 1962). These third-party payment agencies also often make it difficult for elders to claim their
financial benefits, forcing the elder to fill out numerous complex forms and
engage in lengthy correspondence to receive reimbursement.

Elders are not always well informed about the different health care
services available to them (Long, 1977). Modern health care has developed
many relatively new health care specialty areas, such as occupational
therapy or dietary counseling, that may offer health care services of great
utility to elderly health care consumers. Yet, often elders are not aware of
these specialty areas, the services they offer, nor how to access these
services. Likewise, the aged are not always well informed about new
technologies, diagnoses, medications, and treatments relevant to their
health care. The health care system must be able to communicate more
meaningfully with the aged to provide information about health care
services, helping to make these health care services more available to elderly
health care recipients.

## Alienation, Loneliness, and Boredom

The aged have been alienated from the mainstream of modern society due
in part to the stigma of age, discussed earlier in this paper (Tamir, 1979).
Mandatory retirement, the breakdown of the nuclear family, and the
increasing development of age-segregated housing and living communities
have served to separate and alienate the aged from most other segments of
society (House Select Committee on Aging, 1977; Harris & Associates,

1975; Brown, 1960). The separation of the elderly from the rest of modern society removes the aged from public view, negating their presence and their needs.

Alienation of the aged is a society wide issue, but has become an especially significant problem for elderly health care recipients. Long term health care facilities have become a societal repository for the aged. "An increasingly large number of aged individuals are living within the boundaries of health care organizations such as geriatric centers, hospitals for the chronically ill, nursing homes, and rehabilitation hospitals" (Kreps, 1982). In 1974, the National Center for Health Statistics reported that almost 1.2 million elderly individuals were residing in nursing home institutions. Illich (1976, p. 77) reports,

> As more old people became dependent on professional services, more people are pushed into specialized institutions for the old, while the home neighborhood becomes increasingly inhospitable to those who hang on. These institutions seem to be the contemporary strategy for the disposal of the old, who have been institutionalized in more frank and arguably less hideous forms by most other societies.

The growth of such long term health care organizations providing housing for the aged has removed a large segment of the elderly population from public view, causing the aged to become an unseen and largely forgotten segment of modern society.

Within many health care facilities that serve a broad range of consumers of different ages, elderly health care recipients are segregated from other consumers. Butler and Lewis (1973, p. 226) question the wisdom of age-segregated health care for the aged, noting that "... restriction to an age-segregated unit can end up with monotony and difficulties in recruiting and keeping, well-trained, dedicated staff." Additionally, they point out the fact that "some studies have indicated that older persons show greater improvement in age-integrated facilities." The separation of elderly health care recipients from health care consumers of other ages leads to the alienation of the aged in the modern health care system.

The growing alienation of the aged in society and in the health care system has isolated elders from others. This isolation has caused many elderly individuals to experience profound loneliness. Several factors contribute to the growing loneliness of many elders. "With the death of loved ones, there is a diminishing circle of significant people who are not readily replaceable. Former compensations of work may be gone" (Butler and Lewis, 1973, p. 38). Organizational regulations in many health care facilities outlawing communal and conjugal living arrangements between elderly residents limit the peer companionship and emotional support elders might provide for one another (I. Rubin, 1980; Albrecht and Adelman, 1984). "Children and grandchildren, if they exist may live far away" (Butler and Lewis, 1973, p. 38). The Stigma surrounding nursing homes and other live-in health care facilities for the aged often discourage visits from family or friends, increasing the isolation of the elderly individual. "The all too limited outlets of religion, hobbies, television, pets, and a few acquaintances, which form the daily existence of so many of the elderly are not enough to satisfy emotional needs" (Butler and Lewis, 1973, p. 38). Loneliness has become a pervasive part of the lives of many elderly health care recipients.

Boredom has also become a reality of life for many elderly individuals. Social alienation and loneliness coupled with decreasing external stimulation for the aged has led to growing boredom in elders' lives. Boredom is especially problematic for the aged living within long term health care organizations. In many cases, there is little mental or physical stimulation provided for elderly health care recipients in live-in health care organizations. Often, live-in health care facilities are more concerned with keeping elderly patients quiet than keeping them mentally and physically occupied and stimulated. Lack of mental and physical stimulation can have a strongly negative impact upon the health of elders. Alienation, loneliness, and boredom can speed the aging process while detrimentally affecting health and shortening lifespans (Woelfel, 1976; Lynch, 1977). Isolation and lack of meaningful communication with others can have a deleterious impact on the health of the aged; thus, many elderly individuals become increasingly more dependent upon the health care system.

## Fraud and Misrepresentation in Health Care

Perhaps the most deplorable of the problems facing elderly health care recipients is criminal malfeasance and dishonesty toward the aged. There is growing evidence of improprieties and abuses directed at aged individuals seeking health care services (Mendelson, 1974). These elderly individuals are often "easy marks" for many unethical individuals who promise health care products and services to the aged but who are really intent on taking money without delivering honest health care. Nursing homes have received a great deal of public attention in recent years. Evidence of fraudulent and unethical behaviors in the treatment of elderly residents has come to light (U.S. Congress, Senate, 1974, 1975; Stannard, 1973). Some of the major areas of nursing home abuse identified by the media were the overmedication of aged residents to keep them quiet and compliant, the neglect of residents' hygienic and nutritional needs, and the misappropriation of residents' retirement incomes and insurance benefits. Certainly not all nursing homes were guilty of these abuses, but several health care facilities were identified and prosecuted. The results of public awareness of the abuses of many nursing homes has resulted in the tightening of licensing regulations for such homes and similar long term health facilities for the aged (Hasler and Hasler, 1967).

Another form of misrepresentation and fraud directed toward elderly health consumers is quackery. Today many older Americans are victimized by quacks and charlatans. Quackery is a major industry in the United States. "It is reported that some 10 million Americans spend about $50 million a year for such products as royal-bee jelly, alfalfa, and ground bones, guaranteed by some 50,000 food and drug salesmen, who peddle such wares from door to door, to do anything from clearing complexions to curing cancer and restoring sexual potency" (Somers and Somers, 1962, p. 139). The elderly person, alone and frightened, may be easy prey to the glib-talking salesman who promises "to restore youth or health" (Somers and Somers, 1962, p. 286). Many health ailments associated with aging do not have ready cures. Illich (1976, p. 76) explains, "Medicine just cannot do much for the illness associated with aging, and even less about the process and experience of aging itself." Yet, "medical quackery flourishes most in areas of unresolved medical problems" (Hasler and Hasler, 1967, p. 286). The aged individual is a natural mark for medical quacks offering cures for health conditions common to aging, such as wrinkled skin, discolored spots on the skin, baldness, or arthritis.

## Directions for Future Health Care Policy and Practice

The five primary issues causing difficulties for elderly individuals seeking health care services addressed in this paper [1. loss of social status within the health care system; 2. loss of personal independence and control over their health care treatment; 3. limitations in the availability of health care services to the aged; 4. the growing alienation, loneliness, and boredom of the elderly within the health care system; and 5. the increase of fraud and misrepresentation in health care for the aged] cannot be resolved with any one suggestion or solution. Several directions for study, change, and improvement in health care systems must be initiated to improve the quality and sensitivity of health care services for the aged. The suggestions for improvement to be offered in this chapter center around improving health communication with elderly health care recipients.

## Health Communication and Education

The quality of health communications with the aged can be enhanced by preparing health care providers to deal sensitively and effectively with the

specific health care needs of aged health care recipients. Several authors
propose the merging of health communication and gerontology in
educational programs for health care providers serving the elderly in order
to train health care professionals to deliver health services to the elderly as
effectively and humanely as possible (Kreps, 1981; Fritz, Russell, and
Wilcox, 1980; Hershman, Fritz, Russell, and Wilcox, 1981). The
development and introduction of such health communication training
programs for health care practitioners working with the aged can be a
productive first step in humanizing internal organizational communication
with elderly health care recipients. By educating health care professionals to
recognize the special communicative needs of the aged and to develop skills
in communicating sensitively with patients, the quality of internal
communication between health providers and elderly consumers can be
enhanced. Increased knowledge of the aging process can counteract
stereotypes about aging and reduce the social stigma surrounding old age,
encouraging health providers to recognize the elderly health care recipient
as an individual with social status. Additionally, health communication
education can facilitate improved dissemination of health care information
by training health providers to educate the public about the process of aging
and about specific services available to the aged (Clinton, 1981; Davis and
Miller, 1982).

Bacus (1982) argues convincingly for development and implementation of
specific courses focusing on communication and aging in college curricula;
such courses would be designed to help students develop increased
knowledge about elders and how to communicate effectively with the aged.
Furthermore, Bacus urges communication educators to include the subject
of communication and aging as units in communication courses such as
interpersonal communication and family communication. Education about
communication and aging can improve individual's abilities to interact
effectively with elders and to counteract the isolation and alienation many
elders experience.

Education is an important avenue of mental stimulation available for
many elders. Traditional educational systems and structures, such as high
schools and colleges, have not generally been highly amenable to the special
needs and interests of the aged. Many of the same problems of accessibility,
stigma, and control that were discussed earlier in this chapter in reference to
health care services are also issues facing elders seeking educational services.
Innovative educational programs for the aged have been developed to
eliminate these problems and to make education truly accessible and
relevant for elderly individuals. Life-long learning has grown as an
educational model appropriate to the needs of the aged (Schuetz, 1980;
Jessup, 1969; Berryman-Fink, 1982). Several of these educational programs
designed for the elderly have emphasized intergenerational programs,
integrating the aged with people of varying age levels (Gifford, 1981;

Woelfel, 1976; Davis and Westbrook, 1981). Geragogical educational programs providing the aged with relevant information about communication, health, and life skills have been introduced. Traditional educational topics, such as art, literature, social sciences, and physical sciences, can also be offered with consideration given to the special learning abilities and needs of the aged (Reynolds and Koon, 1981; Schuetz, 1982).

Geragogical education provides elders with opportunities to explore intriguing ideas and perspectives on reality. Elders are encouraged to examine their unique potentials. The educational interaction is designed to stimulate elders' thinking, as well as to give them opportunities to make informed choices and decisions. Geragogy gives elders information that can empower their choices about health care. This form of education not only combats the stigma surrounding elders' perceptions of self but also encourages them to display assertive communication behavior, personal independence, and control in health care situations.

## Health Communication and Peer Support Programs

To combat the dual problems of loneliness and lack of self-worth affecting many health care recipients, communication programs must be developed for elders to provide them with both emotional support and meaningful activities. A program that has been effective at reaching these goals is peer support groups and counselors for elderly health care recipients (Gronning, 1982). Peer counselors are elders who are trained to communicate effectively in one-on-one counseling interviews with other elders. Peer counselors provide elderly health care recipients with information about health care methods and services, problem solving interaction, referral services, as well as friendly visitations. Additionally, the peer counselors listen supportively to the needs and concerns of their peers, helping them make effective choices about health care options available to them. These programs help elders feel good about themselves and suggest ways to take control of their health care treatment.

Peer counseling programs have been used successfully to provide high quality interpersonal communication for aged health care recipients (Gronning, 1982). Peer counselor training programs for the aged have been introduced in several health care facilities across the nation (Campbell and Chenoweth, 1981; Gronning, 1982; Fowler, 1981). Peer counseling and peer support groups are used internally in health care organizations with elderly residents of health care facilities, as well as in outpatient health care services. "The peer counselors are taking their services to places where older adults live and meet together in the community" (Gronning, 1982, p. 7).

Peer support programs provide meaningful activities for the elders chosen as peer counselors, for the elderly health care recipients, and for members of peer support groups. The process of communicating with others in a supportive manner enables elders to provide each other with information, insight, and reorientation as to how to improve the quality of their lives. Peer counseling can help elders provide mutual support and therapy for each other, helping to relieve some of the isolation and loneliness many elders experience.

Closely related to peer support groups is the development of supportive community senior citizens' centers throughout the United States, such as the Aliyah Senior Citizens' Center described by Meyerhoff (1978, pp. 8-9) in her anthropological study, *Number Our Days:*

> Officially about three hundred members pay dues of six dollars a year, but these figures do not reflect the actual importance of the Center to the community. Many more use it than join, and they use it all day, every day. The Center is more halfway house than voluntary association, making it possible for hundreds of people to continue living alone in the open community, despite their physical and economic difficulties. Daily hot meals are provided there, and continuous diverse programs are offered—cultural events, discussions, classes of all kinds, along with social affairs, religious ceremonies, celebrations of life crises, anniversaries, birthdays, memorials, and occasional weddings. The gamut of political and social processes found in larger societies are well developed in Center life. Here is an entire, though miniature, society, a Blakeian "world in a grain of sand," the setting for an intricate and rich culture, made up of bits and pieces of people's common history.

These supportive community centers provide important affiliation, peer interaction, mental and physical stimulation, as well as a sense of identity, organizational control, and belonging for many elderly individuals.

Senior citizen centers are very successful sites for health promotion and referral services. Classes dealing with health care for the aged are common activities in many centers. Health care experts from the larger community often present such classes in an environment where the elder is comfortable and supported. Senior centers provide elders with an opportunity to direct their daily activities and to seek health care information and services from the larger health care community.

## Health Communication and Home Health Care

Home health care services have allowed the infirm aged to live at home and to avoid much of the stigma and dehumanization of residing in long term health care facilities. Elders who cannot live alone can often live with their offsprings where they receive home health care services (Silverstone and Hyman, 1976). The primary home health care service available to the aged is the visiting nurse program, where nurses travel to the patient's home to deliver skilled care to patients and their families. Often occupational therapists, physical therapists, speech pathologists, nutritionists, social workers, home health aides, and homemakers are also available to provide home health care services to the aged. Receiving health care at home helps put the patient at ease. The elder is far less intimidated by the health care provider when in his or her own home environment. The aged are more likely to be assertive at home, exerting more control over the health care system than they would in a hospital or nursing home. Home health care promotes the self-determination of the elderly health care recipient by teaching the patient and his or her family the skills needed to keep the elder as independent as possible. The traditional health care system often leads the elderly individual to become dependent on the rules and structure of a health care organization.

Community wellness centers are being developed in many neighborhoods to provide health promotion and health maintenance for local health care consumers. These centers often offer classes to community residents on topics such as retirement planning, physical fitness, stress management, nutritional awareness, and other health related topics. These centers also provide community residents with information about health and health care and give health service referrals when needed. Elderly residents of the community can easily partake in the health promoting activities of nearby wellness centers without the stigma or hassle of seeking help at more bureaucratic health care organizations.

Home emergency response systems have been developed for use by elderly health care recipients. These systems generally consist of a small, wireless call unit that the elder may carry or attach to their clothing. In an emergency, the elder need only push the button on the emergency response unit. This, in turn, signals a small digital communicator attached to the elder's telephone to call a nearby health care center, where trained operators answer calls for help 24 hours a day. When a call is received via the system the operator calls the user to learn the nature of the emergency. If the telephone line is busy, or if there is no answer, a pre-selected responder is sent to the the elder's home. (Responders are usually close neighbors, family, friends, or a community support person). After arriving at the elder's home the responder calls the health care center to report the nature of the emergency. If emergency health care treatment is needed, the responder either brings the elder to the hospital or the health care center will dispatch appropriate emergency services. These emergency response systems are provided in many communities as a free service to elderly health care recipients, helping these individuals maintain their independence while providing emergency health care services (St. Vincent Hospital and Health Care Center, 1982).

# Health Communication and Participative Decision Making

Health care providers can humanize their communication with elderly consumers by offering the opportunity to participate actively in directing health care treatment programs. The more the health care provider can involve the elder in making choices about his or her own activities and treatment, the more likely it is that the elder will feel positively about the health care system and become involved in treatment, rehabilitation, and health maintenance. It is relatively simple for the health care provider to consult with the elder about scheduling appointments, selecting menus for meals, and choosing recreational activities, yet such cooperative communication strategies can have profoundly positive impact on the development of effective practitioner/client relationships (Kreps and Thornton, 1984).

Health care providers must provide the elder with different, interesting and challenging recreational activities to keep the elder active and involved in health care treatment. Allowing elderly health care recipients to choose different therapeutic and recreational regimens can make these activities more meaningful. Giving the elder the opportunity to make decisions empowers them within the health care system and makes them more willing to cooperate with health care activities.

Many health care organizations are implementing participative decision making programs where the patient, in collaboration with members of the health care team, evaluates the adequacy of health care treatment and decides on future courses of action (Gifford, 1981; Thornton, 1978; Klinger-Vatabedian, 1982; Petrulli, 1982). Often these programs involve group meetings, on a weekly or bi-weekly basis, between several members of the elder's health care team (doctor, nurse, therapist, social worker, nutritionist) and the elder. These meetings serve several purposes. First, they help the elder to understand the different health care treatments being offered. Second, it allows the elder to exert some control over these services. Third, it enables the health providers to check their ideas and assumptions about treatment with the patient and with each other. Fourth, it facilitates information exchange and cooperation between all members of the health care team, including the patient.

## Health Communication and Consumer Protection of the Aged Health Care Client

Consumer advocates can help the elderly health care recipient cope with health care fraud and misrepresentation. These advocates can help the elder seek legal and financial recourse after they have been taken advantage of, as well as help elders avoid health care "rip-offs." In the past several years, consumer advocates have become popular in the public media. Television shows (including portions of news programs), magazine articles, and newspaper articles have been introduced to address fraud in health care (Davis and Miller, 1982). Providing people with knowledge about consumer fraud discourages unethical practices in health care and helps the elder resist health care rip-offs (Kreps, 1986).

Government programs have been developed to provide health care consumers with information and to protect these consumers from health care fraud. Recently the Surgeon General's office released a report stating that there were no known cures for baldness and that any product advertised to cure baldness was fraudulent. Frequently government prosecutors' offices have taken different nursing homes, who were taking advantage of the aged, to court, causing these health care facilities to stop their unethical practices. Better business bureaus provide consumers with information about the integrity of different health care organizations and specialized health care products and services. Additionally, government agencies have introduced programs to "... transfer information about state and local public health agencies to federal policy decision makers," to help direct government legislation and decision making towards protecting the consumer (Tilletson, 1981). These programs also provide consumers with information about available health care services.

# Conclusion

Introducing health communication education for health care providers, geragogical educational programs for elders, peer support for elders, home health care for elders, encouraging elders to participate in health care decision making, and providing consumer protection and information to elderly health care recipients will offer solutions to the health communication problems facing the elderly.

## ❧ 14 ❧

# Communication in Nursing Homes

## James R. Wilcox, Leslie J. Young, and Ethel M. Wilcox

Current organizational communication research reflects concern for contemporary social issues (Richetto, 1977, p. 337). One such issue is the nursing home as a source of long term health care. This essay will elaborate the nature and magnitude of this issue, discuss the nursing home in organizational terms, and identify what qualify as primary organizational communication problems. Communication is thought to serve functions of integration, socialization, and adaptation in an organization. This chapter will reveal the particular challenges nursing homes pose to this set of functions, showing how communication may be either facilitated or impeded by nursing home organizational structures and practices.

### A Relevant Concern

Nursing homes are the fastest growing health care facilities in the United States (Aiken, 1981). Since the 1960s, the number of nursing home beds has tripled, and there are more beds in long term care facilities than in hospitals (American Health Care Association, 1978). Current government statistics

185

indicate that long term care has become a $30 billion industry which annually meets the needs of approximately 1.5 million older Americans (Special Committee on Aging, United States Senate, 1986a).

Data from the American Association of Retired Persons and the United States Administration on Aging (A profile of older Americans, 1985) reveal that 27 million Americans are over 65 years of age. By the year 2030, this number will jump to 60 million of whom 33% will be older than 75; the 65 and older group will constitute 21.2% of the total U.S. population. In 1983, the United States Bureau of the Census reported that approximately half of the 2 million Americans over age 85 were limited in or unable to perform daily activities due to chronic illness. "Ours is the first generation on record called upon to directly address the implications of a progressively aging population...." (Seltzer, 1983, p. 28).

The Federal Council on Aging (1981) defined a person who needs long term care as "one who because of social, physical and/or mental condition is unable to cope with the tasks of daily living without assistance for an extended period of time." Long term care facilities (nursing homes) focus on the problems of chronic illness and rehabilitation services while hospitals are primarily concerned with acute care needs (Burger and D'Erasmo, 1976). While only 5% of the elderly population reside in a nursing home at any point in time (Manton et al., 1984); 9% will need to receive nursing home care at some time during any given calendar year (Liu and Palesch, 1981). There is a 20% (Kerzner, 1981) to 25% (Palmore, 1976) chance that a person 65 years or older will use the services of a nursing home during his/her lifetime.

Why would an older person require long term care services? Knight and Lower-Walker (1985) studied a sample of 500 elderly and concluded that the following risks contribute to a person's need for nursing home care: (1) medical disorders producing disability or dependency, (2) memory-impairment disorders [the most common form being Alzheimer's disease which affects between 50-70% of all nursing home residents (Lincoln, 1983)], (3) other mental disorders such as depression, paranoia, schizophrenia [Kahn (1977) reports early deinstitutionalization moved elderly mental patients from public mental hospitals to skilled nursing facilities. Redick and Taube (1980) concur that in addition to residents with physical illness, increasing numbers of the elderly with various psychiatric disorders are being placed in nursing homes], (4) behavior dangerous to others, (5) behavior dangerous to self, (6) bizarre behavior, (7) support system breakdown (p. 359). Although strokes, chronic heart disease, and cancer are prevalent reasons for nursing home admission, the National Nursing Home Survey of 1977 lists the third and fourth most common admission disgnoses as "senility" and "chronic brain syndrome" (p. 26).

## Quality of Care

Historically, nursing homes of the 1950s were custodial in nature (Vladeck, 1980). Researchers Lowenthal (1964) and Townsend (1965) perceived institutionalization of the elderly as "dumping" or "abandonment." The Report of the Special Senate Subcommittee on Aging, *Nursing Home Care in the United States: Failure in Public Policy* (U.S. Congress, 1974) concluded that "nursing homes seldom deliver the kind of care which even meets minimal standards." When a profession undergoes rapid growth in size, scope, social demands or social significance, it will have problems defining its structure and limitations (Marx, 1969). The nursing home industry has undergone a tremendous growth rate and the health care needs of the residents have become more demanding and complex. This has serious implications for the administrator and his/her staff.

Nursing homes of the 1980s are serving a more heterogeneous population (Stein et al., 1985); however, they still generally fail to recognize the multifaceted needs of aged clients (Munley et al., 1982). Books like *Tender Loving Greed,* Ralph Nader's *Old Age: The Last Segregation, Living and Dying in Murray Manor, Too Old, Too Sick, Too Bad: Nursing Homes In America,* or the made for television movie *Amos* portray the overall inability of long term care facilities to maintain high standards. Questions continue to arise regarding the value American society places on human services for the elderly in nursing homes. What is the worth and importance of employees in this field? Of what usefulness is the care they provide? (Butler, 1985).

Varying degrees of care and treatment exist among long term care facilities (Moss, 1977). Formal investigations have shown a broad spectrum regarding the quality of care delivered by the nursing home industry. Senator John Heinz, Chairman of the Special Committee on Aging, reports in the findings from a two year study, "What we found is that thousands of our oldest, sickest citizens living in nursing homes which more closely resemble 19th century asylums than modern health care facilities..." (United States Senate, 1986b, p. iii. Senator John Glenn ranking democratic member of the Senate Special Committee on Aging, who introduced the "Nursing Home Quality Reform Act of 1986" with Senator Heinz, stated "I must stress that the majority of America's nursing homes are honest and above board—many of them provide excellent care. The enforcement provisions of the Nursing Home Quality Reform Act are aimed at... those who insist on providing poor care and violating the rights of nursing home patients" *(Congressional Record,* No. 89 - Part II, June 26, 1986, p. 1). Recently, more attention is being focused on the importance of providing quality care in nursing homes and the means of achieving that goal (Devit and Checkoway, 1982; Monk and Kaye, 1982; Munley et al., 1982; Stein et al., 1985).

"The great majority of people want to be part of something that is well regarded" (Reinhardt, 1983, p. 26). A progressive administrator realizes that the quality of care is only as good as the nursing staff (RNs, LPN/LVNs, orderlies, and aides) who provide it. He/she must be concerned with proper training, attitudes toward/interactions with residents, and the interpersonal working environment. Residents deserve care-givers who are well trained and confident of their skills.

Today's nursing home administrator faces the tasks of supplying the best possible care to residents (within budget constraints) and ensuring the job satisfaction and productivity of the nursing staff which provides this physical and psycho/social care. To complicate this situation, "Nursing homes bring together personnel with wide ranging backgrounds and expectations" (Grau, 1983, p. 31). Isolated administrators, nurses, and nurses' aides cannot ensure quality care; they must function as a team. This feeling of team responsibility can best be established through open communication channels and mutual respect. However, many nursing homes suffer from the lack of a sense of teamwork; there are tensions between the paraprofessional and professional employees (Gunter, 1984). With the exception of directors of nursing, nursing home staff feel removed from the "front office" and do not perceive their input is warranted (Holtz, 1982).

Employee stress, burnout, absenteeism and high turnover appear to be almost universal problems in nursing homes (Mullen, 1985). High turnover is a behavioral reflection and dissatisfaction which ultimately affects the administrator's priorities of: (1) acquisition and retention of competent staff, (2) the delivery of quality care, and (3) effective cost containment. However, studies by Goldin (1985) assert that nursing homes which maintain a good human relations environment will benefit from: less employee stress, more financial success, and fewer staff-resident complaints.


## The Nursing Home as a Specialized Organization

Studies by Weisbord (1976) and Jablin (1984) suggest that health care organizations have unique organizational structures and communication dimensions. Through their financial arrangements nursing homes are considered philanthropic, proprietary, or government controlled. Staff/resident ratios, education requirements of the nursing staff, reimbursement policies, and state and federal regulations are all dependent on the nursing home's care level assessment. The three levels of classification include: residential, intermediate, and skilled.

> *Residential Care:* "care which provides assistance with personal needs such as food, shelter, dressing, etc."
>
> *Intermediate Care:* "personal care including simple medical procedures such as special diets, uncomplicated dressing changes, and injections."
>
> *Skilled Nursing Care:* "comprehensive planned care incorporating rehabilitation and restorative services including: drug therapy, reality orientation, inhalation therapy, and the administration of intravenous fluids" (Burger and D'Erasmo, 1976, p. 134).

However, with the profile of the "average" nursing home resident as: being 82 years old, having 4 or more chronic or crippling disabilities, having a 50% chance of suffering from mental impairment, taking an average of 7 drugs, and living an estimated 3 years in the facility (Peragrin, 1983; Saul, 1983), the two predominant levels of classification may be consolidated. "Several states are moving in the direction of granting a single SNF/ICF license and then assessing individual residents as a basis of reimbursement and staffing decisions" (Vladeck, 1980, p. 46).

Residents in intermediate and skilled nursing facilities have multiple physical, emotional, and/or mental problems; they are unable to manage the routines of daily living without assistance and are dependent on the registered and paraprofessional nursing staff to meet their needs. These needs are not limited to physical care. In long term care facilities, the nursing staff spends three-fourths of their time caring for residents' emotional needs and one-fourth of their time administering to the physical needs (Cobis, 1975). "Their importance to patient care goes beyond routine maintenance. They are often in the position to provide close personal and emotional support to residents in nursing homes and are depended upon to satisfy a variety of their patients' needs" (Waxman, Carner, and Berkenstock, 1984, p. 503).

## Centralized Organization

In the nursing home setting organizational control is centralized.

> The nursing home administrator more than any other person, is responsible for control within the organization. Control... is usually centralized, as partially reflected in the lack of vertical differentiation (layers of hierarchy) within the nursing home. Only one level of supervision usually separates the administrator from nursing aides, housekeepers, dietary aides, maintenance workers, and other key operational employees (Smith and Fottler, 1982, p. 10).

**Administrator**                            **Medical Director**


**Department Heads** (Nursing, Accounting, Social
Services, Dietary, Occupational Therapy...)

Floor Nurses, Aides, Orderlies, Activities, Housekeep-
ing, Maintenance...


**Residents**


This diagram represents the "in house" structure. Residents' personal
physicians, family members, friends, and the state ombudsmen, in a limited
way, influence the organization from the "outside."

The administrator is in the leadership position to establish a sense of
teamwork and cooperation among all levels of staff.

> Good administration can be defined as the accomplishment of clearly
> established goals and objectives by a team of individuals working to-
> gether in a health care environment conducive to achievement of maxi-
> mum results.... The primary role of the administrator of the nursing
> home is to get people representing various disciplines to carry out what
> they have been hired to do in the most efficient manner possible. The
> administrator does this by creating a favorable working environment.
> (Schneeweiss and Davis, 1974, pp. 14-15).

The administrator sets the general tone of the long term care facility
(Schneeweiss and Davis, 1974). One question included on the survey
conducted by Young and Hendrix (1985) asked 40 nurses' aides, "Who sets
the tone of the facility?" Results of the open-ended question are reported
below.


| Who Sets the Tone | Number of Facilities | Per cent |
|---|---|---|
| The Administrator | 11 | 27.5 |
| The Director of Nursing | 6 | 15.0 |
| The Licensed Nurses | 6 | 15.0 |
| The Aides | 10 | 25.0 |
| The Residents | 5 | 12.5 |
| No One | 2 | 5.0 |


"The Administrator" and "the aides" drew the highest responses from
the interviewees indicating to the researchers that the paraprofessional

nursing staff not only look to the administrator for leadership and decision making, but when the key element of direction is missing from the working relationship, aides disregard the administrator and place greater emphasis on their own opinions. Staff perceive administrators' positive and negative behavioral cues. The following sample of answers illustrate the aides varied experiences with "Who sets the tone?":

> I suppose the administrator, at least on paper. But, the aides have the most contact so they are the ones who really set the tone for how things run" (Interview No. 4). "The administrator sets the rules and policies, but on the real down-to-earth level, it was the aides who really made the place hum! So, I guess we set the tone more than anyone else" (Interview No. 17). "I would say the aides, but the administrator didn't realize it" (Interview No. 27). (Young and Hendrix, 1985, p. 14).

The administrator is the catalyst for the development and implementation of all services. In order to be effective, he/she needs rapport with his/her employees. "The formation of attitudes and establishment of rapport greatly affects his ability to establish policies, recognize problems, and inspire solutions" (Schneeweiss and Davis, 1974, p. 8). The attitudes of the administrator not only influence social policy but also directly affect the quality of care the residents will receive (Keith, 1971).

## Nursing Homes' Susceptibility to Organizational Problems

"While individuals holding different roles may work closely together, differences in their roles have been shown to affect their degree of interaction" (Costello and Pettegrew, 1979, p. 611). For the nursing home administrators, registered nurses, and paraprofessional nursing staff to function as an integrated health care team delivering quality care, they must have knowledge of each other's roles, approaches, and contributions. An effective flow of information is central to team functioning and collaborative efforts (Thompson, 1965). Costello and Pettegrew (1979) summarize the meaning of "integration" and its relationship with organizational communication [as previously researched by Georgopoulos (1975)] as: "the ability of an individual, group or the organization to understand and appreciate the contributions of various parts of the health care system so that there can exist an identification with common objectives through a shared value system" (p. 607). The degree of integration is dependent on hierarchical communication networks (Costello and Pettegrew, 1979). A lack of integrative relationships can lead to a decline in employee morale and job satisfaction, and promote higher job turnover rates (Holloway, 1976).

Organizational socialization is "the process by which a person learns the values, norms and required behaviors which permit him to participate as a member of the organization" (Van Maanen, 1975, p. 67). New staff members have certain expectations about their job duties and work environments, including the type of supervision they will receive (Jones, 1983; Porter et al., 1975; Porter and Steers, 1973). Supervisor communication behaviors have been linked with employee perceptions of job related stress (Pettegrew et al., 1981). Beehr (1976) indicates that employees who view their supervisors as supportive are less likely to be affected by job related stress due to role ambiguity.

Adaptation refers to the demands of a changing environment (Buckley, 1968; Costello and Pettegrew, 1979; Georgopoulos, 1974; Huse, 1975). The nursing home has proven to be a changing environment for residents as well as all levels of the care-giving staff. Tolerance for ambiguity (Norton, 1975), behavioral flexibility, ability to handle stress, capacity for empathy (Costello and Pettegrew, 1979), and the ability of individuals to communicate about their relationships (Watzlawick, Beavin, and Jackson, 1967) are factors contributing to adaptation. Frequently, the development of interpersonal relationships among staff members, among residents, or between staff members and residents is neglected due to time constraints, emphasis by management on measurable/accountable care-giver tasks, or role rigidity. These factors adversely affect adaptation.

The culmination of successful integration, organizational socialization and adaptation is organizational assimilation. "Organizational assimilation refers to the process by which the organizational members become a part of, or are absorbed into, the culture of an organization" (Jablin, 1982, p. 256). The person feels a sense of being a team member or integral identification with the organization yet also develops or retains a strong sense of self-identity (Jablin, 1984). Assimilation will not occur if there is a breakdown in the integration, organizational socialization, or adaptation phases. Communication, specifically, the exchange between the organization member and his/her immediate supervisor has been identified by Graen (1976) as the vital component to this process.

The following discussion will show how communication occurs in the nursing home so as to serve, inadequately and/or effectively, the functions of integration, socialization, and adaptation. Nursing home characteristics and organizational problems sometimes make these goals difficult to achieve, hence the frequent absense of organizational assimilation.

## Integration

"The nature of the communication system in an organization is an important factor in shaping perceptions of the climate of the organization" (Albrecht, 1979, p. 343). The hierarchy and isolation of roles in the current nursing home organization encourages an "us-them" environment. "When top staff appears on the floors, it observes mere slices of patient/staff inter-action. Rarely does it seek to know the daily floor history of an event it has witnessed" (Gubrium, 1975, p. 62). "Each world (the world of the admini-strator and the world of the floor staff)—has its own logic: its own ideals, sense of justice and fair treatment, method of expedience, prescribed duties, rhetorical style, and proper mode of making decisions" (Gubrium, 1975, p. 37). The isolation and specialization of employee roles in nursing homes may deter open accurate communication.

Nursing home administrators typically work in isolation; that is, they manage the business but with minimal involvement in patient care and maximal insulation from staff. They direct but do not participate in the culture of the organization. This isolation is the result of:

1. The physical placement of the administrator's office. It is often found near the main entrance and away from the nurses' station and general floor activities.

2. Many administrators do not have an "open door policy." They learn about floor concerns from the director of nursing or department heads at care conferences or interdepartmental meetings from which non-administrative staff are usually excluded. Aides, orderlies and floor nurses are expected to "go through channels"; the administrator must rely on second and third hand information.

3. The working hours of an administrator are filled with busi-ness meetings, care conferences, and paperwork. Therefore, most administrators spend little or no time on the floors. They don't eat lunches with the employees, make the rounds with the charge nurse, or solicit suggestions from non-professional staff.

"The administrator's personal influence on the health care environment is directly related to his visibility" (Schneeweiss and Davis, 1974, p. 18). "This is not true at all homes, but it is true in many of the homes... many people don't even know the name of their administrator because he is never visible.... If the administrator does not care, does not show himself, then the staff works along the same lines" (Subcommittee on Health and Long-Term Care of the Select Committee on Aging, House of Representatives, 1986, p. 36). Residents notice when the administrator is too busy to say "hello" (Gubrium, 1975). One seventy-year-old resident commented, "I never met those people in the front office. No one ever introduced us. Who are they? I see them everyday." (De Paul, 1983, p. 31). The administrator rarely mingles on the floors and when he/she is found there, it is to complete a managerial task not to observe resident/staff interactions. The numerous state and special interest inspections keep the administrator informed of any safety, procedure, or building code violations; but seldom is he/she aware of the staff's psycho/social concerns.

Directors of nursing supervise charge nurses, charge nurses supervise floor nurses, and floor nurses supervise the aides and orderlies. Administrators rely on the judgment of the director of nursing for developing staffing standards (Shukla, 1982). In 1971, the White House Council on Aging called for long term care nurses to assume leadership roles in improving geriatric nursing. However, a survey by Almquist and Bates (1980) reports that 59% of the nurses felt their management and training skills were greatly deficient, and 66% indicated they received little support from the administrator. Nurses often feel uncomfortable handling personnel problems. "Even if a supervisor observed improper care, she might do nothing about it because she didn't want to make waves or offend and possibly lose the aide, lacked time or occasion for corrective instruction, or thought the problem was not solvable" (Barney, 1983, p. 46). Such avoidance behavior by supervisors causes uncertainty in employees and adversely affects their dependability, productivity and length of service (Reinhardt, 1983). White (1980) suggests that an effective supervising nurse in a long term care facility needs the following administrative skills: team leadership, teaching ability, patient care assessment, planning and management.

According to Gunter (1984), some "professional" nurses (those who have attained an RN or LPN degree) have questioned, "Why should you be concerned about the nurses' aides?" (p. 6). This condescending attitude is communicated through remarks and actions to the nurses' aides. "Nurses' aide has been labeled a job, an occupation, unskilled labor, or a non-profession. Yet, nurses' aides have he greatest amount of direct responsibility for patient care of any personnel (Jones, 1982). "Aides play a crucial, if unappreciated, role in the operation of a nursing home. Although the comprise only 43% of all nursing home personnel, it has been estimated that they deliver close to 90% of the actual patient care" (Waxman, Carner and Berkenstock, 1984, p. 503). Currently, nurses' aides are likely to receive minimum recognition and minimum contact with supervising LPNs or RNs. Despite their responsibilities for direct patient care, many nurses' aides believe "the administrators and directors of nursing homes place a very low value on their nursing assistants..." (Almquist and Bates, 1980, p. 625). Gunter (1984) warns that "... too many nurses and administrators have used and continue to use and exploit the nurse aide" (p. 6). Administrators must realize that nurses' aides are an important source of information. By seeking the opinions of the nurses' aides, the administrator will begin to bridge the values, opinions, and perceptions of management and the paraprofessional staff (Waxman, Carner, and Berkenstock, 1984).

To facilitate understanding communication patterns within the nursing home hierarchy, Young and Hendrix (1985) interviewed 40 nurses' aides who were currently working in or who had recently worked in rural or urban nursing homes in the Northwest Ohio area. The nursing homes ranged in size from less than 50 to over 300 bed facilities. The nurses' aides were asked in taped interviews, "What is/was the hierarchy structure? Did messages tend to flow in a downward pattern? From bottom to top? Across status levels?" A transcript of those perceptions from Young and Hendrix (1985) pp. 35-46 follows:

> We had administrators, nurses and aides. Communication would go down sometimes through channels. Sometimes the administrator would come in and talk to us. Communication would go down through channels but it would all get confused. Once in a while the nursing supervisor would say something. And messages in both places traveled upward if you even opened your mouth. It got all mixed up and stuff and confused (Interview No. 2).

> There was the couple who owned the facility, nurses, and aides. The director of nurses usually initiated conversations with the aides. Aides would talk to each other. More messages went from a higher up person to the aides. I never thought about it before but there seemed to be this unspoken feeling that aides don't initiate conversations with higher ups. You wait till you are called in (Interview No. 11).

> The aides always went to the nurses on the floor with questions and that's where we got any information that we needed to hear. There was a head nurse at each nurses' station who was in charge but above that I'm not exactly sure. The doctors were not permanent fixtures around the place that I could see so I'm not sure how they fit into the structure (Interview No. 15).

> The aides were at the bottom, that's for sure. On every shift there was an LPN supervisor and an RN director of nurses. Above that was the administrator of the place and I think she was a nurse too. Orders about changes in anything came down from the top and filtered down to us finally. I wasn't there that long but the staff that was in a position of "authority" on my shift pretty much shoved off the jobs they didn't like on somebody else. (Interview No. 17).

> I don't know that there really was one, in a real structured sort of way. I never really knew who was the boss except for the nurses on the wing at any given shift. Beyond that I'm not sure (Interview No. 18).

> The hierarchy of communication was that if you had a problem you would first ask another aide who had run into the problem before. Then if they didn't know, we would ask the nurse on that day. She usually knows, but if she's not sure we go to Mary Ann who is the head of nursing. She always tells us. It never goes as far as the administrator — at least not from the aides' point of view (Interview No. 22).

The degree of integration is dependent on hierarchical communication networks (Costello and Pettegrew, 1979). A lack of integrative relationships can lead to a decline in employee morale and job satisfaction, and promote higher job turnover rates (Holloway, 1976). The quality of resident/staff/ supervisor interpersonal relationships was cited by nursing home employees as the primary factor in their job satisfaction; surprisingly, salary ranked No. 6 as a reason for satisfaction (Holtz, 1982). "... your morale and productivity is governed by how you are treated" (Subcommittee on Health and Long-Term Care of the Select Committee on Aging, House of Representatives, 1986, p. 52). When positive verbal feedback is used, intrinsic motivation increases (Deci, 1975). "It is possible that turnover in the nursing home industry may actually be related less to economic conditions or staff characteristics per se than to how the management style of nursing home administrators makes the employees feel that they are perceived" (Waxman et al., 1984, p. 504).

Statistics from the report by the Subcommittee on Health and Long-Term Care of the Select Committee on Aging, House of Representatives (1986) indicate that the national turnover rate for nursing home administrators is 29%; it is 50% for directors of nursing and ranges from 110%-300% for nurses' aides. Wallace and Brubaker (1982) report that nursing homes have annual turnover rates of 40%-60%. Schwartz (1974) cites higher rates of 75%-100% and figures rocket to 500% according to Stannard (1973).

This high turnover can produce devastating financial and social results. "A stable staff is more cost efficient to a facility than one with high turnover" (Holtz, 1982, p. 270). Each terminated employee will cost the nursing home an additional $800 to replace. This conservative figure is based on the costs of recruiting, interviewing, orientation, supervision, records, downtime of experienced personnel helping new personnel, overtime or pool replacement, and low productivity of new personnel (Stryker, 1982). Schwartz (1974) reports that the cost of hiring, training and supervising a new nurses' aide may reach as high as four times the previous aide's salary and these costs are passed on to the consumer.

"It was rough on a resident when an aide left because they had built up a trust" (Interview No. 38), (Young and Hendrix, 1985). "The constant turnover of staff is confusing. The staff is confused, the residents are confused. Every second or third day, there is another aide on the floor. They do not know the patients. The patients do not know them. They become a little irritated and the patients became more confused" (Subcommittee on Health and Long-Term Care of the Select Committee on Aging, House of Representatives, 1986, p. 38). High turnover is a behavioral reflection and dissatisfaction which adversely affects the administrator's priorities: (1) acquisition and retention of competent staff, (2) the delivery of quality care, and (3) effective cost containment.

## Organizational Socialization

"... as a result of an individual's education, previous work experience, cultural background... and the organization's recruitment procedures...

the prospective employee acquires a set of expectations about what life will be like in the organization'' (Jablin, 1984, p. 595).

Communication regarding job expectations and how to best fulfill these physical and emotional care-giving tasks should ideally be clearly and continually expressed to the staff by the nursing home administrators. Administrators and nursing supervisors should also be willing to listen to the questions and concerns of the floor staff. Managers need to spend between one-third and two-thirds of their time communicating with subordinates (Porter and Roberts, 1976). Lack of training, lack of clear job descriptions, lack of open communication channels, and lack of proper recognition undermine organizational socialization. It is management's responsibility to reduce the environmental uncertainty resulting from: (1) lack of information about relevant factors, (2) lack of knowledge about organizational decisions (Duncan, Featherman, Duncan, 1972).

The nursing home administrator is probably the person best prepared to enter the organization. However, even though they are required to be licensed by the state (Vladeck, 1980), Mullen (1985) reports that before their present employment, many nursing home administrators had some supervising experience but few had formal or informal training in management or administration. "Most often administrators of large nursing homes tend more toward the authoritarian than the participative end of the management continuum" (Grau, 1983, p. 31). Employees usually resent a dictatorial approach. In contrast, the participative leadership style ensures the nursing staff have a voice, but the administrator still retains the appropriate amount of control after consulting with his/her employees. An administrator needs open, straightforward communication channels among all nursing home personnel. Subordinates report being suspicious of the type of administrator who (1) issues ambiguous orders, (2) plays favorites, (3) seeks a scapegoat for his own mistakes (Schneeweiss and Davis, 1974).

Registered nurses and licensed practical nurses are somewhat less prepared for their responsibilities. They are often hired immediately following their graduation from nursing programs which range from one to four years and which rarely contain gerontological nursing preparatory experience (Butler, 1985; Hagen, 1980; McNally, 1972; Penner et al., 1984). In contrast, programs in England have required student participation in eight to twelve weeks of long term nursing care as part of their general nursing education (Reid, 1981). Most long term care directors of nursing assume the position without preparation beyond their basic nursing degree; in contrast, hospital nursing directors usually have a Master's degree (Eliopoulous, 1982).

Regardless of their employment classification, long term care nurses have greater autonomy regarding medical decisions than do nurses in any other setting (White, 1980). They also face accountability for those decisions. For example, "Tranquilizers are mostly prescribed "PRN" which means they

may be administrated as needed at the discretion of the floor nurses"
(Gubrium, 1975, p. 148). As managers, they need to be able to define the
duties of the staff they supervise, effectively deal with their problems, and
recognize their efforts (Holtz, 1982).

Regardless of the demands, "medicine consistently has demonstrated
disinterest in long-term care and has verbalized its feelings that professional
employees who choose employment in long-term care do so because of some
inability to be successful in another field" (Butler, 1985, p. 43). "Nurses
working in nursing homes traditionally have been stigmatized by their
professional peers, being assigned lower role status" (Brower, 1981,
p. 297). Rose Hnatiuk, a staff nurse explains, "Inevitably, someone will say
to you, 'The only job you could find was in a nursing home?'" (Hnatiuk,
1981, p. 41). Most long term care directors of nursing have incomes less
than one-half of the average salary of an acute care director of nursing. The
overwhelming diversity of responsibilities and lack of proper preparation
may lead to "burnout." Lack of administrative support and recognition
lead to feelings of futility. "Burnout" and feelings of futility account for
the job related stress and high turnover rate found among nurses in long
term care.

> A persistent problem area in long-term care is the scarcity of trained
> nurse assistants or aides. This has led to the undesirable practice of
> employing large numbers of untrained personnel to do most of the per-
> sonal, physical, and difficult care necessary to deliver quality patient
> care. There are no universal standards for orientation or training prob-
> lems. A few nursing homes have a full staff of instructors, others have
> an aide follow an experienced aide on his/her rounds, and many have
> no provisions for staff education (Walston and Walston, 1980, p. vii).

Waxman et al.'s (1984) study provides the demographic data that 95% of
their aide population was female, 65.4% were black, the average age was
33.8 and 28.2% had not completed high school. In inner cities, nurses' aides
are predominantly black or hispanic while white aides predominate in rural
and suburban areas (Vladeck, 1980). Racial issues sometimes cause
interpersonal conflict between residents and staff or among staff members
(Kart and Beckham, 1976).

A 1982 demographic profile shows the composites of the nurses' aide to
be: female, mid 20's, high school education, and no previous health care
experience. Most have worked as an aide for less than four years, are full
time, and have no other training than a brief orientation (usually two weeks
or less) and possible on-the-job inservice. They see this job as their niche
and do not view it as a stepping stone to other work (Holtz, 1982, pp. 269-
270). Aides are likely to receive minimum wage, minimum recognition, and
minimum contact with supervising LPNs or RNs.

With the problems of high turnover and low wages, most nursing homes do not carefully screen prospective nurses' aides or require any previous experience or training (Bergen, 1986). Provisions in the "Nursing Home Quality Reform Act of 1986" will require that after September 30, 1987, "all nurse aides or nurse assistants providing direct patient care have completed a state-approved training program in a state-accredited institution," and "all employees providing direct patient care have cleared an appropriate criminal background check" (U.S. Congress, Senate, 1986b, p. 3). Of the 40 nurses' aides surveyed by Young and Hendrix (1985), 60% reported they had an orientation program; training usually entailed following an experienced aide around for one day to two weeks. Of the 24 aides who received an orientation/training program, only seven spoke of the program in a positive manner or felt their training prepared them for their responsibilities; ten aides were neutral, and seven aides were highly critical.

State laws require written, uniform job descriptions for nursing home administrators and registered or licensed practical nurses; however, nurses' aides are not always provided with written job descriptions or made aware of terms for dismissal (Bergen, 1986). Sometimes job descriptions are in the administrator's or director of nursing's office files but are never given to new employees. An overwhelming 80% of the aides in the Young and Hendrix (1985) survey reported not being provided with a list of their duties in writing (p. 29); 82.5% responded that they were not provided with terms for dismissal in writing (p. 34). Absence of a clearly explained, written job description and uniform, printed terms of dismissal add to job related stress and the nurses' aide's environmental uncertainty. 80% of the aides in the Young and Hendrix (1985) survey reported that they performed duties or faced care-giving situations for which they did not feel prepared.

It might appear that management's dispensing of information would reduce the employee's environmental uncertainty and that management's receptiveness to employee questions would ensure a more confident, satisfied employee and better quality care. However, 85% of the nurses' aides surveyed by Young and Hendrix (1985) reported being confused about their duties and reluctant to ask for clarification (p. 30). Unfortunately, confusion about procedures and lack of effective communication can lead to devastating consequences:

> Except for administering medicine, the nurses didn't really interact with the patients; that was our area. Each day I was responsible for cleaning, feeding, dressing and turning about 40 people, and I learned my "trade" by trial and error. Sometimes the errors were grave. There was one woman who screamed in pain each time we turned her. "Do I have to turn her?" I asked the nurse. "Yes," she said. So—until she was taken half-conscious to the hospital—we turned Eliza while she screamed in pain. What we didn't know was that, thanks to her bone cancer, with every turn we were literally breaking bones all over her body. Why didn't we know? Why wasn't a high-skill facility, supposedly equipped

to handle delicate patients, equipped with the knowledge that turning a
bone cancer patient breaks bones? I wish I knew the answer to that
(testimony by Nurses' Aide X) (Subcommittee on Health and Long-
Term Care of the Select Committee on Aging, House of Representatives, 1986, p. 42).

## Adaptation

The process of adaptation to the changes in the nursing home
environment are often difficult for both residents and staff. Entry into the
organization can be a "reality shock" (Hughes, 1958). It often "involves a
pattern of day-to-day experiences in which the individual is subjected to the
reinforcement policies and practices of the organization and its members"
(Porter et al., 1975, p. 164).

Residents in skilled or intermediate long term care facilities have lost
control over their environment. They have lost control over their bodies and
over their physical surroundings: 50% have heart disease, hypertension or
arthritis; 40% are incontinent; 50% have some state of Alzheimer's disease;
33% have impaired vision; 33% require assistance being fed; 50% require
assistance being toileted; 70% require assistance being dressed; and 90%
require assistance being bathed (Subcommittee on Health and Long-Term
Care of Select Committee on Aging, House of Representatives, 1986, p. 5).
Residents frequently suffer from anxiety or depression associated with their
feelings of helplessness and loss of control (Higgins-Vogel, 1982). Their
depression is often ignored by staff members and considered "normal."
Residents respond to this disinterest by either passive withdrawal or by
angry outbursts, abrupt tears, or combative behavior.

The residents' daily routines are set to the convenience of the nursing
home. They are told when to get up, when to eat, what to eat, when to go to
bed. Their physical environment has changed from the family home to a
semi private room which restricts their ability to keep personal possessions.
The loss of personal items and familiar surroundings contributes to a lack
of individuality and a diminished sense of security.

Residents have also lost control over their social environment. 90% have
no living spouse according to the Subcommittee on Health and Long-Term
Care of the Select Committee on Aging, House of Representatives (U.S.
Congress, House, 1986, p. 5). With few exceptions, the residents fit the
description of one nurses' aide, "In some ways they are like throw-away
kids, only they are old; hardly have any family or anyone come visit them."

White (1980) gives the following reasons why staff may have problems
adapting to the nursing home environment: (1) the stress of coping with
death and dying, (2) communication difficulties with patients, (3) emotional
drain of being a family member surrogate, and (4) the inability to separate
work pressures from family life.

Most of the nursing staff in long term care facilities feel a personal concern for the residents; they take on a surrogate family member role. "We assign this group of workers the role and function of family members. They give care which relatives and friends are not able to give. We believe that most often they do it with gentleness and compassion" (Nursing Home Care in the United States: Failure in Public Policy, 1975, pp. 370-371). They give care which relatives and friends are not able to give. We believe that most often they do it with gentleness and compassion" (U.S. Congress, Senate, 1975b, pp. 370-371). There are individual exceptions: "There didn't seem to be much of a bond between aides and some of the patients got real combative, especially on the total care wing... I got pretty frustrated with that but I guess if I was in their place, I'd get cranky too" (Interview No. 18) (Young and Hendrix, 1985, p. 55).

When management doesn't take the time to help the nurses' aides understand the residents and develop an empathy for the residents' concerns and limitations the following types of insensitive communication occur:

> My guess is that if you walked into a nursing home tomorrow, your big-gest shock would be the absolute insensitivity toward the patient as a person. I saw active, vital members of my community reduced to "pet" for 17 year old nurses' aides to boss around. And the elderly person — anxious to reduce tensions in his or her living environment — generally tried to obey their commands. Hurried aides, not thinking, constantly resorted to "dog talk" when addressing an elderly patient. "Come, Vern. Sit, Myrtle. Stay, cat." Is that how you talk to your mother? Worse yet were the demoralizing "third person" conversations — talking about a person to his face as though he wasn't there. When I was introduced to Myrtle, the aide looked at her and said, "That's Myrtle. She's confused and she wets herself." Is that how you'd like your mother introduced? (Testimony by Nurses' Aide X) (Subcommittee on Health and Long-Term Care of the Select Committee on Aging, House of Representatives, 1986, p. 43).

Patients are prone to stress which can affect their ability to adapt (West, 1975). Their unexplained behaviors intensify feelings of frustration among the nurses' aides. "Individuals accused of having a bad attitude, hot temper, or a bad day are often suffering from undue amounts of stress" (Caldwell, 1976, p. 21). Sometimes the staff dealt with the tensions in a positive manner, "We had an area for breaks where we could release tension and talk about them" (Interview No. 15) (Young and Hendrix, 1985, p. 63). And sometimes they were channeled in a less positive manner.

For residents to adapt to the nursing home environment, the care-givers need to encourage the development of positive interpersonal relationships. It seems that development is still idiosyncratic with the individual nursing staff member. "It was easy to ignore the residents who can't talk" (Interview No. 29) (Young and Hendrix, 1985, p. 61). "To the extent they kept people clean, that was good; but in terms of communicating with residents while they were cleaning them up, it was minimal'' (Interview No. 1) (Young and Hendrix, 1985, p. 31).


## Recommendations for the Communication Environment

The nursing home environment as described in this chapter makes a set of guidelines for communication policies and practices which would facilitate the goals of integration, socialization, and adaptation imperative. That a nursing home typically has a centralized organizational structure with few hierarchical levels makes the design of guidelines somewhat less problematic than for the large corporation. Nonetheless, as in any organization, whatever its size and scope, the head administrator is a key figure upon whom considerable responsibility rests for establishing a system of managerial communication.

For enhancing the goal of integration, establishment and articulation of a philosophy of nursing home care for every employee is strongly recommended. Such a philosophy needs frequent reiteration and reinforcement. It should consist of the goals and values the nursing home administration wishes to utilize.

Whether participative or not, management style should exhibit a consistent means of communication (both written and face-to-face links) which achieve maximum clarity and elicit upward directed feedback (suggestions, recommendations, aspirations, and even "bad news"). Such upward feedback, when evoked, should be responded to quickly and directly. Both feedback receptiveness and feedback responsiveness should characterize the managerial communication system.

Administrators should work with department heads who should in turn work with nurses, aides, etc. to establish clear job descriptions where needed, to set goals periodically and to assess periodically the degree to which such goals are being realized. Ideally this would be accomplished in work groups representing more than one level of the organization. Obviously an important secondary function served by this arrangement is familiarizing administrators, nurses, and paraprofessional staff with one another's roles, approaches and contributions.

In a relatively small organization, the current MBWA (Management by Walking Around) is a fairly simple and potentially very desirable approach to achieving visibility, recognition, and the perception among employees of an interested supervisor.

The goal of organizational socialization seems most appropriately met by developing orientation and training programs as well as a formal support group system. Such programs would provide orientation for new employees, ongoing training for all employees and an opportunity for employees to directly confront the stresses, frustrations, etc., which seem associated with burnout, absenteeism, and turnover. Administrators and supervisors can assist by clarifying accountability guidelines, providing recognition for excellent performance, and displaying an attitude of respect for the functions employees perform.

Adaptation may be served by developing and articulating an understanding regarding patient and staff rights, developing a system of "care conferences" which elicit staff input, providing workshops for employees which help them understand patient problems such as depression, confusion, displays of inappropriate behavior, and death and dying. Finally, serious consideration should be given to a program to develop guest relations skills in providing an appropriate image for patients' families.

These are modest as well as fairly obvious suggestions considering the analysis of organizational communication difficulties which may be encountered in today's nursing homes. They represent a small but potentially significant step in responding to a particularly critical contemporary social issue.

# ❧ 15 ❧

# Communication and Lifelong Learning

## Janice E. Schuetz

During the 1980s, federal and state legislators focused their attention on three policy areas—education, aging, and health care. This emphasis reflected the agenda of the public who wanted a quality education for their children, independence for their elders, and the availability of good health care for all. In one sense, these policy concerns represented progress toward an American dream of success, economic well-being, and health. On the other hand, these concerns pointed to a frustrating reality; that is, many citizens were not benefactors of the American dream and therefore new policies were needed so that this dream would be available to more persons.

This chapter suggests an agenda, a plan of action by which the nearly 30 million elderly in this country can participate in policy changes affecting education, aging, and health. The highest priority of this approach is lifelong learning.

Lifelong learning is an educational approach emphasizing continuous learning through new experiences which promote growth and develop coping strategies. This type of learning takes place outside of traditional educational settings, features learners who are not traditional students, requires teachers who are co-learners, and considers personally relevant subject matter. Hiemstra (1972) defines lifelong learning as "a process of learning that continues throughout one's lifetime, depending on individual needs, interests, and learning skills" (p. 17).

When adapted to the elderly population, lifelong learning takes on an even more specific meaning. Cross and Florio (1978, p. 61) stress that continuing education is not only desirable for elders but this process is essential to their well-being. Specifically, they quote James E. Birren: "Education plays a role in enabling the aged to maintain their intellectual effectiveness" (Cross & Florio, 1978, p. 61).

Although lifelong learning is essential to the elderly's survival skills, this segment of the population possesses some unique learner characteristics resulting from their educational attainment, their tendencies for sociability, and their propensity for physical impairments.

First, their educational achievement differs from the larger population. As a group, 38 percent of the elderly hold high school diplomas and over 3 million are functionally illiterate (Davis and Davis, 1985). Even though this population is not well-educated in a general sense, elders need to know how to adapt to radical and gradual changes resulting from retirement, death of loved ones, new living situations, physical impairments, increasingly complicated technology, lack of mobility, and cumbersome government bureaucracies. Moreover, elders have the ability to learn. Marcus (1978) notes that the old differ from young learners in that they "tend to respond more slowly, are often sensitive to interference while engaged in the learning task." Even though they show a decline in short-term memory, they "surpass younger learners in verbal and integrating ability" (p. 127).

Second, Atchley (1985) notes that elders seem to socialize less than other segments of the population. Despite this fact, Neugarten (1982) concludes elders report positive self-images and feel that life in general is better than they expected. Because lifelong learning needs to be learner centered and self-directed, a first step in learning programs for the elderly should emphasize communication skills that assist the development of their socialization process through self-expression, relationship development, and group interaction.

A final characteristic of elderly learners is their potential for physical impairments. Even though many elders experience good health, physical changes occur during old age. Among these changes affecting learning are loss of energy, failing eyesight, impairments in hearing, lower reaction time, and lapses in short-term memory (Schuetz, 1982). Elders can offset these physical changes by their psychological assets as learners such as their ability to organize experience, self-knowledge, and strong motivation (Kalish, 1975).

To enhance the opportunities for elders to take advantage of public policies designed to serve them, they need to engage in lifelong learning activities. To achieve this purpose, this chapter will propose a six-part explanation of lifelong learning. The first three explanations stress learning *for, about,* and *in.* The second three characterize the process of lifelong learning by emphasizing communication *with, through,* and *to.*

## Lifelong Learning *For*

Several reasons explain the purposes *for* lifelong learning. Bunting (1978) characterizes the ideal lifelong learning program as having three components: Elders "successfully guiding and fostering their own development and growth; local providers offering... learning resources to those individuals; and public policies directed toward encouraging... learning opportunities" (p. 4).

The purpose *for* learning differs from elder to elder depending on their health and well-being. Neugarten (1982) differentiates between the young-old and the old-old. The young-old are healthy, want to work, seek out new educational experiences, and engage in community service. Because the young-old have a great deal of vitality and talent, they pursue a wide variety of lifestyles. For them, lifelong learning produces opportunities for personal growth, new roles, assistance in the community, and development of new interests. For this healthy group, learning might include: participating in classes, workshops, seminars; conducting classes themselves; working as a volunteer grandparent; writing their own history; or becoming a docent at a museum or zoo.

In contrast to this group, Neugarten (1982) describes the old-old. This group has suffered physical and mental deteriorations; thus, they require assistance from their families and health and social service providers. Because of the impairments of the old-old, lifelong learning programs should be focused on very specific needs. For example, coping skills for dealing with health care providers such as how to question doctors, how to schedule and use medication, or how to maintain a physical therapy routine might be particularly beneficial. Additionally, the lifestyle of the old-old may require that they learn to use public transportation, take advantage of meals on wheels, use hearing aids, walkers, or wheel chairs, find phone companions or home nursing services, or make their residences more safe and secure. For the old-old, learning is just as essential as for the young-old, but the content of programs needs to be adjusted to their specific needs.

For both groups, lifelong learning strives to prepare persons for emerging life experiences through increased consciousness of aging, preparation for independent living, and encouragement to become involved with persons in their families and communities of the same or different generations.

### Age Consciousness

Sherman, Ward, and LaGlory (1985) define age consciousness broadly as personal self-identification as elders, behavioral preferences for elderly or young associates, sensitivity to concerns shared by other elderly, and active participation in or on behalf of older persons. This broad definition suggests several learning objectives such as (1) understanding the myths and realities of growing old; (2) recognizing elders' roles in the family, community, work environment, and economic system; (3) awareness of the unique problems of the old-old; (4) observing how patterns of interaction have evolved through a long life cycle; (5) identifying the effects and preferences of elders' interaction patterns; (6) recognizing means that can be used to assist other elders; (7) participating with elders to improve the environments in which elders live. In short, one reason justifying lifelong learning for elders is their need to understand what it means to be old and to improve the status of the elderly in society.

## Independence

In addition to age consciousness, lifelong learning attempts to foster independence as a goal for the elderly population as a whole. Davis and Davis (1985) note that four out of five men and three of five elderly women live with a spouse or other family member, 33 percent live alone, and only 5 percent reside in institutions. Since independent living is already the norm and institutionalization the exception, lifelong learning seeks to assist elders to remain independent so they can maintain their autonomy, retain self-esteem, and possess life satisfaction (Smith, 1973).

Several factors force elders to become dependent on others such as loss of financial security, declining health, lack of public transportation, and the loss of mental capacity. None of these factors needs to result in total dependence of elders on others. To maintain independence, learning programs should create options for elders by assisting them to live according to their budgets, showing them how to qualify for government programs, offering strategies and skills for coping with failing health, showing them how to take advantage of existing transportation networks, and assisting them to gain access to in-home companion or nursing services if needed.

## Involvement

Smith (1973) emphasizes the importance of involvement. He says, "If isolation is the ultimate abandonment, then involvement is the imperative commitment" (p. 186). Elderly persons should be involved with their families, neighborhoods, communities, political organizations, religious groups, and their own self-enhancement. A well-known historian, Will Durant, highlighted this point: "To be busy is the secret of grace, and half the secret of content. Let us not ask for possessions but for things to do" (Smith, 1973, p. 188). The goal of education for elders centers on elders becoming involved themselves and soliciting the involvement of others.

Percy (1974) emphasizes that isolation is the opposite of involvement; it is a major factor that contributes to the physical and mental decline of elders. Lifelong learning by definition focuses on new information and experiences demanding involvement of learners in activities and relationships. Specifically, several learning objectives encourage involvement of elders such as helping others and accepting the help of others; expressing self and listening to others; seeking and using information from the mass media; going places, meeting new people, and using one's own talents for the benefit of family and community. Clearly, no shortage of activity exists. However, elders often need to be invited, solicited, or asked to become involved; once they become involved, learning is the likely result.

## Lifelong Learning *About*

Many purposes exist for lifelong learning processes for the elderly. What this learning is about is the second perspective. Taking a macroscopic view, lifelong learning can be as broad as any individual's experiences, cover all disciplines, and include many kinds of new information. Thus, learning need not be restricted to certain ideas or programs. This chapter takes a microscopic view and discusses three subject areas for learning identified by elders as topics of special concern—health care, government and community programs, and life transitions.

### Health Care

Neugarten (1982) recognizes that the main distinction between the young-old and the old-old is the condition of their health. A Congressional fact sheet (U.S. Congress, Senate, 1984) reports that the main fear of the elderly is poor health. Eighty percent of the population over sixty-five suffer from chronic health problems; twenty percent of the average income of the elderly is spent on health care; and health care costs have increased 130 percent since 1980. Thus, the health issue should interest many elderly learners.

Many topics about health issues are suitable for educational programs including the following:

exercise and physical fitness

medications—their use and abuse

chronic illness—arthritis, heart disease, diabetes

mental health

inherited disease

preventive care, health maintenance organizations

in-home health care

diet nutrition

environmental hazards

home safety

doctor-nurse-patient communication

patients' rights

paying the costs of health care

support groups for chronic illnesses

private and government insurance

Elders need to know what to do to prevent health problems as well as how to handle health impairments when they occur. Such programs can help alleviate elders' fear of health loss by increasing their consciousness about health, helping them to maintain an independent lifestyle, and encouraging them to get involved with issues related to their health.

**Government and Community Programs**

Holstein (1983) identifies the decades of the 60's and 70's as the "age of the aged." She justifies this claim because of the large number of pro-elderly policies put into place by government agencies during this period. Examples are: the Older Americans Act of 1965, Supplemental Security Income in 1974, Medicare in 1965, and automatic cost of living adjustments to Social Security in the 1970's. However, the 1980's brought cutbacks in many programs for the elderly. This change in government policies combined with the emergence of new community programs created a plethora of information and misinformation. The net result was confusing to elderly benefactors of these programs and services. Regardless of the circumstances of elderly persons, the complicated guidelines for the use of government services such as the "means test" and the "needs test" and cuts and limitations in existing programs suggest a need for elders to learn about these programs. Educational topics about government programs include the following:

Social Security retirement benefits

Social Security disability benefits

Medicare health benefits

Medicaid benefits

medigap insurance

private pensions

taxation for retirees

survivors' benefits

age discrimination in employment

compulsory retirement

Many states and local communities provide recreational, social, and educational programs for elders. Topics related to education about these programs might include the following:

    community and business discounts for elders
    health fairs and free or low cost health screening
    senior center activities
    day care centers for elders
    tours and recreational activities
    volunteer work for elders
    meal sites
    social groups for elders
    educational benefits — tuition reduction, auditing, teaching
    job programs for elders
    political advocacy groups for elders
    intergenerational groups
    arts and crafts

This large variety of topics illustrate educational avenues lifelong learning might take to assist understanding about government and community programs.

## Life Transitions

A third area of interest to elders is topics about life transitions such as retirement, death of a spouse, changing residences, or personal physical or mental setbacks. Life transitions are changes brought about by unpredictable and unpreventable life accidents (Sheehy, 1981). Elders may experience several life transitions in a short period of time. Since any single transition is a major source of stress, the combination of several abrupt and unexpected changes requires elders to develop coping skills to get through change with the assistance of personal support systems. Preparation can and should be made for life transitions prior to the time they occur (Sheehy, 1981). This preparation includes topics *about:*

    retirement preparation
    financial planning
    leisure time
    death and dying
    stress management
    grieving
    widowhood
    living alone
    congregate housing

retirement communities

role changes

intergenerational change in families

living with a family member

relocation

The prevalence of life transitions in the experiences of the elderly population suggests many topics about how elders can deal with change, topics well suited to the formal and informal educational pursuits of elders.


## Learning *In*

The discussion of purposes for lifelong learning and topics about ideas of interest to elders is incomplete without a discussion of where this learning can and does take place. Lifelong learning occurs in publicly designated areas and in private settings. The public places include locations such as YMCA's and YWCA's, churches and synagogues, community centers, senior centers, parks and recreation departments, museums, libraries, social groups, and professional organizations (Cross and Florio, 1978).

Additionally, educational opportunities are available through colleges and universities. Elders can get tuition free courses in 28 states and at 700 different colleges. Elders can audit or take classes for credit at most private and public colleges. Moreover, many colleges offer free admission for elders to cultural events, provide free assistance on legal matters or taxes, and offer special health services to elders.

Other colleges offer special programs such as Elderhostel to persons over 60. This program features one and two week classes where elders live and eat on campus while they attend classes. Every state has at least one Elderhostel program. Special educational institutes for retired persons are available at Mercyhurst College in Erie, Pennsylvania, Pace University in New York City, the University of San Francisco, Case Western Reserve in Cleveland, Ohio, the New School for Social Research in New York City, and Duke University in Durham, North Carolina. Some of these programs entitle elders to take special classes or to enroll in any university class at a reduced rate. Some universities offer special courses for elders taught by retired professors.

Other learning activities take place in private settings such as in conversations, private reading, museum and zoo tours, television and radio programs, visits to the homes of friends and relatives, or from inquiries made to businesses as a consumer.

The places in which learning occurs are not so much a matter of location as they are of attitude. If persons want to learn, make inquiry, understand how to use new information and experiences, and approach life with a receptive mind, they are likely to learn in most places where they spend their time.

The chapter's first three perspectives—for, about, and in—emphasize why, what, and where elders learn. The remaining three perspectives stress the role of communication in the process of learning. By communication, I mean the processes of speaking, listening, sending messages, giving feedback, and understanding the verbal and nonverbal symbols used to share meaning with others. For elders, this process involves learning with, through, and to.

## Learning *With*

Learning takes place both with age cohorts and between generations. Learning among age cohorts often increases age consciousness. That is, persons of the same generation disclose to each other their attitudes and past times, ways of coping with change, their approaches to leisure, and their experiences of family life. Through communication with age cohorts, elders gain a more complete view of what aging means to others and are likely to become conscious of the assets and liabilities of their own aging process.

Cherlin (1983) enunciates the importance of the elderly communicating with persons of other generations. He believes that intergenerational communication is the primary means for elders to be integrated into society, affirm their purpose, and give value and meaning to their lives.

Intergenerational communication among families gives the opportunity to persons of each generation to share experiences with each other. Quinn (1983) explains that intergenerational communication in families depends on several factors such as the degrees of affection and liking between family members, their ability to share thoughts and feelings, the confirmation and approval of family members' strengths and weaknesses, and the mutual ability of members to negotiate conflict.

Obviously, all of the conditions are not always present. Therefore, communication with family members is uneven; exchanges will sometimes be confirming and positive and at other times discussions may be disconfirming and negative. Despite the inevitable problems of intergenerational communication with families, persons of each generation report satisfaction with the relationships they have with members of a different generation (Burnett, 1984).

Elders learn from children the goals, directions, and values of the young. Elders learn from their adult children about the world of work and technology. In return, of course, adults and children learn from their elders.

Despite common assumptions, the interaction between generations of a family is frequent. Silverstone and Hyman (1976) report that three quarters of all the elderly have living children, that 85 percent of these have a child living less than an hour away, and that many elders see and talk to their children every day. Specifically then, elders' communication with children is frequent and makes an important connection between elders and society.

In particular, first and third generations of the same family are often called "generation gap allies" because their roles are similar to each other within the family. They both are a segregated age group, have little influence on decision making, and live in relatively unstructured time (Hartshorne and Monaster, 1982). The advantage of such interaction is to promote a sense of continuity between old and young so that the young understand what it means to be old and the old remember what youth was (Gore, 1976). Clearly, the old and young in families can learn from each other.

Communication with elders and persons of different generations outside of the family is also important. To achieve this goal, Field (1972) recommends that the young and old work together to implement ways and means for handling the problems that face both generations. Programs that bring together the old and young generate several kinds of learning. First, interaction between generations reduces negative stereotypes that one generation has about the other. For example, elders tend to see young people as disrespectful, unsympathetic, and lawless (Grosswith, 1982); young people view elders as unhealthy, lonely, resistant to change, and dependent (Dangott and Kalish, 1979). Second, more contact between generations increases understanding and appreciation of the other (Wood, 1982) so that the generations gain positive attitudes toward each other.

Communication with age cohorts, with other generations in the same family, and with other generations outside of the family shows the importance of relationships to the learning process.

## Learning *Through*

Elders learn through a variety of avenues such as traditional instruction in classrooms, interaction with others, personal reflection, leisure activities, and mass media. Earlier segments of this chapter have outlined places in which elders can learn through traditional teacher-student environments and through interactions with other persons. This section concentrates on how elders can learn through personal reflection and through the mass media, two avenues not usually considered as channels for learning.

## Personal Reflection

The first channel is personal reflection, that is, a systematic process of reviewing, assessing and interpreting the life experiences that a person has had. Gerontologists frequently label this type of reflection, "the life review." Specifically, Birren and Renner (1977) explain the process as involving five R's which can integrate the physical, mental, and spiritual dimensions of an elder's life.

The first R is *review*, an assessment of one's own present circumstance through the windows of the past. In a process of systematic reflection, the elder may review his or her life through the following questions. What have been the major events in my life? How has each of these events led me to include certain persons and values and, at the same time, exclude others? How have these events in my life contributed to who I am now? What are my great accomplishments and failures? What are my strongest personal resources?

The second R is *reconciliation*. This process encourages elders to understand the good and bad relationships they have had and to try to learn from these relationships. Reconciliation especially stresses working through the negative relationships, seeking to understand why they were negative, and trying to understand components of self through the way one has dealt with relationships.

A third R is *relevance*, that is, deciding what has been important in the past and choosing those alternatives that are of value to the present and future. This process discerns what is valuable and then contrasts the valued matters with those of little consequence. Deciphering relevance then is a way of recognizing and establishing priorities among values.

A fourth R is *reverence*, a recognition of the spiritual dimension in one's own life. This is a means for acknowledging the spiritual and transcendent feelings and experiences and using them to understand the meaning of life and death. Reflection on these matters is a type of meditation about the wonders of the universe and the mysteries and puzzles of one's own life and relationships.

The final R is *release*. This final means of reflection gives a type of catharsis for getting rid of resentments, letting go of jealousies, accepting loss of power, and willingness to become interdependent rather than dependent or independent. This release frees an elder's consciousness so that he or she can enjoy the role of their age group in society.

Books, diaries, oral histories, religious retreats, photo albums are all tangible vehicles that can be used by elders to work through the processes of review, reconciliation, relevance, reverence, and release. Unlike other methods of lifelong learning, reflection does not require a teacher other than self, a formal learning context, or new information; it simply enables elders to reflect on the meaning of their lives.

**Mass Media**

Learning can also occur through the media, an obvious but neglected resource for elderly learners. Davis and Davis (1985) report that the average person over 65 views 5 hours of television daily, prefers programs that present news and information, and responds to television as an effortless and convenient source for information. Davis and Davis (1985) also identify three uses of media by elders—entertainment, companionship, and passing time.

Despite the fact that most elderly watch a considerable amount of television, listen to radio daily, and read a daily newspaper, very little programming or column space is directed to issues specifically designed for elderly audiences such as health, government and community programs for elders, or age consciousness. Instead, the media target their contents to the entire population.

Several notable exceptions illustrate media concern for issues related to elderly. Some newspapers regularly print information about the activities of senior social groups, community centers, and meal sites, provide a daily advice column from U.S. Representative Claude Pepper on problems of elders, feature a weekly page entitled "Over Fifty," and give information about federal and state legislation and its potential or actual impact on elders.

Public television has in the past produced shows designed specifically for elders including "Over Easy," a magazine format show that ran for six years and "Old Friends, New Friends," a short-lived program about intergenerational relationships. Network television has recently cast well-known actors into positive roles about elderly characters such as George Burns in "Two of a Kind" and Bette Davis in "Right of Way."

Radio stations specializing in news and information frequently feature call-in programs, guests, or panels that deal with salient concerns of elders. However, in general, specialized information about the elderly and their concerns is the exception rather than the rule. As a result, the 28.3 million elderly viewers and readers in this country rely on media for information, but they receive very little information addressed directly to their needs and concerns. In the absence of specialized programming directed to elders, this population can still learn from existing information about consumer issues, politics, community affairs, and general health issues.

Although the content of the programming and column space is not directed to elders, they gain other insights through their uses of media. For example, elders find companions; that is, persons who are familiar and likeable individuals who provide parasocial relationships for them (Davis and Davis, 1985). Talk show personalities, television characters, radio personalities, and newspaper columnists can become substitutes for real relationships. Because elders feel that they know these media personalities well, the relationship of the media personalities to the elderly viewers approximates that of companions.

Another relational type of learning results from media use by elders. Davis and Davis (1985) note that listeners and readers use media as a way of "marking off time," a way of passing time that replaces the time related events associated with work schedules, coffee breaks, lunch, and committee meetings. Elders can mark off time by a morning radio program at 7:30 a.m., a game show on television at 10 a.m., radio news at noon, a television soap opera at 2 p.m., the arrival of the newspaper at 4:30 p.m., and The Bill Cosby Show on television at 7 p.m. Not only can media fill time for elders, but it can simultaneously provide information, entertainment, and companionship. In these ways, media work as avenues for education for the elderly.

## Learning *To*

A final characteristic of learning focuses directly on the communication skills elders need to succeed in lifelong education. To learn for (purpose), about (topics), in (where), with (how), and through (channels), elders need to be competent communicators.

Communicative competence is the ability of persons to interact effectively with others, to create and respond to verbal and nonverbal messages. More specifically, Bochner and Kelly (1974) list three general principles of communicative competence. These include "(1) ability to formulate and achieve objectives; (2) ability to collaborate effectively with others..., and (3) ability to adapt to situational and environmental variations" (p. 288). Each of these skills assist elders to learn.

Learning is most productive when elders set some objectives for themselves or when others set objectives for them. Achieving these objectives then becomes a marker, an indication of new knowledge, skill, or attitudes acquired by elders. For example, instead of thinking about the past, elders can do a systematic life review. Instead of tuning in randomly to watch television, elders can establish objectives to learn about a particular show or artist or watch a five-part series on a particular subject. Elders might have as their objective to learn more about medigap insurance, and they might pursue that goal by asking other elders about their coverage, seeking information on the subject through the newspapers, or attending a lecture on the subject at a local senior center.

Lifelong learners follow the principles of communicative competence by specifying objectives and then searching for the means available to achieve those objectives. Although this approach does not deny the fact that some learning is accidental and spontaneous, it does elmphasize that elderly learners should not expect knowledge to flow mysteriously in their direction. The pursuit of knowledge is intentional and demands active participation by the learner.

Learners benefit from their abilities to collaborate with others. By collaboration, I mean an attitude of joint participation in the experience of learning. This attitude results in giving messages and accepting and respecting the messages received from others. Using collaborative communication permits the learner to be an active agent in the learning process. Collaborative communication involves asking questions, seeking clarification, listening empathically, giving frequent and appropriate feedback, taking turns at talking and responding, discouraging interruptions, and participating fully in the verbal and nonverbal exchanges that result in learning.

An example of collaborative learning is illustrated in the following scenario. An elderly woman, May recently lost her spouse. She read about a workshop on bereavement sponsored by the local Methodist church. She made a reservation and attended the workshop. When she arrived, the workshop was preceded by a coffee reception. May introduced herself, inquired to the other participants about their backgrounds and reasons for attending. She shared with them the recent loss of her husband and related the difficulties she was experiencing. Other participants, in turn, shared their experiences with her. A counselor, minister, and doctor presented a panel discussion on the subject. May took notes, wrote down questions, and made notations of her personal reactions. When a small group discussion followed the panel, May offered her reactions, sought reactions from other group members, expressed her support of their feelings, and acknowledged the value of others' experiences. At the close of the day, May was very satisfied with the workshop. She had been an active participant, a competent communicator, and consequently learned a great deal from the experience.

Finally, learners need to adapt to different situations and environments for learning. This begins when learners seek enough information so that they understand the norms of the learning context. It is quite clear that a formal classroom setting is substantially different from a political forum or a guided tour of a museum. Besides situational norms, elders need to adapt to the differing roles and intensities of interaction that distinguish an intergenerational family celebration from a neighborhood meeting on safety conducted by a local police officer. In each learning situation, the learner needs to adjust so that his or her interaction fits the context. A competent communicator selectively chooses the pattern of responses that best fits the norms, roles, and channels of a particular context.

Lifelong learning is a worthwhile quest for all learners of all generations. For elders, education is an opportunity for them to take advantage of recent policy decisions on education, health, and aging to improve their knowledge about their role in society. Several distinct advantages result from lifelong education. First, this approach assists elders to achieve goals for themselves related to age consciousness, independence, and involvement. Second, lifelong education provides an opportunity for learning about salient topics. Third, these learning opportunities are readily available in formal, informal, and private settings. Fourth, learning can occur with age cohorts or between elders and other generations inside the family or within the community. Fifth, learning occurs through many channels including private reflection and through mass media. Finally, lifelong learning is most successful when elders define objectives, act as collaborates, and adjust to the learning style of particular contexts.

## ❧ 16 ❧

# Elder Abuse
# and Communication

## Robert Hawkins and Anthony Traxler

The elderly face a number of problems in society today: low income, lack of transportation, inadequate housing, unreasonable fuel costs, unafford-able medical care, and elder abuse. For each of these problems, communi-cation plays a significant role. Oral and written advocacy is used by large organizations and individual service providers. For example, the American Association of Retired Persons has been leading the crusade at the national level through lobbying and political activism to force utility companies to develop fairer policies for older adults' home fuel payments. Social workers represent individual clients in arguing for protection in the face of family abuse and neglect as well as for specific benefits related to the medicare program. In the final analysis, however, it is the individual older person him/herself who must, in many cases, "make his/her own case" with his/her own family or with state and local agencies. Thus an understanding of the process and skills of communication is necessary in any program to help older persons to cope with these difficulties.

To attempt a thorough analysis of the communication dimensions of all the social problems or even the major problems faced by the elderly is beyond the scope of this chapter. We have selected the topic of elder abuse and shall study it in some detail. The rationale for this selection is that elder abuse is recognized by most gerontologists and health care professionals as an increasingly important social problem for seniors today (Quinn and

Tomita, 1986). It is our hope that our readers will translate what we say about communication and elder abuse into terms that can be applied to the other social issues listed above.

Further, we shall concentrate on one particular area of elder abuse, namely that found in the family. There are, of course, instances of institutional abuse (e.g., nursing homes) and a myriad other contexts (the market place, medical services, politics, etc.) in which older adults' rights and safety are infringed upon. It is in the multigenerational family, however, that we find a significantly large majority of cases of elder abuse. Thus, while we confine our consideration to the multi-generation family circle: mother, father, aged grandparent(s), son(s), and daughter(s), the discussions should have applications in other contexts.

## Scope of the Problem

In 1978, the House Select Committee on Aging initiated the first Congressional examination of elder abuse in the United States. The Committee's landmark report published in 1981 entitled, *Elder Abuse: An Examination of a Hidden Problem,* forcefully called attention to the issues of elder abuse. (U.S. Congress, House, 1981) The Committee's report indicated that over 1,000,000 older Americans are physically, financially and emotionally abused by their loved ones, relatives and other caregivers annually. This examination of elder abuse also revealed that elder abuse was a hidden problem and that only one of every six elder abuse victims comes to the attention of the appropriate authorities.

A 1985 study conducted by the Subcommittee on Health and Long-Term Care of the House Select Committee on Aging entitled *Elder Abuse: A National Disgrace,* underscored the findings of the 1981 study and indicated that abuse of the elderly was increasing nationally, resulting in approximately four percent of the nation's elderly becoming victims of abuse. (U.S. Congress, House, 1985) This represents an increase of 100,000 abuse cases annually since 1981.

### Definitions

What is elder abuse? How does one define it? These are important questions that need to be addressed in any study, discussion or intervention program. Galbraith (1986), Quinn and Tomita (1986), and others have pointed out that definitional problems are perhaps the most significant impediment in the development of an adequate knowledge base on elder abuse. There are considerable variations in the definitions of elder abuse within the research literature and state statutes (Traxler, 1986), making it difficult to compare findings from study to study and to establish effective elder abuse intervention programs. Douglass and Hickey (1983) point out that the meaning of the term abuse is generally avoided or confused with the term neglect and have stressed the need to differentiate between these two terms. Douglass, Hickey and Noel (1980) defined neglect in terms of active and passive and suggested that the actions or inactions of the caregivers formed the basis for definitions. O'Malley, et al., (1983) distinguish abuse from neglect on the basis of intent. Thus abuse is an act of commission whereas neglect refers to an act of omission.

In most states, the definition of abuse includes physical injury or the infliction of pain caused by accident. Some states list sexual abuse and assault as a subcategory under physical abuse.

Research indicates that the abuses sustained by the elderly are generally suffered at the hands of their family, relatives or caregivers. Caregivers are unrelated individuals placed in the role of providing care and services to the elderly; the need for a caregiver frequently results from the absence of living relatives or someone to accept responsibility.

Listed below are definitions of abuse frequently appearing in the state statutes (Traxler, 1986). These definitions are highlighted with case studies reported in the research conducted by the House of Representatives Select Committee on Aging (U.S. Congress, House, 1985).

> *Physical Abuse:* The infliction of physical injury or pain not caused by accident.
>
> A woman from Nevada related the abuse of her mother by her sister. When the abuses were reported to the legally appointed guardian, who was a good friend of the sister, they were ignored. The mother was beaten; when she was incontinent, feces were rubbed in her face as punishment. The abusive daughter would not allow a visiting nurse to clear or examine the mother who suffered from bed sores. When she was finally taken to the hospital, the mother died as a result of complications from abusive treatment by the daughter, who by this time had depleted the estate of the mother.
>
> *Negligence:* May be defined as the breach of duty or carelessness that results in injury or the violation of rights.
>
> *Financial Exploitation:* Involves the theft or conversion of money or objects of value belonging to an elderly person by a relative or caretaker. It may be accomplished by force or through misrepresentation.
>
> A heartbroken 88-year-old grandmother from New York trusted her most beloved grandson with everything she owned. She is now destitute because the grandson has taken everything she entrusted to his care. Up to this point the elderly woman had never

needed or accepted outside financial help and now she feels hurt and embarrassed that this is her only means of survival at her age.

*Psychological Abuse:* At one end of the spectrum, psychological abuse includes simple name calling, verbal assaults and threats of placement in a nursing home. At the other end, it is a protracted and systematic effort to dehumanize the elderly. Usually, psychological abuse is accompanied by other types of abuse.

An elderly woman in Oregon was forbidden by her daughter-in-law from seeing her three grandchildren although they lived less than 2 miles away. She overheard telephone conversations in which the daughter-in-law told one of the grandchildren "Grandma is crazy" and "Grandma hates you. She never wants to see you again."

*Violation of Rights:* The breaching of rights that are guaranteed to all citizens by the Constitution, federal statutes, federal courts, and the states. This includes the right to personal liberty, adequate medical treatment, not to have one's property taken without due process of law, the right to freedom from forced labor, etc.

A California case involved a middle-aged man and his sister who were arrested for holding their 90-year-old aunt a prisoner for four years in a metal shed behind their house. The neighbors ignored her cries for help because the sister said she was crazy.

Oklahoma officials reported a case where the title to a woman's home had been turned over to her son, an attorney, apparently without the woman's knowledge or permission. Caseworkers were unable to restore title of the home because of the unavailability of legal assistance.

*Neglect:*

1. *Active:* Withholding of needed medicine, food, clothing, housing, social contact, assistance with daily functions (Bath, toilet, etc.)

An 84-year-old woman from Washington, D.C., terminally ill of cancer, was denied proper medical attention by her grandson because he didn't want to "dissipate" her income and property on hospital and doctors' bills.

2. *Passive:* The failure to provide an elderly person with the necessities of life, such as food, clothing, shelter or medical care because of a failure to understand the elder's needs, lack of awareness of services to help meet needs, or a lack of capacity to care for the elderly.

3. *Self-Neglect:* Includes self-inflicted physical harm and the failure to take care of one's personal needs. More succinctly, the elderly person is taking actions or failing to take actions that are jeopardizing his/her health.

A 67-year-old Texas woman was reported to be lying in her bed hemorrhaging profusely and in severe pain. She had refused medical assistance because she had no income or insurance. Family members and friends had been unsuccessful in convincing her to enter a hospital, even though "free services" had been arranged. Only after she was found lying on the floor unable to move did she accept hospitalization. Within a month, after other hospital admissions, an SSI application and plans for nursing home care, she died in a hospital.

## Nature and Dimensions of the Problem

Representative Claude Pepper, a long-time advocate of America's elderly and Chairman of the Subcommittee on Health and Long-Term Care, U.S. House Select Committee on Aging, has stated that the phrase "elder abuse" still sends shock waves among the majority of Americans since it flies in the face of traditional American ideals built around the concept of a strong, caring and supportive family structure. However, Stearns (1986), in a historical review of old age family conflict, pointed out that familial conflict surrounding the elderly in Western society is not just a contemporary phenomenon. Nevertheless, today's demographic revolution pertaining to the "graying of America" has heightened the visibility of any problems or issues surrounding the older adult population. In 1985, there were 28.5 million persons 65 years or older, representing 12% of the U.S. population. By the year 2030, there will be 65 million persons over the age of 65. Never before have so many individual families had as many elderly relatives to deal with in some capacity.

Moreover, the explosive growth of the old-old population (85 + ), with its increased need for medical, economic and social support can be a demanding experience and a major burden for many families.

Societal factors, in addition to the sheer increase in numbers, which predispose families and caregivers to elder abuse include: (1) changes in the young-old ratio which affects support for many programs for the elderly such as social security, retirement and various pension programs; (2) the fact that the elderly fared better economically during the 1970s than other segments of the population, fueling potential antagonism over generational equity issues; (3) a tendency toward segregating the elderly due to residential separation; (4) societal attitudes and stereotypes about aging and the elderly which depict the aging as generally incompetent, helpless and dependent persons; and (5) the traditional position in society which states that behavior inside the home is a private affair and that one's home should be a sanctuary from governmental interference of any kind. The position that behavior in the home is a private affair is so strong that it works to prevent victims from seeking help.

Quinn and Tomita (1986) point out that many older people are concerned about their family's privacy and the privacy of their relationships. For this reason, they do not report the abuse and neglect they are suffering, and they often tell practitioners they do not want to take any action against the abuser. The thought of public exposure, the embarassment, shame and humiliation at having raised a child who would hurt them in any way is a tremendous blow to the older person's ego. Often the elder abuse victim prefers to suffer in silence rather than to break the family code of solidarity by sharing his plight with others outside the family circle (Jacobs, 1984). The victim may also fear, quite realistically, that the abuser or perpetrator will retaliate with further mistreatment if the abuse is reported. Quinn and Tomita (1986) report that victims of elder abuse and neglect also worry that reporting may mean incarceration for the perpetrator who may be the only caretaker or represent the only relationship the elder has. Moreover, many older persons feel that their only alternative to the abusive situation within a family context is nursing home placement, a fate which they view as more threatening and less acceptable than their current abusive environment.

Elder abuse victims often fear rejection and the loss of affection of their abusers and this fear of rejection may be even more intolerable than the abusive relationship. Older female abuse victims who have had a history of unassertive behavior find it especially difficult to report their plight.

## Characteristics of the Elder Abuse Victims

Research on elder abuse (Block & Sinnott, 1979; Douglass, Hickey & Noel, 1980; Lau & Kosberg, 1979; O'Malley, et al., 1979; Crouse, et al., 1981; Pillemer & Wolf, 1986; Quinn & Tomita, 1986; Galbraith, 1986) has produced a fairly consistent profile of the potentially abused older victim, the abuser and forms of elder abuse that result from their interactions. For example, the typical elder abuse victim is a frail, physically or mentally impaired white female 75+ years of age who is living with a relative on whom she is highly dependent for her daily needs.

Important exceptions to the typical elder abuse case certainly occur, and practitioners need to be cognizant of this. Older men, elderly couples, wealthy elderly persons and even individuals in good health may find themselves victims of abuse and neglect.

## Characteristics of the Abuser

The typical perpetrator of elder abuse is likely to be a relative of the elderly victim. A son, daughter or spouse experiencing stresses due to the lack of financial, social and psychological resources are prime candidates. The abuser is often dependent either psychologically or economically on the elder abuse victim and may feel "trapped" and "overloaded" if the victim requires extensive care such as the Alzheimer's patient. Alcohol and/or drug abuse is also a frequent characteristic among the abusers (Galbraith, 1986).

## Sources of Stress and Change in the Lives of Older Persons and Their Families

Edinberg (1986) points to the importance of age-related events such as chronic illnesses and disability (including senile dementia), divorce, death, moving in with family, institutionalization and role reversal which may cause stress for older persons as they and their families age. He suggests that while each potential stressor may have dramatic consequences for the older person, these are likely to cause equally consequential changes in family functioning. In addition to the above factors, Cicirelli (1986) points to the increasing egocentrism of older people, their increasing disinhibition of certain negative behaviors that were repressed or otherwise controlled during earlier years (such as screaming and yelling, name-calling, and hitting), and the loss of power that often accompanies aging. He indicated that older people often become absorbed in their own concerns and needs and show less interest in others, thereby making it more difficult for them to see the perspective of the other person and to negotiate a compromise solution to a conflict situation. Yelling, name-calling, etc., not only increases the likelihood of conflict, but also engenders negative feeling in the caregiver. The loss of power coordinates with the phenomenon of role reversal wherein the adult child becomes a major source of emotional and material support for an older parent.

## Identifying Elder Abuse and Neglect

As indicated earlier in this chapter, a significant impediment in the development of an adequate knowledge base on elder abuse and neglect is deciding exactly what constitutes abuse and neglect. Both researchers and practitioners must confront definitional problems and concomitant issues in the identification of elder abuse and neglect. Hudson (1986) states that "Basic questions are still unanswered regarding what is and is not, elder neglect or abuse." In her review of current research, she points out that some of the studies provided extrinsic definitions (typologies) without formulating an intrinsic definition (conceptulization). This situation leads to illustrations of the concept of elder abuse and neglect without having first defined it. Hudson indicated that there seems to be the assumption that the intrinsic meaning of elder abuse and neglect are understood, creating a tautology: elder abuse and neglect are often lumped together and defined as elder abuse and neglect!

## Identifying the Communication Correlates
## of Elder Abuse and Neglect

The communicative behaviors manifested in elder abuse cases may generally be categorized as verbal and nonverbal. We have already noted examples of the verbal spoken messages, probably uttered in anger and dispair: "Grandma is crazy; she hates you; she never wants to see you again."

Nonverbal factors include the paralanguage of screaming, yelling, and strident name-calling; the physical behaviors of gesturing with fists and flailing arms, hitting and beating; and the "non-behaviors" of remaining silent for prolonged periods of time, and the withholding of food, shelter, clothing, and medical attention. Such nonverbal phenomena are clear examples of two basic axioms in communication theory: (1) human actions in interpersonal contexts carry meaning and (2) no matter how hard we try, we cannot not communicate (Watzlawick, Beavin, & Jackson, 1967).

Further communicative indicators in families in which elder abuse and neglect exist may be extrapolated from the work of Galvin and Brommel (1986). Their research has dealt with the language of conflict in family settings. Both covert and overt conflict are examined. *Covert,* or hidden conflict, usually relies on one or more of the following strategies: denial, disqualification, displacement, disengagement, and pseudomutuality. *Denial* is manifested in such words as: "Forget it, it's no big deal; No, you didn't harm me," or "Everything's OK, I'm fine!" accompanied by contradictory nonverbal signals. *Disqualification* occurs when a person expresses anger and then discounts, or disqualifies, the angry reaction. "I'm sorry, I was angry about your being late and got carried away," or "I wouldn't have gotten so upset except that your mother was really making unreasonable demands on my time." *Displacement* occurs when an individual cannot bring himself to vent his anger on his ailing mother-in-law, whose demands have broken his patience, and therefore he transfers his hostility to his wife or children. *Disengagement* is seen in the behavior of the couple who continue with an empty, just-barely-alive relationship because they choose not to confront each other with anger over their unresolved bitter disagreement as to whether their aged parents should be placed in a nursing home. *Psuedomutuality* is just the opposite of *disengagement.* Pseudomutuality occurs when the family members make every effort possible to cover up their conflict by "putting on a happy face." This is sometimes referred to as the "peace at all costs" strategy. Eventually the costs surface in the form of ulcers, nervous disorders, and bizaare behavior.

The next step after identifying elder abuse and neglect and its communication correlates is to discuss prevention and intervention techniques and their communication dimensions.

# A Prevention and Communication Approach to the Problem of Elder Abuse and Neglect

## The Concept of Prevention: General Considerations

The concept of prevention derives from the public health movement and more recently the community mental health and the health and wellness movements. Prevention indicates an action that stops something from happening. Theoretically, it means doing something so that problems will not develop. Prevention may be defined on three levels: (1) primary, (2) secondary and (3) tertiary. *Primary prevention* includes health promotion and specific protection. Examples of health promotion are health education and motivation that concern the general health and well-being of the aging population and are not directed at any particular disease or disorder. Examples of specific protection include such measures as sound nutrition and sanitation practices. Thus, primary prevention encompasses those activities directed to specifically identified, vulnerable, high-risk groups within the community for whom measures can be taken to avoid the onset of conflict, abuse and neglect and to enhance their level of effective functioning.

The practitioner working within a prevention framework would pay particular attention to the impact of change, and subsequent stress, in the lives of older persons and their families as discussed earlier in this chapter. Also, they should be cognizant of the profiles of the typical elder abuse victim and the abuser. There are many high-risk situations that offer fertile ground for conflict, neglect and abuse. For example, some caregivers are incapable of caring for a dependent elder because of their own problems which might include alcohol and drug abuse. Other caregivers may have poor mental health, financial problems or very little understanding of the abilities and disabilities of the older person entrusted to their care. Unfortunately, the match between the older person and his caregiver is often a poor one, and thus the potential for abuse and neglect to occur is high. The alert and knowledgeable practitioner functioning within a prevention framework is in a better position to help prevent and to intervene in elder abuse and neglect cases. The primary prevention framework would include education and training for potential abusers as well as for elder abuse victims. Since most abuse and neglect occurs within the family context, the family would necessarily be the focus of the educational interventions. Social service and health care professionals and paraprofessionals working with the elderly in the community and institutional settings would also be included as part of educational interventions.

Communicative perspectives on the educational intervention associated with primary prevention may be inferred from the work of DeVito (1986).

He presents two models of interpersonal communication that are at work in the lives of people who are centered and who are well-adjusted to one another. It is fair to assume, moreover, that he would include multi-generation families who have been trained, or who have trained themselves, to be well-functioning and interpersonally communicative.

DeVito's first model is characterized by certain humanistic values which may be listed as follows: supportiveness, positiveness, equality, openness, empathy. Each of these factors will be discussed in turn.

*Supportiveness.*    Jack Gibb (1961) has developed this concept in careful detail. He argues that families can develop supportiveness among themselves by being descriptive rather than evaluative, spontaneous rather than strategic and provisional rather than certain. Within the category of supportiveness, three subtopics should be addressed. *Descriptiveness.* This factor helps to develop a supportive climate. When we perceive an incoming message from a family member as being a description of another person, a situation, a feeling, or an idea, we are not apt to feel as threatened as we would if we perceived that message as being a judgment or evaluation. *Spontaneity.* A spontaneous rather than a strategic style also helps to develop supportiveness. Most of us feel threatened if we sense that another person is employing some kind of strategem to manipulate our behavior. *Provisionalism.* This value stresses an open-minded, tentative approach rather than an approach of certainty which, in effect, calls for an end to the debate. The person who "has all the answers" and is unwilling to accept an alternative plan, does not contribute much to a climate of supportiveness in intergenerational family communication.

*Positiveness.*    We communicate positiveness in interpersonal communication by stating positive attitudes and "stroking" the person with whom we interact. The two key elements are *positive attitudes* and *stroking.* A positive attitude toward the aging person can do much to lift the spirits and enhance the positiveness of family communication. Everyone, regardless of age, wants and needs to be stroked, to be made to feel positive about themselves. This holds true in all families and certainly in the family with an older parent who senses a growing alienation from younger family members.

*Equality.*    Complete equality is probably never possible, but effectiveness in interpersonal communication can be improved if the communicators can see themselves as equal partners rather than as partners with differing amounts of power or influence.

*Openness.*    Openness is another humanistic value that characterizes the interpersonal communication of a well-functioning, multi-generation family. There are three factors involved here. The first is openness to self. This implies being honest and straightforward with oneself in communicating with another family member. The second is openness to the other person. This implies being willing to see the other person as worthwhile and valuable in his/her own right. The third factor is openness to the other's messages. This implies being careful to take in what is being communicated as well as *how* it is being communicated, without judging and evaluating.

*Empathy.* Empathy refers to the capacity to "feel in" with another person. The key concept here is that of identification. One who is empathic tries to identify with the feelings that another is experiencing.

DeVito's second model suggests that a well-functioning, interpersonally communicative multi-generation family is characterized by certain pragmatic or behavioral values. These may be listed as follows: confidence, immediacy, interaction management, expressiveness, and other-orientation. *Confidence* connotes a feeling of comfortableness, an at-east feeling and an avoidance of self-consciousness. ("It feels good spending the afternoon with you, Grandma."). *Immediacy* suggests a sense of contact and togetherness, a feeling of interest and liking. ("So that's how your father taught you to ride a horse! Interesting!"). *Interaction management* suggests the control of interaction to the satisfaction of both parties; the managing of conversational turns, oral fluency, and message consistency. ("It's easy talking with you; I can so easily follow what you're saying."). *Expressiveness* indicates genuine involvement in speaking and listening, expressed verbally and nonverbally. ("Gosh, grandson, the time just flies when we're talking."). Finally *other-orientation* suggests attentiveness, interest and concern for the other. ("Tell me more about what you did when you were growing up in the 1920s."). [For further comment on the importance of relational communication in families trying to cope with elder abuse, see Winter (1986) and Quinn and Tomita (1986).]

With these two models of communication in mind, let us continue with secondary and tertiary prevention strategies.

*Secondary prevention* of elder abuse includes early diagnosis of a disorder or problem and prompt treatment or intervention. The aim of this level is to relieve distress and to shorten duration of the disorder or problem and to reduce symptoms generated by the abuse and neglect. Secondary prevention can be especially effective when both the abused elder and his abuser have relatively good coping skills and adequate resources at their disposal. Unfortunately, by the time the practitioner gets involved in elder abuse and neglect cases, the situation has escalated beyond the secondary prevention level.

*Tertiary prevention* is focused mainly on chronic and serious illness and other problems and includes attempts to reduce pain and suffering. The preventive measures in the tertiary level are primarily therapeutic and are directed toward the patient in order to arrest the disease process or problem situation and to prevent further complication. The positive objective of tertiary prevention is to return the affected individuals to a useful place in society and make maximum use of their remaining capacities. At the tertiary level, abuse and neglect is obviously apparent and in many cases the practitioner will be required to provide information which will result in the elder being removed from the abuser and the abusive environment.

It will now be helpful to identify those communication skills that can be used to manage the conflicts inherent in situations requiring secondary and tertiary prevention. The five steps to follow in conflict resolution are: 1) define the conflict; 2) define possible decisions; 3) test the decisions; 4) evaluate the decisions, and 5) accept or reject a particular decision (DeVito, 1986). Application of these steps to communication strategies might include the following.

1) *Define the conflict.* This requires careful, honest, and open communication. Too often the parties to a conflict want to discuss the solution before they have fully communicated with one another what the conflict is all about. Thus, a couple might define their conflict in terms of long-standing psychological abuse heaped upon an aged grandparent by ungrateful and spoiled grandchildren. Let us assume that the couple has been so busy with their own lives that they have completely ignored the way their children have been acting toward their grandparents.

2) *Define possible decisions.* We do not use the word "solution" because there is no guarantee that a solution can be reached. Possible decisions, which might result in a lessening of the conflict, should be considered. Returning to our hypothetical case above, decisions could be considered which would either remove the aged parent from the company of the grandchildren or confront the grandchildren directly to persuade them to cease their malicious behavior. Another possible decision could involve the determination to arrange the couple's lifestyle so that they could spend more time with both their children and their aged parents.

3) *Test the decisions.* This testing process would involve the careful "checking out" of the decisions. Thus, assuming the decision is for the parents to spend more time with both grandparents and grandchildren, the parameters would have to be carefully explained and understood by all parties concerned. Of course, if the decision fails, then the next best decision would need to be tested.

4) *Evaluate the decision.* These questions would have to be asked: Does the decision "feel" right? Does it make for improved interpersonal communication? Does it significantly lessen the conflict?

5) *Accept or reject the decision.* This implies staying with the decision to give it an adequate test. If the decision fails, then it needs to be rejected and a search for a new one should commence.

For further study, Beebe and Masterson (1986) offer an excellent introduction to the management of conflict in multi-generation families.

This chapter has highlighted the problem of elder abuse and neglect and the role that communication plays in dealing with the problem. We have seen how gerontologists, other practitioners, and older adults themselves, all working within a multidisciplinary prevention framework, can apply communication skills to the tasks before them by working within a multi-disciplinary prevention framework.

# Part V
# THE RESEARCH CHALLENGE

Part V discusses research issues in communication and aging. The first issue is the scattered nature of much of the research which has often not addressed identifiable central themes. Chapter 17 illustrates how meta-analysis can be used to draw scattered lines of research together to identify an overarching theme, in this case autonomy. Chapter 18 examines methodological considerations in communication and aging which must be addressed in order to move the research agenda forward.

# ❧ 17 ❧

# Communication Research on Autonomy and Aging

## Paul Fritz

## Introduction

How does aging affect communication? What do we know about communication and aging? What do we still need to know about communication and aging? The answers to these questions would be a godsend to health professionals, community leaders, and businesses. If health professionals knew the intricate cues aging persons use to encode motivations, physicians and nurses could provide more sensitive care. Media specialists, architects, retailers, and political leaders could offer services fostering independent living if they knew how aging persons perceived their environment and communicated those perceptions to others. Providing answers to these questions would also generate entire career paths (Edmonson, 1985) for communication students and researchers patient enough to engage in systematic observations among aging persons.

These questions beg communication researchers for answers. Much existing research tends to focus on the stereotype held by youth about how frail and dependent elders are. Communication scholars might provide a valuable service by focusing on ways to enhance aging persons' independence. This chapter will survey some current research topics in the literature and will suggest ways to enhance our research of the communication patterns of aging persons as they strive to retain personal autonomy.

## Autonomy and Aging

Where does one begin researching the communication patterns among the aging? The relevant topics appear myriad: elder abuse, crime, nutrition, forced retirement, social security benefits.

There appears to be no easy way of organization by discrete categories. However, a pervasive theme dominating the literature is "How do aging persons preserve their autonomy?" (Achenbaum, 1986; Pifer, 1986). This theme is depicted on a continuum with increasing intensity as the person ages. At one end, aging persons prepare for retirement and collect resources they think they will need to preserve their autonomy during leisure years. At last they can do as they please unincumbered by the constraints of house mortgages or providing children with costly college educations. The more these persons age the more they become concerned with the preservation and stewardship of autonomy. How persons express that need is a relevant theme for communication and aging research.

At the other end of the continuum are aged persons in sheltered care facilities who are still able to express their needs for autonomy. Although they may not have the wide array of choices enjoyed in previous years, they still need to express free choice in selecting preferred foods, roommates, health care options, or favored nurses. These choices give life meaning and order. Since communication is a major means for maintaining autonomy, many topics of communication and aging are really dimensions of how this theme appears in communication patterns.

### Living Arrangements

How can elders be assisted to cope with independent living and stay in their own home? Phillips and Roman (1984) and Harvey (1983) argue that elders can be independent and can be taught how to cope with living alone. Smithers (1985) examined 245 case histories of elders in a residential hotel to determine how they maintained independence. Boston (1985) provides practical suggestions to explain how homes could be made more suitable for independent elders. The Urban Institute (1983) illustrates how elders can adjust the architecture of their homes to facilitate independent living. These design needs are discussed in detail in Duffy and Willson (1984) and Birch (1985). Bender (1987) discusses how a kitchen is often made into a formidable trap; dangers include cabinets which are difficult to open and heavy objects. Convincing aging persons to alter their homes or apartments is a communication goal and a research topic. A wealth of useful information is available for aging persons to use.

Wister (1985) examined how living patterns affect the communication networks of the elderly. Mindel and Wright (1985) differentiated the speech patterns of those who live alone from those who live with relatives. Two extensive surveys should not be overlooked. Nasar and Farokhpay (1985) and Riddick (1985) surveyed elders to learn what they wanted from housing and how elders spoke about housing needs in conjunction with their health needs.

How do elders obtain groceries and household supplies when they do not have access to transportation? What effect does dependence have on the communication quality of persons forced to live within walking range of their staples and groceries? How do residents join forces for protection or building improvement? What are the range and variety of topics discussed by persons who have access to community events? Communication researchers would serve the community well by surveying elders who live independently. How do these elders elicit help from non-relatives? How do these elders prevent isolation? What discourse patterns characterize unhappy and satisfied elders who live alone?

## Assisted Care

Convincing elders that they need some assisted care may be another area of communication research. The main problem lies in identifying the assisted care needs of elders. At the present time, this identification is minimal. Day care may meet a need of persons too frail to live alone but who have some transportation assistance.

Arling, et al. (1984) help to distinguish between elders who need day care and those who need long term care. Meinke (1984) discusses how to train staff members to supervise a day care center and Butrin (1985) describes how nurses can elicit community support for day care centers. An excellent case study on establishing and maintaining a day care center is given in Neustadt (1985).

Home care is another fruitful area for research. Market surveys indicate that home care will become a greater necessity as families find they are unable to afford long term care. It is estimated that ninety percent of all elder care will be home care in the next two decades (Day, 1985; deLaski-Smith, 1984; Halamandaris, 1985). The literature contains helpful articles on how nurses can train home caregivers (Hewner, 1986), how cognitive therapy is used to help elders redefine their situation (Jarrett, 1985), how role play helps to train caregivers (Levine, et al., 1984), and how to adjust the elder's behavior to fit the patterns of the family (Linsk and Pinkston, 1984).

An excellent case study produced by the Andrus Foundation describes sixty-four elders and their caregivers as they attempt to wrestle with "guilt" (Todd, 1984). This feeling is common among both caregivers (Who may feel they should be doing more for their relatives) and the elders (who may fear they are unwanted burdens to host families). These studies could enhance our understanding of aging persons by identifying, explaining, and testing the delicate conversational strategies aging persons may use when they move in with a caregiving family. Communication researchers can help identify strategies aging persons use in this new environment to express independence. From what we know of group expectations toward new members, we may assume aging persons would function far more productively in family units if they were treated as if they were capable of maintaining some type of independent living. Stoller (1985) used path analysis to learn the salient variables elders used when speaking with their primary caregivers and identified "control contests" used by caregivers and care recipients. Elders' participation in contests for control in the family environment were also studied by Corbin and Strauss (1985).

Many programs exist to help elders cope with the task of sheltered living. Hoffman (1985) discusses an innovative program called the Hilltop Alternative Homesharing Program which matches elders discharged from hospitals to homes where they may receive temporary care. Many caregivers are not aware of the various services and products which can be purchased to alleviate the drudgery of home sanitation needs, drug administration needs and monitoring devices. Edmonson (1985) describes how pharmacists can disseminate information for home care providers on medications, infusion therapy, disposables, and home respiratory units.

Senior centers provide another excellent opportunity for communication researchers to study discourse patterns. Schneider, et al. (1985) learned that persons who were active in a senior center were not at high risk for institutionalization and were active communicators. Yet other scholars complain that essential communication needs may not be met by these centers. Krout (1985) noted that many senior centers did not offer programs on the most frequently requested topics: counseling and income supplement.

Life care centers (sometimes called retirement communities) provide an excellent way for aging persons to obtain a sheltered environment and yet maintain autonomy. Morrison (1985) discusses the legal regulations attached to retirement communities. Thompson and Swisher (1983) and Hartwigsen (1984/85) focus on the environmental features of a retirement center that enhance autonomy. Unanswered are questions such as: What common strategies help elders to smooth the transition to assisted care? What types of training programs would assist elders in this transition? What types of persons do well in assisted care scenes and how do they communicate? We need *synthesis* studies of aging persons in these environments. We have abundant "analysis" studies which examine one or two components of home care or of a senior center. What communication scholars really need are studies that examine how the full range of components in a research setting fit together as a whole. How the aging person communicates to integrate or differentiate the components of his or her environment is a topic communication scholars should study.

## Retirement

Retirement has been studied from a variety of perspectives: history of retirement (Brahce, 1983), changes in behavior in retirement (Birren, et al., 1986), how marriages cope with retirement (Cassidy, 1985) and expectations toward retirement (Schnore, 1985). A few synthesis studies emerge on this topic.

Roza (1985) interviewed retirees in a phased retirement program to classify successful and unsuccessful participants. Hornstein and Wapner (1985) surveyed retirees and described coping techniques for four phases of retirement. Retirement satisfaction may be linked to a specific scene. To aid our understanding of retirement and to generate large amounts of data for the same scene, communication researchers should compile case studies on one organization to determine how satisfied retirees perceive their environment and speak about it. What do these persons perceive as threatening their autonomy; how do they speak about it? What do these persons believe would enhance their autonomy; how do they speak about it?

## Widowhood

Widowhood has been studied in a variety of settings. However, more investigations need to focus on communication problems and not on the widows' attitudes. Hagestad (1986) decries the "only stand and wait" or "kin-keeper" role widows may be forced to accept upon the death of a husband. The entire issue of *Journal of Geriatric Psychiatry* addressed problems experienced by homemakers returning to the workplace after a husband's death (Displaced Homemaker, 1982).

Kennedy and Silverman (1984/85) learned that older women fear crime but that interaction with others helps to reduce that fear. Communication researchers need to know what types of interactions alleviate these fears. Ferraro (1984) discovered that the loss of a spouse intensified social interactions. The literature today focuses on how women can equip themselves to change roles prior to the death of a husband (Hagestad, 1986). Apparently, strategies of independence must be learned in marriage long before death severs a relationship.

## Networks

Networks and group information processing are fruitful ways of studying the communication processes of aging persons. Ward (1985) and Sauer and Coward (1985) describe ways for researchers to operationalize communication network variables and ways to study networks. Apparently, networks function as buffers for stress and may help alleviate anxiety

(Cohen, et al., 1985; Simons and West, 1984). Other factors studied include: emotional closeness of friends in networks (Adams, 1985/86), proximity of friends in a residential hotel (Cohen, et al., 1985), community gatekeepers (Raschoko, 1985), status in the community (Usui, et al., 1985), and perceived companionship as a predictor of satisfaction in networks (Baldassare, et al., 1984).

Networks perform a valuable community service. The Program on Gerontology at Oregon State University studied ways to stimulate links between informal and formal community networks (Clayton, et al., 1984/85). Ehrlich (1985) learned those who were extremely active in the community were those who participated in networks and who interacted with more passive members. Noberini and Berman (1983) described a swapping service network for community members. Oktay (1985) used informal networks to advocate the merits of formal programs. Cole (1985) described how nurses could use patients' informal networks to assess aging patients' abilities to care for themselves when released from the hospital. Communication researchers can also study how one gains access to an existing network, what are commonalities of discourse of network gatekeepers, how gatekeepers select information for network transmission, and how networks are activated by stress. The formation and maintenance of information networks may be one area where aging persons can exert control and exercise autonomy within the community. Public school super-intendents know the wisdom of appealing to elders when asking the community to vote in favor of bond issues. In the future, with increased numbers of retired persons living in the community, such networks could influence local elections, public works expenditures, and investments in education. How these networks are maintained could be a vital area for communication research.

## Volunteerism

Frequently, volunteers are treated as if they possess an inferior role in formal organizations, yet their participation is vital. Euster (1984/85) argues that graduate students in social work should be educated in training and maintaining volunteers. Aging persons or retirees, as volunteers, perform an invaluable function among peers. Volunteer programs cited in the literature include: identifying the needs of frail elders (Gallagher, 1985; Ventura and Worthy, 1982), peer counseling (Brumell, 1984; Byrd, 1984) to lead self-help groups (Lidoff and Harris, 1985), and hospice volunteers (Downe-Wamboldt and Ellerton, 1985/86). Some communication questions that need answers follow. What types of persons interact best in volunteer groups? What effective communication strategies are used by successful volunteers to enhance group identity? What techniques can be used to teach these traits to new volunteers?

**Public Policy**

A final area for communication research includes how elders might use existing public or governmental programs to help maintain independence. Fricke (1985) examined the range of available programs and the role of state and federal programs in the Older Americans Act. Rich and Baum (1984) summarized state and local government programs and how they may change with shifting population trends. Hales (1985) described how to increase the links between libraries and gerontology centers to help elders seeking policy information. Other topics on public policy include: the social security system and how it is perceived by elders (Yankelovich, Skelly and White, Inc., 1985), economic policies that determine the quality of health care aging persons receive (Everitt, 1985), and age discrimination as viewed by elder women reentering the marketplace (Weiss, 1984). Communication researchers can aid aging persons by developing lobby techniques they can use with state, local, or national governments. Legislatures may be more receptive to changes in policy decisions if elders themselves influenced law makers.

**Additional Topics Relevant to Independent Living**

Many other topics appear to help the aging person retain and regain some degree of autonomy. These topics are discussed in detail elsewhere in this text but take on a new face when they are examined from a perspective of independence instead of dependence.

Education for elders (discussed in Chapter 15) sometimes centers on "safe" topics for elders to learn: clubs (Cook, 1985), art and literature (Balkema, 1986). More research efforts are needed on how elders learn and how they interact with students and teachers (Knowles, 1984a), how they are motivated to learn (Brockett, 1985), and the cognitive factors brought to the learning scene (Cavanaugh, et al., 1985; Lumsden, 1985; Pease, 1985; and O'Dowd, 1984).

Aging persons want to enhance their skill repertoire. The more practical the application, the more elders prefer to learn the topic. Favored topic areas are: career planning (Bass, 1986), grant writing (Manheimer, 1984), assessing existing educational programs (Jacobs and Ventura-Merkel, 1984; Ostwald and Williams, 1985) return to the job market (Kahne, 1985), and nutrition (U.S. Congress, Office of Technology Assessment, 1985). The AARP published a list of possible training subjects for the elderly together with the National Older Workers Information System (Root, 1985).

Health care communication, discussed in detail in Chapter 13, confronts researchers with questions which need answering. How do healthy elders speak about their motivation to maintain, retain, and regain their health? What communication patterns are displayed by elders enjoying good health? Lantz (1985), Birren and Livingston (1985), Lalonde and Fallcreek

(1985), Dychtwald and MacLean (1986), and Milligan, et al., (1985) all describe how elders perceive their health status. Apparently, research monies are available to study how persons retain their health independence.

Intergenerational communication is discussed in Chapter 10. Researchers should be encouraged to continue their initial investigations on how aging persons find useful and functional roles in families, organizations, and communities. Programming ideas and resources are cited in Murphy (1984), Slaybaugh (1984), Struntz and Reville (1985), and Klatt and Heeter (1985). Some intergenerational communication variables have been identified: support groups (Nasatir, 1985; Schmidt and Keys, 1985) conflict (Hawranik, 1985), coping workshops (Roberto, 1985), leisure activities (Weiss and Bailey, 1985), family norms (Moss, et al., 1985), media representation of those norms (Davis and Davis, 1985; Passuth and Cook, 1985), and case studies (Lund, et al., 1985; Mancini and Simon, 1984).

Younger family members are rapidly gaining respect for aging members of the family. The older members may have enough financial resources to help younger members with a down payment on a home, or they might provide child care or act as buffers in parent-child conflicts. Aging persons may be gaining new independence accorded to them by new positions of power in the extended family.

## Sheltered Care

Now we move to the opposite end of the independent-dependent continuum: sheltered care. Even here, contrary to popular opinion, aging persons still need autonomy and apparently will struggle to cultivate patterns of independent choice. A different set of communication problems arises when elders can no longer maintain independent living but wish to be independent.

## Mental Health

The chief complaint voiced by members of this group is: "People treat us as if we're crazy." Communication and aging scholars need a clear understanding of the main issues of aging and mental health in order to avoid improper assumptions about their research subjects. Many articles address elders' mental hygiene. Aronson and Jarvik (1984), Abrahams and Crooks (1984), and Sherman (1984) discuss topics of depression, cognitive disorders, emotional problems, and intervention strategies. Turnbull and Turnbull (1985) describe how stress and anxiety may be masked as physical pathologies. Stress may give rise to dysfunctional coping patterns among elders (Sinnott, 1984/85; West and Simons, 1983), and among ethnic groups (Conway, 1985/86). Patterns of stress can also affect nursing strategies (Gioiella and Bevil, 1985). An entire issue of *Physical and Occupational Therapy in Geriatrics* (Dementia and Depression, 1984) is devoted to the topic of depression and dementia in a subject's discourse style. Lazarus (1985), Waxman, et al. (1985), and Weeks and Cuellar (1983) discuss how depression may be masked as somatic complaints.

A review of literature of dementia and cognition disorders is presented in Woodruff (1983). Of special interest to the communication researcher is Woodruff's survey of qualitative assessment tools appropriate for use with dementia victims. Gates (1986) treats dementia as a family problem and discusses treatment from a communication systems perspective. Rosen, et al., (1985) discuss nonpharmaceutical therapies to reverse dementia. Frequently, researchers assume that dementia is a permanent state. They may overlook the fact that communicative therapies may reverse an aging person's confused state of mind. Precise research in this area would be of immense humanitarian value.

Alzheimer's type dementia (ATD) disease commands much attention in the literature. Montgomery and Still (1985) provide an excellent bibliography of ATD and discuss how the disease affects family structures. Cummings and Benson (1983) provide an inventory of symptoms of Alzheimer's and how it often masquerades as other pathologies. There appears to be no accurate assessment tool yet for the disease aside from autopsy. In the literature, there is an urgent call for communication research because medical science urgently needs an index of communicative behaviors which correlate with the disease (Capuano, 1983; Filinson, 1984; Klein, et al., 1985).

Family support groups are needed for victims of Alzheimer's disease. Training the support groups, establishing guidelines for the groups, discussing the stress on family members, and suggesting practical hints for coping with the disease are given in Kahan, et al., (1985), Middleton (1984), Morycz (1985), and Mobily and Hoeft (1985). Of interest for communication researchers is the way friends, family, and practitioners speak to AD victims, a topic dealt with more fully in Chapter 9. From this writer's experience, AD victims are frequently conversed with as if they were in a coma.

On a more positive side, some researchers focus on how elders may prevent cognitive disorders. Case studies show that early attention to cognitive disorders and stimulation may prevent problems such as isolation (Ravish, 1985) and suicide (Osgood, 1985). Hussian and Davis (1985), Busch (1984), MacLennan (1983), Stacey, et al., (1985), and Taylor and Yesavage (1984) all argue that non-pharmaceutical therapy interventions may improve memory, cognitive skills, and conversational fluency.

## Nursing Homes

Weissert (1985) projects that the need for nursing home care will double by the year 2000, according to the National Nursing Home Survey and the

National Health Interview Survey, 1977-80. Many nursing homes are attempting to upgrade services and to render more than custodial care. Oriol (1985) offers an annotated list of active nursing home organizations which are attempting to sensitize administrators to offer more intensive care to resident patients.

Nursing home administration could use the services of communication researchers in the area of financing. Kane (1986) states that residents must be accurately assessed in the first three months of their stay in the nursing home for successful funding from state and federal assistance programs. Communication researchers can assist nursing homes by providing more accurate assessment tools. These tools may determine a resident's projected length of stay at a nursing home.

The teaching nursing home may offer a way for nursing homes to maintain solvency. Cincinnati nursing homes and the Gerontology Center at Miami University cooperate to maintain teaching nursing homes. The Robert Wood Johnson Foundation Teaching Nursing Home Program (Aiken, et al., 1985) also encourages this innovative type of extended care facility. The administration and educational techniques of such institutions would prove to be rich research areas.

The marketing needs of nursing homes can be examined as homes attempt to enhance their community image. The residents themselves can assist in this marketing program by being encouraged to assess the mission of a nursing home and the quality of care received (American Association of Homes for the Aging, 1982). Nursing homes could market their preadmission counseling (Boling, 1984) or humanistic care (Boling, 1983). An entire issue of *American Health Care Association Journal* (Marketing for Long Term Care, 1985) is devoted to marketing strategies for the nursing homes.

Nursing homes can also promote their image with assurances of quality care. Some sources in the literature suggest how this might be done. Spalding and Frank (1985) focus an entire issue of the *American Health Care Association Journal* on programs to assure and assess quality care. Residents may also be taught how to assess health care. Lichtenstein, et al. (1985) found that residents rated help performing routine daily activities as the most accurate marker of quality care. A consumer protection group, The National Citizens' Coalition for Nursing Home Reform (A Consumer perspective, 1985) asked residents themselves what they thought of health care.

Staff development is a major factor in improving nursing home care. Czirr and Rappaport (1984) provided a bibliography of staff problems including residents accusing staff members of pilfering personal property, residents falling in love with staff, and family members' guilt reflected in accusations of staff malfeasance. Such information would be invaluable for communication consultants. Zarit and Sommers (1985) described case histories of caregivers and the reaction to caregivers. Blumenfield (1985) showed readers how to establish a journal club to help staff members avoid burnout and to help practitioners remain current on staff issues. Baum and Gallagher (1985/86) provided strategies for alleviating depression among caregivers.

Numerous communication teaching projects are cited in the literature. The low level of empathy of health care workers with patients is described in Yturri-Byrd and Glazer-Waldman (1984). Low empathy levels among nurses (the younger the nurse the higher the empathy) were found with Pennington and Pierce (1985), Lewis (1983), and Bagshaw and Adams (1986). A whole range of training programs to foster communication skills among staff are seen in Portnoy (1985), McCracken-Knights (1985), Jenkins, et al., (1983), and Hollinger (1986). One workshop was designed to enhance patient autonomy (Kaplan, 1985). Kaplan found little relation between how nurses said they were interacting with patients and actual practice. Kahana and Kiyak (1984) observed nursing personnel in action and came to the same conclusion.

There are numerous nursing home projects to enhance residents' lives. These projects could be studied by the communication researcher to investigate how people decide to go to a nursing home and the process of decision making for nursing home placement (Van Meter and Johnson, 1985), preadmission counseling (Moore, 1984), preadmission screening (Palestis, 1986), an ombudsman program for nursing home residents (Monk and Kaye, 1984), using pets for therapy among nursing home residents (Erickson, 1985), incorporating residents into the nursing home social structure (Dresser, 1985; Retsinas and Garrity, 1985).

## Additional Topics Relevant to Dependent Living

In the case of elder abuse even frail elders can be taught to exert some independence for self-protection. Johnson, et al., (1985), presented an annotated bibliography on elder abuse. Thobaben and Anderson (1985) discussed the legal aspects of the problem, specifically who must report an abuse problem. Guinn (1985) described the types of interventions that can be accomplished in abuse cases. Phillips and Rempusheski (1986) discussed how to detect abuse from the discourse of an elder. And, of course, Chapter 16 in this book discusses the communication aspects of elder abuse.

Speech and hearing problems were addressed by Wilder and Weistein (1984) who discussed ways to manage patients with speech and hearing problems in institutional settings. Dunkle and Hooper (1983) discussed how language therapists and speech therapists can work in tandem on patients' rehabilitation regimen. Hooper and Dunkle (1985) presented aphasia rehabilitation guides. Of chief interest is the victim's attitude state. Additional topics discussed are: locus of control (McDavis, 1983/84), presbycusis (Miller, 1983) and ATD coupled with hearing loss (Uhlmann, et al., 1986).

On questions of hospitalization and medication, medical practitioners sometimes assume the worst when dealing with frail elders. Practitioners may assume they are beyond treatment or rehabilitation. From a medical perspective, the following sources argued that elders can be guided toward autonomous choice in their own health care. Barket, et al., (1985) described techniques to motivate patients in therapy, to move patients off a backlog list, and to prepare them for early release from the hospital. Burton (1985) urged that physicians be trained in making house calls on old-olds so elders may stay in their own homes longer. Physicians can also gain a better understanding of the elder's health problem if they can assess the elder's domestic environment. Other care problems were discussed under physician or nurse bias in prescription practice (Frengley, 1985). Physicians may routinely prescribe a tranquilizer if an aged person is "too talkative" and "shouts too much." The quality of care after installation of DRG's (Diagnostic Related Groups) were discussed by Harron and Schaeffer (1986). Many nursing homes argue that patients are being released too early from hospital stays. How elders present pain (Kwentus, et al., 1985) and prescription compliance rates (Darnell, et al., 1986) are other topics presented from a medical perspective. Physicians and nurses need training to identify characteristic communication patterns of the aging. These practitioners also need to know how to encourage the elders' motives for independence and how to elicit their desire to return to health.

Especially among the dying aged persons, researchers find the "independence" theme sounded. Foster and Paradis (1985) provided an annotated bibliography on providing the dying with humane treatment and hospice care. Dush (1985) described the communication characteristics of hospice patients and how they resist patronizing attitudes from both practitioners and visitors. Other communication aspects discussed in the literature include: pre-death counseling of family members (Fredrick and Fredrick, 1985; Mitrowshi, 1985). The interpersonal variables presented by dying patients (Gonda and Ruark, 1984), the advantages and disadvantages of hospice care (Coleman, 1985), the effects on the staff from the "do not resuscitate" order often seen on nursing care plans (Miles and Ryden, 1985), and the patterns of death in a large nursing home (Brown, 1983).

## Conclusion

Communication researchers would make a valuable contribution by devising ways to enhance aging persons' levels of independence. Our discipline has the opportunity to research and to become involved with our subjects by devising ways to increase their autonomy. How can elders be aided in staying out of the hospital? How can elders be aided in finding supplemental incomes? How can elders be prepared to enter educational programs? How can elders enhance their mobility? How can elders be helped to find means for home care rather than institutional care. As a society we would be far richer if we sought ways of weaving the frail elderly back into the social fabric of our community rather than isolating them from their environment.

# ❖ 18 ❖

# Methodological Considerations in Communication and Aging Research

## Jon F. Nussbaum

This text is an excellent example of the current explosion of social scientific literature relating human communication to the aging process. The purpose of this chapter is twofold. First, the chapter is written to familiarize the reader with the unique methodological considerations which must be understood in order to appreciate the discoveries to be found within the vast gerontological literature. Second, this chapter can serve as an introduction for the reader who wishes to contribute sound research to the growing field of Communication and Aging.

The chapter is divided into four major sections. The initial section introduces the notion of Life-Span Communication and the effects of such a process-related paradigm for the methodologies utilized to describe and explain communication and aging. The second section of the chapter outlines the two most common developmental methodologies utilized by researchers within the gerontological literature: cross-sectional and longitudinal designs. In addition, this section briefly presents three sequential designs which have been advanced to better "explore" developmental change. The third section of this chapter relates several practical considerations of data collection from elderly subjects. The chapter concludes with a summary section discussing the costs, the rewards, and the ethics of conducting human communication research within an elderly population.

## Life-Span Communication

Theorists within the field of Communication have long stressed the importance of "process" within any interactive exchange. Communication, in fact, is often defined as the "process" of shared meaning or the "process" by which two or more individuals interact to achieve some goal. These theorists, however, have only concerned themselves with the immediate process involved in each communicative transaction. What they have ignored is the continuing process of interaction over an extended period of time throughout the duration of one's life.

The task of Life-Span Communication is to describe and explain the process of change in human interaction throughout the life-span. Thus, individuals interested in life-span communication are concerned with the changing functions and purposes of communication from birth to old age. This concern presents many unique theoretical problems. For instance, communication scholars with an interest in friendship must explain and describe how friendships are formed when an individual is 3 years old compared to friendship formation at 16 years old compared to friendship formation at 70 years old. In addition, the communication scholar must build theory which explains the functional nature of friendships at different times during the life-span. Do adolescent friendships have the same interpersonal goals and satisfaction as old-age friendships?

These new theoretical issues can only be explored with research methodologies specifically constructed to test for the lifelong communication process and the inherent change within that process. This text is primarily concerned with communication during the more advanced stages of one's life. Yet, if we are to understand the dynamic changes in communicative behavior which take place in old age, we must place that change into the context of the entire life-span. Methodologies which place primary emphasis upon uncovering change, the process of the change, and the possible patterns of that change are the most appropriate methodologies for communication scholars investigating the elderly.

## Developmental Methodologies[1]

Researchers studying change throughout the life-span have constructed and utilized several methodologies to measure age-related change. Cross-sectional designs and longitudinal designs are the most traditional and the

---

[1]For a more in-depth discussion of developmental methodologies please see: Baltus, Reese, and Nesselroade, 1977; Nesselroade and Reese, 1973; or Nesselroade and Labouvie, 1985.

most utilized of these methodologies. In response to several flaws within the traditional designs, a series of sequential designs were first proposed in the 1960s. The sequential designs, however, have not as yet been utilized to the extent of the more popular cross-sectional and longitudinal designs. This section of the chapter reviews these research designs.

## Cross-Sectional Design

Baltes, Reese, and Nesselroade (1977) describe the cross-sectional design as a method used to compare different age groups observed at one point in time. If, for example, a researcher was interested in answering the question as to whether communication apprehension scores change over the life-course, the researcher can assess the change with a cross-sectional design. Individuals of different ages (5, 10, 15, ... 60, 65, 75, 80) would complete a measure of communication apprehension at approximately the same time and the scores of each age group would be compared to determine change in apprehension across the life-span.

Two major reasons for performing a cross-sectional study have been advanced by Nunnally (1973). First, the design permits the study of differences in some human attribute across the life-span at one point in time. This type of study is outlined in the above example. Second, the cross-sectional study permits the investigator to estimate developmental sequences. If the data suggests that communication apprehension increases with age, the investigator could predict that any given individual will experience an increase in apprehension as he or she ages.

The cross-sectional design has two major advantages as a research methodology designed to investigate age-related change. The first major advantage concerns the ability to obtain a sample to answer age-change research questions. Although the researcher is responsible for sampling different age groups, the fact that those age groups are measured at one point in time simplifies the data collection process. The researcher must work to locate individuals of different ages and ensure that comparable samples are obtained at each age level. Once located, those individuals only need to complete the measure at one point in time and the data collection is accomplished.

A second major advantage of the cross-sectional design is the minimal sophistication of the data analysis. The researcher must compare scores across differing age groups. This can be accomplished by simple mean comparison tests or a correlation coefficient often accompanied by a graphic representation of the change from one age group to the next.

The cross-sectional design has two major disadvantages which developmental researchers need to be aware of before they select this design as appropriate. First, "cross-sectional studies completely confound age at time of testing and generation of subjects" (Nunnally, 1973, p. 91).

Individuals not only differ in terms of age, but also in terms of the kinds of lives they have led up to the time of testing. Results from data analysis may suggest that older individuals score higher on a communication apprehension measure than younger individuals. This difference may not be due to age change but rather to the effects of environmental factors such as lack of television when the elderly subjects were teens.

A second major disadvantage centers around the generalization of the results of cross-sectional designs to developmental sequences. The cross-sectional design investigates inter-individual change. Often, however, the researcher wants to make a statement about change within individuals across the life-span. This type of an intra-individual causal statement is problematic since individuals are only measured at one point in time. True longitudinal designs are required to make valid intra-individual change statements.

## Longitudinal Design

Researchers interested in studying change throughout the life-span "have long felt that the understanding of lawful relationships pertaining to the developmental processes must sooner or later require that the same organisms be observed over that period of time during which the developmental phenomena of interest are thought to occur" (Schaie, 1983a, p. 1). Baltes, Reese, and Nesselroade (1973) define the longitudinal design as the method which "follows the same persons through all age levels with repeated observations" (p. 122). A researcher who asks the question whether communication apprehension scores change during the life-course can select a longitudinal design to assess the change. The researcher would select a sample of five year olds and test those individuals at age 5, age 10, and at five year intervals through age 60, 65 or older. Changes manifested by each individual throughout the life-course would be plotted and compared.

Most researchers agree that longitudinal designs have three major advantages over cross-sectional designs for investigating age changes. First, longitudinal studies do not confound age change with generational effects. This is true since the measure of change is the individual himself or herself. Second, the researcher utilizing a longitudinal design need not worry about comparable samples at each age level. Within the longitudinal design, each subject is measured at each age level. The third major advantage of the longitudinal design is that the design permits for more powerful statistical analysis. The increased power results from the fact that each subject is compared against himself or herself which decreases error variance. (For a more complete analysis of the advantages of longitudinal designs please see Schaie, 1983a).

A series of major limitations are of concern to researchers utilizing the longitudinal design. First, since longitudinal designs are not true experiments, they suffer from the threats to internal validity inherent within all quasi-experiments. Campbell and Stanley (1966) and Cook and Campbell (1979) outline in great detail the most serious threats to internal validity. For our purposes, the most serious of these threats include: maturation, attrition, historical effects, testing effects which are due to practice and repeated measurement, instrumentation problems, statistical regression, and experimental mortality (both in subjects and researchers).

Schaie, 1983a) cites threats to external validity as a second major limitation of longitudinal designs. These threats, which Schaie (1983a) describes as centering around the experimental units, the experimental setting, the treatment variables, and the measurement variables, all concern limitations with the generalizability of the findings within longitudinal studies. Quite simply, since each individual is measured repeatedly and serves as his or her own control, statements concerning the general population are speculative at best.

A third limitation or disadvantage inherent within longitudinal designs is the "confounding of genetically programmed unraveling of behavioral characteristics with cumulative effects on the interaction of organismic status with the environment" (Nunnally, 1973, p. 92). This problem is quite complex and deals primarily with factors external to the design such as learning to cope with whatever is being studied. Thus, if we are attempting to plot the developmental nature of communication apprehension in old age and the subject continually learns to adapt to apprehension, change would not be observed even though change had taken place. We often have no way of indicating the adaptability of the subject and our results are therefore questionable.

A final major disadvantage of the longitudinal design is inherent within the lifelong nature of the method. Very few researchers are willing to devote their entire lives to a longitudinal study. This is partly true because researchers are rewarded for quick results not necessarily quality results.

The disadvantages of both the cross-sectional design and the longitudinal design have prompted researchers to explore other methods of assessing change. The most popular of these alternative methods are known as sequential designs.

## Sequential Designs

Schaie (1965) proposed three strategies of data collection to provide not only descriptive information but also explanations of developmental change. He labelled these new designs the cross-sequential, the cohort-sequential, and the time-sequential methods. The "sequential designs were developed in order to study intra-individual change in a changing world and to separate age changes to cohort effects" (Nunnally, 1973, p. 137). These designs ignited new interest in developmental methodology and to this day remain quite controversial. For most researchers, the sequential designs as outlined by Schaie (1965) serve only as good descriptive designs and have never showed promise in the arena of explanation.

The designs themselves are quite complex and are best illustrated with a schematic showing the design. The schematic also indicates the more traditional cross-sectional and longitudinal design. Briefly, the cohort-sequential design as shown in the schematic involves measuring individuals during the years 1970, 1980, and 1990. Two groups of individuals, those born in 1920 and those born in 1930, are measured in 1980. Inbedded within this design is both cross-sectional information (comparing the 1920 cohort with the 1930 cohort) and longitudinal information (comparing the 1920 cohort at age 50 and 60 and the 1930 cohort at age 50 and 60). The time-sequential design involves two times of measurement (2000 and 2010) with these cohorts (1930, 1940, and 1950) who are either 60 or 70 years old. The cross-sequential design involved two cohorts (1960 and 1970) measured at two times (2020 and 2030) who are either 50, 60, or 70 years old.

The advantage of each sequential design is the inherent imbeddedness of the cross-sectional and longitudinal design. In addition, a researcher can utilize any of these designs and not spend an entire lifetime measuring change.

The major disadvantage of these sequential designs is that each design confounds either age, time of measurement or cohort. To solve this problem, many methodologists suggest combining sequential designs. These designs are quite complex and the reader should consult texts written for advanced methodology courses for a more in-depth discussion of the various sequential designs.

## Practical Considerations of Data Collection[2]

The selection of an appropriate design for studying Communication and Aging is but the first of several complex judgments to be made by social researchers. This section of the chapter discusses the practical problems of locating the elderly subjects for communication investigations and actually collecting information (data) from the elderly. The section is based upon this author's personal experiences in conducting Communication and Aging research over the past decade (Nussbaum, 1980; 1981; 1983a, b; 1985; Nussbaum and Robinson, 1984; Nussbaum, Robinson and Grew, 1985).

---

[2]Sinnott, Harris, Block, Cullusano, and Jacobson (1983) provide a great source book for those who are interested in locating resources for research on aging.

# Figure 1

## Schematic Showing Sequential Designs

### (Table Entries Represent Times of Measurement)

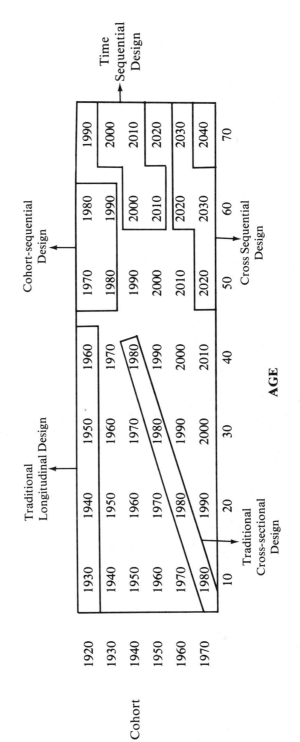

## The Elderly as Subjects

The demographics of the aged population are quite impressive. The U.S. Department of Health and Human Services in concert with the Program Resources Department, the American Association of Retired Persons and the Administration on Aging have published information based on data from the U.S. Bureau of the Census which states that in 1984 persons 65 years or older numbered 28 million of 11.9% of the U.S. population. (Profile of Older Americans, 1985). By the year 2030, at which time the "baby boom" generation reaches 65, 60 million Americans will be over 65. In 1980, the fastest growing segment of the population were individuals over the age of 85. Stated quite simply, we are a maturing society.

The interesting paradox concerning the ever growing numbers of elderly people is the fact that the elderly are getting harder to find. Our society is age-segregated to the extent that we (the "younger generation") rarely interact with the older generation. This fact is made clear when, during various classes each semester, I ask the students how many "know" at least one individual over the age of 65 other than a grandparent. With over 3,000 students responding during the last five years, only 12% say that they "know" an individual over 65 who is not their grandparent and only 2% say that they have interacted with an individual over 65 in the last month including their grandparents. This raises the question as to where the elderly are in this society.

The vast majority of the elderly in the U.S. live in and own their own homes. Approximately 15% of the elderly live either with their family or in retirement communities, while, at any one time, approximately 4% of the elderly are institutionalized. The overwhelming majority of studies done within the field of communication utilize students as subjects. The elderly are typically not part of the student population. Therefore, researchers must go to the elderly if they wish to include them in their investigations. The researcher must leave campus and often "hunt" for the elderly.

Two "hunting" strategies have been quite successful for this author. First, simply go to the older neighborhoods within any given community, knock on the doors and visit with the residents. This obviously is time consuming but often leads to good elderly network contacts. The second strategy involves locating "lists" of elderly from those institutions which serve or in some way cater to the elderly. Senior citizen centers and churches are the most likely institutions to have actual lists of elderly individuals. Once the researcher obtains the list, he or she can then meet the elderly in the institution itself or visit with them at home.

A third strategy for locating elderly subjects for an investigation involves the local newspaper. Elderly individuals typically read the daily newspaper at higher rates than others within the population. Thus, placing an ad and offering a small stipend for participation can be quite rewarding.

A demographic characteristic which may be problematic in obtaining a proper sample of elderly subjects is the sex ratio. Women tend to live much longer than men and elderly women outnumber elderly men. Thus, one will have to work much harder to include the proper number of elderly men in any investigation.

Perhaps the most important element within any research project is to obtain cooperation from the subject pool. Elderly individuals did not grow up in a society dominated by social research. In addition, many individuals dedicate themselves to "ripping off" the elderly. These factors contribute to a skepticism on the part of the elderly which makes the job of social scientist much harder. To gain the proper cooperation from the elderly, the researcher must prove that he or she is sincerely interested in the needs and attitudes of the aged and will not use or abuse the privilege of their help. One must be respectful, courteous and never forget that the elderly are doing us a favor by participating in our research projects. Letters of introduction from the university or sponsor of the research project are a must. In addition, follow-up thank you notes are much appreciated by the elderly. If at all possible, it is appropriate to send a copy of the final paper to each elderly participant. Sensitive treatment of the elderly by the researcher will permit that researcher to continue the research relationship at future points in time. (This would obviously be essential if a longitudinal design was being utilized).

## Data Collection

Once the elderly subjects have been located and the researcher has obtained their cooperation, the task of collecting information from the elderly is at issue. Several techniques of collecting data are quite popular within the field of communication. Face-to-face distribution of questionnaires, mailings, phone interviews and face-to-face interviews are all utilized when students serve as subjects. The strengths and weaknesses of each technique is well documented (Babbie, 1983; Bailey, 1982). Collecting data from the elderly is quite different than collecting data from "captive" students and demands a much more "personal touch." For this reason, it is strongly recommended to collect data with the use of face-to-face interviews. Although this technique is both time-consuming and costly, the experience of interacting with the elderly and the validity checks possible with the interview technique make this procedure of data collection superior to other procedures.

The interview procedure itself is a skill which can be improved with proper training. First, the researcher must decide whether to invite the elderly subjects to his or her office or to go directly to the elderly subjects' homes. If the researcher invites the subjects to his or her office, problems of transportation will arise (who is driving, carfare, token). It is advisable for the researcher to visit the elderly in their homes. If the researcher visits the elderly in their homes, the researcher must be invited in and behave as a guest. A rule of thumb most social gerontology researchers utilize is to employ female interviewers. An interviewer who is female is less threatening and perceived to be more personable by both elderly women and men. The bottom line is that the female interviewer is more likely to be invited into the home than a male interviewer.

Once invited into the home, the researcher must obviously collect the required information. However, it has been this author's experience that an interview which would normally require 30 minutes with a twenty-year-old student subject will average 90 minutes with an elderly subject. The researcher must be prepared for small talk as well as in-depth personal responses to personal questions. For instance, a simple question requesting information on the number of children will elicit a response about each child, their jobs, their families, their history in the neighborhood and the last time each child visited. The researcher must remain patient and utilize the additional information to probe or to learn about the communicative world of this elderly individual. In addition, the interviewer must respond to the self-disclosure of the subject. The interviewer should not be afraid to wander from the interview schedule to reciprocate the disclosure. This will build cohesion and, in the long run, improve the interviewer-subject relationship.

A final caution when utilizing elderly individuals involves subject fatigue. Fatigue is a serious problem for experimental researchers who bring the elderly into the laboratory and test for reaction time or some other behavioral response. Yet, for social scientists who conduct interviews which last up to 90 minutes, fatigue can also be a factor. The good interviewer will look for possible fatigue symptoms and take frequent breaks. The interviewer also should be aware of his or her own concentration level and take precautions against fatigue factors which could result in a poor interview.

## Summary

Communication and Aging research depends upon unique methodologies as well as unique data collection procedures. The methodologies are complex and the data collection procedures are tedious. At some point, the question must be asked as to the worth of such research.

A life-span communication approach is based on the belief that knowing the past allows us to understand the present and to predict the future. The methodologies which have been developed to describe and explain developmental change help us to understand better the complex nature of communication throughout the entire life-course. To truly "come to grips" with communication and the aging process, we must gain some understanding of what has transpired prior to old age and what is happening now that old age is here. The intricacies involved in such a developmental process prohibit simple methodological tools as a means to valid description and explanation.

The work involved in collecting data from elderly subjects adds even more "costs" to the worth of doing life-span communication research. After all, it is much easier to study the communication behavior of college sophomores and never leave the safe environment of a college campus. Yet, college sophomores can tell us very little about communication as we age and practically nothing about communication when we are old. There is simply no other way of describing, explaining and perhaps someday modifying the communication and aging process other than utilizing the developmental methodologies along with the data collection procedures advanced within this chapter. The costs in terms of time (this is especially true if one is doing longitudinal work) and expense are great. However, if a true understanding of communication and aging are important, the rewards of knowledge far outweigh the costs of researcher inconvenience.

A final note needs to address ethics in aging research. Communication, by its very nature, is an intimate social science. When researchers begin to unravel the communicative world of the aged, personal information will abound. The researcher must protect this information and never "push" the elderly subject too hard to acquire this information. In addition, the elderly individual has the right not to participate in the investigation and to drop out of the study at any time. Researchers need not place a "guilt-trip" upon those elderly individuals who wish to leave the research project. The researcher must respect the rights of the elderly subject and never question those rights.

This chapter introduces the notion of life-span communication and the unique developmental methodologies which have been constructed to describe and explain such a process-related paradigm. Practical considerations of data collection from elderly subjects were reviewed with special emphasis given to collecting information utilizing a face-to-face interview format. Finally, a short discussion of the "worth" of communication and aging research with an emphasis toward ethics concludes the chapter.

# References

Aaronson, B.S. (1966). Personality Stereotypes of Aging. *Journal of Gerontology, 21,* 458-62.

Abrahams, J.P., & Crooks, V. (Eds.). (1984). *Geriatric mental health.* Orlando, FL: Grune & Stratton.

Achenbaum, W.A. (1986). America as an aging society: Myths and images. *Daedalus, 115,* 13-30.

Adamowicz, J. (1976). Visual short-term memory and aging. *Journal of Gerontology, 31*(1), 39-46.

Adams, G.R. (1977). Physical attractiveness research: Toward a developmental social psychology of beauty. *Human Development, 20,* 217-39.

_____. (1985). Attractiveness through the ages: Implications of facial attractiveness over the life cycle. In J.A. Graham & A.M. Kligman (Eds.), *The psychology of cosmetic treatments.* New York: Praeger.

_____. (1985-86). Emotional closeness and physical distance between friends: Implications for elderly women living in age-segregated and age-integrated settings. *International Journal of Aging and Human Development, 22,* 55-76.

_____. (1986). A look at friendship and aging. *Generations, 10,* 40-43.

Adams, G.R., & Huston, T.L. (1975). Social perception of middle-aged persons varying in physical attractiveness. *Developmental Psychology, 11,* 657-58.

Ahammer, I.M. (1973). Social-learning theory as a framework for the study of adult personality development. In P.B. Baltes & K.W. Schaie (Eds.), *Life-span development psychology: Personality and Socialization* (pp. 253-84). New York: Academic Press.

Aiello, J.R., Nicosia, G., & Thompson, D.E. (1979). Physiological, social, and behavioral consequences of crowding on children and adolescents. *Child Development, 50,* 195-202.

Aiken, L.H. (1981). Nursing priorities for the 1980's: Hospitals and nursing homes. *American Journal of Nursing, 81,* 324-33.

Aiken, L.H., Mezey, M.D., Lynaugh, J.E., & Buck, C.R. (1985). Teaching nursing homes: Prospects for improving long-term care. *Journal of the American Geriatrics Society, 33,* 196-201.

Albrecht, T.L. (1979). The role of communication perceptions of organizational climate. In D. Nimmo (Ed.), *Communication Yearbook, 3,* 343-57.

_____. (1982). Coping with occupational stress: Relational and individual strategies of nurses in acute health care settings. In M. Burgoon (Ed.), *Communication Yearbook, 6,* 832-49.

Albrecht, T., & Adelman, M. (1984). Social support and life stress: New Directions for communication research. *Human Communication Research, 11,* 3-33.

Aldrich, N. (Ed.). (1985). *Aging Research and Training News, 8*(5), May, 33-36.

Allan, G. (1979). Sibling solidarity. *Journal of Marriage and the Family, 39,* 177-84.

Allen, V.L. (1981). The role of nonverbal behavior in children's communication. In W. Patrick Dickson (Ed.), *Children's oral communication skills.* New York: Academic Press.

Almquist, E., & Bates, D. (1980). Training programs for nursing assistants and LPNs in nursing homes. *Journal of Gerontological Nursing, 6,* 623-27.

Altergott, K. (1985). Marriage, gender and social relations in later life. In W.A. Peterson & J. Quadagno (Eds.), *Social bonds in later life* (pp. 51-70). Beverly Hills: Sage.

Altman, I., & Taylor, D.A. (1973). *Social penetration: The development of interpersonal relationships.* New York: Holt, Rinehart and Winston.

American Association of Homes for the Aging. (1982). *How do we look?: A guide to corporate self-assessment and ethical reflection in non-profit homes for the aging.* Washington, DC: American Association of Homes for the Aging.

American Cancer Society. (1984). *Cancer facts and figures 1984.* New York: American Cancer Society.

American Health Care Association. (1978). Long term care facts. Washington, DC: American Health Care Association.

Anderson, B., & Palmore, E. (1974). Longitudinal evaluation of ocular function. In E. Palmore (Ed.), *Normal Aging* (pp. 24-32). Durham, NC: Duke University Press.

Andersson, L. (1984). Intervention against loneliness in a group of elderly women: A process of evaluation. *Human Relations, 37,* 295-310.

*Annual Review of Gerontology and Geriatrics, 5,* (1985). New York: Springer.

Appel, F.W., & Appel, E.M. (1942). Intracranial variation in the weight of the human brain. *Human Biology, 14,* 48-68, 235-50.

Aristotle. (1932). *The rhetoric,* Trans. L. Cooper. New York: Appleton Century.

Arling, G., Harkins, E.B., & Romaniuk, M. (1984). Adult day care and the nursing home: The appropriateness of care in alternative settings. *Research on Aging, 6,* 225-42.

Aronoff, C. (1974). Old age in prime time. *Journal of Communication, 24*(4), 86-87.

Aronson, M.K., & Jarvik, L.F. (Eds.). (1984). *Generations, 9,* (entire issue).

Asai, R. (1972). Laryngoplasty after total laryngectomy. *Archives of Otolaryngology, 75,* 114.

Atchley, R.C. (1980). *The social forces in later life* (3rd ed.). Belmont, CA: Wadsworth.

_____. (1985). *Social forces and aging: An introduction to social gerontology* (4th ed.). Belmont, CA: Wadsworth.

Atchley, R.C., & Miller, S.J. (1983). Types of elderly couples. In T.H. Brubaker (Ed.), *Family relationships in later life* (pp. 77-90). Beverly Hills: Sage.

Atkin, C.K. (1976). Mass media and aging. In H.J. Oyer & E.J. Oyer (Eds.), *Aging and communication* (pp. 98-119). Baltimore: University Park Press.

Atkinson, J.W., & Shiffrin, R.M. (1968). Human memory: A proposed system and its control processes. In K.W. Spence & J.T. Spence (Eds.), *The psychology of learning and motivation, 2*. New York: Academic Press.

Austin, D.R. (1985). Attitudes toward old age: A hierarchical study. *The Gerontologist, 25,* 431-34.

Babbie, E. (1983). *The practice of social research* (4th ed.). Belmont, CA: Wadsworth.

Babchuck, N., Peters, G.R., Hoyt, D.R., & Kaiser, M.A. (1979). The voluntary associations of the aged, *Journal of Gerontology, 34,* 579-87.

Bacus, K. (1982). *Communication and aging: An imperative for the communication educator.* Paper presented to the Indiana Speech Association annual conference, Indianapolis.

Bagshaw, M., & Adams, M. (1986). Nursing home nurses' attitudes, empathy, and ideologic orientation. *International Journal of Aging and Human Development, 22,* 235-46.

Bailey, K.D. (1982). *Methods of social research* (2nd ed.). New York: The Free Press.

Baldassare, M., Rosenfield, S., & Rook, K. (1984). The types of social relations predicting elderly well-being. *Research on Aging, 6,* 549-59.

Balkema, J.B. (1986). *The creative spirit: An annotated bibliography on the arts.* Washington, DC: National Council on the Aging.

Baltes, P.B., & Schaie, K.W. (1974). Aging and the I.Q.: The myth of the twilight years. *Psychology Today, 7*(10), March, 35-40.

Baltes, P.B., Reese, H.W., & Nesselroade, J.R. (1977). *Life-Span developmental psychology: Introduction to research methods.* Monterey, CA: Brooks/Cole Publishing.

Barbato, C.A., & Feezel, J.D. (1987). The language of aging in different age groups. *The Gerontologist, 27,*

Bardach, J.L. (1969). Group sessions with wives of aphasic patients. *International Journal of Group Psychology, 19,* 361-65.

Barker, W.H., Williams, T.F., Zimmer, J.G., Van Buren, C., & Pickrel, S.G. (1985). Geriatric consultation teams in acute care hospitals: Impact on back-up of elderly patients. *Journal of the American Geriatrics Society, 33,* 422-28.

Barnard, C. (1938). *The functions of the executive.* Cambridge: Harvard University Press.

Barney, J.L. (1983). Common concern: A new perspective on nurses' aide training. *Geriatric Nursing, 4,* 44-48.

Barrow, G.M., & Smith, P.A. (1979). *Aging, ageism and society.* New York: West Publishing.

Bartol, M.A. (1979). Nonverbal communication in patients with Alzheimer's disease. *Journal of Gerontological Nursing, 5*(4), 21-31.

Barton, R.L., & Schreiber, E. (1978). Media and aging: A critical review of an expanding field of communication research. *Central States Speech Journal, 29, 173-86.*

Bass, S.A. (1986). Matching educational opportunities with the able elderly. *Life-long Learning, 9,* 4-7.

Bassili, J.N., & Reil, J.E. (1981). On the dominance of the old-age stereotype. *Journal of Gerontology, 36,* 682-88.

Batza, E.M. (1977). Adventures in vocal rehabilitation. In M. Cooper & M.H. Cooper (Eds.), *Approaches to vocal rehabilitation.* Springfield, IL: Charles C. Thomas.

Baum, D., & Gallagher, D. (1985-86). Case Studies of psychotherapy with depressed caregivers. *Clinical Gerontologist, 4,* 19-29.

Baum, S.K. (1983-84). Age identification in the elderly: Some theoretical considerations. *International Journal of Aging and Human Development, 18,* 25-30.

Baum, W. (1980). Therapeutic value of oral history. *International Journal of Aging and Human Development, 12,* 49-51.

Bayles, K.A. (1984). Language and dementia. In A.L. Holland (Ed.), *Language disorders in adults: Recent advances.* San Diego: College-Hill Press.

_____. (1986). Management of neurogenic communication disorders associated with dementia. In R. Chapey (Ed.), *Language intervention strategies in adult aphasia* (2nd ed.). Baltimore: Williams & Wilkins.

Beard, B.B. (1969). Sensory decline in very old age. *Gerontological Clinician, 11,* 149-58.

Beasley, D.S., & Davis, G.A. (Eds.). (1981). *Aging: Communication processes and disorders.* New York: Grune & Stratton.

Becker, D.G., Blumenfield, S., & Gordon, N. (1984). Voices from the eighties and beyond: Reminiscences of nursing home residents. *Journal of Gerontological Social Work, 8,* 83-100.

Beckman, C.J., & Houser, B.B. (1982). The consequences of childlessness on the social-psychological well-being of older women. *Journal of Gerontology, 37,* 243-50.

Beebe, S.A., & Masterson, J. (1986). *Family talk: Interpersonal communication in the family.* New York: Random House.

Beehr, T.A. (1976). Perceived situational moderators of the relationships between subjective role ambiguity and role strain. *Journal of Applied Psychology, 61,* 35-40.

Bell, R. (1979). *Marriage and family interaction* (5th ed.). Homewood, IL: Dorsey Press.

Belsky, J. (1984). *The psychology of aging: Theory, research and practice.* Monterey, CA: Brooks/Cole.

Bender, M. (1987). Packaging for the elder consumer: Housing and product design. *Vital Speeches of the Day, 53,* 490-92.

Bengston, V.L. (1979). Research perspectives on intergenerational interaction. In P.K. Ragan (Ed.), *Aging parents* (pp. 37-57). University of Southern California Press: The Ethel Percy Andrus Gerontology Center.

Bengston, V.L., & Cutler, N.E. (1976). Generations and intergenerational relations. In R.H. Binstock & E. Shanas (Eds.), *Handbook of aging and the social sciences.* New York: Van Nostrand Reinhold.

Benjamin, B. (1986). Dimensions of the older female voice. *Language and Communication, 6,* 35-45.

Bennett, R., & Eckman, J. (1973). Attitudes toward aging: A critical examination of recent literature and implications for future research. In C. Eisdorfer & M.P. Lawton (Eds.), *The psychology of adult development and aging.* Washington, DC: American Psychological Association.

Bergen, T.J. (1986). *Nursing care requirements in nursing homes in the states of the Union as compiled by the National Geriatrics Society.* Milwaukee, WI: National Geriatrics Society.

Berger, C.R., & Bradac, J.J. (1982). *Language and social knowledge: Uncertainty in interpersonal relations.* Baltimore: Edward Arnold.

Berryman-Fink, C. (1982). Communication education in a lifelong learning program. *Communication Education, 31,* 335-49.

Berscheid, E., & Walster, E. (1974). Physical attractiveness. In L. Berkowitz (Ed.), *Advances in experimental social psychology,* (Vol. 7). New York: Academic Press.

Berscheid, E., Walster, E., & Bohrnstedt. (1973). The happy American body: A survey report. *Psychology Today, 7,* 119-31.

Biegel, D.E., Shore, B.K., & Gordon, E. (1984). *Building support networks for the elderly: Theory and applications* (Sage Human Services Guides, vol. 36). Beverly Hills: Sage.

Binstock, R.H., & Shanas, E. (Eds.). (1985). *Handbook of aging and the social sciences* (2nd ed.). New York: Van Nostrand Reinhold.

Birch, E.L. (Ed.). *Unsheltered woman: Women and housing in the 80's.* New Brunswick, NJ: Rutgers, The State University, Center for Urban Policy Research.

Birren, J.E., & Renner, V.J. (1977). *A brief history of mental health and aging.* Washington, DC: National Institute of Mental Health.

Birren, J.E., Robinson, P.K. & Livingston, J.E. (Eds.). (1986). *Age, health, and employment.* Englewood Cliffs, NJ: Prentice-Hall.

Birren, J.E., & Schaie, K.W. (Eds.). (1985). *Handbook of the psychology of aging.* New York: Van Nostrand Reinhold.

Blau, Z.S. (1973). *Old age in a changing society.* New York: New Viewpoints.

―――. (1981). *Aging in a changing society.* New York: Franklin Watts.

Block, M., & Sinnott, J. (Eds.). (1979). *The battered elder syndrome: An exploratory study.* College Park: University of Maryland Center on Aging.

Blom, E.E., & Singer, M.I. (1979). Surgical-prosthetic approaches for post laryngectomy voice restoration. In R.L. Keith & F.L. Darley (Eds.), *Laryngectomee rehabilitation.* Houston, TX: College-Hill Press.

Blood, R.O., & Wolfe, D.N. (1960). *Husbands and wives: The dynamics of married living.* New York: Free Press.

Blumenfield, S. (1985). Gerontology journal Club: A continuing education modality for experienced social workers in an acute hospital setting. *The Gerontologist, 25,* 11-14.

Bochner, A.P., & Kelly, C.W. (1974). Interpersonal competence: rationale, philosophy, and implementation of a conceptual framework. *The Speech Teacher, 23,* 279-301.

Boling, T.E. (1984). A new image of long-term care: A challenge to management. *Journal of Long-Term Care Administration, 12,* 15-17.

Boling, T.E., Vrooman, D.M., & Sommers, K.M. (1983). *Nursing home management: A humanistic approach.* Springfield, IL: Charles C. Thomas.

Borgatta, E.F., & Hertzog, C. (Eds.). (1985). Methodology and aging research. *Research on Aging, 7,* (entire issue).

Boston, H.S. (1985). *Housing and living arrangements for the elderly: A selective bibliography.* Washington, DC: The National Council on the Aging.

Botan, C.H., & Frey, L.R. (1983). Do workers trust labor unions and their messages? *Communication Monographs, 50,* 223-45.

Botwinick, J. (1967). *Cognitive processes in maturity and old age.* New York: Springer.

_____. (1973). *Aging and behavior: A comprehensive integration of research findings.* New York: Springer.

Bourne, B. (1982). Effects of aging on work satisfaction, performance and motivation. *Aging and Work, 5,* 37-46.

Bowen, M.A. (1978). *Family therapy in clinical practice.* New York: Aronson.

Bower, R.T. (1973). *Television and the public.* New York: Holt, Rinehart and Winston.

Bradford, V. (1981). *Advertising images and societal stereotypes.* Paper presented to the Speech Communication Association conference on Communication and Aging, Edwardsville, Illinois.

Brahce, C.I. (1983). *Preretirement planning: Individual, institutional, and social perspectives.* Columbus, OH: The ERIC Clearing House on Adult, Career, and Vocational Education.

Britton, J.H. & Britton, J.O. (1972). *Personality changes in aging.* New York: Springer.

Britton, J.O., & Britton, J.H. (1970). Young people's perceptions of age and aging. *Gerontologist, 10,* 39.

Brockett, R.G. (1985). The relationship between self-directed learning readiness and life satisfaction among older adults. *Adult Education Quarterly, 35,* 210-219.

Brody, E. (1985). Parent care as a normative family stress. *The Gerontologist, 25,* 19-29.

Brody, H. (1985). Neuronal changes with increasing age. In H.K. Ulatowska (Ed.), *The Aging Brain: Communication in the Elderly.* San Diego: College-Hill Press.

Brookshire, R.H. (1986). *An introduction to aphasia.* Minneapolis: BRK Publishers.

Brower, H.T. (1981). Social organization and nurses' attitudes toward older persons. *Journal of Gerontological Nursing, 7,* 293-98.

Brown, G. (1960). Family structure and social isolation of older persons. *Journal of Gerontology, 15,* 170-74.

Brown, I. (1983). A study of patterns of dying in a multilevel geriatric setting. *Canadian Journal on Aging, 2,* 79-85.

Brubaker, T.H. (1985). Responsibility for household tasks: A look at golden anniversary couples aged 75 years and older. In W.A. Peterson & J. Quadagno (Eds.), *Social bonds in later life* (pp. 27-36). Beverly Hills: Sage.

Brumell, S.W. (1984). Senior companions: An unrecognized resource for long term care. *Pride Institute Journal of Long Term Health Care, 3,* 3-12.

Buber, M. (1957). Distance and relation. *Psychiatry, 20,* 94-104.

Buck, M. (1978). *Dysphasia: Professional guidance for family and patient.* Englewood Cliffs, NJ: Prentice Hall.

Buckley, W. (1968). *Modern systems research for the behavioral sciences.* Chicago: Aldine.

Bulcroft, K., & Bulcroft, R. (1985). Dating and courtship in late life: An exploratory study. In W.A. Peterson and J. Quadagno (Eds.), *Social bonds in later life* (pp. 115-28). Beverly Hills: Sage.

Bull, R. (1985). The general public's reactions to facial disfigurement. In J.A. Graham & A.M. Kligman (Eds.), *The psychology of cosmetic treatments.* New York: Praeger.

Bunting, C.I. (1978). The federal lifelong learning project. In *Current issues in higher education.* Washington, DC: American Association of Higher Education.

Bureau of the Census. (1984). *Statistical abstract of the United States 1985.* Washington, DC: U.S. Government Printing Office.

Burger, S.G., & D'Erasmo, M. (1976). *Living in a nursing home.* New York: The Seabury Press.

Burgoon, J.K. (1980). Nonverbal communication research in the 1970s: An overview. In D. Nimmo (Ed.), *Communication Yearbook 4.* New Brunswick, NJ: Transaction.

_____. (1985). Nonverbal signals. IN M.L. Knapp and G.R. Miller (Eds.), *Handbook of interpersonal communication.* Beverly Hills: Sage.

Burke, R., & Weir, T. (1982). Husband-wife helping relationships as moderators of experienced stress: "The mental hygiene" function in marriage. In H. McCubbin (Ed.), *Family stress, coping and social support.* Springfield, IL: Charles C. Thomas.

Burnett, K. (1984). Teens and seniors sharing through music: Using music to change attitudes between generations. Masters project, University of New Mexico, Albuquerque.

Burnside, I.M. (1979). Alzheimer's disease: An overview. *Journal of Gerontological Nursing, 5*(4), 14-20.

Burr, W.R. (1970). Satisfaction with various aspects of marriage over the life cycle: A random middle class sample. *Journal of Marriage and the Family, 32,* 29-37.

Burton, J.R. (1985). The house call: An important service for the frail elderly. *Journal of the American Geriatrics Society, 33,* 291-93.

Busch, C.D. (1984). Common themes in group psychotherapy with older adult nursing home residents: A review of selected literature. *Clinical Gerontologist, 2,* 25-38.

Busse, E.W., & Eisdorfer, C.F. (1970). Two thousand years of married life. In E. Palmore (Ed.), *Normal aging* (pp. 266-69). Durham, NC: Duke University Press.

Butler, A. (1985). Societal values impact on the role of the professional nurse in long-term care. *Nursing Homes, 34,* 41-44.

Butler, R.N. (1968). The life review: An interpretation of reminiscence in the aged. In B. Neugarten (Ed.), *Middle age and aging* (pp. 486-96). Chicago: University of Chicago Press.

_____. (1969). Age-ism: Another form of bigotry. *The Gerontologist, 9,* 243-46.

_____. (1974). Successful aging and the role of the life review. *Journal of the American Geriatrics Society, 22,* 529-35.

Butler, R., & Lewis, M. (1973). *Aging and mental health.* Saint Louis: C.V. Mosby Company.

Butrin, J. (1985). Day care: A new idea? *Journal of Gerontological Nursing, 11,* 19-22.

Byrd, M. (1984). Personal growth aspects of peer counselor training for older adults. *Educational Gerontology, 10,* 369-85.

Cabletelevision Advertising Bureau. (1987). *1987 cable TV facts.* New York: Cabletelevision Advertising Bureau.

Caldwell, M.M. (1976). Staff stress: What can you do about it? *Journal of Educational Nursing, 2,* 21-23.

Campbell, D.T., & Stanley, J.C. (1966). *Experimental and Quasi-Experimental Designs for Research.* Chicago: Rand McNally.

Campbell, R., & Chenoweth, B. (1981). *Peer support for older adults.* Ann Arbor: University of Michigan Press.

Caporael, L.R., & Culbertson, G.H. (1986). Verbal response modes of baby talk and other speech at institutions for the aged. *Language and Communication, 6,* 99-112.

Capella, J.N., & Street, R.L. (1985). Introduction: Functional approach to the structure of communicative behavior. In R.L. Street & J.N. Cappella (Eds.), *Sequence and pattern in communicative behavior* (pp. 1-29). Baltimore: Edward Arnold.

Capuano, E. (1983). Substituting the behavioral model for the diagnostic model as an admission standard for the demented elderly. *Activities, Adaptation, and Aging, 4,* 29-32.

Carey, B., & Hansen, S.S. (1985-86). Social support groups with institutionalized Alzheimer's disease victims. *Journal of Gerontological Social Work, 9,* 15-26.

Carlson, E. (1986). New study looks at the state of the nation's old-old citizens. *Wall Street Journal,* August 5, 31.

Carmichael, C.W. (1976). Communication and gerontology: Interfacing disciplines. *Journal of the Western Speech Communication Association, 40,* 121-29.

_____. (1979). Attitudes toward aging throughout the life span. *Journal of the Communication Association of the Pacific, VIII,* 129-51.

_____. (1983). Intrapersonal communication and aging: the effects of age related sensory losses. Paper presented at International Communication Association, Albuquerque, New Mexico.

_____. (1985). Cultural patterns of the elderly. In L.A. Samovar and R.E. Porter (Eds.), *Intercultural communication: A reader* (4th ed.) (pp. 136-41). Belmont, CA: Wadsworth.

Carson, D.H., & Pastalan, L.A. (1970). *Spatial behavior of older people.* Ann Arbor: University of Michigan Press.

Cassata, D. (1979). Death and dying: Communication papameters and perspectives. Paper presented to the Speech Communication Association conference, San Antonio, Texas.

Cassell, C.K. (1985). Ethical issues in research in geriatrics. *Generations, 10,* 45-48.

Cassidy, M.L. (1985). Role conflict in the postparental period: The effects of employment status on the marital satisfaction of women. *Research on Aging, 7,* 433-54.

Cavanaugh, J.C., Kramer, D.A., Sinnott, J.D., Camp, C.J., & Markley, R.P. (1985). On missing links and such: Interfaces between cognitive research and everyday problem-solving. *Human Development, 28,* 146-68.

Chaffee, S., & Wilson, D. (1975, August). Adult life cycle changes in mass media use. Paper presented at the Association for Education in Journalism convention, Ottawa, Canada.

Chapey, R. (Ed.). (1986). *Language intervention strategies in adult aphasia* (2nd ed.). Baltimore: Williams & Wilkins.

Chellam, G. (1977-78). Awareness of death and self-engagement in later life: The engagement continuum. *Journal of Aging and Human Development, 8,* 111-27.

Cherlin, A. (1983). A sense of history: Recent research on aging and the family. In M.W. Riley, B.B. Hess, and K. Bond, *Aging in society.* Hillsdale, NJ: Erlbawn Associates.

Cherlin, A.J., & Furstenberg, F.F., Jr. (1986). *The new American grandparent: A place in the family, a life apart.* New York: Basic Books.

Chiriboga, D., & Thurner, M. (1975). Concept of self. In M. Lowenthal, M. Thurner, & D. Chiriboga (Eds.), *Four states of life* (pp. 62-83). San Francisco: Jossey-Bass.

Chown, S.M. (1977). Morale, careers, and personal potentials. In J.E. Birren & K.W. Schaie (Eds.), *Handbook of the psychology of aging.* New York: Van Nostrand Reinhold.

Christoph, D., & Li, A.K.F. (1985). Cognitive versus social rigidity in old age; Implications for therapy. *Canadian Journal on Aging, 4,* 59-65.

Chwat, S., & Gurland, G.B. (1981). Comparative family perspectives on aphasia: Diagnostic, treatment, and counseling implications. In R.H. Brookshire (Ed.), *Proceedings of the Clinical Aphasiology Conference.* Minneapolis: BRK Publishers.

Cicirelli, V.G. (1977). Relationship of siblings to the elderly person's feelings and concerns. *Journal of Gerontology, 32,* 317-22.

_____. (1979).*Social services for the elderly in relation to the kin network.* Report to the NRTA-AARP. Washington, DC: Andrus Foundation.

_____. (1981). *Helping elderly parents: The role of adult children.* Boston: Auburn House.

_____. (1983a). Adult children and their elderly parents. IN T.H. Brubaker (Ed.), *Family relationships in later life* (pp. 31-46). Beverly Hills: Sage.

_____. (1983b). Adult children's attachment and helping behavior to elderly parents: A path model. *Journal of Marriage and the Family, 45,* 815-23.

_____. (1986). The helping relationship and family neglect in later life. In K.A. Pillemer & R.S. Wolf (Eds.), *Elder abuse: Conflict in the family* (pp. 49-66). Dover, MA: Auburn House Publishing.

Clarke, C.H., & Feezel, J.D. (1982, November). The triangular forces of change in the aging process. Paper presented at the Speech Communication Association Annual Conference.

Clausen, J.A. (1972). The life courses of individuals. In M.W. Riley, M. Johnson, & A. Foner, (Eds.), *Aging and society: A sociology of age stratification.* New York: The Russell Sage Foundation, 457-514.

Clayton, D.E., Schmall, V.L., & Pratt, C.C. (1984-85). Enhancing linkages between formal services and the informal support systems of the elderly. *Gerontology and Geriatrics Education, 5,* 3-11.

Clinton, L. (1981). Pretesting techniques for health information targeted at the elderly. Paper presented to the Speech Communication Association Summer Conference on Communication and Gerontology, Edwardsville, Illinois.

Cobis, J. (1975). Administration of quality care. In *Proceedings of the first North American symposium on long term care administration,* American College of Nursing Home Administrators, 79-84.

Coe, R. (1980). Professional perspectives on the aged. In J. Quadagno (Ed.), *Aging, the individual and society: Readings in social gerontology* (pp. 472-81). New York: St. Martin's Press.

Cohen, C.I., Teresi, J., & Homes, D. (1985). Social networks and adaptation. *The Gerontologist, 25,* 297-304.

_____. (1985). Social networks, stress, adaptation, and health: A longitudinal study of an inner-city elderly population. *Research on Aging, 7,* 409-31.

Cohen, J. (1957). The factorial structure of the WAIS between early adulthood and old age. *Journal of Consulting Psychology, 21,* 283-90.

Cohler, B.J. (1983). Autonomy and interdependence in the family of adulthood: A Psychological perspective. *The Gerontologist, 23,* 33-39.

Colavita, F.B. (1978). *Sensory changes in the elderly.* Springfield, IL: Charles C. Thomas.

Cole, E. (1985). Assessing needs for elders' networks. *Journal of Gerontological Nursing, 11,* 31-34.

Coleman, B. (1985). *Consumer guide to hospice care.* Washington, DC: National Consumers' League.

Comfort, A. (1976). Age prejudice in America. *Social Policy, 7*(3), 3-8.

Comstock, G., Chaffee, S., Katzman, N., McCombs, M., & Roberts, D. (1978). *Television and human behavior.* New York: Columbia University Press.

*Congressional Record,* (1986). 99th Cong., 2nd Sess., June 26, No. 89, Part II p. 1.

Conner, K.A., Powers, E.A., & Bultena, G.L. (1979). Social interaction and life satisfaction: An empirical assessment of late-life patterns. *Journal of Gerontology, 34,* 116-21.

A consumer perspective on quality of institutional care in the U.S. (1985). *Ageing International, 12,* 16-17.

Conway, K. (1985/86). Coping with the stress of medical problems among black and white elderly. *International Journal of Aging and Human Development, 21,* 39-48.

Cook, J.D. (1985). *Innovations in activities for the elderly.* New York: Haworth Press.

Cook, T.D., & Campbell, D.T. (1979). *Quasi-experimentation: Design and analysis issues for field settings.* Chicago: Rand McNally.

Corbin, J.M., & Strauss, A.L. (1985). Issues concerning regimen management in the home. *Aging and Society, 5,* 249-65.

Corso, J. (1963). Age and sex differences in puretone thresholds. *Archives of Otolaryngology, 77,* 376-405.

_____. (1977). Auditory perception and communication. In J.E. Birren and K.W. Schaie (Eds.), *Handbook of the psychology of aging.* New York: Van Nostrand Reinhold.

_____. (1981). *Aging sensory systems and perception.* New York: Praeger.

Cortes, J.B., & Gatti, F.M. (1965). Physique and self-description of temperament. *Journal of Consulting Psychology, 29,* 432-39.

Costello, D., & Pettegrew, L.S. (1979). Health communication theory and research: An overview of health organizations. In D. Nimmo (Ed.), *Communication Yearbook, 3,* (pp. 605-23). Beverly Hills: Sage.

Coval, M. (1985). A multi-focus assessment scale for use with frail elderly populations. *Canadian Journal on Aging, 4,* 101-9.

Covey, H.C. (1985). Qualitative research of older people: Some considerations. *Gerontology and Geriatrics Education, 5,* 41-50.

Cowgill, D.O., & Baulch, N. (1962). The use of leisure time by older people. *The Gerontologist, 2,* 47-50.

Crane, D. (1975). The social potential of the patient: An alternative to the sick role. *Journal of Communication, 25,* 131-39.

Cross, W., & Florio, C. (1978). *You are never too old to learn.* New York: McGraw Hill.

Crouse, J., Cobbs, D., Harris, B., Kopecky, E.F., & Poertner, J. (1981). *Abuse and neglect of the elderly in Illinois: Incidence and characteristics, legislation and policy recommendations.* Springfield, IL: Illinois Department on Aging.

Cuber, J.F., & Haroff, P.B. (1965). *The significant Americans.* New York: Meredith.

Cumming, E. (1963). Further thoughts on the theory of disengagement. *International Social Science Journal, 3,* 377-93.

Cumming, E., & Henry, W.E. (1961). *Growing old: The Process of disengagement.* New York: Basic Books.

Cummings, H.W., & Renshaw, S.L. (1979). SLCA III: A metatheoretical approach to the study of language. *Human Communication Research, 5,* 291-300.

Cummings, J., & Benson, D. (1983). *Dementia: A Clinical approach.* Boston: Butterworth.

*Current Literature On Aging.* (1983-). Washington, DC: Publications Office, National Council on Aging, 600 Maryland Avenue, S.W., West Wing 100.

Cushman, D.P., & Cahn, D.D. (1985). *Communication in interpersonal relationships.* Albany: State University of New York Press.

Cutlip, S., Center, A., & Broom, G. (1986). *Effective public relations* (6th ed.). Englewood Cliffs, NJ: Prentice-Hall.

Czaja, S. (1983). *Hand anthropometrics.* Washington, DC: U.S. Architectural and Transportation Barriers Compliance Board.

Czirr, R., & Rappaport, M. (1984). Toolkit for teams: Annotated bibliography on interdisciplinary health teams. *Clinical Gerontologist, 2,* 47-54.

Czvik, P.S. (1977). Assessment of family attitudes toward aphasic patients with severe auditory processing disorders. In R.H. Brookshire (Ed.), *Proceedings of the Clinical Aphasiology Conference.* Minneapolis: BRK Publishers.

Dance, F.E.X. (1967). Toward a theory of human communication. In F.E.X. Dance (Ed.), *Human Communication theory: Original essays* (pp. 288-309). New York: Holt, Rinehart, and Winston

Dance, F.E.X., & Larson, C.E., (1976). *The functions of human communication: A theoretical approach.* New York: Holt, Rinehart, and Winston.

Dangott, L.R., & Kalish, R.A. (1979). *A time to enjoy the pleasures of aging.* Englewood Cliffs, NJ: Prentice Hall.

Danowski, J. (1976). Communication specialists in aging-related organizations. In H.J. Oyer & E.J. Oyer (Eds.), *Aging and communications* (pp. 275-88). Baltimore: University Park Press.

Darley, F.L. (1982). *Aphasia.* Philadelphia: W.B. Saunders.

Darley, F.L., Aronson, A.E., & Brown, J.R. (1975). *Motor speech disorders.* Philadelphia: W.B. Saunders.

Darnell, J.C., Murray, M.D., Martz, B.L., & Weinberger, M. (1986). Medication use by ambulatory elderly: An in-home survey. *Journal of the American Geriatrics Society, 34,* 1-4.

Davis, G.A., & Baggs, T.W. (1984). Rehabilitation of speech and language disorders. In L. Jacobs-Condit (Ed.), *Gerontology and communication disorders* (PP. 185-243). Rockville, MD: American Speech-Language-Hearing Association.

Davis, G.A., & Holland, A.L. (1981). Age in understanding aphasia. In D.S. Beasley and G.A. Davis (Eds.), *Aging: Communication processes and disorders.* New York: Grune & Stratton.

Davis, P.B. (1949). An investigation of the suggestion of age through voice in interpretative reading. M.A. Thesis, University of Denver.

Davis, R.H. (1971). Television and the older adult. *Journal of Broadcasting, 15,* 153-59.

_____ (1980). *Television and the aging audience.* Los Angeles: University of Southern California.

Davis, R.H., & Davis, J.A. (1985). *TV's image of the elderly.* Lexington, MA: D.H. Heath.

Davis, R.H., Edwards, A.E., Bartel, D.J., & Martin, D. (1976). Assessing television viewing behavior of older adults. *Journal of Broadcasting, 20,* 69-76.

Davis, R.H., & Kubey, R.W. (1982). Growing old on television and with television. In D. Pearl, L. Bouthilet, & J.B. Lazar (Eds.), *Television and behavor: Ten years of scientific progress and implications for the eighties,* (Vol. 2: *Technical Reports*) (DHHS No. ADM 82-1196, pp. 201-8). Rockville, MD: National Institute of Mental Health.

Davis, R.H., & Miller, R. (1982). Communications media and the aged. Paper presented to the Speech Communication Association Annual Conference, Louisville, Kentucky.

Davis, R.H., & Westbrook, G.J. (1981). Intergenerational dialogues: A tested educational program for children. *Journal of Educational Gerontology, 7,* 223-37.

_____ (1985). Television in the lives of the elderly: Attitudes and opinions. *Journal of Broadcasting & Electronic Media, 29,* 209-14.

Day, A.T. (1985). *Who cares?: Demographic trends challenge family care for the elderly.* Washington, DC: Population Reference Bureau, Inc.

Deci, E.L. (1975). *Intrinsic motivation.* New York: Plenum Press.

Decker, D.L. (1980). *Social gerontology.* Boston: Little, Brown.

DeGrazia, S. (1961). The uses of time. In R.W. Kleemeier (Ed.), *Aging and leisure* (pp. 113-53). New York: Oxford University Press.

deLaski-Smith, D.L. (1984). Housing the elderly: Intergenerational family settings. *Journal of Housing for the Elderly, 2,* 61-70.

Dementia and depression: Behavior dysfunction in the elderly. (1984). *Physical and Occupational Therapy in Geriatrics, 3,* 1-59.

De Paul, A.V. (1983). Aunt Edna and the nursing home. *Journal of Gerontological Nursing, 9,* 29-31.

Derman, S., & Manaster, R. (1967). Family counseling with relatives of aphasic patients at Schwab Rehabilitation Hospital. *Asha, 9,* 175-77.

Deutsch, F.M., Clark, M.E., & Zalenski, C.M. (1983). Is there a double standard of aging? Paper presented at the Eastern Psychological Association, Philadelphia.

Deutscher, I. (1968). The quality of postparental life. In B. Neugarten (Ed.), *Middle age and aging* (pp. 263-68). Chicago: University of Chicago Press.

Deutschman, M. (1985). Environmental competence and environmental management. *The Journal of Long-Term Care Administration,* Fall, 78-84.

Devit, M., & Checkoway, B. (1982). Participation in nursing home resident councils: Promise and practice. *The Gerontologist, 22,* 49-53.

DeVito, J. (1986). *The interpersonal communication book* (4th ed.). New York: Harper and Row.

Dimmick, J.W., McCain, T.A., & Bolton, W.T. (1979). Media use and the life span. *American Behavioral Scientist, 23,* 7-31.

Displaced homemaker: A crisis of later life. (1982). *Journal of Geriatric Psychiatry, 15,* 131-91.

Doering, M., Rhodes, S.R., & Schuster, M. (1983). *The aging worker: Research and recommendation.* Beverly Hills: Sage.

Doolittle, J.C. (1979). News media use by older adults. *Journalism Quarterly, 56,* 311-17, 345.

Douglass, R., & Hickey, T. (1983). Domestic neglect and abuse of the elderly: Research findings and a systems perspective for service delivery planning. In J.I. Kosberg, (Ed.), *Abuse and maltreatment of the elderly: Causes and intervention* (pp. 115-33). Littleton, MA: John Wright.

Douglass, R., Hickey, T., & Noel, C. (1980). A study of maltreatment of the elderly and other vulnerable adults. *Final report to the United States Administration on Aging and the Michigan Department of Social Services.* Ann Arbor, MI: The Institute of Gerontology, The University of Michigan.

Dowd, J.J. (1980). *Stratification among the aged.* Monterey, CA: Brooks/Cole Publishers.

Downe-Wamboldt, B., & Ellerton, M. (1985-86). A study of the role of hospice volunteers. *Hospice Journal, 1,* 17-31.

Doyle, D., & Forehand, M.J. (1984). Life satisfaction and old age. *Research On Aging, 6,* 432-48.

Dreher, B. (1987). *Communication skills for working with elders.* New York: Springer Publishing.

Dresser, R. (1985). When patients resist feeding: Medical, ethical, and legal considerations. *Journal of the American Geriatrics Society, 33,* 790-94.

Duffy, M., & Willson, V.L. (1984). The role of design factors of the residential environment in the physical and mental health of the elderly. *Journal of Housing for the Elderly, 2,* 37-45.

Duncan, O.D., Featherman, D.L., & Duncan, B. (1972). *Socioeconomic background and achievement.* New York: Seminar Press.

Dunkle, R.E., & Hooper, C.R. (1983). Using language to help depressed elderly aphasic persons. *Social Casework, 64,* 539-45.

Dunn, H.L. (1969). Communication and purpose—ingredients for longevity. *Journal of Speech and Hearing Disorders, 26*(2), 114.

Dush, D.M. (Ed.). (1985). *The Hospice Journal, 1,* 1-101.

Dychtwald, K., & MacLean, J. (Eds.). (1986). *Wellness and health promotion for the elderly.* Rockville, MD: Aspen Systems Corporation.


Edinberg, M. (1986). Developing and integrating family-oriented approaches in care of the elderly. In K.A. Pillemer & R.S. Wolf (Eds.), *Elder abuse: Conflict in the family* (pp. 267-82). Dover, MA: Auburn House Publishing.

Edmonson, B. (1985). The home health care market. *American Demographics, 7,* 48-51.

Ehrlich, P. (1985). Informal support networks meet health needs of rural elderly. *Journal of Gerontological Social Work, 9,* 85-98.

Eisdorfer, C., Nowlin, J., & Wilkie, F. (1970). Improvement of learning in the aged by modification of autonomic nervous system activity. *Science, 170,* 1327-29.

Eisenson, J. (1973). *Adult aphasia: Assessment and treatment.* Englewood Cliffs, NJ: Prentice-Hall.

Eliopoulous, C. (1982). The director of nursing in the nursing home setting: An emerging dynamic role in gerontological nursing. *Journal of Gerontological Nursing, 8,* 448-50.

Elmore, J., & Elmore, G. (1982). Communication and community health for the aged. Paper presented to the Speech Communication Association Annual Conference, Louisville, Kentucky.

Emery, O.B. (1985). Language and aging. *Experimental Aging Research, 11,* (entire issue).

Engen, T. (1977). Taste and smell. In J.E. Birren and K.W. Schaie (Eds.), *Handbook of the psychology of aging.* New York: Van Nostrand Reinhold.

_____. (1982). *The perception of odors.* New York: Academic Press.

Enright, R.D., Roberts, P., & Lapsley, D.K. (1983). Belief discrepancy reasoning in the elderly. *International Journal of Aging and Human Development, 17,* 213-21.

Erber, J.T. (1981). Remote memory and age: a review. *Experimental Aging Research, 1,* 189-99.

_____. (1982). Memory and age. In T. Field, W. Overton, H. Quay, L. Troll, & G. Finley (Eds.). *Review of human development.* New York: Wiley.

Erickson, R. (1985). Companion animals and the elderly. *Geriatric Nursing, 6,* 92-96.

Erickson, R.D., & Hyerstay, B.J. (1974). The dying patient and the double-bind hypothesis. *Omega, 5,* 287-98.

Euster, G.L. (1984-85). Volunteerism with the elderly: An innovative interdisciplinary course in graduate education. *Gerontology and Geriatrics Education, 5,* 13-23.

Evans, D.L., Millicovsky, L., & Tennison, C.R. (1984). Aging, reminiscence and mourning. *Psychiatric Forum, 12,* 19-32.

Everitt, D.E. (1985). Cost containment and the elderly: Making financial incentives more explicit. *Journal of Geriatric Psychiatry, 18,* 155-76.


"Face the nation," aired August 31, 1986.

Farace, R.V., Monge, P.R., & Russell, H.M. (1977). *Communicating and organizing.* Reading, MA: Addison-Wesley.

Federal Council on Aging. (1981). *The need for long-term care.* Washington, DC: U.S. Government Printing Office.

Federal regulations title 45. (1983). Office for protection from research risks. Part 46: Protection of Human subjects. Revised March 8, 1983.

Feezel, J.D., & Shepherd, P.E. (1987). Cross-generational coping with interpersonal relationship loss. *Western Journal of Speech Communication, 51,* Summer, 317-27.

Feier, C.D., & Gerstman, L.J. (1980). Sentence comprehension abilities throughout the adult life span. *Journal of Gerontology, 35,* 722-28.

Feil, N.W. (1985). Resolution: The final life task. *Journal of Humanistic Psychology, 25,* 91-105.

Fein, D.J. (1983a). The prevalence of speech and language impairments. *Asha, 25*(11), 31.

_____. (1983b). Projection of speech and hearing impairments to 2050. *Asha, 25*(11), 31.

Feldman, R.S. (Ed.). *Development of nonverbal behavior in children.* New York: Springer-Verlag.

Fengler, A.P. (1984). Life satisfaction of subpopulations of elderly: The comparative effects of volunteerism, employment, and meal site participation. *Research on Aging, 6,* 189-212.

Ferguson, C. (1977). Baby talk as a simplified register. In C. Snow & C. Ferguson (Eds.), *Talking to children.* New York: Cambridge University Press.

Ferraro, K.F. (1984). Widowhood and social participation in later life: Isolation or compensation? *Research on Aging, 6,* 451-68.

Field, M. (1972). *The aged, the family and the community.* New York: Columbia University Press.

Fieweger, M., & Smilowitz, M. (1984). Relational conclusion through interaction with the dying. *Omega, 15,* 161-72.

Filinson, R. (1984). Diagnosis of senile demental Alzheimer's type: The state of the art. *Clinical Gerontologist, 2,* 3-23.

Fillenbaum, G.G. (1985). Screening the elderly: A brief instrumental activities of daily living measure. *Journal of the American Geriatrics Society, 33,* 698-706.

Fishbein, M., & Ajzen, I. (1975). *Belief, attitude, intention and behavior: An introduction to theory and research.* Reading, MA: Addison-Wesley.

Fitzgerald, J.M. (1978). Actual and perceived sex and generational differences in interpersonal style: Structural and quantitative issues. *Journal of Gerontology, 33,* 394-401.

Florance, C.L. (1979). The aphasic's significant other: Training and counseling. In R.H. Brookshire (Ed.), *Proceedings of the clinical aphasiology conference.* Minneapolis: BRK Publishers.

Foner, A. (1974). Age stratification and age conflict in political life. *American Sociological Review, 39,* 187-96.

———. (1979). Ascribed and achieved bases of stratification. In A. Inkeles, J. Coleman, and R. Turner (Eds.), *Annual Review of Sociology* (Vol. 5). Palo Alto, CA: Annual Reviews.

Fontana, A. (1980). Growing old between walls. In J. Quadagno, (Ed.), *Aging, the individual and society: Readings in social gerontology* (pp. 482-99). New York: St. Martin's Press.

Foster, L.W., & Paradis, L.F. (1985). Hospice and death education: A resource bibliography. *The Hospice Journal, 1,* 3-61.

Fowler, N. (1981). The administration on aging ombudsman developmental specialist program in Illinois as a means of enhancing the visability of the older American. Paper presented to the Speech Communication Association Summer Conference on Communication and Gerontology, Edwardsville, Illinois.

Fozard, J.L., Wolf, E., Bell, B., McFarland, R.A., and Podolsky, S. (1977). Visual perception and communication. In J.E. Birren and K.W. Schaie (Eds.), *Handbook of the psychology of aging.* New York: Van Nostrand Reinhold.

Francher, J.S. (1973). "It's the Pepsi generation..." accelerated aging and the television commercial. *International Journal of Aging and Human Development, 4,* 245-55.

Franke, J.L. (1984). Representation in age-based interest groups. *Research on Aging, 6,* 346-71.

———. (1985). Citizens input and aging policy: The case of Florida. *Research on Aging, 7,* 517-33.

Fredrick, J.F., & Fredrick, N.J. (1985). The hospice experience: Possible effects in altering the biochemistry of bereavement. *The Hospice Journal, 1,* 81-90.

Frengley, J.D. (1985). The special knowledge of geriatric medicine. *Rehabilitation Literature, 46,* 133-37.

Fricke, S.C. (Ed.). (1985). *An orientation to the older Americans Act.* (Rev. ed.) Washington, DC: National Association of State Units on Aging.

Friedson, E. (1966). Disability as deviance. In M. Sussman, (Ed.), *Sociology and rehabilitation.* Washington, DC: American Sociological Association.

Fritz, P., Russell, C., & Wilcox, E. (1980). The chronic, non-compliant older patient: A method for teaching norm sensitivity to nurses. Paper presented to the Speech Communication Association Annual Conference, New York.

Froehlich, J., & Nelson, D.L. (1986). Affective meanings of life review through activities and discussion. *American Journal of Occupational Therapy, 40,* 27-33.

Fry, D. (1977). *Homo Loquens: Man the talking animal.* Cambridge: Cambridge University Press.

Fuchs, V. (1974). *Who shall live?: Health, economics, and social choice.* New York: Basic Books.

Galbraith, M.W. (1983). *The older employee as a concern of staff developers.* ERIC Document Reproduction Service No's. ED238383, HE 016924.

Galbraith, M.W. (Ed.). (1986). *Elder abuse: Perspectives on an emerging crisis.* Kansas City, KS: Mid-American Congress on Aging.

Gallagher, F.M. (1985). Capitalize on elder strengths. *Journal of Gerontological Nursing, 11,* 13-14.

Galvin, K.M., & Brommel, B.J. (1986). *Family communication: Cohesion and change.* Glenview, IL: Scott, Foresman, and Company.

Gantz, W., Gartenberg, H.M., & Rainbow, C.K. (1980). Approaching invisibility: The portrayal of the elderly in magazine advertisements. *Journal of Communication, 30*(1), 56-60.

Gates, K. (1986). Dementia: A family problem. *Gerontion, 1,* 12-17.

Genevay, B. (1986). Intimacy as we age. *Generations, 10*(4), 12-15.

George, L.K. (1986). Life satisfaction in later life: The positive side of mental health. *Generations, 10,* 5-8.

Georgopoulos, B.S. (Ed.). (1974). *Organization research on health institutions.* Ann Arbor, MI: Institute for Social Research.

――――. (1975). *Hospital organization research: Review and source book.* Philadelphia: Saunders.

Gerbner, G., Gross, L., Signorielli, N., & Morgan, M. (1980). Aging with television: Images on television drama and conceptions of social reality. *Journal of Communication, 30*(1), 37-47.

Gibb, J.R. (1961). Defensive communication. *The Journal of Communication, 11,* 141-48.

Gifford, C. (1981). Across ages: Generations communicate in unique Multidisciplinary Learning Retreat at Temple University. Paper presented at the Speech Communication Association Conference on Communication and Gerontology, Edwardsville, Illinois.

――――. (1983). Health team literature: A review and application with implications for communication research. Paper presented to the Eastern Communication Association conference, Ocean City, Maryland.

Gilford, R. (1986). Marriages in later life. *Generations, 10*(4), 16-20.

Gioiella, E.C., & Bevil, C.W. (1985). *Nursing care of the aging client: Promoting healthy adaptation.* Norwalk, CT: Appleton-Century-Crofts.

Glenn, J. (1986). Statement of Senator John Glenn at a hearing before the U.S. Senate Special Committee on Aging, "Nursing Home Care: The Unfinished Agenda." *News Release,* May 21, 1-4.

Glick, I.O., & Levy, S.J. (1962). *Living with television.* Chicago: Aldine.

Glosser, G., & Wexler, D. (1985). Participants' evaluation of educational/support groups for families of patients with Alzheimer's disease and other dementias. *The Gerontologist, 25,* 232-36.

Goffman, E. (1963). *Stigma: Notes on the management of spoiled identity.* Englewood Cliffs, NJ: Prentice-Hall.

Golden, H.M. (1976). Blake ageism. *Social Policy, 7,*(3), 40-42.

Goldhaber, G. (1986). *Organizational communication* (4th ed.). Duguque, IA: Wm. C. Brown.

Goldin, G.J. (1985). The influence of self-image upon the performance of nursing home staff. *Nursing Homes, 34,* 33-38.

Gonda, T.A., & Ruark, J.E. (1984). *Dying dignified: The health professionals's guide to care.* Menlo Park, CA: Addison-Wesley.

Goodglass, H., & Kaplan, E. (1983). *The assessment of aphasia and related disorders* (2nd ed.). Philadelphia: Lea & Febiger.

Goodman, C.C. (1984). Natural helping among older adults. *The Gerontologist, 24,* 138-43.

Gore, I. (1976). *The generation jigsaw.* London: George Allen Ltd.

Gouldner, A.W. (1960). The norm of reciprocity: A preliminary statement. *American Sociological Review, 25,* 161-78.

Graen, G. (1976). Role making processes within complex organizations. In M.D. Dunnette (Ed.), *Handbook of industrial and organizational psychology.* Chicago: Rand McNally.

Graney, M.J. (1975). Communication uses and the social activity constant. *Communication Research, 2,* 347-66.

Graney, M.J., & Graney, E.E. (1974). Communications activity substitutions in aging. *Journal of Communication, 24*(4), 88-96.

Grau, L. (1983). Management styles: Application to nursing homes. *Nursing Homes, 32,* 28-31.

Green, I., Fedewa, B.E., Johnston, C.A., Jackson, W.M., & Deardorff, H.L. (1975). *Housing for the elderly: The development and design process.* New York: Van Nostrand Reinhold.

Green, R.F. (1969). Age-intelligence relationship between ages sixteen and sixty-four: A rising trend. *Developmental Psychology, 1,* 618-27.

Greenberg, B.S., Korzenny, F., & Atkin, C. (1979). The portrayal of the aging: Trends on commercial television. *Research on Aging, 1,* 319-34.

Griew, S. (1964). *Job redesign.* Paris: Organization for Economic Co-Operation and Development.

Gronning, N. (1982). Peer counselor training in gerontology. Paper presented to the Speech Communication Association Conference, Louisville, Kentucky.

Grosswith, M. (1982). How to soften up the thoughts. *50 Plus, 22,* 32-35.

Grunebam, H. (1979). Middle age and marriage: Affiliative men and assertive women. *American Journal of Family Therapy, 7*(3), 46-50.

Gubrium, J.F. (1975). *Living and dying in Murray Manor.* New York: St. Martin's Press.

_____. (1976). Being single in old age. In J.F. Gubrium (Ed.), *Times, roles and self in old age* (pp. 179-97). New York: Human Sciences Press.

_____. (1980). Patient exclusion in geriatric staffings. *The Sociological Quarterly, 21,* 335-47.

Guinn, M.J. (1985). Elder abuse and neglect raise new dilemmas. *Generations, 10,* 22-25.

Gunter, L.M. (1984). Editorial. *Journal of Gerontological Nursing, 10,* 6.

Hagen, D. (1980). Nursing homes as a training site for LPNs/LVNs. *The journal of Long-Term Care Administration,* September, 1-11.

Hagestad, G.L. (1978). Patterns of communication and influence between grand-parents and grandchildren in a changing society. Paper presented at the World Congress of Sociology, Uppsala, Sweden.

Halamandaris, V.J. (1985). *Nursing care of the aging client: Promoting healthy adaptation.* Norwalk, CT: Appleton-Century-Crofts.

Hales, C. (1985). How should the information needs of the aging be met?: A Delphi response. *The Gerontologist, 25,* 172-76.

Halpern, H. (1986). Therapy for agnosia, apraxia, and dysarthria. In R. Chapey (Ed.), *Language intervention strategies in adult aphasia* (2nd ed.). Baltimore: Williams & Wilkins.

Hampe, G.D., & Bievins, A.L., Jr. (1975). The therapeutic role of the life review in the elderly. *Academic Psychology Bulletin, 6,* 287-99.

Haney, V. (1967). *Communication and organizational behavior: Text and cases.* Homewood, IL: Richard D. Irwin.

Hardiman, C.J., Holbrook, A., & Hedrick, D.L. (1979). Nonverbal communication systems for the severely handicapped. *The Gerontologist, 19*(1), 96-101.

Harel, Z. (1978). Organizational analysis of institutions for the aged. *Journal of Sociology and Social Welfare, 5, 792-801.*

Harper, R.G., Wiens, A.N., & Matarazzo, J.D. (1978). *Nonverbal communication: The state of the art.* New York: Wiley & Sons.

Harris, D.K. (1985). *The sociology of aging: An annotated bibliography and source-book.* New York: Garland.

Harris, L. & Associates (1975). *The myth and reality of aging in America.* Washing-ton, DC: The National Council on the Aging.

Harris, A.J., & Feinberg, J.F. (1977). Television and aging: Is what you see what you get? *The Gerontologist, 17,* 464-68.

Harris, J.E., & Bodden, J.L. (1978). An activity group experience for disengaged elderly persons. *Journal of Consulting Psychology, 25,* 325-30.

Harron, J., & Schaeffer, J. (1986). DRG's and the intensity of skilled nursing. *Geriatric Nursing, 7,* 31-33.

Hartley, J.T., Harker, J.O., & Walsh, D.A. (1980). Contemporary issues and new directions in adult development of learning and memory. In L.W. Poon (Ed.), *Aging in the 1980's.* Washington, DC: American Psychological Association.

Hartman, P.E., & Danhauer, J.L. (1976). Perceptual features of speech for males in four perceived age decades. *Journal of the Acoustical Society of America, 59,* 713-15.

Hartshorne, T.S., & Monaster, G.J. (1980). Relationships with grandparents: Con-tact, importance, role conception. *International Journal of Aging and Human Development, 15,* 233-45.

Hartwigsen, G. (1984/85). The appeal of the life care facility to the older widow. *Journal of Housing for the Elderly, 2,* 63-75.

Harvey, L.M. (1983). The activist self-help program: An alternative service for the aged. *Activities, Adaptation and Aging, 4,* 1-10.

Hasler, D., & Hasler, N. (1967). *Personal, home, and community health.* New York: MacMillan Company.

Hatfield, E., & Sprecher, S. (1986). *Mirror, Mirror...: The importance of looks in everyday life.* Albany: State University of New York Press.

Havighurst, R.J. (1968). A social-psychological perspective on aging. *The Gerontologist, 8,* 67-71.

Hawranik, R. (1985). Caring for aging parents: Divided allegiances. *Journal of Gerontological Nursing, 11,* 19-22.

Haynie, W.E. (1983). Cypen Tower: A design for retirement living. *Retirement,* January-February, 18-24.

Hayslip, B. (1984/85). Idiographic assessment of the self in the aged: A case for the use of the Q-sort. *International Journal of Aging and Human Development, 20,* 293-311.

Heinemann, G.D. (1985). Interdependence in informal support systems: The case of elderly urban widows. In W.A. Peterson & J. Quadagno (Eds.), *Social bonds in later life* (pp. 165-86). Beverly Hills: Sage.

Helfrich, H. (1979). Age markers in speech. In K.R. Scherer & H. Giles (Eds.), *Social markers in speech.* New York: Cambridge University Press.

Helmick, J.W., Watamori, T.S., & Palmer, J.M. (1976). Spouses' understanding of the communication disabilities of aphasic patients. *Journal of Speech and Hearing Disorders, 41,* 238-43.

Henderson, S.A. (1980). A development in social psychiatry: The systematic study of social bonds. *The Journal of Nervous and Mental Disease, 168,* 63-68.

Hendricks, J., & Hendricks, C.D. (1977). *Aging in mass society: Myths and realities* (2nd ed.). Cambridge: Winthrop.

Hennon, C.B. (1983). Divorce and the elderly: A neglected area of research. In T.H. Brubaker (Ed.), *Family relationships in later life* (pp. 149-72). Beverly Hills: Sage.

Hepner, J. & Hepner, D. (1973). *The health strategy game.* Saint Louis: C.V. Mosby Company.

Herr, J.J., & Weakland, J.H. (1979). Communications within family systems: Growing older within and with the double bind. In P.K. Ragan (Ed.), *Aging parents.* (pp. 144-53). University of Southern California Press: The Ethel Percy Andrus Gerontology Center.

Hershman, P., Fritz, P., Russell, C., & Wilcox, E. (1981). Recognition of status norms among the non-compliant elderly: A communication course for nurses. Paper presented to the Speech Communication Association Summer Conference on Communication and Aging, Edwardsville, Illinois.

Heslin, R., & Patterson, M.L. (1982). *Nonverbal behavior and social psychology.* New York: Plenum.

Hess, B.B. (1974). Stereotypes of the aged. *Journal of Communication, 24,* 74-84.

———. (1984). Social aspects of communication in later years. In R.E. Dunkle, M. Haug, & M. Rosenberg (Eds.), *Communication Technology and the Elderly: Issues and Forecasts.* New York: Springer.

Hewner, S.J. (1986). Bringing home the health care. *Journal of Gerontological Nursing, 12,* 29-35.

Hickey, T., & Kalish, R.A. (1968). Young peoples perceptions of adults. *Journal of Gerontology, 23,* 215-19.

Hiemstra, R.P. (1972). Continuing education for the aged: A survey of needs and interests. *Adult Education, 3,* 100-109.

Higgins-Vogel, C. (1982). Anxiety and depression among the elderly. *Journal of Gerontological Nursing, 8,* 213-16.

Hinton, J.M. (1981). Sharing or withholding awareness of dying between husband and wife. *Journal of Psychosomatic Research, 25,* 337-43.

Hnatiuk, R. (1981). The challenge of gerontological nursing in a nursing home. *Journal of Gerontological Nursing, 7,* 41-44.

Hoffman, V. (1985). Homesharing: A new tool for keeping patients out of institutions. *Continuing Care Coordinator, 4,* 22-24.

Holland, A.L., & Bartlett, C.L. (1985). Some differential effects of age on stroke-produced aphasia. In H.K. Ulatowska (Ed.), *The aging brain: Communication in the elderly.* San Diego, CA: College-Hill Press.

Hollinger, L.M. (1986). Communicating with the elderly. *Journal of Gerontological Nursing, 12,* 8-13.

Holloway, R.G. (1976). Management can reverse declining employee work attitudes. *Hospitals, 50,* 71-77.

Holstein, M. (1983). Today's policies for elders have roots in the past. *Generations, 7,* 28-29.

Holtz, G.A. (1982). Nurses' aides in nursing homes: Why are they satisfied? *Journal of Gerontological Nursing, 8,* 265-71.

Hooper, C.R., & Dunkle, R.E. (1985). *The older aphasic person: Strategies in treatment and disgnosis.* Rockville, MD: Aspen Systems Corporation.

Hornstein, G.A., & Wapner, S. (1985). Modes of experiencing and adapting to retirement. *International Journal of Aging and Human Development, 21,* 291-315.

Hoyer, W.J., & Plude, D.J. (1980). Attentional and perceptual processes in the study of cognitive aging. In L.W. Poon (Ed.), *Aging in the 1980's.* Washington, DC: American Psychological Association.

Hudson, M.F. (1986). Elder mistreatment: Current research. In K.A. Pillemer & R.S. Wolf (Eds.), *Elder abuse: Conflict in the family,* (pp. 125-66). Dover, MA: Auburn House Publishing.

Hughes, E.C. (1958). The study of occupations. In R.K. Merton, L. Broomand, and L. Cottrell (Eds.), *Sociology Today,* New York: Basic Books.

Huse, E.F. (1975). *Organization development and change.* St. Paul: West.

Huss, A. J. (1977). Touch with a Care or a Caring Touch, *American Journal of Occupational Therapy, 31,* 11-18.

Hussian, R.A., & Davis, R.L. (1985). *Responsive care: Behavioral interventions with elderly persons.* Champaign, IL: Research Press.

Huyck, M.H., & Hoyer, W.J. (1982). *Adult development and aging.* Belmont, CA: Wadsworth.

Hwang, J.C. (1972). Information seeking and opinion leadership among older Americans. Doctoral dissertation, University of Oregon, Eugene.

Illich, I. (1976). *Medical nemesis.* New York: Random House.

International Association of Laryngectomees. (1975). *Laryngectomized speaker's source book.* New York: International Association of Laryngectomees.

Isquick, M.F. (1981). Training older people in empathy: Effects of empathy, attitudes, and self-exploration. *International Journal of Aging and Human Development, 13,* 1-14.

Itzin, F.H. (1983). Social relationships and activities. In W.W. Morris & I.M. Bader, (Eds.), *Hoffman's daily needs and interests of older people* (pp. 95-118). Springfield: Charles C. Thomas Publisher. (Original work published in 1970.)

Ivester, C., & King, K. (1977). Attitudes of adolescents toward the aged. *The Gerontologist, 17,* 85-89.


Jablin, F.M. (1982). Organizational communication: An assimilation approach. In M.E. Roloff and C.R. Berger (Eds.), *Social cognition and communication* (pp. 255-86). Beverly Hills: Sage.

_____. (1984). Assimilating new members into organizations. In Robert Bostrom, (Ed.), *Communication Yearbook, 8,* (pp. 594-626). Beverly Hills: Sage.

Jacobs, B., & Ventura-Merkel, C. (1984). *A guidebook for the educational goals inventory: Establishing goals for older adult educational programs.* Washington, DC: The National Council on Aging, Inc.

Jacobs, M. (1984). More than a million older Americans abused physically and mentally each year. *Perspectives on Aging, 13*(6), 19-20.

Jacobs-Condit, L. (Ed.). (1984). *Gerontology and communication disorders.* Rockville, MD: American Speech-Language-Hearing Association.

Jacobs-Condit, L. & Ortenzo, M.L. (1984). Physical changes in aging. In L. Jacobs-Condit (Ed.), *Gerontology and communication disorders.* Rockville, MD: American Speech-Language-Hearing Association.

Jarrett, W.H. (1985). Caregiving within kinship systems: Is affection really necessary? *The Gerontologist, 25,* 5-10.

Jenkins, T.S., Parham, I.A., & Jenkins, T. (1985). Alzheimer's disease: Caregivers' perceptions of burden. *Journal of Applied Gerontology, 4,* 40-57.

Jenkins, T.S., Roberts, N.J., Johnson, J.W., & Windsor, V.K. (1983). *Mental health and aging: A guide to training and program development.* Odessa, FL: Psychological Assessment Resources.

Jessup, F. (1969). *Lifelong learning.* London: Pergamon.

Johnson, C.L. (1983). Dyadic family relations and social support. *The Gerontologist, 23,* 377-83.

Johnson, D.F. (1985). Appearance and the elderly. In J.A. Graham & A.M. Kligman (Eds.), *The psychology of cosmetic treatments.* New York: Praeger.

Johnson, D.F., & Pittenger, J.B. (1984). Attribution, the attractiveness stereotype, and the elderly. Unpublished paper, Department of Psychology, University of Arkansas at Little Rock.

Johnson, E.S. (1978). "Good" relationships between older mothers and their daughters: A causal model. *The Gerontologist, 18,* 301-6.

Johnson, E.S., & Bursk, B.J. (1977). Relationships between the elderly and their adult children. *The Gerontologist, 17,* 90-96.

Johnson, T.F., O'Brien, J.G., & Hudson, M.F. (Eds.). (1985). *Elder neglect and abuse: An annotated bibliography.* Westport, CT: Greenwood Press.

Jones, C.C. (1982). *Caring for the aged: An appraisal of nursing homes and alternatives.* Chicago: Nelson-Hall.

Jones, G.R. (1983). Psychological orientation and the process of organizational socialization: An interactionist perspective. *Academy of Management Review, 8,* 464-74.

Jones, R.M., & Adams, G.R. (1982). Assessing the importance of physical attractiveness across the life-span. *Journal of Social Psychology, 118,* 131-32.

Kahan, J., Kemp, B. Staples, F.R., & Brummel-Smith, K. (1985). Decreasing the burden in families caring for a relative with a dementing illness: A controlled study. *Journal of the American Geriatrics Society, 33,* 664-70.

Kahana, E.F., & Kiyak, H.A. (1984). Attitudes and behavior of staff in facilities for the aged. *Research on Aging, 6,* 395-416.

Kahane, J.C. (1981). Anatomic and physiologic changes in the aging peripheral speech mechanism. In D.S. Beasley and G.A. Davis (Eds.), *Aging: Communication processes and disorders.* New York: Grune and Stratton.

Kahn, R. (1977). Perspectives in evaluation of psychological mental health programs for the aged. In W.D. Gentry (Ed.), *Geropsychology.* Cambridge, MA: Ballinger.

Kahne, H. (1985). *Reconceiving part-time work: New perspectives for older workers and women.* Totowa, NJ: Rowman & Allanheld.

Kalish, R. (1975). *Late adulthood: Perspectives on human development.* Monterrey, CA: Wadsworth.

Kalish, R.A. (1976). Death and dying in a social context. In R.H. Binstock & E. Shanas (Eds.), *Handbook of aging and the social sciences* (pp. 483-507). New York: Van Nostrand Reinhold.

_____. (1979). The new ageism and the failure of models: A polemic. *The Gerontologist, 19,* 398-402.

Kaminsky, M. (1984). The uses of reminiscence: A discussion of the formative literature. *Journal of Gerontological Social Work, 7,* 137-56.

Kane, R.L. (1986). Outcome-based payment: A new beginning? *Health Progress, 67,* 36-41.

Kaplan, A.L. (1985). Let wisdom find a way: The concept of competency in the care of the elderly, *Generations, 10,* 10-14.

Kart, C.S., & Beckham, B.L. (1976). Black-white differentials in the institutionalization of the elderly: A temporal analysis. *Social Forces, 54,* 901-10.

Kastenbaum, R., & Aisenberg, R. (1972). *The psychology of death.* New York: Springer.

Kastenbaum, R., & Durkee, N. (1964). Young people view old age. In R. Kastenbaum (Ed.), *New Thought on old age.* New York: Springer.

Katz, D., & Kahn, R.L. (1978). *The social psychology of organizations* (2nd ed.). New York: John Wiley & Sons.

Kearney, P., Plax, T.G., & Lentz, P.S. (1985). Participation in community organizations and socioeconomic status as determinants of seniors' life satisfaction. *Activities, Adaptation, and Aging, 6,* 31-37.

Kearns, K.P. (1986). Group therapy for aphasia: Theoretical and practicl considerations. In R. Chapey (Ed.), *Language intervention strategies in adult aphasia* (2nd ed.). Baltimore: Williams & Wilkins.

Keith, P. (1971). An exploratory study of sources of stereotypes of old age among administrators. *Journal of Gerontology, 32,* 463-69.

Keither, P.M., & Schafer, R.B. (1985). Equity, role strains, and depression among middle aged and older men and women. In W.A. Peterson and J. Quadagno (Eds.), *Social bonds in later life* (pp. 37-49). Beverly Hills: Sage.

Keller, J. and Rozema, H. (1981). Patients' impressions of physicians: Age-related differences in patient's behavioral responses to persuasive appeals by physicians. Paper presented to the Speech Communication Association Summer Conference on Communication and Gerontology, Edwardsville, Illinois.

Kemper, T. (1984). Neuroanatomical and neuropathological changes in normal aging and dementia. In M.L. Albert (Ed.), *Clinical neurology of aging.* New York: Oxford University Press.

Kennedy, L.W., & Silverman, R.A. (1984/85). Significant others and fear of crime among the elderly. *International Journal of Aging and Human Development, 20,* 241-56.

Kenshalo, D.R. (1977). Age changes in touch, vibration, temperature, kinesthesis and pain sensitivity. In J.E. Birren & K.W. Schaie (Eds.), *Handbook of the psychology of aging.* New York: Van Nostrand Reinhold.

Kent, R.D., & Burkard, R. (1981). Changes in the acoustic correlates of speech production. In D.S. Beasley & G.A. Davis (Eds.), *Aging: Communication processes and disorders.* New York: Grune and Stratton.

Kermis, M.D. (1984). *The psychology of human aging: Theory, research, and practice.* Boston: Allyn & Bacon.

Kerzner, L. (1981). Medical education opportunities offered by long-term care institutions. In K. Steel (Ed.), *Geriatric education,* Lexington, MA: The Collamore Press.

Kiernat, J.M. (1983). Retrospection as a life span concept. *Physical and Occupational Therapy in Geriatrics, 3*(2), 35-48.

Kivinck, H. (1981). Grandparenthood and the mental health of grandparents. *Aging and Society, 1,* 365-91.

Klatt, P., & Heeter, K. (1985). *Hand in hand... bringing generations together: A guide to intergenerational programming.* Monticello, MN: Karla Heeter.

Kleck, R.E., & Strenta, A.C. (1985). Physical deviance and the perception of social outcomes. In J.A. Graham & A.M. Kligman (Eds.), *The psychology of cosmetic treatments.* New York: Praeger.

Klein, L.E., Roca, R.P., McArthur, J., Vogelsang, G., Klein, G.B., Kirby, S.M., & Folstein, M. (1985). Diagnosing dementia: Univariate and multivariate analyses of the mental status examination. *Journal of the American Geriatrics Society, 33,* 483-88.

Klinger-Vartabedian, L. (1982). *The group setting: A viable mental health alternative for the elderly.* Paper presented to the Speech Communication Association Annual Conference, Louisville, Kentucky.

Knapp, M.L. (1978a). *Nonverbal communication in human interaction.* New York: Holt, Rinehart & Winston.

———. (1978b). *Social intercourse: From greeting to goodbye.* Boston: Allyn and Bacon.

———. (1985). The study of physical appearance and cosmetics in western culture. In J.A. Graham & A.M. Kligman (Eds.), *The psychology of cosmetic treatments.* New York: Praeger.

Knapp, M.R. (1977). The activity theory of aging. *The Gerontologist, 17,* 553-59.

Knight, B., & Lower-Walker, D. (1985). Toward a definition of alternatives to alternatives to institutionalization for the frail elderly. *The Gerontologist, 25,* 358-63.

Knowles, M.S. (1984a). *Andragogy in action: Applying modern principles of adult learning.* San Francisco: Jossey-bass.

_____. (1984b). *The adult learner: A neglected species.* Houston: Gulf Publishing Company.

Koncelik, J.A. (1976). *Designing the open nursing home.* Stroudsberg, PA: Dowden, Hutchinson, and Ross, Inc.

Kopac, C.A. (1983). Sensory loss in the aged: The role of the nurse and the family. *Nursing Clinics of North America, 18,* 373-84.

Korzenny, F., & Neuendorf, K. (1980). Television viewing and self-concept of the elderly. *Journal of Communication, 30*(2), 71-80.

Krauskopf, J.M., & Burnett, M.E. (1983). The elderly person: When protection becomes abuse. In H. Cox (Ed.), *Aging: Annual editions* (4th ed.), (pp. 219-25). Guilford, CT: Dushkin Publishing Group.

Kreps, G. (1981). Communication and gerontology: Health communication training for providers of health services to the elderly. Paper presented to the Speech Communication Association Summer Conference on Communication and Gerontology, Edwardsville, Illinois.

_____. (1982, November), Humanizing organizational communication for elderly health care recipients. Paper presented to the Speech Communication Association Annual Conference, Louisville, Kentucky.

_____. (1986). *Organizational communication.* New York: Longman.

Kreps, G., and Thornton, B., (1984). *Health communication: Theory and practice.* New York: Longman.

Krout, J.A. (1985). Senior center activities and services: Findings from a national study. *Research on Aging, 7,* 455-71.

Kubey, R.W. (1980). Television and aging: Past, present, and future. *The Gerontologist, 20,* 16-35.

Kukol, R.J. (1979). *Perceptual speech and voice characteristics of aging male and female speakers.* Doctoral Dissertation, Wichita State University.

Kurocz, Janos, Feldmar, Gabriel, Werner, & William. (1979). Prosopo-affective agnosia associated with chronic organic brain syndrome. *Journal of the American Geriatrics Society, 27*(2), 91-95.

Kurtzke, J., & Kurland, L. (1973). The epidemiology of neurologic disease. In A. Baker (Ed.), *Clinical neurology.* Hagarstown, MD: Harper & Row.

Kwentus, J.A., Harkins, S.W., Lignon, N., & Silverman, J.J. (1985). Current concepts of geriatric pain and its treatment. *Geriatrics, 40,* 48-54.

Laing, R.D. (1961). *Self and others..* London: Tavistock.

Lakin, M., Bremer, J., & Oppenheimer, B. (1983/84). Group processes in helping groups: Toward a developmental perspective. *International Journal of Aging and Human Development, 18,* 13-24.

Lalonde, B.I.D., & Fallcreek, S.J. (1985). Outcome effectiveness of the Wallingford Wellness Project: A model health promotion program for the elderly. *Journal of Gerontological Social Work, 9,* 49-64.

Lantz, J.M. (1985). In search of agents for self-care. *Journal of Gerontological Nursing, 11,* 10-14.

LaRue, A. & D'Elia, L.F. (1985). Anxiety and problem solving in middle-aged and elderly adults. *Experimental Aging Research, 11,* 215-20.

Lasch, C. (1977). *Haven in a heartless world.* New York: Basic Books.

Lau, E., & Kosberg, J. (1979). Abuse of the elderly by informal care providers. Aging, September-October, 10-15.

Lawton, M.P. (1975). *Planning and managing housing for the elderly.* New York: John Wiley & Sons.

Lawton, M.P. (Ed.). (1979). Special Issue on Housing. *Generations, III, Winter,* 1-40.

Lazarus, L.W. (1985). Geriatric depression: A guide to successful therapy. *Geriatrics, 40,* 43-53.

Levin, J., & Levin, W.C. (1981). Willingness to interact with an old person. *Research on Aging, 3,* 211-17.

Levine, J. (1986). AIDS: Prejudice and progress. *Time,* September 8, p. 68.

Levine, N.B., Gendron, G.E., Dastoor, D.P., Poitras, L.R., Sirota, S.E., Barza, S.L., & Davis, J.C. (1984). Supporter endurance training: A manual for trainers. *Clinical Gerontologist, 2,* 15-23.

Levinson, D. (1978). *The seasons of a man's life.* New York: Knopf.

Lewis, S.C. (1983). *Providing for the older adult: A gerontological handbook.* Thorofare, NJ: Slack, Inc.

Lewkwart, J.F. (1967). *Social distance as an interpersonal dimension of vertical relationships.* Western Reserve University.

Lichtenstein, M.J., Federspiel, C.F., & Schaffner, W. (1985). Factors associated with early demise in nursing home residents: A case control study. *Journal of the American Geriatrics Society, 33,* 315-19.

Lidoff, L., & Harris, P. (1985). *Idea book on caregiver support groups.* Washington, DC: The National Council on the Aging, Inc.

Lincoln, R. (1983). What do nurses know about confusion in the aged? *Journal of Gerontological Nursing, 10,* 26-32.

Linebaugh, C.W., & Young-Charles, H.Y. (1978). The counseling needs of the families of aphasic patients. In R.H. Brookshire (Ed.), *Proceedings of the Clinical Aphasiology Conference.* Minneapolis: BRK Publishers.

Linsk, N.L., & Pinkston, E.M. (1984). Training gerontological practitioners in home-based family interventions. *Educational Gerontology, 10,* 289-305.

Lipman, A. (1961). Role conceptions and morale of couples in retirement. *Journal of Gerontology, 16,* 267-71.

_____. (1962). Role concepts of couples in retirement. In C. Tibbitts & W. Donahue (Eds.), *Social and psychological aspects of aging* (pp. 475-83). New York: Columbia University Press.

Lipman, J.L. (1984). Popular "granny flats" help elderly stay close to home. *The Wall Street Journal,* March 28, 35.

Litwak, A. (1985). *Helping the elderly: The complementary role of informal networks and formal systems.* New York: Guilford.

Liu, K., and Palesch, Y. (1981). The nursing home population: Different perspectives and implications for policy. *Health Care Financing Review, 3,* 1815-23.

Livson, F.B. (1983). Changing sex roles in the social environment of later life. In G.D. Rowles & R.J. Ohta (Eds.), *Aging and milieu: Environmental perspectives on growing old* (pp. 131-52). New York: Academic Press.

Long, N. (1977). *Information and referral services: Research findings* (Vol. 1). Washington, DC: DHEW publication No. (OHDS) 77-16251, Office of Human Development, Administration on Aging.

Longino, C.F., Jr, & Lipman, A. (1981). Married and spouseless men and women in planned retirement communities: Support network differentials. *Journal of Marriage and the Family. 43,* 169-77.

Lopata, H.Z. (1973). *Widowed in an American city.* Cambridge, MA: Schenckman.

_____. (1977). The meaning of friendship in widowhood. In L. Troll, J. Israel, & F. Israel (Eds.), *Looking ahead* (pp. 93-105). Englewood Cliffs, NJ: Prentice-Hall.

_____. (1981). Widowhood and husband sanctification. *Journal of Marriage and the Family, 43,* 439-50.

Lowenthal, M.F. (1964). *Lives in distress.* New York: Basic Books.

Lowenthal, M.F., & Haven, L. (1968). Interaction and adaptation: Intimacy as a critical behavior. *American Sociological Review, 33,* 20-30.

Lowenthal, M.F., & Robinson, B. (1976). Social networks and isolation. In R.H. Binstock & E. Shanas (Eds.), *Handbook of aging and the social sciences* (pp. 432-56). New York: Van Nostrand Reinhold.

Lowry, J.H. (1984). Life satisfaction time components among the elderly: Toward understanding the contribution of predictor variables. *Research on Aging, 6,* 417-31.

Lubinski, R. (1981). Environmental language intervention. In R. Chapey (Ed.), *Language intervention strategies in adult aphasia.* Baltimore: Williams & Wilkins.

Luke, Aviva S. (1973). The Study of Social Interactions among Senile Dementia Patients, *Annales Medico-Psychologiques,* March, *1*(3), 349-85.

Lumsden, D.B. (Ed.). (1985). *The older adult as learner: Aspects of educational gerontology.* Washington, DC: Hemisphere Publishing.

Lund, D.A., Feinhauer, L.L., & Miller, J.R. (1985). Living together: Grandparents and children tell their problems. *Journal of Gerontological Nursing, 11,* 29-33.

Lynch, J. (1977). *The broken heart: The medical consequence of loneliness.* New York: Basic Books.


McClone, R.E., & Hollien, H. (1963). Vocal pitch characteristics of aged women. *Journal of Speech and Hearing Research, 6,* 164-70.

McConnell, S.R. (1979). House sharing: An alternative living arrangement for the elderly. *Generations,* III, Winter, 24-26.

McCormick, G.P., & Williams, P. (1976). The Midwestern Pennsylvania Stroke Club: Conclusions following the first year's operation of a family-centered program. In R.H. Brookshire (Ed.), *Proceedings of the Clinical Aphasiology Conference.* Minneapolis: BRK Publishers.

McCracken-Knights, A. (1985). Look beyond your clients' answers. *Journal of Gerontological Nursing, 11,* 20-22.

McDavis, K.C. (1983/84). The effects of severity of hearing impairment and locus of control on the denial of hearing impairment in the aged. *International Journal of Aging and Human Development, 18,* 47-60.

McGhee, J.C. (1985). The effects of siblings on the life satisfaction of the rural elderly. *Journal of Marriage and the Family, 47,* 85-91.

McKain, W. (1969). *Retirement marriage.* Storrs: University of Connecticut, Agricultural Experiment Station.

Maclay, E. (1977). *Green winter: Celebrations of old age.* New York: Reader's Digest Press & Thos. Y. Crowell.

MacLennan, B.A. (1983). Some possible implications for adapting the milieu in nursing homes. *Activities, Adaptation and Aging, 4,* 33-38.

McMahon, A.W., & Rudrick, P.J. (1964). Reminiscing: Adaptational significance in the aged. *Archives of General Psychiatry, 10,* 292-98.

McNally, J.M. (1972). *Continuing education for nurses: A survey of current programs.* Kansas City: American Nurses Association.

Malone, P.E. (1969). Expressed attitudes of families of aphasics. *Journal of Speech and Hearing Disorders, 34,* 146-50.

Mancini, J.A., & Simon, J. (1984). Older adults' expectations of support from family and friends. *Journal of Applied Gerontology, 3,* 150-60.

Manheimer, R.J. (1984). *Developing arts and humanities programming with the elderly.* Chicago: American Library Association, Reference and Adult Services Division.

Manton, K.G., Woodbury, M.A., & Liu, K. (1984). Life table methods for assessing the dynamics of U.S. nursing home utilization: 1976-1977. *Journal of Gerontology, 39,* 79-87.

Marcus, L. (1978). Aging and education. In D. Hohman (Ed.), *The social challenge of aging.* (p. 128). London: Croom Helm Ltd.

Marketing for long term care. (1985). *American Health Care Association Journal, 11,* (entire issue).

Marshall, V.W. (1983). Generations, age groups, and cohorts: Conceptual distinctions. *Canadian Journal on Aging, 2,* 51-62.

Marx, J.H. (1969). A multidimensional conception of ideologies in professional arenas: The case of the mental health field. *Pacific Sociological Review, 12,* 75-85.

Matthews, S.H. (1986). *Friendships through the life cycle: Oral biographies in old age.* Beverly Hills: Sage.

Maurer, J.F. (1984). Introduction. In L. Jacobs-Condit (Ed.), *Gerontology and communication disorders* (pp. 9-25). Rockville, MD: American Speech-Language-Hearing Association.

Mayo, C., & LaFrance, M. (1978). On the acquisition of nonverbal commmunication: A review. *Merrill-Palmer Quarterly, 24,* 213-28.

Medina, S.C. (1986). People. *Time,* August 25, 59.

Mehrabian, A. (1969). Significance of posture and position in the communication of attitude and status relationships. *Psychological Bulletin, 71,* 359-72.

Meinke, G. (1984). *Staff training manual for adult day health care programs.* San Francisco: On Lok Senior Health Services.

Mendelson, M. (1974). *Tender loving greed*. New York: Knopps.

Meyerhoff, B. (1978). *Number our days*. New York: Simon and Schuster.

Meyersohn, R. (1961). A critical examination of commercial entertainment. In R.W. Kleemeier (Ed.), *Aging and leisure* (pp. 243-72). New York: Oxford University Press.

Middleton, L. (1984). *Alzheimer's family support groups: A manual for group facilitators*. Tampa, FL: University of South Florida Medical Center, Suncoast Gerontology Center.

Miles, S.H., & Ryden, M.B. (1985). Limited-treatment policies in long-term care facilities. *Journal of the American Geriatrics Society, 33*, 707-11.

Miller, W.E. (1983). Research and family factors in aural rehabilitation of the elderly. *Activities, Adaptation and Aging, 3*, 17-29.

Milligan, W.L., Powell, D.A., Harley, C., & Furchgott, E. (1985). Physical health correlates of attitudes toward aging in the elderly. *Experimental Aging Research, 11*, 75-80.

Milt, H. (1982). Family neglect and abuse of the aged: A growing concern. *Public Affairs* (pamphlet no. 603). New York: Public Affairs Pamphlets.

Mindel, C.H., & Wright R. (1985). Characteristics of the elderly in three types of living arrangements. *Activities, Adaptation and Aging, 6*, 39-51.

Mitrowshi, C.A. (1985). Social work intervention with geriatric cancer patients and their children. *Social Casework, 66*, 242-45.

Mobily, K.E., & Hoeft, T.M. (1985). The family's dilemma: Alzheimer's disease. *Activities, Adaptation and Aging, 6*, 63-71.

Monk, A., & Kaye, L.W. (1982). The ombudsman volunteer in the nursing home: Differential role perceptions of patient representatives for the institutionalized aged. *The Gerontologist, 22*, 194-99.

_____. (1984). Patient advocacy services in long-term care facilities: Ethnic perspectives. *The Journal of Long-term Care Administration, 12*, 5-9.

Montgomery, D.R., & Still, J.A. (1985). Alzheimer's disease: A select bibliography relating to the families of victims of this disease. *Activities, Adaptation and Aging, 6*, 73-79.

Moody, H.R. (1984). Reminiscence and the recovery of the public world. *Journal of Gerontological Social Work, 7*, 157-66.

Moore, J. (1984). Pre-admission education brings early involvement. *American Health Care Association Journal, 10*, 14-19.

Morris, W.W., & Bader, I.M. (Eds.). (1983). *Hoffman's daily needs and interests of older people*. Springfield: Charles C. Thomas Publisher. (Original work published in 1970.)

Morrison, I.A. (Ed.). (1985). *Continuing care retirement communities: Political, social, and financial issues*. NY: Haworth Press.

Morrison, M.H. (1983). The aging of the U.S. population: Human resource implications. *Monthly Labor Review, 106*, 13-19.

Morycz, R.K. (1985). Caregiving strain and the desire to institutionalize family members with Alzheimer's disease. *Research on Aging, 7*, 329-61.

Moss, F. (1977). *Too old, too sick, too bad: Nursing homes in America*. Germantown, MD: Aspen Systems Corporation.

Moss, M.S., Moss, S.Z., & Moles, E.L. (1985). The quality of relationships between elderly parents and their out-of-town children. *The Gerontologist, 25*, 134-40.

Mouser, N.F., Powers, E.A., Keith, P.M., & Goudy, W.J. (1985). Marital status and life satisfaction: A study of older men. In W.A. Peterson and J. Quadagno (Eds.), *Social bonds in later life* (pp. 71-90). Beverly Hills: Sage.

Mueller, D. (1980). Social networks: A promising direction for research on the relationship of the social environment and psychiatric disorder. *Social Science and Medicine. 14A,* 147-61.

Mueller, P.B., & Peters, T.J. (1981). Needs and services in geriatric speech-language pathology and audiology. *Asha, 23,* 627.

Mullen, W.E. (1985). Identification and ranking of stressors in nursing home administration. *The Gerontologist, 25,* 370-75.

Munley, A., Powers, C.S., & Williamson, J.B. (1982). Humanizing nursing home environments: The relevance of hospice principles. *International Journal of Aging and Human Development, 15,* 263-84.

Murdock, B.B., Jr. (1960). The immediate retention of unrelated words. *Journal of Experimental Psychology, 60,* 222-34.

Murphy, M.B. (1984). *A guide to intergenerational programs.* Washington, DC: National Association of State Units on Aging.

Myers, P.S. (1984). Right hemisphere impairment. In A.L. Holland (Ed.), *Language disorders in adults: Recent advances.* San Diego: College-Hill.

———. (1986). Right hemisphere communication impairment. In R. Chapey (Ed.), *Language intervention strategies in adult aphasia* (2nd ed.). Baltimore: Williams & Wilkins.

Mysak, E.D. (1959). Pitch and duration characteristics of older males. *Journal of speech and hearing research, 2,* 46-54.


Nadol, J.B. (1981). The aging peripheral hearing mechanism. In D.S. Beasley & G.A. Davis (Eds.), *Aging: Communication processes and disorders.* New York: Grune and Stratton.

Nasar, J.L. & Farokhpay, M. (1985). Assessment of activity priorities and design preferences of elderly residents in public housing: A case study. *The gerontologist, 25,* 251-57.

Nasatir, M. (1985). Aging parents: A support group at work. *Activities, Adaptation and Aging, 6,* 81-87.

National Center for Health Statistics. (1974). *Monthly vital statistics.* Washington, DC: U.S. Government Printing Office.

Nerbonne, G.P. (1967). The identification of speaker characteristics on the basis of aural cues. Ph.D. dissertation, Michigan State University.

Nesselroade, J.R., & Labouvie, E.W. (1985). Experimental Design in Research on Aging. In J.E. Birren & K.W. Schaie (Eds.), *Handbook of the Psychology of Aging,* (pp. 35-60). New York: Van Nostrand Reinhold.

Nesselroade, J.R., & Reese, H.W. (1973). *Life-span developmental psychology: Methodological issues.* New York: Academic Press.

Neugarten, B.L. (1972). Personality and the aging process. *The Gerontologist, 12,* 9-15.

_____. (1982). Policy for the 1980's. In B.L. Neugarten (Ed.), *Age or need?: Public policies for older people* (pp. 1-7). Beverly Hills: Sage.

Neugarten, B.L., & Weinstein, K.K. (1964). The changing American grandparent. *Journal of Marriage and the Family, 26,* 199-204.

Neustadt, L.E. (1985). Adult day care: A model for changing times. *Physical and Occupational Therapy in Geriatrics, 4,* 53-66.

Newhoff, M., & Davis, G.A. (1978). A spouse intervention program: Planning, implementation, and problems of evaluation. In R.H. Brookshire (Ed.), *Proceedings of the Clinical Aphasiology Conference.* Minneapolis: BRK Publishers.

Noberini, M.R., & Berman, R.U. (1983). Barter to beat inflation: Developing a neighborhood network for swapping services on behalf of the aged. *The Gerontologist, 23,* 467-70.

Norman, D., & Lindsey, P. (1972). *Human information processing.* New York: Academic Press.

Northcott, H.C. (1975). Too young, too old — Age in the world of television. *The Gerontologist, 15,* 184-86.

Norton, R.W. (1975). Measurement of ambiguity tolerance. *Journal of Personality Assessment, 39,* 607-19.

Nuessel, F. (1984). Old age needs a new name. *Research on Aging, 6,* 4-6.

Nunnally, J.C. (1973). Research strategies and measurement methods for investigating human development. In J. Nesselroade & H. Reese (Eds.), *Life-span developmental psychology: Methodological issues,* (pp. 87-110). New York: Academic Press.

Nussbaum, J.F. (1980, April). Attitudes toward aging: A critical review of a popular medium throughout the 70's. Paper presented at the Eastern Communication Association Convention, Pittsburgh.

_____. (1981, July). An initial investigation into the interactive behavior of elderly individuals across three living environments. Paper presented at the Speech Communication Association — International Communication Association, Communication and Gerontology Summer Conference, Edwardsville, Illinois.

_____. (1983a). Relational closeness of elderly interaction: Implications for life satisfaction. *Western Journal of Speech Communication, 47,* 229-43.

_____. (1983b). Perceptions of communication content and life satisfaction among the elderly. *Communication Quarterly, 31,* 313-19.

_____. (1985). Successful aging: A communicative model. *Communication Quarterly, 33,* 262-69.

Nussbaum, J.F., & Robinson, J.D. (1984). Attitudes toward aging. *Communication Research Reports, 1,* 21-27.

Nussbaum, J.F., Robinson, J.D., & Grew, D.J. (1985). Communicative behavior of the long-term health care employee: Implications for the elderly resident. *Communication Research Reports, 2,* 16-22.

Obler, L.K., & Albert, M.L. (1981). Language in the elderly aphasic and in the dementing patient. In M.T. Sarno (Ed.), *Acquired aphasia.* New York: Academic Press.

O'Dowd, S.C. (1984). Does vocabulary decline qualitatively in old age? *Educational Gerontology, 10,* 357-68.

Offenbacher, D.I., & Poster, C.H. (1985). Aging and the baseline code: An Alternative to the "Normless Elderly." *The Gerontologist, 25,* 526-31.

Oktay, J.S. (1985). Maintaining independent living for the impaired elderly: The role of community support groups. *Aging, 349,* 14-18.

Oldrich, N. (Ed.). (1985, May). *Aging Research and Training News, 8*(5), 33-36.

Oliver, R. & Bock, F.A. (1985). Alleviating the distress of caregivers of Alzheimer's disease patients: A rational-emotive therapy model. *Clinical Gerontologist, 3,* 17-34.

Olsho, L.W., Harkins, S.W., & Lenhardt, M.L. (1985). Aging and the auditory system. In J.E. Birren & K.W. Schaie (Eds.), *Handbook of the Psychology of Aging* (2nd ed.). New York: Van Nostrand Reinhold.

O'Malley, H., Bergman, J., Segars, H., Perex, R., Mitchell, V., & Kruepfel, G. (1979). *Elder abuse in Massachusetts: A survey of professionals and paraprofessionals.* Boston, MA: Legal Research and Services for the Elderly.

O'Malley, T.A., Everett, E.D., O'Malley, H.C., & Campione, E.W. (1983). Identifying and preventing family mediated abuse and neglect of elderly persons. *Annuals of Internal Medicine, 90*(6), 998-1005.

Orchik, D.J. (1981). Peripheral auditory problems and the aging process. In D.S. Beasley & G.A. Davis (Eds.), *Aging: Communication processes and disorders.* New York: Grune and Stratton.

Ordy, J.M., Brizzee, K.R., & Beavers, T.L. (1980). Sensory function and short-term memory in aging. In G.J. Maletta & F.J. Pirozzolo (Eds.), *The aging Nervous system.* New York: Praeger.

Oriol, W.E. (1985). *The complex cube of long term care: The case for next-step solutions—now.* Washington, DC: American Health Planning Association.

Osgood, N.J. (1985). *Suicide in the elderly: A practitioner's guide to diagnosis and mental health intervention.* Rockville, MD: Aspen Systems Corporation.

Oster, H., & Ekman, P. (1978). Facial behavior in child development. In W. Andrew Collins (Ed.), *Minnesota symposia on child psychology,* (Vol. 11). Hillsdale, NJ: Erlbaum.

Ostwald, S.K., & Williams, H.Y. (1985). Optimizing learning in the elderly: A model. *Lifelong Learning, 9,* 10-13.

Owens, W.A. (1966). Age and mental abilities: A second adult follow-up. *Journal of Educational Psychology, 57,* 311-25.

Oyer, E.J. (1976). Summary. In Oyer, H.J., & Oyer, E.J. (Eds.), *Aging and communication.* (pp. 289-99). Baltimore: University Park Press.

Oyer, H.J., & Oyer, E.J., (Eds.). (1976). *Aging and communication.* Baltimore: University Park Press.

Palestis, E. (1986). The admission ward concept. *Geriatric Nursing, 7,* 40-41.

Palmore, E. (1976). Total chance of institutionalization among aged. *The Gerontologist, 16,* 504-7.

_____. (1977). Facts on aging: A short quiz. *The Gerontologist, 17,* 315-20.

_____. (1980). The facts on aging quiz: A review of findings. *The Gerontologist, 20,* 669-72.

_____. (1981). *Social patterns in normal aging: Findings from the Duke longitudinal study.* Durham, NC: Duke University Press.

Palmore, E.B. (Ed.). (1984). *Handbook on the aged in the United States.* Westport, CT: Greenwood Press.

Panek, P.E., Barrett, G.V., Alexander, R.A., & Sterns, H.E. (1979). Age and self-selected performance pace on a visual monitoring task. *Aging and Work, 2,* 183-91.

Parsons, T. (1951). *The social system.* New York: The Free Press.

Parsons, T. (1958). Definitions of health and illness in the light of American values and social structure. In E. Jaco, (Ed.), *Patients, physicians, and illness* (pp. 165-87). New York: The Free Press.

Passuth, P.M., & Cook, F.L. (1985). Effects of television viewing on knowledge and attitudes about older adults: A critical reexamination. *The Gerontologist, 25,* 69-77.

Pearson, F. (1977). Language facility and aging. Doctoral dissertation, University of Oregon, Eugene.

Pease, R.A. (1985). Praise elders to help them learn. *Journal of Gerontological Nursing, 11,* 16-20.

Pegels, C. (1980). *Health care and the elderly.* Rockville, MD: Aspen Systems Corporation.

Penner, L., Ludenia, K., & Mead, G. (1984). Staff attitudes: Image or reality? *Journal of Gerontological Nursing, 10,* 110-17.

Pennington, R.E., & Pierce, W.L. (1985). Observations of empathy of nursing home staff: A predictive study. *International Journal of Aging and Human Development, 21,* 281-90.

Peragrin, J.V. (1983). Editorial. *Journal of Gerontological Nursing, 9*(1), 9.

Percy, C.H. (1974). *Growing old in the country of the young.* New York: McGraw-Hill.

Perrotta, P., & Meachan, J.A. (1981). Can a reminiscing intervention alter depression and self-esteem? *International Journal of Aging and Human Development, 14,* 23-30.

Peters, G.R. (1971). Self-conceptions of the aged, age identification and aging. *The Gerontologist, 11,* 69-73.

Petersen, M. (1973). The visibility and image of old people on television. *Journalism Quarterly, 50,* 569-73.

Petrulli, J. (1982). Practical approaches to improving communication with the elderly in nursing homes. Paper presented to the Speech Communication Association Annual Conference, Louisville, Kentucky.

Pettegrew, L.S., Thomas, R.C., Ford, J., & Costello, D.E. (1981). The effects of job-related stress on medical center employee communication style. In Michael Burgoon (Ed.), *Communication yearbook, 5* (pp. 529-46). Beverly Hills: Sage.

Philblad, C.T., & McNamara, R.L. (1965). Social adjustment of elderly people in three small towns. In A.M. Rose & W.A. Peterson (Eds.), *Older people and their social world* (pp. 49-73). Philadelphia: F.A. Davis.

Phillips, A.H., & Roman, C.K. (1984). *A practical guide to independent living for older people.* Seattle: Pacific Search Press.

Phillips, G. (1982). *Communicating in Organizations.* New York: McMillan.

Phillips, L.R., & Rempusheski, V.E. (1986). Making decisions about elder abuse. *Social Casework, 67,* 131-40.

Pifer, A. (1986). The public policy response to population aging. *Daedalus, 115,* 373-95.

Pillemer, K.A., & Wolf, R.S. (Eds.). (1986). *Elder abuse: Conflict in the family.* Dover, MA: Auburn House Publishing.

Pineo, P.C. (1961). Disenchantment in the later years of marriage. *Marriage and Family Living, 23,* 3-11.

Poon, L.W. (1985). Differences in human memory with aging: Nature, causes, and clinical implications. In J.E. Birren & K.W. Schaie (Eds.), *Handbook of the Psychology of Aging* (2nd ed.). New York: Van Nostrand Reinhold.

Porter, L.W., Lawler, E.E., & Hackman, J.R. (1975). *Behavior in organizations.* New York: McGraw-Hill.

Porter, L.W., & Roberts, K.H. (1976). Communication in organizations. In M.D. Dunnette (Ed.), *Handbook of industrial and organizational psychology* (pp. 1553-89). New York: Rand-McNally.

Porter, L.W., & Steers, R.M. (1973). Organizational, work, and personal factors in employee turnover and absenteeism. *Psychological Bulletin, 80,* 151-76.

Portnoy, E.J. (1985). Communication and the elderly patient. *Activities, Adaptation and Aging, 7,* 25-30.

Prater, R.J., & Swift, R.W. (1984). *Manual of voice therapy.* Boston: Little, Brown.

Preston, T. (1973). When words fail. *American Journal of Nursing,* December, 2064-66.

Priefer, B.A., & Gambert, S.R. (1984). Reminiscence and life review in the elderly. *Psychiatric Medicine, 2,* 91-100.

A profile of older Americans. (1985). Program for Resources Development, American Association of Retired Persons and Administration on Aging, Department Health and Human Services. Compiled by Donald G. Fowles. Publication No. P.F. 3049 (1085) (.D996). Rockville, MD: U.S. Government Printing Office.

Ptacek, P.H., & Sander, E.K. (1966). Age recognition from voice. *Journal of Speech Hearing Research, 9,* 273-77.

Ptacek, P.H., Sander, E.K., Maloney, W.H., & Jackson, C. (1966). Phonatory and related changes with advanced age. *Journal of Speech and Hearing Research, 9,* 353-60.


Quattrochi-Tubin, S., & Jason, L.A. (1983). The influence of introversion-extroversion on activity choice and satisfaction among the elderly. *Activities, Adaptation, and Aging, 4,* 19-28.

Quinn, M.I., & Tomita, S.K. (Eds.). (1986). *Elder abuse and neglect.* New York: Springer.

Quinn, W.H. (1983). Anatomy, interdependence, and developmental delay in older generations of the family. In W.H. Quinn and G.A. Hughston (Eds.), *Independent aging.* Rockville, MD: Aspen Systems Corporation.

Rabinowitz, J.C., Craik, F.I.M., & Ackerman, B.P. (1982). Processing resource account of age differences in recall. *Canadian Journal of Psychology, 36,* 325-44.

Ragsdale, J.D., & Dauterive, R. (1986). Relationships between age, sex, and hesitation phenomena in young children. *Southern Speech Communication Journal, 52,* 22-34.

Ramig, L.A., & Ringel, R.L. (1983). Effects of physiological aging on selected acoustic characteristics of voices. *Journal of Speech and Hearing Research, 26,* 22-30.

Raschko, B.A. (1982). *Interior design for the elderly.* New York: Van Nostrand Reinhold.

Raschoko, R. (1985). Systems integration at the program level: Aging and mental health. *The Gerontologist, 25,* 460-63.

Ravish, T. (1985). Prevent social isolation before it starts. *Journal of Gerontological Nursing, 11,* 10-13.

Reddick, J. (1984/85). The interdependence of health and housing for the elderly. *Journal of Housing for the Elderly, 2,* 77-82.

Redick, R., & Taube, C. (1980). Demographic and mental health care of the aged. In J. Birren and R.B. Sloane (Eds.), *Handbook of mental health and aging.* Englewood Cliffs, NJ: Prentice-Hall.

Reed, W.L., & Washington, B.B. (1984). Social well-being of institutionalized elderly persons. *International Journal of Aging and Human Development, 19,* 311-18.

Reid, E. (1981). Nursing care of the aged: An overview of education research and practice in England Wales. *Journal of Gerontological Nursing, 7,* 733-38.

Reinhardt, R.L. (1983). Do employees know where they stand with you? *Nursing Homes, 32,* 24-26.

Reiter, M. (1985). Age discrimination in the workplace. *50 Plus, 25,* 14-20.

Retsinas, J., & Garrity, P. (1985). Nursing home friendships. *The Gerontologist, 25,* 376-81.

Reynolds, M., & Koon, A. (1981). Combining intrapersonal communication with andragogical methods: An effective approach in adult/retiree education. Paper presented to the Speech Communication Association Conference on Communication and Aging, Edwardsville, Illinois.

Rich, B.M., & Baum, M. (1984). *The aging: A guide to public policy.* Pittsburgh: University of Pittsburgh Press.

Richetto, G.M. (1977). Organizational communication theory and research: An overview. In Brent Ruben (Ed.), *Communication Yearbook, 1,* (pp. 331-46). New Brunswick: Transaction/ICA.

Riddick, C.C. (1985). Life satisfaction of older female homemakers, retirees, and workers. *Research on Aging, 7,* 383-93.

Rippy, J., Dancer, J., Pryor, R., & Stamper, J. (1985). A field experience: Rating the communication difficulty of home-bound older persons. *Home Health Care Services Quarterly, 6,* 33-47.

Robbins, S.P. (1983). *Organizational theory: Structure, design, and applications.* Englewood Cliffs, NJ: Prentice-Hall.

Roberto, K.A. (1985). Adult children and aging parents: A report of a program design and evaluation. *Activities, Adaptation, and Aging, 6,* 89-101.

Roberto, K.A., & Scott, I.P. (1986). Equity consideration in the friendships of older adults. *Journal of Gerontology, 30,* 103-7.

Roberts, G. (1985). Beauty is any age. In J.A. Graham & A.M. Kligman (Eds.), *The psychology of cosmetic treatments.* New York: Praeger.

Roberts, R. (1985). The British Red Cross beauty care and cosmetic camouflage service in hospitals. In J.A. Graham & A.M. Kligman (Eds.), *The psychology of cosmetic treatments.* New York: Praeger.

Rokeach, M. (1970). *Beliefs, attitudes and values: A theory of organization and change.* San Francisco: Jossey-Bass.

Rollins, B.C., & Feldman, H. (1970). Marital satisfaction over the family life cycle. A reevaluation. *Journal of Marriage and the Family, 32,* 20-28.

Root, L.S. (1985). Corporate programs for older workers. *Aging, 351,* 12-16.

Roper Organization. (1987). *America's watching: Public attitudes toward television.* New York: Television Information Office.

Rosen, A.J., Abramowitz, L., Diamond, J., & Jesselson, P. (1985). Environmental management of senile dementia. *Social Work in Health Care, 11,* 33-43.

Rosen, W.G., Mohs, R.C., & Davis, K.L. (1984). A new rating scale for Alzheimer's disease. *The American Journal of Psychiatry, 141,* 1356-64.

Rosenbek, J.C., & LaPointe, L.L. (1981). Motor speech disorders and the aging process. In D.S. Beasley & G.A. Davis (eds.), *Aging: Communication processes and disorders.* New York: Grune & Stratton.

Rosencranz, H.A., & McNevin, T.E. (1969). A factor analysis of attitudes toward the aged. *The Gerontologist, 9,* 55-59.

Rosenweike, I., & Logue, B. (1985). *The extreme aged in America: A portrait of an expanding population.* Westport, CT: Greenwood Press.

Rosow, I. (1967). *Social integration of the aged.* New York: Free Press.

_____. (1974). *Socialization to old age.* Berkeley: University of California Press.

Roza, V.K. (1985). Phased retirement—an experimental view. *Activities, Adaptation and Aging, 6,* 9-30.

Ruben, D.H. (1984). Comparison of two analogue measures for assessing and teaching assertiveness to physically disabled elderly: An exploratory study. *Gerontology and Geriatrics Education, 5,* 63-71.

Rubin, A.M. (1980). Patterns in age differences. *Feedback, 22*(2), 5-10.

_____. (1982). Directions in television and aging research. *Journal of Broadcasting, 26,* 537-51.

_____. (1986). Television, aging and information seeking. *Language & Communication, 6,* 125-37.

Rubin, A.M., Perse, E.M., & Powell, R.A. (1985). Loneliness, parasocial interaction, and local television news viewing. *Human Communication Research, 12,* 155-80.

Rubin, A.M., & Rubin, R.B. (1981). Age, context and television use. *Journal of Broadcasting, 25,* 1-13.

_____. (1982a). Contextual age and television use. *Human Communication Research, 8,* 228-44.

_____. (1982b). Older persons' TV viewing patterns and motivations. *Communication Research, 9,* 287-313.

_____. (1985). Interface of personal and mediated communication. *Critical Studies in Mass Communication, 2,* 36-53.

_____. (1986). Contextual age as a life-position index. *International Journal of Aging and Human Development, 23,* 27-45.

Rubin, I. (1980). The "sexless" older years—a socially harmful stereotype. In J. Quadagno (Ed.), *Aging, the individual and society: Readings in social gerontology* (pp. 472-81). New York: St. Martin's Press.

Rubin, R.B., & Rubin, A.M. (1982). Contextual age and television use: Reexamining a life-position indicator. In M. Burgoon (Ed.), *Communication yearbook, 6,* (pp. 583-604). Beverly Hills: Sage.

Ryan, E.B., & Capadano, H.L. (1978). Age perception and Evaluative reactions toward adult speakers. *Journal of Gerontology, 33,* 98-102.

Ryan, W.J. (1972). Acoustic aspects of the aging voice. *Journal of Gerontology, 27,* 265-68.

Ryan, W.J., & Burk, K.W. (1974). Perceptual and acoustic correlate of aging in the speech of males. *Journal of Gerontology, 33,* 98-102.

Sable, L.M. (1984). Life review therapy: An occupational therapy treatment technique with geriatric clients. *Physical and Occupational Therapy, 3*(4), 49-54.

St. Vincent Hospital and Health Care Center. (1982). *V-line: St. Vincent home emergency response system.* Indianapolis: St. Vincent Hospital.

Sanders, S., Hamby, E.I., & Nelson, M. (1984). *You are not alone.* Nashville, TN: American Heart Association-Tennessee Affiliate.

Sauer, W.J., & Coward, R.T. (Eds.). (1985). *Social support networks and the care of the elderly: Theory, research, and practice.* New York: Springer.

Saul, S. (1983). The interdisciplinary component of education in a long-term care facility. *Nursing Homes, 32,* 6-10.

Sayles, A.H., & Adams, J.K. (1979). *Communication problems and behaviors of older Americans.* Rockville, MD: American Speech-Language-Hearing Association.

Schaie, K.W. (1965). A general model for the study of developmental problems. *Psychological Bulletin, 64,* 92-107.

_____. (1979). Age changes in intelligence. In R.L. Sprott (Ed.), *Aging and intelligence.* New York: Van Nostrand Reinhold.

_____, (1980). Cognitive development in aging. In L.K. Obler & M. Alpert (Eds.), *Language and communication in the elderly.* Lexington, MA: Heath.

_____. (1983a). *Longitudinal Studies of Adult Psychological Development.* New York: Guilford.

_____. (1983b). Consistency and change in cognitive functioning of the young-old and old-old. In M. Bergener, U. Lehr, E. Lang, & R. Schmitz-Scherzer (Eds.), *Aging in the eighties and beyond.* New York: Springer.

_____. (1983c). The Seattle longitudinal study: A twenty-one year exploration of psychometric intelligence in adulthood. In K.W. Schaie (Ed.), *Longitudinal studies of adult psychological development.* New York: Guilford.

Schaie, K.W., & Geiwitz, J. (1982). *Adult Development and Aging.* Boston: Little, Brown.

Schaie, K.W., & Hertzog, C. (1985). Toward a comprehensive model of adult intellectual development: Contributions of the Seattle Longitudinal Study. In R.J. Sternberg (Ed.), *Advances in human intelligence* (Vol. 3). New York: Academic Press.

Schalinske, T.F. (1968). The role of television in the life of the aged person. Doctoral dissertation, Ohio State University, Columbus.

Scheman, J.D., & Lockard, J.S. (1979). Development of gaze aversion in children. *Child Development, 50,* 594-96.

Scherer, K.R. (1979). Personality markers in speech. In K.R. Scherer and H. Giles (Eds.), *Social markers in speech.* New York: Cambridge University Press.

Schmidt, G.L., & Keys, B. (1985). Group psychotherapy with family caregivers of demented patients. *The Gerontologist, 25,* 347-50.

Schmitt, F.A., Murphy, M.D., & Sanders, R.E. (1981). Training older adults free recall rehearsal strategies. *Journal of Gerontology, 36,* 329-37.

Schneeweiss, S.M., & Davis, S.W. (1974). *Nursing home administration.* Baltimore: University Park Press.

Schneider, M.J., Chapman, D.D., & Voth, D.E. (1985). Senior center participation: A two step approach to impact evaluation. *The Gerontologist, 25,* 194-200.

Schneider, R.L. & Decker, T., (Eds.) (1984). *Specialized course outlines for gerontological social work education.* Washington, DC: Council on Social Work Education.

Schnore, M.M. (1985). *Retirement: Bane or blessing?* Atlantic Highlands, NJ: Humanities Press.

Schow, R.L., Christensen, J.M., Hutchinson, J.M., & Nerbonne, M.A. (1978). *Communication disorders of the aged: A guide for health professionals.* Baltimore: University Park Press.

Schramm, W. (1969). Aging and mass communication. In M.W. Riley, J.W. Riley, & M.E. Johnson (Eds.), *Aging and society, volume 2: Aging and the professions* (pp. 352-75). New York: Russell Sage Foundation.

Schreiber, E.S., & Boyd, D.A. (1980). How the elderly perceive television commercials. *Journal of Communication, 30*(2), 61-70.

Schroeder, A.B. (1977). Effectiveness and attractiveness as a function of communicator style in triads. *Dissertation Abstracts International, 38,* 6401A-6402A, University Microfilms No. 7804807.

Schuetz, J. (1980). Lifelong learning: Communication education for the elderly. *Communication Education, 33,* 33-41.

Schuetz, J. (1982). Geragogy: Instructional programs for elders. *Communication Education, 31,* 339-47.

Schumm, W.R., & Bugaighis, M.A. (1986). Marital quality over the marital career: Alternative explanations. *Journal of Marriage and the Family, 48,* 165-68.

Schwartz, A.N. (1974). Staff development and morale building in nursing homes. *The Gerontologist, 14,* 50-53.

Scott, W.G. (1967). *Organizational Theory.* Homewood, IL: IRW.

Seltzer, S. (1983). Some Jewish perspectives on aging. *Generations, 8,* 28-30.

Shadden, B.B. (1982). Communication process and aging: Information needs and attitudes of older adults and professions. Project report to the American Association of Retired Persons Andrus Foundation.

Shadden, B.B., Raiford, C.A., & Shadden, H.S. (1983). *Coping with communication disorders in aging.* Tigard, OR: C.C. Publications.

Shannon, C., & Weaver, W. (1949). *The mathematical theory of communication.* Urbana, IL: University of Illinois Press.

Sheehy, G. (1981). *Pathfinders.* New York: Bantam Books.

Sherman, D., Ward, R., & LaGlory, M. (1985). Socialization and aging group consciousness: The effect of neighborhood age concentration. *Journal of Gerontology, 40,* 102-10.

Sherman, E. (1984). *Working with older persons: Cognitive and phenomenological methods.* Boston: Kluwer-Nijhoff.

Shock, N.W. (1984). *Normal human aging: The Baltimore longitudinal study of aging.* Washington, DC: U.S. Government Printing Office.

Shukla, R. (1982). Organizational philosophy and nurse staffing: Three-step process. *The Journal of Long-Term Care Administration,* Fall, 22-28.

Sigman, S.J. (1985). Some common mistakes students make when learning discourse analysis. *Communication Education, 34,* 119-27.

Silverstone, B., & Hyman, H. (1976). *You and your aging parent: The modern family's guide to emotional, physical, and financial problems.* New York: Pantheon Books.

Simmons, S., & Given, B. (1980). Nursing care of the terminal patient. *Perspectives on death and dying, 2,* 115-23.

Simons, R.L., & West, G.E. (1984). Life changes coping resources, and health among the elderly. *International Journal of Aging and Human Development, 20,* 173-89.

Simos, B.G. (1973). Adult children and their aging parents. *Social Work, 18,* 78-85.

Singh, B.R., & Williams, J.S. (1982). Childlessness and family satisfaction. *Research on Aging, 3,* 231-40.

Sinnott, J.D. (1984/85). Stress, health, and mental health symptoms of older women and men. *International Journal of Aging and Human Development, 20,* 123-32.

Sinnott, J.D., Harris, C.S., Block, M.R., Collesano, S., & Jacobsen, S.G. (1983). *Applied research in aging: A guide to methods and resources.* Boston: Little, Brown.

Slaybaugh, C.S. (Ed.). (1984). *The Grandparents' catalogue: An idea book for family sharing.* Mogadore, OH: Charles S. Slaybaugh & Associates.

Sluzki, C.E., & Ransom, D.C. (1976). *Double bind: The foundation of the communicational approach to the family.* New York: Grune and Stratton.

Smith, B.K. (1973). *Aging in America.* Boston: Beacon Press.

Smith, H.L., & Fottler, M.D. (1982). Cost containment practices among nursing home administrators. *The Journal of Long-Term Care Administration,* Fall, 9-17.

Smith, J.E. (1965). Family interaction patterns of the aged: A review. In A.M. Rose and W.A. Peterson (Eds.), *Older people and their social world* (pp. 143-61). Philadelphia: F.A. Davis.

Smith, N.R., Kielhofner, G., & Watts, J.H. (1986). The relationships between volition, activity pattern, and life satisfaction in the elderly. *American Journal of Occupational Therapy, 40,* 278-83.

Smithers, J.A. (1985). *Determined survivors: Community life among the urban elderly.* New Brunswick, NJ: Rutgers University Press.

Somers, H., & Somers, A. (1962). *Doctors, patients, and health insurance: The organizing and the financing of medical care.* New York: Doubleday.

Sommer, R. (1969). *Personal space.* Englewood Cliffs, NJ: Prentice Hall, Inc.

Sontag, S. (1972). The double standard of aging. *Saturday Review, 55,* 29-38.

Spalding, J., & Frank, B.W. (1985). Quality care from the residents' point of view. *American Health Care Association Journal, 11,* 3-7.

Special issue on history and aging. (1984). *Aging and Society, 4,* 379-524 (entire issue).

Stacey, C., Kozma, A., & Stones, M.J. (1985). Simple cognitive and behavioral changes resulting from improved physical fitness in persons over 50 years of age. *Canadian Journal on Aging, 4,* 67-74.

Stagner, R. (1985). Aging in industry. In J.E. Birren & K.W. Schaie (Eds.), *Handbook of the psychology of aging* (pp. 789-817). New York: Van Nostrand Reinhold.

Stanley, B. (Ed.). (1985). *Geriatric psychiatry: Ethical and legal issues.* Washington, DC: American Psychiatric Press.

Stannard, C. (1973). Old folks and dirty work: The social conditions for patient abuse in a nursing home. *Social problems, 20,* 329-42.

Stearns, P.J. (1986). In K.A. Pillemer & R.S. Wolf (Eds.), *Elder abuse: Conflict in the family* (pp. 3-24). Dover, MA: Auburn House Publishing.

Steere, G.A. (1981). The family and the elderly. In F.J. Berghorn & D.E. Schafer (Eds.), *The dynamics of aging* (pp. 289-309). Boulder, CO: Westview Press.

Stein, S., Linn, M.W., & Stein, E.M. (1985). Patients' anticipation of stress in nursing home care. *The Gerontologist, 25,* 88-94.

Steinfatt, T.M., & Infante, D.I. (1976). Attitude-behavior relationships in communication research. *Quarterly Journal of Speech, 62*(3), 267-78.

Steinfeld, E. (1983). *Multiple disabilities through the lifespan.* Washington, DC: U.S. Architectural and Transportation Barriers Compliance Board.

Stinnett, N., Carter, L.M., & Montgomery, J.E. (1972). Older person's perceptions of their marriages. *Journal of Marriage and the Family, 34,* 665-70.

Stoller, E.P. (1985). Elder-caregiver relationships in shared households. *Research on Aging, 7,* 175-93.

Street, R.L., & Cappella, J.N. (Eds.). (1985). *Sequence and pattern in communicative behavior.* Baltimore: Edward Arnold.

Streib, G.F., Folts, W.E., & LaGreca, A.J. (1985). Autonomy, power, and decision-making in thirty-six retirement communities. *The Gerontologist, 25,* 403-5.

Struntz, K.A., & Reville, S. (Eds.). (1985). *Growing together: An intergenerational sourcebook.* Washington, DC: American Association of Retired Persons — Elvirita Lewis Foundation.

Stryker, R. (1982). The effect of managerial interventions on high personnel turnover in nursing homes. *The Journal of Long-Term Care Administration,* Summer, 21-33.

Sudnow, D. (1967). *Passing on.* Englewood Cliffs, NJ: Prentice Hall.

Sussman, M.A. (1983). Family relations, supports, and the aged. In Morris, W.W. and Bader, I.M. (Eds.), *Hoffman's daily needs and interests of older people* (pp. 219-39). Springfield: Charles C. Thomas. (Original work published in 1970).

Sussman, M.B. (1976). The family life of old people. In R.H. Binstock & E. Shanas (Eds.), *Handbook of aging and the social sciences.* New York: Van Nostrand Reinhold.

Sussman, M.B., & Burchinal, L. (1962a). Kin family network: Unheralded structure in current conceptualizations of family functioning. *Marriage and Family Living, 24,* 231-40.

_____. (1962b). Parental aid to married children: Implications for family functioning. *Marriage and Family Living, 24,* 320-32.

Suzuki, S. (1970). *Zen mind, beginners mind.* New York: Weatherhill.

Swank, C. (1979). Media uses and gratifications: Need salience and source dependence in a sample of the elderly. *American Behavioral Scientist, 23,* 95-117.

Tamir, L.M. (1979). *Communication and the aging process: Interaction throughout the life cycle.* New York: Pergamon Press.

Tanner, D.C. (1980). Loss and grief: Implications for the speech-language pathologist and audiologist. *Asha, 22,* 916-28.

Tardelli, M.M., & Bocage, M. (1985). A team approach to family support groups in Alzheimer's disease. Paper presented at the Annual Convention of the American Speech-Language-Hearing Association, Washington, D.C.

Taylor, L.L., & Yesavage, J.A. (1984). Cognitive retraining programs for the elderly: A case study of cost/benefit issues. *Clinical Gerontologist, 2,* 51-63.

Templer, J., Lewis, D., & Sanford, J. (1983). *Ground and floor surface treatments.* Washington, DC: U.S. Architectural and Transportation Barriers Compliance Board.

Thobaben, M., & Anderson, L. (1985). Legal side: Reporting abuse—it's the law. *American Journal of Nursing, 85,* 371-74.

Thomas, J.L. (1986). Age and sex differences in perceptions of grandparenting. *Journal of Gerontology, 41,* 417-23.

Thompson, B., & Swisher, M. (1983). An assessment, using the multiphasic environmental assessment procedure (MEAP) of a rural life-care residential center for the elderly. *Journal of Housing for the Elderly, 1,* 41-56.

Thompson, T. (1984). The invisible helping hand: The role of communication in health and social service professions. *Communication Quarterly, 32,* 148-63.

Thompson, V. (1965). Bureaucracy and innovation. *The Administrative Science Quarterly, 10,* 1-10.

Thornton, B. (1978). Health care teams and multimethodological research. In B. Ruben (Ed.), *Communication yearbook 2.* New Brunswick, NJ: Transaction/ International Communication Association, 538-53.

Tibbits, C. (1962). Politics of aging: Pressure for change. In W. Donahue & C. Tibbitts (Eds.), *Politics of age.* Ann Arbor: University of Michigan.

Tilletson, A. (1981). *Intergovernmental communication of health care services for the elderly: A case study of the national public health program reporting system.* Paper presented to the Speech Communication Association Summer Conference on Communication and Gerontology, Edwardsville, Illinois.

Todd, P.A. (1984). *Differences over time in subjective burden between men and women caregivers.* Los Angeles: University of Southern California, Andrus Gerontology Center.

Townsend, P. (1965). The effects of family structure on the likelihood of admission to an institution in old age: The application of a general theory. In E. Shanas & G.F. Streib (Eds.), *Social structure and the family: Generational relations.* Englewood Cliffs, NJ: Prentice Hall.

Traupmann, J., Eckels, E., & Hatfield, E. (1982). Intimacy in older women's lives. *The Gerontologist, 22,* 493-98.

Traxler, A.J. (1980a). Mental health and primary prevention for the aging. Paper presented at conference on a "New wave: Primary preventions for mental health," Southern Illinois University at Edwardsville School of Nursing, Edwardsville, IL, April 29.

_____. (1980b). Let's get gerontologized: Developing a sensitivity to aging. In *The multi-purpose senior center concept: A training manual for practitioners working with the aging.* Springfield, IL: Illinois Department on Aging.

_____. (1986). Elder abuse laws: A survey of state statutes. In M.W. Galbraith (Ed.), *Elder abuse: Perspectives on an emerging crisis* (pp. 139-67). Kansas City, KS: Mid-America Congress on Aging.

Treas, J. (1975). Aging and the family. In D.S. Woodruff & J.E. Birren (Eds.), *Aging,* 92-108. New York: Van Nostrand Reinhold.

_____. (1979). Intergenerational families and social change. In P.K. Ragan (Ed.), *Aging parents.* (pp. 58-65). University of Southern California Press: The Ethel Percy Andrus Gerontology Center.

Treas, J., & Van Hilst, A. (1976). Marriage and remarriage rates among older Americans. *The Gerontologist, 16,* 132-35.

Troll, L.E. (1980). Grandparenting. In L.W. Poon (Ed.), *Aging in the 1980s: Psychological Issues.* Washington, DC: American Psychological Association.

_____. (1982). *Continuations: Adult development and aging.* Monterey, CA: Brooks/Cole.

_____. (1983). Grandparents: The family watchdogs. In T.H. Brubaker (Ed.), *Family relationships in later life.* Beverly Hills: Sage.

_____. (1986). Parents and children in later life. *Generations, 10,* 23-25.

Tuckman, J., & Lorge, I. (1953). Attitudes toward old people. *Journal of Social Psychology, 37,* 249-60.

Turnbull, J.M., & Turnbull, S.K. (1985). Management of specific anxiety disorders in the elderly. *Geriatrics, 40,* 75-82.

Turow, J. (1974). Talk show radio as interpersonal communication. *Journal of Broadcasting, 18,* 171-79.

Uhlmann, R.F., Larson, E.B., & Koepsell, T.D. (1986). Hearing impairment and cognitive decline in senile dementia of the Alzheimer's type. *Journal of the American Geriatrics Society, 34,* 207-10.

United States National Health Survey. (1968). *Monocular-binocular visual acuity of adults.* Public Health Service Publication No. 100 Series 11 No. 30. 1960-62. Washington, D.C.: U.S. Department of Health, Education and Welfare.

Unruh, D.R. (1983). *Invisible lives: Social worlds of the aged.* Beverly Hills: Sage.

Urban Institute (1983). *Housing for a maturing population.* Washington, DC: Urban Institute in cooperation with the Housing Committee, American Institute of Architects.

U.S. Bureau of the Census. (1983). *America in transition: An aging society. Current Population Reports,* Series P-23, No. 128, Washington, DC: U.S. Government Printing Office.

U.S. Bureau of the Census. (1984). *Demographic and socioeconomic aspects of aging in the United States.* J.S. Siegel & M. Davidson. Current Population Reports, Series P-23, Special Studies, No. 138. August, 1984.

U.S. Bureau of the Census (1985). *Statistical Abstract 1985* (105th ed.). Washington, DC: U.S. Government Printing Office.

U.S. Congress. House of Representatives. Select Committee on Aging. (1977). *Mandatory retirement: The social and human cost of enforced idleness.* Washington, DC: U.S. Government Printing Office.

U.S. Congress. House of Representatives. Select Committee on Aging (1981). *Elder abuse: Examination of a hidden problem.* (Committee Publication No. 97-277). Washington, DC: U.S. Government Printing Office.

U.S. Congress. House of Representatives. Select Committee on Aging, Subcommittee on Health and Long-Term Care. (1985). *Elder abuse: A national disgrace.* (Committee Publication No. 99-502). Washington, DC: U.S. Government Pringint Office.

U.S. Congress. House of Representatives. Select Committee on Aging, Subcommittee on Health and Long-Term Care. (1986). *The rights of America's institutionalized aged: Lost in confinement.* Hearing, September 18, 1985. Washington, DC: U.S. Government Printing Office.

U.S. Congress, Office of Technology Assessment. (1985). *Technology and aging in America.* Washington, DC: U.S. Government Printing Office.

U.S. Congress Senate. (1986, June 23). Senate Bill No. 604, An amendment to the Older Americans Act of 1965. Washington, DC: U.S. Government Printing Office.

U.S. Congress. Senate. Special Committee on Aging, Subcommittee on Long-Term Care (1974). *Nursing home care in the United States, failure in public policy: Introductory report.* Washington, DC: U.S. Government Printing Office.

U.S. Congress, Senate. Special Committee on Aging, Subcommittee on Long-Term Care (1975a). *Nursing home care in the United States: Failure in public policy, supporting paper No. 4, nurses in nursing homes, the heavy burden (the reliance on untrained and unlicensed personnel).* (pp. 360, 372-73, 381). Washington, DC: U.S. Government Printing Office.

U.S. Congress. Senate. Special Committee on Aging, Subcommittee on Long-Term Care. (1975b). *Nursing home care in the United States, failure in public policy: Introductory report and nine supporting papers.* Washington, DC: U.S. Government Printing Office.

U.S. Congress. Senate. Special Committee on Aging. (1980). Developments on aging 1979: (Part I Report No. 96-613). 96th Congress, 2nd session. Washington, DC: U.S. Government Printing Office.

U.S. Department of Health and Human Services. (1982). More older workers want part-time work after retirement. *Aging, 39,* 337.

U.S. Department of Health, Education, and Welfare. (1977). *Papers on the national health guidelines: Baselines for setting health goals and standards.* Washington, DC: DHEW Publication No. (HRA) 77-640.

Usui, W.M., Keil, T.J., & Durig, K.R. (1985). Socioeconomic comparisons and life satisfaction of elderly adults. *Journal of Gerontology, 40,* 110-14.

Van Maanen, J. (1975). Breaking in: Socialization to work. In R. Dublin (Ed.), *Handbook of work, organization and society.* Chicago: Rand McNally.

Van Meter, M.J., & Johnson, P. (1985). Family decision making and long-term care for the elderly: A Review, Part II. *Journal of Religion and Aging,* 59-72.

Ventura, C.A., & Worthy, E.H. (1982). *Voluntary action and older Americans: A synthesis of significant data.* Washington, DC: The National Council on The Aging, Inc.; National Polity Center on Education, Leisure, and Continuing Opportunities for Older Americans.

Vickers, W.D. (1983). Project looking back: A structured reminiscence experience. *Activities, Adaptation and Aging, 3,* 31-38.

Vinick, B.H. (1978). Remarriage in old age. *The Family Coordinator, 27,* 359-63.

Vladeck, B.C. (1980). *Unloving care, the nursing home tragedy.* New York: Basic Books.

Vogel, D., & Costello, R.M. (1985). Relatives and aphasia clinicians—do they agree? In R.H. Brookshire (Ed.), *Processings of the Clinical Aphasiology Conference.* Minneapolis: BRK Publishers.

Wallace, R.W., & Brubaker, T.H. (1982). Biographical factors related to employment tenure: A study of nurse aides in nursing homes. *The Journal of Long-Term Care Administration,* Summer, 11-17.

Walsh, D.A. (1975). Age differences in learning and memory. IN D.S. Woodruff & J.E. Birren (Eds.), *Aging: Scientific perspectives and social issues* (pp. 125-51). New York: Van Nostrand Reinhold.

Walston, B.J., & Walston, K.E. (1980). *The nursing assistant in long-term care, a new era.* St. Louis: C.V. Mosby Company.

Ward, R. (1985). Informal networks and well-being in later life: A research agenda. *The Gerontologist, 25,* 55-61.

Ward, R.A. (1984). *The aging experience: An introduction to social gerontology* (2nd ed.). New York: Harper and Row.

Watson, W.H. (1975). The meanings of touch: Geriatric nursing. *Journal of Communication, 25,*(3), 104-12.

Watson, W.H. (1973). Body idiom in social interaction: A field study of geriatric nursing, Ph.D. Dissertation, University of Pennsylvania, in *Dissertation Abstracts International, 33* (7-A), January, 3778.

Watzlawick, P., Beavin, J.H., & Jackson, D.D. (1967). *Pragmatics of human communication* (pp. 48-49). New York: W.W. Norton.

Waxman, H.M., Carner, E.A., & Berkenstock, G. (1984). Job turnover and job satisfaction among nursing home aides. *The Gerontologist, 24,* 503-9.

Waxman, H.M., McCreary, G., Weinrit, R.M., & Carner, E.A. (1985). A comparison of somatic complaints among depressed and non-depressed older persons. *The Gerontologist, 25,* 501-7.

Weber, M. (1947). *The theory of social and economic organizations,* trans. A.M. Henderson & T. Parsons. New York: Oxford University Press.

Webster, E.J., & Newhoff, M. (1981). Intervention with families of communicatively impaired adults. In D.S. Beasley & G.A. Davis (Eds.), *Aging: Communication processes and disorders.* New York: Grune & Stratton.

Weeks, J.R. (1984). *Aging: Concepts and social issues.* Belmont, CA: Wadsworth.

Weeks, J.R., & Cuellar, J.B. (1983). Isolation of older persons: The influence of immigration and length of residence. *Research on Aging, 5,* 369-88.

Weg, R. (1975). Changing physiology of aging: Normal and pathological. In D. Woodruff & J. Birren, (Eds.). *Aging: Scientific perspectives and social issues.* New York: Van Nostrand Reinhold.

Weinberger, L.E., & Millham, J. (1975). A multi-dimensional, multiple method analysis of attitudes toward the elderly. *Journal of Gerontology, 30,* 343-48.

Weinfeld, F.D. (1981). The 1981 national survey of stroke. *Stroke, 1*(12), 1-22.

Weisbord, M.R. (1976). Why organization development hasn't worked (so far) in medical centers. *Health Care Management Review, 1,* 17-28.

Weiss, C.R., & Bailey, B.B. (1985). The influence of older adults' activity selection on their progeny's expectations for their own future. *Activities, Adaptation and Aging, 6,* 103-14.

Weiss, F.K. (1984). *Older women and job discrimination: A primer.* Washington, DC: Older Women's League.

Weissert, W.G. (1985). Estimating the long-term care population: Prevalence rates and selected characteristics. *Health Care Financing Review, 6,* 83-91.

Welford, A.T. (1983). Social skill and aging: Principles and problems. *International Journal of Aging and Human Development, 17,* 1-5.

Wells, W., & Siegel, B. (1961). Stereotyped somotypes. *Psychological Reports, 8,* 77-78.

Wenner, L. (1976). Functional analysis of TV viewing for older adults. *Journal of Broadcasting, 20,* 77-88.

West, G.E., & Simons, R.L. (1983). Sex differences in stress, coping resources, and illness among the elderly. *Research on Aging, 5,* 235-68.

West, N.D. (1975). Stresses associated with ICUs affect, patients, families, staff. *Hospitals, 49,* 62-63.

White, K. (1980). Nursing recruitment and retention in long-term care. *The Journal of Long-Term Care Administration,* September, 25-36.

Wilcox, K.A., & Horii, Y. (1980). Age and changes in vocal jitter. *Journal of Gerontology, 35,* 194-98.

Wilder, C.N., & Weistein, B.E. (Eds.). (1984). *Aging and communication: Problems in management.* Belmont, CA: Wadsworth.

Williams, J.B., Evans, L., & Powell, L.A. (1982). *The politics of aging: Power and policy.* Springfield, IL: Charles C. Thomas.

Williams L. (1986). Alzheimer's: The need for caring. *Journal of Gerontological Nursing, 12,* 20-28.

Williamson, D.S. (1981). Personal authority via termination of the intergenerational hierarchical boundary: A new "stage" in the family life cycle. *Journal of Marital and Family Therapy, 7,* 441-52.

Wilson, G.L., Goodall, H.L., & Waagen, C.L. (1986). *Organizational Communication.* New York: Harper & Row.

Winter, A. (1986). The shame of elder abuse. *Modern Maturity, 29*(5), Lakewood, CA: American Association of Retired Persons.

Wister, A.V. (1985). Living arrangement choices among the elderly. *Canadian Journal on Aging, 4,* 127-44.

Woelfel, J. (1976). Communication across age levels. In H.J. Oyer and E.J. Oyer, (Eds.), *Aging and communication* (pp. 63-73). Baltimore: University Park Press.

Wood, V. (1982). Grandparenthood: An ambiguous role. *Generations, 7,* 22.

Wood, V., & Robertson, J. (1976). The significance of grandparenthood. In J. Gubrium (Ed.), *Times, roles and self in old-age* (pp. 278-304). New York: Human Sciences Press.

Woods, W. (1983). *Windows.* Washington, DC: U.S. Architectural and Transportation Barriers Compliance Board.

Woodruff, D.S. (1983). A review of aging and cognitive processes. *Research on Aging, 5,* 139-53.

Yairi, E., & Clifton, N.F. (1972). Disfluent speech behavior of preschool children, high school seniors and geriatric persons. *Journal of Speech and Hearing Research, 15,* 714-19.

Yankelovich, Skelly and White, Inc. (1985). *A fifty-year report card on the Social Security System: The attitudes of the American public.* Washington, DC: Yankelovich, Skelly and White, Inc.

Young, L., & Hendrix, C. (1985). The candid perceptions of nursing home aides to their environmental uncertainty. Paper presented as one of the top three competitively selected papers in health communication at the 1985 Eastern Communication Association Convention, Providence, Rhode Island.

Young, T.J. (1979). Use of the media by older adults. *American Behavorial Scientist, 23,* 119-36.

Your home, your choice: A workbook for older people and their families. (1985). Washington, DC: American Association of Retired Persons.

Yturri-Byrd, K., & Glazer-Waldman, H. (1984). The physician assistant and care of the geriatric patient. *Gerontology and Geriatrics Education, 5,* 33-41.

Zaks, P.M., & Labouvie-Vief, G. (1980). Spatial perspective taking and referential communication skills in the elderly: A training study. *Journal of Gerontology, 35,* 217-24.

Zarit, S.H. (1982). Gerontology: Getting better all the time. In S.H. Zarit, (Ed.), *Readings in aging and death: Contemporary perspectives,* (pp. 15-20). New York: Harper & Row. (Original work published in 1977).

Zarit, S.N., & Sommers, T. (Eds.). (1985). Caregivers. *Generations, 10,* (entire issue).